新世纪双语系列
New Century Bilingual Series

NCBS

国际贸易实务

International Trade Practice

●英汉对照版●

主　编　刘　毅　郭　琛
副主编　郭　琳　宫伟建　宋壮基　于丽艳
主　审　薛文礼

哈尔滨工程大学出版社
Harbin Engineering University Press

内容简介

本书介绍了当今国际贸易中的前沿问题和最新发展，介绍了国际贸易实务的基本原理、基本知识和基本技能。本书分为国际贸易实务英文与国际贸易实务中文两部分，分别有5章。其中，第一章为国际贸易术语，第二章为国际货物销售合同的基本条款，第三章为国际货款支付，第四章为国际货物销售合同的商订，第五章为跟单信用证统一惯例。

本书可作为高等院校有关专业学生的教材，还可供企业经营管理人员的外贸业务培训使用，对参加国际商务师、外销员、报关员以及其他相关资格考试的人员也大有裨益。

图书在版编目(CIP)数据

国际贸易实务/刘毅，郭琛主编.—哈尔滨：
哈尔滨工程大学出版社，2008.2
ISBN 978-7-81133-140-0

Ⅰ.国… Ⅱ.①刘… ②郭… Ⅲ.国际贸易—贸易实务—
汉、英 Ⅳ.F740.4

中国版本图书馆CIP数据核字(2008)第204304号

出版发行 哈尔滨工程大学出版社
社　　址 哈尔滨市南岗区东大直街124号
邮政编码 150001
发行电话 0451-82519328
传　　真 0451-82519699
经　　销 新华书店
印　　刷 肇东粮食印刷厂
开　　本 16开
印　　张 20
字　　数 340千字
版　　次 2008年2月第1版
印　　次 2008年2月第1次印刷
定　　价 30.00元
http://press.hrbeu.edu.cn
E-mail:heupress@hrbeu.edu.cn

前言

改革开放、市场经济的发展和加入WTO把中国推向了国际舞台，也标志着我国在融入世界经济全球化、参与国际竞争方面又迈出了决定性的一步，更使我国的经济发展从此步入了一个崭新的阶段。众所周知，经济领域竞争的实质是人才竞争，而人才的培养有赖于教育，教育质量则直接关系到人力资源的质量，而教材的质量则直接关系到教育质量。培养和造就一大批基础理论雄厚、专业知识扎实、计算机技能熟练、外语交流通畅的复合型人才，正在成为我国高等院校尤其是重点高校追求的主要目标。

国际贸易实务是高等院校国际经济与贸易等专业的一门主课，适宜采用外语讲授。《国家贸易实务》(英汉对照版)正是为了适应入世后国际贸易的需要而编写的，其目的是为有志于从事国际经贸事业的人员，提供适应新形势要求的必备理论知识和实践技能，以提高国际经济贸易人员的理论和实际操作能力，不断增强其国际竞争力。

本书编者借鉴了国内外学者的研究成果，在教材结构上作出了一些尝试性的创新，在内容上既有简单基本常识的阐述，又有重点难点的讲解；既有理论知识的框架体系，又注意理论联系实际，用案例分析着眼于实务操作、技能训练。这种结合我国对外经贸实践、我国外贸发展，利用外贸和外贸实务的引导式学习方式，必将有助于读者提高分析和解决问题的能力。全书结构完整，内容翔实，简明易懂，符合国情。

本书由哈尔滨理工大学、哈尔滨工程大学、黑龙江科技学院的学者及教师共同编写，并由多年从事国际贸易实践工作的薛文礼博士担任主审。本书由黑龙江省社会科学基金项目(批准号:06D701)资助，特此感谢！

国际贸易的理论与实践都在不断的发展完善之中，加之作者水平有限，错误或疏漏之处在所难免，恳请同行专家和广大读者批评指正。

编　者

2008年1月

CONTENTS

目录

English Part

Chapter 1 International Trade Terms

1.1 Summary of International Trade Terms

1.1.1 Role of Trade Terms

Trade terms, also known as price terms or delivery terms, are standardized terms used in sales contracts that describe the place and manner for the transfer of goods from the seller to the buyer. These trade terms, such as Free On Board (FOB) and Cost, Insurance, and Freight (CIF), may also define a variety of other matters, including the price, the time when the risk of loss shifts from the seller to the buyer, and the costs of freight band insurance. The use of trade terms greatly simplifies the process of negotiation of contract, thus saving time and cost for businessmen.

1.1.2 International Rules and Practices on Trade Terms

Trade terms have been developed in practice for many years. However, as different countries might have different interpretations of the terms, misunderstandings occurred frequently. To clear up the confusion, some commercial organizations drew up sets of rules or standard definitions.

1. Warsaw-Oxford Rules 1932

This rule was drafted by the Association of International Law in 1932. It contains 21 clauses, which only stipulate the nature of CIF contract, and the charges, risks and obligations which should be born by the seller or the buyer.

2. Revised American Foreign Trade Definitions 1941

This rule was made out by nine American commercial organizations in 1941. It is a set of foreign trade terms which are considered obsolete, but still sometimes used in domestic U. S. trade. It contains 6 trade terms.

3. International Rule for the Interpretation of Trade Terms 2000

The International Chamber of Commerce (ICC) in Paris developed INCOTerms (International Commercial Terms). It was first published in 1936 and has been periodically revised to account for changing modes of transport and document delivery. The current version is INCOTERMS 2000, which came into force on Jan. 1, 2000. In this rule, there are totally 13 trade terms, which have been divided into 4 different groups.

a. The "E"-term (EXW). The only term where the seller/exporter makes the goods available at his or her own premises to the buyer/importer.

b. The "F"-terms (FCA, FAS and FOB). Terms where the seller/exporter is responsible to deliver the goods to a carrier named by the buyer.

c. The "C"-terms (CFR, CIF, CPT and CIP). Terms where the seller/exporter is responsible for contacting and paying for carriage of the goods, but not responsible for additional costs or risk of loss or damages to the goods once they have been shipped.

d. The "D"-terms (DAF, DES, DEQ, DDU and DDP). Terms where the seller/exporter is responsible for all costs and risks associated with bringing the goods to the place of destination. D terms evidence "arrival" contracts.

1.2 International Practice

1.2.1 Purpose and Scope of INCOTERMS

The purpose of INCOTERMS is to provide a set of international rules for the interpretation of the most commonly used trade terms in foreign trade. Thus, the uncertainties of different interpretation of such terms in different countries can be avoided or at least reduced to a considerable degree.

Frequently, parties to a contract are unaware of the different trading practices in their respective countries. This can give rise to misunderstandings, disputes and litigation, with all the waste of time and money that this entails. In order to remedy these problems, the International Chamber of Commerce first published in 1936 a set of international rules for the interpretation of trade terms. These rules were known as "INCOTERMS 1936". Amendments and additions were later made in 1953, 1967, 1976, 1980, 1990 and presently in 2000 in order to bring the rules in line with current international trade practices.

It should be stressed that the scope of INCOTERMS is limited to matters relating to the rights and obligations of the parties to the contract of sale with respect to the delivery of goods sold (in the sense of "tangible", not including "intangibles" such as computer software).

It appears that two particular misconceptions about INCOTERMS are very common. First, INCOTERMS are frequently misunderstood as applying to the contract of carriage rather than the contract of sale. Second, they are sometimes wrongly assumed to provide for all the duties which parties may wish to include in a contract of sale.

As has always been underlined by ICC, INCOTERMS deal only with the relation between sellers and buyers under the contract of sale, and moreover, only do so in some very distinct respects.

While it is essential for exporters and importers to consider the very practical relationship between the various contracts needed to perform an international sales transaction—where not only the contract of sale is required, but also contracts of carriage, insurance and financing—INCOTERMS relate to only one of these contracts, namely the contract of sale.

Nevertheless, the parties' agreement to use a particular Incoterm would necessarily have implications for the other contracts. To mention a few examples, a seller having agreed to a CFR- or CIF-contract cannot perform such a contract by any other mode of transport than carriage be sea, since under these terms he must present a bill of lading or other maritime document to the buyer which is simply not possible if other modes of transport are used. Furthermore, the document required under a documentary credit would necessarily depend upon the means of transport intended to be used.

Second, INCOTERMS deal with a number of identified obligations imposed on the parties—such as the seller's obligation to place the goods at the disposal of the buyer or hand them over for carriage or deliver them at destination—and with the distribution of risk between the parties in these cases.

Further, they deal with the obligations to clear the goods for export and import, the packing of the goods, the buyer's obligation to take delivery as well as the obligation to provide proof that the respective obligations have been duly fulfilled. Although INCOTERMS are extremely important for the implementation of the contract of sale, a great number of problems which may occur in such breaches as well as exemptions from liability in certain situations. It should be stressed that INCOTERMS are not intended to replace such contract terms that are needed for a complete contract of sale either by the incorporation of standard terms or by individually negotiated terms.

Generally, INCOTERMS do not deal with the consequences of breach of contract and any exemptions from liability owing to various impediments. These questions must be resolved by other stipulations in the contract of sale and the applicable law.

INCOTERMS have always been primarily intended for use where goods are sold for delivery across national boundaries: hence, international commercial terms. However, INCOTERMS are in practice at times also incorporated into contracts for the sale of goods within purely domestic markets. Where INCOTERMS are so used, the A2 and B2 clauses and any other stipulation of other articles dealing with export and import do, of course, become redundant.

1.2.2 Reason of INCOTERMS' Revision

The main reason for successive revisions of INCOTERMS has been the need to adapt them to contemporary commercial practice. Thus, in the 1980 revision the term Free Carrier (now FCA) was introduced in order to deal with the frequent case where the reception point in maritime trade was no longer the traditional FOB-point (passing of the ship's rail) but rather a point on land, prior to loading on board a vessel, where the goods were stowed into a container for subsequent transport by sea or by different means of transport in combination (so-called combined or multimodal transport).

Further, in the 1990 revision of INCOTERMS, the clauses dealing with the seller's obligation to provide proof of delivery permitted a replacement of paper documentation by EDI-messages provided the parties had agreed to communicate electronically. Needless to say, efforts are constantly made to improve upon the drafting and presentation of INCOTERMS in order to facilitate their practical implementation.

1.2.3 INCOTERMS 2000

During the process of revision, which has taken about two years, ICC has done its best to invite views and responses to successive drafts from a wide ranging spectrum of world traders, represented as these various sectors are on the national committees through which ICC operates. Indeed, it has been gratifying to see that this revision process has attracted far more reaction from users around the world than any of the previous revisions of INCOTERMS. The result of this dialogue is INCOTERMS 2000, a version which when compared with INCOTERMS 1990 may appear to have effected few changes. It is clear, however, that INCOTERMS now enjoy world wide recognition and ICC has therefore decided to consolidate upon that recognition and avoid change for its own sake. On the other hand, serious efforts have been made to ensure that the wording used in INCOTERMS 2000 clearly and accurately reflects trade practice. Moreover, substantive changes have made in two areas. the customs clearance and payment of duty obligations under FAS and DEQ; the loading and unloading obligations under FCA.

All changes, whether substantive or formal have been made on the basis of thorough research among users of INCOTERMS and particular regard has been given to queries received since 1990 by the Panel of INCOTERMS Experts, set up as an additional service to the users of INCOTERMS.

1.2.4 Incorporation of INCOTERMS into the Contract of Sale

In view of the changes made to INCOTERMS from time to time, it is important to ensure that where the parties intend to incorporate INCOTERMS into their contract of sale, an express reference is always made to the current version of INCOTERMS. This may easily be overlooked when, for example, a reference has been made to an earlier version in standard contract forms or in order forms used by merchants. A failure to refer to the current version may then result in disputes as to whether the parties intended to incorporate that version or an earlier version as a part of their contract. Merchants wishing to use INCOTERMS 2000 should therefore clearly specify that their contract is governed by "INCOTERMS 2000".

1.2.5 Structure of INCOTERMS

In 1990, for ease of understanding, the terms were grouped in four basically different categories: namely starting with the term whereby the seller only makes the goods available to the buyer at the seller's own premises (the "E"-term Ex works); followed by the second group whereby the seller is called upon to deliver the goods to a carrier appointed by the buyer (the "F"-terms FCA, FAS and FOB); continuing with the "C"-terms where the seller has to contract for carriage, but without assuming the risk of loss of or damage to the goods or additional costs due to events occurring after shipment and dispatch (CFR, CIF, CPT, and CIP); and, finally, the "D"-term whereby the seller has to bear all costs and risks needed to bring the goods to the place of destination (DAF, DES, DEQ, DDU, and DDP). The following chart sets out this classification of the trade terms.

Table 1.1 INCOTERMS 2000

(a)

Group E	**Departure**	
	EXW	Ex Works
Group F	**Main carriage unpaid**	
	FCA	Free Carrier (... named place)
	FAS	Free Alongside Ship (... named port of shipment)
	FOB	Free On Board (... named port of shipment)
Group C	**Main Carriage Paid**	
	CFR	Cost and Freight (... named place of destination)
	CIF	Cost, Insurance and Freight (... named port of destination)

Table 1.1
(b)

	CPT	Carriage Paid To (... named port of destination)
	CIP	Carriage and Insurance Paid To (... named place of destination)
Group D	**Arrival**	
	DAF	Delivered At Frontier (... named place)
	DES	Delivered Ex Ship (... named port of destination)
	DEQ	Delivered Ex Quay (... named port of destination)
	DDU	Delivered Duty Unpaid (... named port of destination)
	DDP	Delivered Duty Paid (... named port of destination)

Further, under all terms, as in INCOTERMS 1990, the respective obligations of the parties have been grouped under 10 headings where each heading on the seller' s side " mirrors" the position of the buyer with respect to the same subject matter.

1.2.6 Terminology

While drafting INCOTERMS 2000, considerable efforts have been made to achieve as much consistency as possible and desirable with respect to the various expressions used throughout the thirteen terms. Thus, the use of different expressions intended to convey the same meaning has been avoided. Also, whenever possible, the same expressions as appear in the 1980 "*UN Convention on Contracts for the International Sale of Goods*" (CISG) have been used.

1. Shipper

In some cases it has been necessary to use the same term to express two different meanings simply because there has been no suitable alternative. Traders will be familiar with this difficulty both in the context of contracts of sale and also of contracts of carriage. Thus, for example, the term "shipper" signifies both the person handing over the goods for carriage and the person who makes the contract with the carrier: however, these two "shippers" may be different persons, for example under a FOB contract where the seller would hand over the goods for carriage and the buyer would make the contract with the carrier.

2. Delivery

It is particularly important to note that the term "delivery" is used in two different senses in INCOTERMS. First, it is used to determine when the seller has fulfilled his delivery obligation which is specified in the A4 clauses throughout INCOTERMS. Second, the term "delivery" is also used in the context of the buyer's obligation to take or accept delivery of the goods, an obligation which appears in the B4 clauses throughout INCOTERMS. Used in this second context, the word "delivery" means first that the buyer "accepts" the very nature of the "C" terms, namely that the seller fulfils his obligations upon the shipment of the goods, and second that the buyer is obliged to receive the goods. This latter obligation is important so as to avoid unnecessary charges for storage of the goods until they have been collected by the buyer. Thus, for example under CFR and CIF contracts, the buyer is bound to accept delivery of the goods and to receive them from the carrier and if the buyer fails to do so, he may become liable to pay damages to the seller who has made the contract of carriage with the carrier or, alternatively, the buyer might have to pay demurrage charges resting upon the goods in order to obtain the carrier's release of the goods to him. When it is said in this context that the buyer must "accept delivery", this does not mean that the buyer has accepted the goods as conforming with the contract of sale, but only that he has accepted that the seller has performed his obligation to hand the goods over for carriage in accordance with the contract of carriage which he has to make under the A3 clauses of the "C"-terms. So, if the buyer upon receipt of the goods at destination were to find that the goods did not conform to the stipulations in the contract of sale, he would be able to use any remedies which the contract of sale and the applicable law gave him against the seller, matters which, as has already been mentioned, lie entirely outside the scope of INCOTERMS.

Where appropriate, INCOTERMS 2000 have used the expression "placing the goods at the disposal of" the buyer when the goods are made available to the buyer at a particular place. This expression is intended to bear the same meaning as that of the phrase "handing over the goods" used in the《United Nations Convention on Contracts for the International Sale of Goods》.

3. Usual

The word "usual" appears in several terms, for example in EXW with respect to the time of delivery (A4) and in the "C"-terms with respect to the documents which the seller is obliged to provide and the contract of carriage which the seller must procure (A8, A3). It can, of course, be difficult to tell precisely what the word "usual" means, however, in many cases, it is possible to identify what persons in the trade usually do and this practice will then be the guiding light. In this sense, the word "reasonable", which requires an assessment not against the world of practice but against the more difficult principle of good faith and fair dealing. In some circumstances it may well be necessary to decide what is "usual" has been generally preferred to the word "reasonable".

4. Charges

With respect to the obligation to clear the goods for import it is important to determine what is meant by "charges" which must be paid upon import of the goods. In INCOTERMS 1990 the expression "official charges payable upon exportation and importation of the goods" was used in DDP A6. In INCOTERMS 2000 DDP A6 the word "official" has been deleted, the reason being that this word gave rise to some uncertainty when determining whether the charge was "official" or not. No change of substantive meaning was intended through this deletion. The "charges" which must be paid only concern such charges as are a necessary consequence of the import regulations. Any additional charges levied by private parties in connection with the import are not to be included in these charges, such as charges for storage unrelated to the clearance obligation. However, the performance of that obligation may well result in some costs to customs brokers or freight forwarders freight forwarders if the party bearing the obligation does not do the work himself.

5. Ports, Places, Points and Premises

So far as concerns the place at which the goods are to be delivered, different expressions are used in INCOTERMS. In the terms intended to be used exclusively for carriage of goods by sea—such as FAS, FOB, CFR, CIF, DES and DEQ—the expressions "port of shipment" have been used. In all other cases the word "place" has been used. In some cases, it has been deemed necessary also to indicate a "point" within the port or place as it may be important for the seller to know not only that the goods should be delivered in a particular area like a city but also where within that area the goods should be placed at the disposal of the buyer. Contracts of sale would frequently lack information in this respect and INCOTERMS therefore stipulate that if no specific point has been agreed within the named place, and if there are several points available, the seller may select the point which best suits his purpose (as an example see FCA A4). Where the delivery point is the seller's place the expression "the seller's premises" (FCA A4) has been used.

6. Ship and Vessel

In the terms intended to be used for carriage of goods by sea, the expressions "ship" and "vessel" are used as synonyms. Needless to say, the term "ship" would have to be used when it is an ingredient in the trade term itself such as in "free alongside ship" (FAS) and "delivery ex ship" (DES). Also, in view of the traditional use of the expression "passed the ship's rail" in FOB, the word "shop" has had to be used in that connection.

7. Checking and Inspection

In the A9 and B9 clauses of INCOTERMS the headings "checking-packaging and marking" and "inspection of the goods" respectively have been used. Although the words "checking" and "inspection" are synonyms, it has been deemed appropriate to use the former word with respect to the seller's delivery obligation under A4and to reserve the latter for the particular case when a "pre-shipment inspection" is performed, since such inspection normally is only required when the buyer or the authorities of the export or import country want to ensure that the goods conform with contractual or official stipulations before they are shipped.

1.2.7 Seller's Delivery Obligations

INCOTERMS focus on the seller's delivery obligation. The precise distribution of functions and costs in connection with the seller's delivery of the goods would normally not cause problems where the parties have a continuing commercial relationship. They would then establish a practice between themselves ("course of dealing") which they would follow in subsequent dealing in the same manner as they have done earlier. However, if a new commercial relationship is established or if a contract is made through the medium of brokers—as is common in the sale of commodities, one would have apply the stipulations of the contract of sale and, whenever INCOTERMS 2000 have been incorporated into that contract, apply the division of functions, costs and risks following therefore.

It would, of course have been desirable if Inconterms could specify in as detailed a manner as possible the duties of the parties in connection with the delivery of the goods. Compared with INCOTERMS 1990, further efforts have been made in this respect in some specified instances (see for example FCA A4). But it has not been possible to avoid reference to customs of the trade in FAS and FOB A4 ("in the manner customary at the port"), the reason being that particularly in commodity trade the exact manner in which the goods are delivered for carriage in FAS and FOB contracts vary in the different sea ports.

1.2.8 Passing of Risks and Costs Relating to the Goods

The risk of loss of or damage to the goods, as well as the obligation to bear the costs relating to the goods, passed from the seller to the buyer when the seller has fulfilled his obligation to deliver the goods. Since the buyer should not be giver the possibility to delay the passing of the risk and costs, all terms stipulate that the passing of risk and costs may occur even before delivery, if the buyer does not take delivery as agreed or fails to give such instructions (with respect to time for shipment and/or place for delivery) as the seller may require in order to fulfill his obligation to deliver the goods. It is a requirement for such premature passing of risk and costs that the goods have been identified as intended for the buyer or, as is stipulated in the terms, set aside for him (appropriation).

This requirement is particularly important under EXW, since under all other terms the goods would normally have been identified as intended for the buyer when measures have been taken for their shipment or dispatch ("F"-and "C"-terms) or their delivery at destination ("D"-terms). In exceptional cases, however, the goods may have been sent from the seller in bulk without identification of the quantity for each buyer and, if so, passing of risk and cost does not occur before the gcods have been appropriated as aforesaid (also article 69. 3 of the "1980 *United Nations Convention on Contracts for the International Sale of Goods*").

1.2.9 Terms

a. The "E"-term is the term in which the seller's obligation is at its minimum: the seller has to do no more than place the goods at the disposal of the buyer at the agreed place—usually at the seller's own premises. On the other hand, as a matter of practical reality, the seller would frequently assist the buyer in loading the goods on the latter's collecting vehicle. Although EXW would better reflect this if the seller's obligations were to be extended so as to include loading, it was thought desirable to retain the traditional principle of the seller's minimum obligation under EXW so that it could be used for cases where the seller does not wish to assume any obligation whatsoever with respect to the loading of the goods. If the buyer wants the seller to do more, this should be made clear in the contract of sale.

b. The "F"-terms require the seller to deliver the goods for carriage as instructed by the buyer. The point at which the parties intend delivery to occur in the FCA term has caused difficulty because of the wide variety of circumstances which may surround contracts covered by this term. Thus, the goods may be loaded on a collecting vehicle sent by the buyer to pick them up at the seller's premises; alternatively, the goods may need to be unloaded from a vehicle sent by the seller to deliver the goods at a terminal named by the buyer. INCOTERMS 2000 take account of these alternatives by stipulating that, when the place named in the contract as the place of delivery is the seller's premises, delivery is complete when the goods are loaded on the buyer's collecting vehicle and, in other cases. Delivery is complete when the goods are placed at the disposal of the buyer not unloaded from the seller's vehicle and, in other cases, delivery is complete when the goods are placer at the disposal of the buyer not unloaded from the seller's vehicle. The variations mentioned for different modes of transport in FCA A4 of INCOTERMS 1990 are not repeated in INCOTERMS 2000.

The delivery point under FOB, which is the same under CFR and CIF, has been left unchanged in INCOTERMS 2000 in spite of a considerable debate. Although the notion under FOB to deliver the goods " across the ship's rail" nowadays may seem inappropriate in many cases, it is nevertheless understood by merchants and applied in a manner which takes account of goods and the available loading facilities. It was felt that a change of the FOB-point would create unnecessary confusion, particularly with respect to sale of commodities carried by sea typically under charter parties.

Unfortunately, the word" FOB"is used by some merchants merely to indicate any point of delivery—such as "FOB factory", "FOB plant", "FOB Ex seller's words" or other inland points—thereby neglecting what the abbreviation means: Free On Board. It remains the case that such use of "FOB" tends to create confusion and should be avoided.

There is an important change of FAS relating to the obligation to clear the goods for export, since it appears to be the most common practice to put this duty on the seller rather than on the buyer. In order to ensure that this change is duly noted it has been marked with capital letters in the preamble of FAS.

c. the "C"-terms require the seller to contract for carriage on usual terms at his own expense. Therefore, a point up to which he would have to pay transport costs must necessarily be indicated after the respective "C"-term. Under the CIF and CIP terms the seller also has to take out insurance and bear the insurance cost. Since the point for the division of costs is fixed at a point in the country of destination, the "C" -terms are frequently mistakenly believed to be arrival contracts, in which the seller would bear all risks and costs until the goods have actually arrived at the agreed point. However, it must be stressed that the "C" -terms are of the same nature as the "F" -terms in that the seller fulfils the contract in the country of shipment or dispatch. Thus, the contracts of sale under the "C" -terms, like the contracts under the "F" -terms, fall within the category of shipment contracts.

It is in the nature of shipment contracts that, while the seller is bound to pay the normal transport cost for the carriage of the goods by a usual route and in a customary manner to the agreed place, the risk of loss of or damage to the goods, as well as additional costs resulting from events occurring after the goods having been appropriately delivered for carriage, fall upon the buyer. Hence, the "C"-terms are distinguishable from all other terms in that they contain two "critical" points, one indicating the point to which the seller is bound to arrange and bear the costs of a contract of carriage and another and for the allocation of risk. For this reason, the greatest caution must be observed when adding obligations of the seller to "C"-terms which seek to extend the seller's responsibility beyond the aforementioned "critical" point for the allocation of risk. It is of the very essence of the "C"-terms that the seller is relieved of any further risk and cost after he has duly fulfilled his contract by contracting for carriage and handing over the goods to the carrier and by providing for insurance under the CIF-and CIP-terms.

The essential nature of the "C"-terms as shipment contract is also illustrated by the common use of documentary credits as the preferred mode of payment used in such terms. Where it is agreed by the parties to the sale contract that the seller will be paid by presenting the agreed shipping documents to a bank under a documentary credit, it would be quite contrary to the central purpose of the documentary credit for the seller to bear further risks and costs after the moment when payment had been made under documentary credits or otherwise upon shipment and dispatch of the goods. Of course, the seller would have to bear the cost of the contract of carriage irrespective of whether freight is per-paid upon shipment or is payable at destination (freight collect); however, additional costs which may result from events occurring subsequent to shipment and dispatch are necessarily for the account of the buyer.

If the seller has to provide a contract of carriage which involves payment of duties, taxes and other charges, such costs will, of course, fall upon the seller to the extent that they are for his account under that contract. This is now explicitly set forth in the A6 clause of all "C"-terms.

If it is customary to procure several contracts of carriage involving transshipment of the goods at intermediate places in order to reach the agreed destination, the seller would have to pay all these costs, including any costs incurred when the goods are transshipped from one means of conveyance to the other. If, however, the carrier exercised his rights under a transshipment—or similar clause—in order to avoid unexpected hindrances (such as ice, congestion, labor disturbances, government orders, war or warlike operations) then any additional cost resulting therefore would be for the account of the buyer, since the seller's obligation is limited to procuring the usual contract of carriage.

It happens quite often that the parties to the contract of sale wish to clarify the extent to which the seller should procure a contract of carriage including the costs of discharge. Since such costs are normally covered by the freight when the goods are carried by regular shipping lines, the contract of sale will frequently stipulate that the goods are to be so carried or at least that they are to be carried under "line terms". In other cases, the word "landed" is added after CFR or CIF. However, it is advisable not to use abbreviations added to the "C"-terms unless, in the relevant trade, the meaning of the abbreviations is clearly understood and accepted by the contracting parties or under any applicable law or custom of the trade.

In particular, the seller should not and indeed could not, without changing the very nature of the "C"-terms-undertake any obligation with respect to the arrival of the goods at destination, since the risk of any delay during the carriage is borne by the buyer. Thus, any obligation with respect to time must necessarily refer to the place of shipment or dispatch, for example, "shipment (dispatch) not later than…" An agreement for example, "CFR Hamburg not later than…" is really a misnomer and thus open to different possible interpretations. The parties could be taken to have meant either that the goods must actually arrive at Hamburg at the specified date, in which case the contract is not a shipment contract but an arrival contract or, alternatively, that the seller must ship the goods at such a time that they would normally arrive at Hamburg before the specified date unless the carriage would have been delayed because of unforeseen events.

It happens in commodity trades that goods are bought while they are at sea and that, in such cases, the word "afloat" is added after the trade term. Since the risk of loss of or damage to the goods would then, under the CFR-and CIF-terms, have passed from the seller to the buyer, difficulties of interpretation might arise. One possibility would be to maintain the ordinary meaning of the CFR-and CIF-terms with respect to the allocation of risk between seller and buyer, namely that risk passes on shipment: this would mean that the buyer might have to assume the consequences of events having already occurred at the time when the contract of sale enters into force. The other possibility would be to let the passing of the risk coincide with the time when the contract of sale is concluded. The former possibility might well be practical, since it is usually impossible to ascertain the condition of the goods while they are being carried. For this reason the 1980 United Nations Convention on Contracts for the International Sale of Goods article 68 stipulates that "if the circumstances so indicate, the risk is assumed by the buyer from the time the goods were handed over to the carrier who issued the documents embodying the contract of carriage". There is, however, an exception to this rule when "the seller knew or ought to have known that the goods had been lost or damaged and did not disclose this to the buyer". Thus, the interpretation of a CFR-or CIF-term with the addition of the word "afloat" will depend upon the law applicable to the contract of sale. The parties are advised to ascertain the applicable law and any solution which might follow therefore. In case of doubt, the parties are advised to clarify the matter in their contract.

In practice, the parties frequently continue to use the traditional expression C&F (or C and F, C + F). Nevertheless, in most cases it would appear that they regard these expressions as equivalent to CFR. In order to avoid difficulties of interpreting their contract the parties should use the correct Incoterm which is CFR, the only world-wide-accepted standard abbreviation for the term "Cost and Freight (…name port of destination)".

CFR and CIF in A8 of INCOTERMS 1990 obliged the seller to provide a copy of the charter party whenever his transport document (usually the bill of lading) contained a reference to the charter party, for example, by the frequent notation "all other terms and conditions as per charter party". Although, of course, a contracting party should always be able to ascertain all terms of his contract—preferably at the time of the conclusion of the contract—it appears that the practice to provide the charter party as aforesaid has created problems particularly in connection with documentary credit transactions. The obligation of the seller under CFR and CIF to provide a copy of the charter party together with other transport documents has been deleted in INCOTERMS 2000.

Although the A8 clauses of INCOTERMS seek to ensure that the seller provides the buyer with "proof of delivery", it should be stressed that the seller fulfils that requirement when he provides the "usual" proof. Under CPT and CIP it would be the "usual transport document" and under CFR and CIF a bill of lading or a sea waybill. The transport documents must be "clean", meaning that they must not contain clauses or notations expressly declaring a declaring a defective condition of the goods and/or the packaging. Of such clauses or notations appear in the document, it is regarded as "unclean" and would then not be accepted by banks in documentary credit transactions. However, it should be noted that a transport document even without such clauses or notations would usually not provide the buyer with incontrovertible proof as against the carrier that the goods were shipped in conformity with the stipulations of the contract of sale. Usually, the carrier would, in standardized text on the front page of the transport document, refuse to accept responsibility for information with respect to the goods by indicating that the particulars inserted in the transport document constitute the shipper's declarations and therefore that the information is only "said to be" as inserted in the document. Under most applicable laws and principles, the carrier must at least use reasonable means of checking the correctness of the information and his failure to do so may make him liable to the consignee. However, in container trade, the carrier's means of checking the contents in the container would not exist unless he himself was responsible for stowing the container.

There are only two terms which deal with insurance, namely CIF and CIP. Under these terms the seller is obliged to procure insurance for the benefit of the buyer. In other cases it is for the parties themselves to decide whether and to what extent they want to cover themselves by insurance. Since the seller takes out insurance for the benefit of the buyer, he would not know the buyer's precise requirements. Under the "*Institute Cargo Clauses*" drafted by the Institute of

London Underwriters, insurance is available in "minimum cover" under Clause C, "medium cover" under Clause B and "most extended cover" under Clause A. Since in the sale of commodities under the CIF term the buyer may wish to sell the goods again, it is impossible to know the insurance cover suitable to such subsequent buyers and, therefore, the minimum cover under CIF has traditionally been chosen with the possibility for the buyer to require the seller to take out additional insurance. Minimum cover is however unsuitable for sale of manufactured goods where the risk of theft, pilferage or improper handling or custody of the goods would require more than the cover available under Clause C. Since CIP, as distinguished from CIF, would normally not be used for the sale of commodities, it would have been feasible to adopt the most extended cover under CIP rather than minimum cover under CIF. But to vary the seller's insurance obligation under CIF would lead to confusion and both terms therefore limit the seller's insurance obligation to the minimum cover. It is particularly important for the CIP-buyer to observe this: should additional cover be required, he should agree with the seller that the latter could take out additional insurance or, alternatively, arrange for extended insurance cover himself. There are also particular instances where the buyer may wish to obtain even more protection than is available under Institute Clause A, for example insurance against war, riots, civil commotion, strikes or other labor disturbances. If he wishes the seller to arrange such insurance he must instruct him accordingly, in which case the seller would have to provide such insurance if procurable.

(4) The "D"-terms are different in nature from the "C"-terms, since the seller according to the "D"-terms is responsible for the arrival of the goods at the agreed place or point of destination at the border or within the county of import. The seller must bear all risks and costs in bringing the goods thereto. Hence, the "D"-terms signify arrival contracts, while the "C"-terms evidence departure/shipment contracts.

Under the "D"-terms except DDP the seller dose not have to deliver the goods cleared for import in the country of destination.

Traditionally, the seller had the obligation to clear the goods for import under DEQ, since the goods had to be landed on the quay and thus were brought into the county of import. But owing to changes in customs clearance procedures in most countries, it is now more appropriate that the party domiciled in the country concerned undertakes the clearance and pays the duties and other charges. Thus, a change in DEQ has been made for the sane reason as the change in FAS previously mentioned. As in FAS, in DEQ the change has been marked with capital letter in the preamble.

It appears that in many countries trade terms not included in INCOTERMS are used particularly in railway traffic ("franco border", "franco-frontiere", "Frei Granze"). However, under such terms it is normally not intended that the seller should assume the risk of or damage to goods circumstances to use CPT indicating the border. If, on the other hand, the parties intend that the seller should bear the risk during the transport DAF indicating the border would be appropriate.

The DDU term was added in the 1990 version of INCOTERMS. The term fulfils an important function whenever the seller is prepared to deliver the goods in the country of destination without clearing the goods for import and paying the duty. In countries where import clearance may be difficult and time consuming, it may be risky for the seller to undertake an obligation to deliver the goods beyond the customs clearance point. Although, according to DDU B5 and B6, the buyer would have to bear the additional risks and costs which might follow from his failure to fulfill his obligations to clear the goods for import, the seller is advised not to use the DDU term in countries where difficulties might be expected in clearing the goods for import.

1.2.10 Expression "No Obligation"

As appears from the expressions "the seller must" and "the buyer must" INCOTERMS are only concerned with the obligations which the parties owe to each other. The words "no obligation" have therefore been inserted whenever one party does not owe an obligation to the other party. Thus, if for instance according to A3 of the respective term the seller has to arrange and pay for the contract of carriage we find the words "no obligation" under the heading contract of carriage" in B3 **a** setting forth the buyer's position. Again, where neither party owes the other an obligation, the words "no obligation" will appear with respect to both parties, for example, with respect to insurance.

In either case, it is important to point out that even though one party may be under "no obligation" towards the other to perform a certain task, this does not mean that it is not in his interest to perform that task. Thus, for example, just because a CFR buyer owes his seller no duty to make a contract of insurance under B4, it is clearly in his interest to make such a contract, the seller being under no such obligation to procure insurance cover under A4.

1.2.11 Variants of INCOTERMS

In practice, it frequently happens that the parties themselves by adding words to an INCOTERMS seek further precision than the term could offer. It should be underlined that INCOTERMS give no guidance whatsoever for such additions. Thus, if the parties cannot rely on a well-established custom of the trade for the interpretation of such additions they may encounter serious problems when no consistent understanding of the additions could be proven.

If for instance the common expressions "FOB stowed" or "EXW loaded" are used, it is impossible to establish a world-wide understanding to the effect that the seller's obligations are extended not only with respect to the cost of actually loading the goods in the ship or on the vehicle respectively but also include the risk of fortuitous loss of or damage to the goods in the process of stowage and loading. For these reasons, the parties are strongly advised to clarify whether they only mean that the function or the cost of the stowage and loading operations should fall upon the seller or whether he should also bear the risk until the stowage and loading has actually been completed. These are questions to which INCOTERMS do not provide an answer: consequently, if the contract too fails expressly to describe the parties' intentions, the parties may be put to much unnecessary trouble and cost.

Although INCONTERMS 2000 do not provide for many of these commonly used variants, the preambles to certain trade terms do alert the parties to the need for special contractual terms if the parties wish to go beyond the stipulations of INCOTERMS.

EXW the added obligation for the seller to load the goods no the buyer's collecting vehicle.
CIF/CIP the buyer's need for additional insurance.
DEQ the added obligation for the seller to pay for costs after discharge.

In some cases sellers and buyers refer to commercial practice in liner and charter party trade. In these circumstances, it is necessary to clearly distinguish between the obligations of the parties under the contract of carriage and their obligations to each other under the contract of sale. Unfortunately, there are no authoritative definitions of expressions such as "liner terms" and "terminal handling charges" (THC). Distribution of costs under such terms may differ in different places and change from time to time. The parties are recommended to clarify in the contract of sale how such costs should be distributed between themselves.

Expressions frequently used in charter parties, such as "FOB stowed", "FOB stowed and trimmed", are sometimes used in contracts of sale in order to clarify to what extent the seller under FOB has to perform stowage and trimming of the goods onboard the ship. Where such words are added, it is necessary to clarify in the contract of sale whether the added obligations only relate to costs or to both costs and risks.

As has been said, every effort has been made to ensure that INCOTERMS reflect the most common commercial practice. However in some cases-particularly where INCOTERMS 2000 differ from INCOTERMS 1990—the parties may wish the trade terms to operate differently. They are reminded of such options in the preamble of the terms signaled by the word "However".

1.2.12 Customs of the Port or of a Particular Trade

Since INCOTERMS provide a set of terms for use in different trades and regions it is impossible always to set forth the obligations of the parties with precision. To some extent it is therefore necessary to refer to the custom of the port or of the particular trade or to the practices which the parties themselves may have established in their previous dealings (refer to article 9 of the 1980 United Nations Convention on Contracts for the International Sale of Goods). It is of course desirable that sellers and buyers keep themselves duly informed of such customs when they negotiate their contract and that, whenever uncertainty arises, they clarify their legal position by appropriate clauses in their contract of sale. Such special provisions in the individual contract would supersede or vary anything that is set forth as a rule of interpretation in the various INCOTERMS.

1.2.13 The Buyer's Options as to the Place of Shipment

In some situations, it may not be possible at the time when the contract of sale is entered into to decide precisely on the exact point or even the place where the goods should be delivered by the seller for carriage. For instance reference might have been made at this stage merely to a "range" or to a rather large place, for example, seaport, and it is then usually stipulate that the buyer has the right or duty to mane later on the more precise point within the range or the place. If the buyer has a duty to mane the precise point as aforesaid his failure to do so might result in liability to bear the risks and additional costs resulting from such failure (B5/B7 of all terms). In addition, the buyer's failure to use his right to indicate the point may give the seller the right to select the point which best suits his purpose (FCA A4).

1.2.14 Customs Clearance

The term "customs clearance" has given rise to misunderstandings. Thus, whenever reference is made to an obligation of the seller or the buyer to undertake obligations in connection with passing the goods through customs of the country of export or import it is now made clear that this obligation does not only include the payment of duty and other charges but also the performance and payment of whatever administrative matters are connected with the passing of the goods through customs and the information to the authorities in this connection. Further, it has although quite wrongfully been considered in some quarters in some quarters inappropriate to use terms dealing with the obligation to clear the goods through customs when, as in intra-European Union trade or other free trade areas, there is no longer any obligation to pay duty and no restrictions relating to import or export. In order to clarify the situation, the words "where applicable" have been added in the A2 and B2, A6 and B6 clauses of the relevant INCOTERMS in order for them to be used without any ambiguity where no customs procedures are required.

It is normally desirable that customs clearance is arranged by the party domiciled in the country where such clearance should take place or at least by somebody acting there on his behalf. Thus, the exporter should normally clear the goods for export, while the importer should clear the goods for import.

INCOTERMS 1990 departed from this under the trade terms EXW and FAS (export clearance duty on the buyer) and DEQ (import clearance duty on the seller) but in INCOTERMS 2000 FAS and DEQ place the duty of clearing the goods for export on the seller and to clear them for import on the buyer respectively, while EXW representing the seller's minimum obligation has been left unamended (export clearance duty on the buyer). Under DDP the seller specifically agrees to do what follows from the very name of the term Delivered Duty Paid namely to clear the goods for import and pay any duty as a consequence thereof.

1.2.15 Packaging

In most cases, the parties would know beforehand which packaging is required for the safe carriage of the goods to destination. However, since the seller's obligation to pack the goods may well vary according to the type and duration of the transport envisaged, it has been felt necessary to stipulate that the seller is obliged to pack the goods in such a manner as is required for the transport, but only to the extent that the circumstances relating to the transport are made known to him before the contract of sale is concluded (refer to articles 35. 1. and 35. 2. b. of the 1980 United Nations Contracts for the International Sale of Goods where the goods, including packaging, must be "fit for any particular purpose expressly or impliedly made known to the seller at the time of the conclusion of the contract, except where the circumstances show that the buyer did not rely, or that it was unreasonable for him to rely, on the seller' skill and judgment").

1.2.16 Inspection of Goods

In many cases, the buyer may be well advised to arrange for inspection of the goods before or at the time they are handed over by the seller for carriage (so-called pre-shipment inspection or PSI). Unless the contract stipulates otherwise, the buyer would himself have to pay the cost for such inspection that is arranged in his own interest. However, if the inspection has been made in order to enable the seller to comply with any mandatory rules applicable to the export of the goods in his own country, the seller would have to pay for that inspection, unless the EXW term is used, in which case the costs of such inspection are for the account of the buyer.

1.2.17 Mode of Transport and the Appropriate INCOTERMS 2000

Table 1.2 Mode of Transport and the Appropriate INCOTERMS 2000

(a) Any Mode of Transport

Group E		
	EXM	Ex Works (... named place)
Group F		
	FCA	Free Carrier (... named place)
Group C		
	CPT	Carriage Paid To (... named place of destination)
	CIP	Carriage and Insurance Paid To (... named place of destination)
Group D		
	DAF	Delivered At Frontier (... named place)
	DDU	Delivered Duty Unpaid (... named place of destination)
	DDP	Delivered Duty Paid (... named place of destination)

(b) Maritime and Inland Waterway Transport Only

Group F		
	FAS	Free Alongside Ship (... named port of shipment)
	FOB	Free On Board (... named port of shipment)
Group C		
	CFR	Cost and Freight (... named port of shipment)
	CIF	Cost, Insurance and Freight (... named port of shipment)
Group D		

(b)

DES	Delivered Ex Ship (... named port of shipment)
DEQ	Delivered Ex Quay (... named port of shipment)

1.2.18 The Recommended Use

In some cases the preamble recommends the use or non-use of a particular term, this is particularly important with respect to the choice between FCA and FOB. Regrettably, merchants continue to use FOB when it is totally out of place thereby causing the seller to incur risks subsequent to the handing over of the goods to the carrier named by the buyer. FOB is only appropriate to use where the goods are intended to be delivered "across the ship's rail" or, in any event, to the ship and not where the goods are handed over to the carrier for subsequent entry into the ship, for example stowed in containers or loaded on lorries or wagons in so-called roll on-roll off traffic. Thus, a strong warning has been made in the preamble of FOB that the term should not be used when the parties do not intend delivery across the ship's rail.

It happens that the parties by mistake use terms intended for carriage of goods by sea also when another mode of transport is contemplated. This may put the seller in the unfortunate position that he cannot fulfill his obligation to tender the proper document to the buyer (for example a bill of lading, sea waybill or the electronic equivalent).

1.2.19 Bill Of Landing and Electronic Commerce

Traditionally, the on board bill of lading has been the only acceptable document to be presented by the seller under the CFR and CIF term. The bill of lading fulfils three important functions, namely:

a. proof of delivery of the foods on board the vessel;

b. evidence of the contract of carriage;

c. a means of transferring rights to the goods in transit to another party the transfer of the paper document to him.

Transport documents other than the bill of lading would fulfill the two first-mentioned functions, but would not control the delivery of the goods at destination or enable a buyer to sell the goods in transit by surrendering the paper document to his buyer. Instead, other transport documents would name the party entitled to receive the goods at destination. The fact that the possession of the bill of lading is required in order to obtain the foods from the carrier at destination makes it particularly difficult to replace by electronic means of communication.

Further, it is customary to issue bills of lading in several originals but it is, of course, of vital importance for a buyer or a bank acting upon his instructions in paying the seller to ensures that all originals are surrendered by the seller (so-called "full set"). This is also a requirement under the ICC Rules for Documentary Credits.

The transport document must evidence not only delivery of the goods to the carrier but also that the goods, as far as could be ascertained by the carrier, were received in good order and condition. Any notation on the transport document which would indicate that the goods had not been in such condition would make the document "unclean" and would thus make it unacceptable under the UCP.

In spite of the particular legal nature of the bill of lading it is expected that it will be replaced by electronic means in the near future. The 1990 version of Incomers had already taken this expected development into proper account. According to the A8 clauses, paper documents may be replaced by electronic messages provided the parties have agreed to communicate electronically. Such messages could be transmitted directly to the parties concerned or though a third party providing added-value services. One such service that can be usefully provided by a third party is registration of successive holders of a bill of lading. Systems providing such service, such as the so-called BOLERO service, may require further support by appropriate legal norms and principles as evidenced by the CMI 1990 Rules for Electronic Bills of Lading and articles 16—17 of the 1996 UNCITRAL Model Law on Electronic Commerce.

1.2.20 Non-negotiable Transport Documents Instead of Bills of Lading

In recent years, a considerable simplification of documentary practices has been achieved. Bills of lading are frequently replaced by non-negotiable documents similar to those which are used for other modes of transport than carriage by sea. These documents are called "sea waybills", "liner waybills", "freight receipts", or variants of such expressions. Non-negotiable documents are quite satisfactory to use except where the buyer wishes to sell the goods in transit by surrendering a paper document to the new buyer. In order to make this possible, the obligation of the seller to provide a bill of lading under CFR and CIF must necessarily be retained. However, when the contracting parties known that the buyer does not contemplate selling the goods in transit, they may specifically agree to relieve the seller from the obligation to provide a bill of lading, or, alternatively, they may use CPT and CIP where there is no requirement to provide a bill of lading.

1.2.21 Right to Give Instruction to the Carrier

A buyer paying for the goods under a "C" -term should ensure that the seller upon payment is prevented from disposing of the goods by giving new instructions to the carrier. Some transport documents used for particular modes of transport (air, road or rail) offer the contracting parties a possibility to bar the seller from giving such new instructions to the carrier by providing the buyer with a particular original or duplicate of the waybill. However, the documents used instead of bills of lading for maritime carriage do not normally contain such a barring function. The Comity International has remedied this shortcoming of the above-mentioned documents by introducing the 1990 "*Uniform Rules for Sea Waybillsp*" enabling the parties to insert a " no-disposal" clause whereby the seller surrenders the right to dispose of the goods by instructions to the carrier to deliver the goods to somebody else or at another place than stipulated in the waybill.

1.2.22 ICC Arbitration

Contracting parties who wish to have the possibility of resorting to ICC Arbitration in the event of a dispute with their contract or, in the event that no single contractual document between them. The fact of incorporating one or more Incomers in a contract or the related correspondence does NOT by itself constitute an agreement to have resort to ICC Arbitration.

The following standard arbitration clause is recommended by ICC.

"All disputes arising out of or in connection with the present contract shall be finally settled under the rules of Arbitration of the International Chamber of Commerce by one or more arbitrators appointed in accordance with the said Rules."

1.3 Trade Terms

1.3.1 EXW

EX WORKS(... named place)

"Ex works" means that the seller delivers when he places the goods at the disposal of the buyer at the seller's premises or another named place (i. e. works, factory, warehouse, etc.) not cleared for cleared for export and not loaded on any collecting vehicle.

This term thus represents the minimum obligation for the seller, and the buyer has to bear all costs and risks involved in taking the goods from the seller's premises.

However, if the parties wish the seller to be responsible for the loading of the goods on departure and to bear the risks and all the costs of such loading, this should be made clear by adding explicit wording to this effect in the contract of sale. This term should not be used when the buyer cannot carry out the export formalities directly or indirectly. In such circumstances, the FCA term should be used, provided the seller agrees that he will load at his cost and risk.

1. Provision of Goods in Conformity with the Contract

A1 The seller must provide the goods and the commercial invoice, or its equivalent electronic message, in conformity with the contract of sale and any other evidence of conformity which may be required by the contract.

B1 The buyer must pay the price as provided in the contract of sale.

2. Licenses, Authorizations and Formalities

A2 The seller must render the buyer, at the latter's request, risk and expense, every assistance in obtaining, where applicable, any export license or other official authorization necessary for the export of the goods.

B2 The buyer must obtain at his own risk and expense any export and import license or other official authorization and carry out, where applicable, all customs formalities for the export of the goods.

3. Contracts of Carriage and Insurance

A3 The seller has no obligation for the contract of carriage and the contract of insurance.

B3 The buyer has no obligation for the contract of carriage and the contract of insurance.

4. Delivery

A4 The seller must place the goods at the disposal of the buyer at the named place of delivery, not loaded on any collecting vehicle, on the date or within the period agreed or, if no such time is agreed, at the usual time for delivery of such goods. If no specific point has been agreed within the named place, and if there are several points available, the seller may select the point at the point at the place of delivery which best suits his purpose.

B4 The buyer must take delivery of the goods when they have been delivered in accordance with A4 and A7 or B7.

5. Transfer of Risks

A5 The seller must, subject to the provisions of B5, bear all risks of loss of or damage to the goods until such time as they have been delivered in accordance with A4.

B5 The buyer must bear all risks of loss of or damage to the goods.

a. From the time they have been delivered in accordance with A4.

b. From the agreed date or the expiry date of any period fixed for taking delivery which arise because he fails to give notice in accordance with B7, provided, however, that the goods have been duly appropriated to the contract, that is to say clearly set aside or otherwise identified as the contract goods.

6. Division of Costs

A6 The seller must, subject to the provision of B6, pay all costs relating to the goods until such time as they have been delivered in accordance with A4.

B6 The buyer must pay:

a. All costs relating to the goods from the time they have been delivered in accordance with A4.

b. Any addition costs incurred by failing either to take delivery of the goods when they have been placed at his disposal, or to give appropriate notice in accordance with B7 provided, however, that the goods have been duly appropriated to the contract, that is to say, clearly set aside or otherwise identified as the contract goods.

c. Where applicable, all duties, taxes and other charges as well as the costs of carrying out customs formalities payable upon export.

The buyer must reimburse all costs and charges incurred by the seller in rendering assistance in accordance with A2.

7. Notice

A7 The seller must give the buyer sufficient notice as when and where the goods will be placed at his disposal.

B7 The buyer must, whenever he is entitled to determine the time within an agreed period and/or the place of taking delivery, give the seller sufficient notice thereof.

8. Proof of Delivery, Transport Document or Equivalent Electronic Message

A8 The seller has no obligation for the proof of delicery and related evidenle.

B8 The buyer must provide the seller with appropriate evidence of having taken delivery.

9. Checking-Packaging-Marking

A9 The seller must pay the costs of those checking operations (such as checking quality, measuring, weighing, and counting) which are necessary for the purpose of placing the goods at the buyer's disposal.

The seller must provide at his own expense packaging (unless it is usual for the particular trade to make the goods of the contract description available unpacked) which is required for transport of goods, to the extent that the circumstance relating to the transport (for example modalities, destination) are made known to the seller before the contract of sale is concluded. Packaging is to be marked appropriately.

B9 The buyer must pay the costs of any pre-shipment inspection, including inspection mandated by the authorities of country of export.

10. Other Obligations

A10 The seller must render the buyer at the latter's request, risk and expense, every assistance in obtaining any documents or equivalent electronic messages issued or transmitted in the country of delivery and/or of origin which the buyer may require for export and/or import of the goods and, where necessary, for their transit through any country.

The seller must provide the buyer, upon request, with the necessary information for procuring insurance.

B10 The buyer must pay all costs and charges incurred in obtaining the documents or equivalent electronic messages mentioned in A10 and reimburse those incurred by the seller in rendering his assistance in accordance therewith.

1.3.2 FCA

Free Carrier (... named place)

"Free Carrier" means that the seller delivers the goods, cleared for export, to the carrier nominate by the buyer at the named place. It should be noted that the chosen place of delivery has an impact on the obligations of loading and unloading the goods at that place. If delivery occurs at the seller's premises, the seller is responsible for loading. If delivery occurs at any other place, the seller is not responsible for unloading.

This term may be use irrespective of the mode of transport, including multimodal transport.

"Carrier" means any person who, in a contract of carriage, undertakes to perform or to procure the performance of transport by rail, road, air, sea, inland waterway or by combination of such modes.

If the buyer nominates a person other than a carrier to receive the goods, the seller is deemed to have fulfilled his obligation to deliver the goods when they are delivered to that person.

1. Provision of Goods in Conformity with the Contract

A1 The seller must provide the goods and the commercial invoice, or its equivalent electronic message, in conformity with the contract of sale and any other evidence of conformity which maybe required by the contract.

B1 The buyer must pay the price as provided in the contract of sale.

2. Licenses, Authorizations and Formalities

A2 The seller must obtain at his own risk and expense any export license or other official authorization and carry out, where applicable, all customs formalities necessary for the export of the goods.

B2 The buyer must obtain at his own risk and expense any import license or other official authorization and carry out, where applicable, all customs formalities for the import of the goods and for their transit through any country.

3. Contracts of Carriage and Insurance

A3 The seller has no obligation. However, if requested by the buyer or if it is commercial practice and the buyer does not give an instruction to the contrary in due time, the seller may contract for carriage on usual terms at the buyer's risk and expense. In either case, the seller may decline to make the contract and, if he dose, shall promptly notify the buyer accordingly.

The seller has no obligation for the contract of insurance.

B3 The buyer must contract at his own expense for the carriage of the goods from the named place, except when the contract of carriage is made by the seller as provided for in A3.

The buyer has no obligation for the contract of insurance.

4. Delivery

A4 The seller must delver the goods to the carrier or another or another person nominated by the buyer, or chosen by the seller in accordance with A3, at the named place on the date or within the period agreed for delivery.

Delivery is completed:

a. If the named place is the seller's premises, when the goods have been loaded on the means of transport provided by the carrier nominated by the buyer or another person acting on his behalf.

b. If the named place is anywhere other than **a**, when the goods are placed at the disposal of the carrier or another person nominated by the buyer, or chosen by the seller in accordance with best suits his purpose.

c. If no specific point has been agreed within the named place, and if there are several points available, the seller may select the point at the place of delivery which best suit his purpose.

Failing precise instructions from the buyer, the seller may deliver the goods for carriage in such a manner as the transport mode and/or the quantity and/or nature of the goods may require.

B4 The buyer must take delivery of the goods when they have been delivered in accordance with A4.

5. Transfer of Risks

A5 The seller must, subject to the provisions of B5, bear all risks of lose of or damage to the goods until such time as they have been delivered in accordance with A4.

B5 The buyer must bear all risks of loss of or damage to the goods:

a. From the time they have been delivered in accordance with A4.

b. From the agreed date or the expiry date if any agreed period fir delivery which arise either because he fails to nominate the carrier or another person in accordance with A4, or because the carrier or the party nominated by the buyer fails to take the goods into his charge at the agreed time, or because the buyer fails to give appropriate notice in accordance with B7, provide, however, that is to say, clearly set aside or otherwise identified as the contract goods.

6. Division of Costs

A6 The seller must pay, subject to the provisions of B6:

a. All costs relating to the goods until such time as they have been delivered in accordance with A4.

b. Where applicable, the costs of customs formalities as well as all duties, taxes, and other charge payable upon export.

B6 The buyer must pay:

a. All costs relating to the goods from the time they have been delivered in accordance with A4.

b. Any additional costs incurred, either because he fails to nominate the carrier or another person in accordance with A4 or because the party nominated by the buyer fails to take the goods into his charge at the agreed time, or because he has failed to give appropriate notice in accordance with B7, provided, however, that the goods have been duly appropriated as the contract goods.

c. Where applicable, all duties, taxes and other charges as well as the costs of carrying out customs formalities payable upon import of the goods and for their transit through any country.

7. Notice

A7 The seller must give the seller sufficient notice that the goods have been delivered in accordance with A4. Should the carrier fail to take delivery in accordance with A4 at the time agreed, the seller must notify the buyer accordingly.

B7 The buyer must give the seller sufficient notice of the party designated in A4 and, where necessary, specify the mode of transport, as well as the date or period for delivering the goods to him and, as the case may be, the point within the place where the goods should be delivered to that party.

8. Proof of Delivery, Transport Document or Equivalent Electronic Message

A8 The seller must provide the buyer at the seller's expense with the usual proof of delivery of the goods in accordance with A4.

Unless the document referred to in the preceding paragraph is the transport document, the seller must render the buyer at the latter's request, risk and expense.

Every assistance in obtaining a transport document for the contract of carriage (for example a negotiable bill of lading, a nonnegotiable sea waybill, an inland waterway document, an air waybill, a railway consignment note, a road consignment note, or a multimodal transport document).

When the seller and the buyer have agreed to communicate electronically, the document referred to in the preceding paragraph may be replaced by an equivalent electronic data interchange (EDI) message.

B8 The buyer must accept the proof of delivery in accordance with A8.

9. Checking-Packaging-Marking

A9 The seller must pay the costs of those checking operations (such as checking quality, measuring, weighing, counting) which are necessary with A4.

The seller must provide at his own expense packaging (unless it is usual for the particular trade to send the goods of the contract description unpacked) which is required for the transport of the goods, to the extent that the circumstances relating to the transport (for example modalities, destination) are made known to the seller before the contract of sale is concluded. Packaging is to be marked appropriately.

B9 The buyer must pay the costs of any pre-shipment inspection except when such inspection except when such inspection is mandated by the authorities of the country of export.

10. Other Obligations

A10 The seller must render the buyer at the latter's request, risk and expense, every assistance in obtaining any documents or equivalent electronic message (other than those mentioned in A8) issued or transmitted in the country of delivery and/or of origin which the buyer may require for the import of the goods and, where necessary, for their transit through ant country.

The seller must provide the buyer, upon request, with the necessary information for procuring insurance.

B10 The buyer must pay all costs and charges incurred in obtaining the documents or equivalent electronic messages mentioned in A10 and reimburse those incurred by the seller in rendering his assistance in accordance therewith and in contracting for carriage in accordance with A3 **a**.

The buyer must give the seller appropriate instructions whenever the seller's assistance in contracting for carriage is required in accordance with A3.

1.3.3 FAS

FREE ALONGSIDE SHIP(... named port of shipment)

"Free Alongside Ship" means that the seller delivers when the goods are placed alongside the vessel at the named port shipment. This means that the buyer has to bear all costs and rises of loss of or damage to the goods from that moment.

The FAS term requires the seller to clear the goods for export.

This is a reversal from previous INCOTERMS versions which required the buyer to arramge for export clearance.

However, if the parties wish the buyer to clear the goods for export, this should be made clear by adding explicit wording to this effect in the contract of sale. This term can be used only for sea or inland waterway transport.

1. Provision of Goods in Conformity with the Contract.

A1 The seller must provide the goods and the commercial invoice, or its equivalent electronic message, in conformity with the contract of sale and any other evidence of conformity which may be required by the contract.

B1 The buyer must pay the price as provided in the contract of sale.

2. Licenses, Authorizations and Formalities

A2 The seller must obtain at his own risk and expense any export license or other official authorization and carry out, where applicable, all customs formalities necessary for the export of the goods.

B2 The buyer must obtain at his own risk and expense any import license or other official authorization and carry out, where applicable, all customs formalities for the import of the goods and for their transit through any country.

3. Contracts of Carriage and Insurance

A3 The seller has no obligation for the contract of carriage and the contract of insurance.

B3 The buyer must contract at his own expense for the carriage if the goods from the named port of shipment. The buyer has no obligation for the contract of insurance.

4. Delivery

A4 The seller must place the goods alongside the vessel nominated by the buyer all the loading place named by the buyer at the named port of shipment on the date or within the agreed period and in the manner customary at the port.

B4 The buyer must delivery of the goods when they have been delivered in accordance with A4.

5. Transfer of Risks

A5 The seller must, subject to the provisions of B5, bear all risks of loss of or damage to the goods until such time as they have been delivered in accordance with A4.

B5 The buyer must bear all risks of loss of or damage to the goods:

a. From the time they have been delivered in accordance with A4.

b. From the agreed date or the expiry date of the agreed period for delivery which arise because he fails to give notice in accordance with B7, or because the vessel nominated by him fails to accordance on time, or is unable to take the goods, or closes for cargo earlier than the time notified in accordance with B7 provided, however, that the goods have been duly appropriated to the contract, that is to say, clearly set aside or otherwise identified as the contract goods.

6. Division of Costs

A6 The seller must pay, subject to provisions of B6:

a. All costs relating to the goods until such time as they have been delivered in accordance with A4.

b. Where applicable, the costs of customs formalities as well as all duties, taxes, and other charges payable upon export.

B6 Division of costs:

a. All costs relating to the goods from the time they have been delivered in accordance with A4.

b. Any additional costs incurred, either because the vessel nominated by him has failed to arrive on time, or is unable to take the goods, or closes for cargo earlier than the time notified in accordance with B7, or because the buyer has failed to give appropriate notice in accordance with B7 provided, however, that the goods have been duly appropriated to the contract, that is to say, clearly set aside or otherwise identified as the contract goods.

c. Where applicable, all duties, taxes and other charges as well as the costs of carrying out customs formalities payable upon import of the goods and for their transit through any country.

7. Notice to the Buyer

A7 The seller must give the buyer sufficient notice that the goods have been deliver alongside the nominated vessel.

B7 The buyer must give the seller sufficient notice of the vessel name, loading point and required delivery time.

8. Proof of Delivery, Transport Document or Equivalent Electronic Message

A8 The seller must provide the buyer at the seller's expense with the usual proof of delivery of the goods in accordance with A4.

Unless the document referred to in the preceding paragraph is the transport document, the seller must render the buyer at the latter's request, risk and expense, every assistance in obtaining a transport document (for example a negotiable bill of lading, a non-negotiable sea waybill, an inland waterway document).

When the seller and the buyer have agreed to communicate electronically, the document referred to in the preceding paragraphs may be replaced by an equivalent electronic data interchange (EDI) message.

B8 The buyer must accept the proof of delivery in accordance with A8.

9. Checking-Packaging-Marking

A9 The seller must pay the costs of those checking operations (such as checking quality, measuring, weighing, counting) which are necessary for the purpose of delivering the goods in accordance with A4.

The seller must provide at his own expense packaging (unless it is usual for the particular trade to shi the goods of the contract description unpacked) which is required for the transport of the goods, to the extent that the circumstances relating to the transport (for example modalities, destination) are made known to the seller before the contract of sale is concluded. Packaging is to be marked appropriately.

B9 The buyer must pay the costs of any pre-shipment inspection, except when such inspection is mandated by the authorities of the country of export.

10. Other Obligations

A10 The seller must render the buyer at the latter's request, risk and expense, every assistance in obtaining any documents or equivalent electronic messages (other than those mentioned in A8) issued or transmitted in the country and/or of origin which the buyer may require for the import of the goods and, where necessary, for their transit through any country. The seller must provide the buyer, upon request, with the necessary information for procuring insurance.

B10 The buyer must pay all costs and charges incurred in obtaining the documents or equivalent electronic messages mentioned in A10 and reimburse those incurred by the seller in rendering his assistance in accordance therewith.

1.3.4 FOB

FREE ON BOARD(... named pore of shipment)

"Free on board" means that the seller delivers when the goods pass the ship's rail at the named port of shipment. This means that the buyer has to bear all cost to and risks of loss of or damage to the goods from that point. The FOB term requires the seller to clear the goods for export. This term can be used only for sea or inland waterway transport. If the parties do not intend to deliver the goods across the ship's rail, the FCA term should be used.

1. Provision of Goods in Conformity with the Contract

A1 The seller must provide the goods and the commercial invoice, or its equivalent electronic message, in conformity with the contract of sale and any other evidence of conformity which may be required by the contract.

B1 The buyer must pay the price as provided in the contract of sale.

2. Licenses, Authorizations and Formalities

A2 The seller must obtain at his own risk and expense any import license or other official authorization and carry out, where applicable, all customs formalities necessary for the export of the goods.

B2 The buyer must obtain at his own risk and expense any import license or other official authorization and carry out, where applicable, all customs formalities for the import of the goods and, where necessary, for their transit through any country.

3. Contracts of Carriage and Insurance

A3 The seller has no obligation for the contract of carriage and the contract of insurance.

B3 The buyer must contract at his own expense for the carriage of the goods from the named port of shipment. The buyer has no obligation for the contract of insurance.

4. Delivery

A4 The seller must deliver the goods on the date or within the agreed period at the named port of shipment and in the manner customary at the port on board the vessel nominated by the buyer.

B4 The buyer must take delivery of the goods when they have been delivered in accordance with A4.

5. Transfer of Risks

A5 The seller must, subject to the provisions of B5, bear all risks of loss of or damage to the goods until such time as the have passed the ship's rail at the named port of shipment.

B5 The buyer must bear all risks of loss of or damage to the goods:

a. From the time they have passed the ship's rail at the named port of shipment.

b. From the agreed date or the expiry date of the agreed period for delivery which arise because he fails to give notice in accordance with B7, or because the vessel nominated by him fails to arrive on time, or is unable to take the goods, or closes for cargo earlier than the time notified in accordance with B7, provided, however, that the goods have been duly appropriated to the contract, that is to say, clearly set aside or otherwise identified as the contract goods.

6. Division of Costs

A6 The seller must pay, subject to the provisions of B6:

a. All cost relating to the goods until such time as they have passed the ship's rail at the named port of shipment.

b. Where applicable, the costs of customs formalities necessary for export as well as all duties, taxes and other charges payable upon export.

B6 The buyer must pay:

a. All costs relating to the goods from the time they have passed the ship's rail at the named port of shipment.

b. Any additional costs incurred, either because the vessel nominated by him fails to arrive on time, or is unable to take the goods, or closes for cargo earlier than the time notified in accordance with B7, or because the buyer has failed to give appropriate notice in accordance with B7, provided, however, that the goods have been duly appropriatde to the contract, that is to say, clearly set aside or otherwise identified as the contract goods.

c. Where applicable, all duties, taxes and other charges as well as the costs of carrying out customs formalities payable upon import of the goods and for their transit through any country.

7. Notice

A7 The seller must give the buyer sufficient notice that the goods have been delivered in accordance with A4.

B7 The buyer must give the seller sufficient notice of the vessel name, loading point and required delivery time.

8. Proof of Delivery, Transport Document or Equivalent Electronic Message

A8 The seller must provide the buyer at the seller's expense with the usual proof of delivery in accordance with A4.

Unless the document referred to in the preceding paragraph is the transport document, the seller must render the buyer, at the latter's request risk and expense, every assistance in obtaining a transport document for the contract of carriages (for example, a negotiable bill of lading, a non-negotiable sea waybill, an inland waterway document, or a multimodal transport document).

Where the seller and the buyer have agreed to communicate electronically, the document referred to in the preceding paragraph may be replaced by an equivalent electronic data interchange (EDI) message.

B8 The buyer must accept the proof of delivery in accordance with A8.

9. Checking-Packaging-Marking

A9 The seller must pay the costs of those checking operations (such as checking quality, measuring, weighting, counting) which are necessary for the purpose of delivering the goods in accordance with A4.

The seller must provide at his own expense packaging (unless it is usual for the particular trade to ship the goods of the contract description unpacked) which is required for the transport of the goods, to the extent that the circumstances relating to the transport (for example modalities, destination) are made known to the seller before the contract of sale is concluded. Packaging is to be marker appropriately.

B9 The buyer must pay the costs of any pre-shipment inspection except when such inspection is mandated by the authorities of the country of export.

10. Other Obligations

A10 The seller must render the buyer at the latter's request, risk and expense, every assistance in obtaining any document or equivalent electronic messages (other than those mentioned in A8) issued or transmitted in the country of shipment and/or of origin which the buyer may require for the import of the goods and, where necessary, for their transit through any country.

The seller must provide the buyer, upon request, with the necessary information for procuring insurance.

B10 The buyer must pay all costs and charges incurred in obtaining the documents or equivalent electronic messages mentioned in A10 and reimburse those incurred by the seller in rendering his assistance in accordance therewith.

1.3.5 CFR

COST AND FREIGHT (…named port of destination)

"Cost and freight" means that the seller delivers when the goods pass the ship's rail in the port of shipment, the seller must pay the costs and freight necessary to bring the goods to the named port of destination. But the risk of loss of or damage to the goods, as well as any additional costs due to events occurring after the time of delivery, are transferred from the seller to the buyer.

The CFR term requires the seller to clear the goods for export.

This term can be used only for sea and inland waterway transport. If the parties do not intend to deliver the goods across the ship's rail, the CPT term should be used.

1. Provision of Goods in Conformity with the Contract

A1 The seller must provide the goods and the commercial invoice, or its equivalent electronic message, in conformity which may be required by the contract.

B1 The buyer must pay the price as provided in the contract of sale.

2. Licenses, Authorizations and Formalities

A2 The seller must obtain at his own risk and expense any inport license or other official authorization and carry out, where applicable, all customs formalities necessary for the export of the goods.

B2 The buyer must obtain at his own risk and expense any import license or other official authorization and carry out, where applicable, all customs formalities for the import of the goods and for their transit through any country.

3. Contracts of Carriage and Insurance

A3 The seller must contract on usual terms at his own expense for the carriage of goods to the named port of destination by the usual route in a seagoing vessel (or inland waterway vessel as the case may be) of the type normally used for the contract description.

The seller has no obligation for the contract of insurance.

B3 The buyer has no obligation for the contract of carriage and the contract of insurance.

4. Delivery

A4 The seller must deliver the goods on board the vessel at the port of shipment on the date or within the agreed period.

B4 The buyer must accept delivery of the goods when they have been delivery in accordance with A4 and receive them from the carrier at the named port of destination.

5. Transfer of Risks

A5 The seller must, subject to the provisions of B5, bear all risks of loss of or damage to the goods until such times as they have passed the ship's rail at the port of shipment.

B5 The buyer must bear all risks of loss of or damage to the goods from the time they have padded the ship's rail at the port of shipment.

The buyer must should he fail to give notice in accordance with B7, bear all risks of loss of or damage to the goods from the agreed date or the expiry date of the period fixed for shipment provide, however, that the goods have been duly appropriated to the contract, that is to say, clearly set aside or otherwise identified as the contract goods.

6. Division of Costs

A6 The seller must pay, subject to the provisions of B6:

a. All cost relating to the goods until such time as they have been delivered in accordance with A4.

b. The freight and all other costs resulting from A3 **a**, including the costs of loading the goods on board and any charges for unloading at the agreed port of discharge which were for the seller's account under the contract of carriage.

c. Where applicable, the costs of customs formalities necessary for export as well as all duties, taxes and other charges payable upon export, and for their transit through any country if they were for the seller's account under the contract of carriage.

B6 The buyer must pay, subject to the provisions of A3:

a. All costs relating to the goods from the time they have been delivered in accordance with A4.

b. All costs and charges relating to the goods whilst in transit until their arrival at the port of destination, unless such costs and charges were for the seller's account under the contract of carriage.

c. Unloading costs including lighter age and wharf age charges, unless such costs and charges were for the seller's account under the contract of carriage.

d. All additional costs incurred if he fails to give notice in accordance with B7, for the goods from the agreed date or the expiry date of the period fixed for shipment, provided, however, that the goods have been duly appropriated to the contract, that is to say, clearly set aside or otherwise identified as the contract goods.

e. Where applicable, all duties, taxes and other charges as well as the costs of carrying out customs formalities payable upon import of the goods and, where necessary, for their transit through any country unless included within the cost of the contract of carriage.

7. Notice

A7 The seller must give the buyer sufficient notice that the goods have been delivered in accordance with A4 as well as any other notice required in order to allow the buyer to take measures which are normally necessary to enable him to take the goods.

B7 The buyer must, whenever his entitled to determine the time for shipping the goods and/or the port of destination, give the seller sufficient notice there.

8. Proof of Delivery, Transport Document or Equivalent Electronic Message

A8 The seller must at his own expense provide the buyer without delay with the usual transport document (for example a negotiable bill of lading, a non-negotiable sea waybill or an inland waterway document) must cover the contract goods, be dated within the period agreed for shipment, enable the buyer to claim the goods from the carrier at the port of destination and, unless otherwise agreed, enable the buyer to sell the goods in transit by the transfer of the document to a subsequent buyer (the negotiable bill of landing) or by notification to the carrier.

When such a transport document is issued in several originals, a full set of originals must be presented to the buyer.

Where the seller and the buyer have agreed to communicate electronically, the document referred to in the proceeding paragraphs may be replaced by an equivalent electronic data interchange (EDI) message.

B8 The buyer must accept the transport document in accordance with A8 if it is in conformity with the contract.

9. Checking-Packaging-Marking

A9 The seller must pay the costs of those checking operations (such as checking quality, measuring, weighing, counting) which are necessary for the purpose of delivering the goods in accordance with A4.

The seller must provide at his own expense packaging (unless it is usual for the particular trade to ship the goods of the contract description unpacked) which is required for the transport of the goods arranged by him.

Packaging is to be marked appropriately.

B9 The buyer must pay the costs of any pre-shipment inspection except when such inspection is mandated by the authorities of the country of export.

10. Other obligations

A10 The seller must render the buyer at the latter's request, risk and expense, every assistance in obtaining any documents or equivalent electronic messages (other than those mentioned in A8) issued or transmitted in the country of shipment and/or of origin which the buyer may require for the import of goods and, where necessary, for their transit through any country.

The seller must provide the buyer, upon request, with the necessary information for procuring insurance.

B10 The buyer must pay all costs and charges incurred in obtaining the documents or equivalent electronic messages mentioned in A10 and reimburse those incurred by the seller in rendering his assistance in accordance therewith.

1.3.6 CIF

COST, INSURANCE AND FREIGHTW(... named port of destination)

"Cost, Insurance and Freight" means that the seller delivers when the goods pass the ship's rail in the port of shipment, the seller must pay the costs and freight necessary to bring the goods to the named port of destination. But the risk of loss of damage to the goods, as well as any additional costs due to events occurring after the time of delivery, are transferred from the seller to the buyer. However, in CIF the seller also has to procure marine insurance against the buyer's risk of loss of or damage to the goods during the carriage.

Consequently, the seller contracts for insurance and pays the insurance premium, the buyer should note that under the CIF term the seller is required to obtain insurance only on minimum cover, he would either need to agree as such expressly with the seller or to make his own extra insurance arrangements.

The CIF term requires the seller to clear the goods for export.

This term can be used only for sea and inland waterway transport. If the parties do not intend to deliver the goods across the ship's rail, the CIF term should be used.

1. Provision of Good in Conformity with the Contract

A1 The seller must provide the goods the commercial invoice, or its equivalent electronic message, in conformity with the contract of sale and any other evidence of conformity which may be required by the contract.

B1 The buyer must pay the price as provide in the contract of sale.

2. Licenses, Authorizations and Formalities

A2 The seller must obtain at his own risk and expense any export license or other official authorization and carry out, where applicable, all customs formalities necessary for the export of goods.

B2 The buyer must obtain at his own risk and expense any export license or other official authorization and carry out, where applicable, all customs formalities for the import of the goods and for their transit through any country.

3. Contracts of Carriage and Insurance

A3 The seller must contract on usual terms at his own expense for the carriage of the good s to the agreed point at the named place of destination by a usual route and in a customary manner. If a point is not agreed or is not determined by practice, the seller may select the point at the named place of destination which best suits his purpose.

The seller must obtain at his own expense cargo insurance as agreed in the contract, such that he buyer, or any other person having an insurable interest in the goods, shall be entitled to claim directly from the insurer and provide the buyer with the insurance policy or other evidence of insurance cover.

The insurance shall be contracted with underwriters or an insurance company of good repute and, failing express agreement to the contrary, be in accordance with minimum cover of the Institute Cargo Clauses (Institute of London Underwriters) or any similar set of clauses. The duration of insurance cover shall be in accordance with B5 and B4. When required by the buyer, the seller shall provide at the buyer's expense war, strikes, riot and civil commotion risk insurances if procurable. The minimum insurance shall cover the price provides in the contract plus ten per cent (i. e. 110%) and shall be provided in the currency of the contract.

B3 The buyer has no obligation for the contract of carriage and the contract of insurance.

4. Delivery

A4 The seller must delivery the goods on board the vessel at the port of shipment on the date or with the agreed period.

B4 The buyer must accept delivery of the goods when they have been delivered in accordance with A4 and receive them from the carrier at the named port of destination.

5. Transfer of Risks

A5 The seller must, subject to the provision of B5, bear all risks of loss of or damage to the goods until such time as they have passed the ship's rail at the port of shipment.

B5 The buyer must bear all risks of loss of damage to the goods from the time they have passed the ship's rail at the port of shipment.

The buyer must, should he fail to give notice in accordance with B7, bear all risks of loss of or damage to the goods from the agreed date or the expiry date of the period fixed for shipment provided, however, that the goods have been duly appropriated to contract, that is to say, clearly set aside or otherwise identified as the contract goods.

6. Division of Costs

A6 The seller must pay, subject to the provisions of B6.

a. All costs relating to the goods until such time as they have been delivered in accordance with A4.

b. The freight and all other costs resulting from A3, including the costs of loading the goods on board, and the costs of insurance resulting from A3 **b.**

c. Any charges for unloading at the agreed port of discharge which were for the seller's account under the contract of carriage.

d. Where applicable, the cost of customs formalities necessary for export as well as all duties, taxes or other charges payable upon export, and for their transit through any country if were for the seller's account under contract of carriage.

B6 The buyer must pay, subject to the provisions of A3:

a. All costs relating to the goods from the time they have been delivery in accordance with A4.

b. All costs and charges relating to the goods whilst in transit until their arrival at the port of destination, unless such costs and charges were for the seller's account under the contract of carriage.

c. Unloading costs including lighterage and wharfage charges, unless such costs and charges were for the seller's account under the contract of carriage.

d. All additional costs incurred if he fails to give notice accordance with B7, for the goods from the agreed date or the expiry date of the period fixed for shipment, provided, however, that the goods have been duty appropriated to the contract, that is to say, clearly set aside or otherwise identified as the contract goods.

e. Where applicable, all duties, taxes and other charges as well as the costs of carrying out customs formalities payable upon import of the goods and, where necessary, for their transit through any country unless included within the cost of the contract of carriage.

7. Notice

A7 The seller must give the buyer sufficient notice that the goods have been delivered in accordance with A4 as well as any other notice required in order to allow the buyer to take measures which are normally necessary to enable him to take the goods.

B7 The buyer must, whenever he is entitled to determine the time for dispatching the goods and/or the destination, give the seller sufficient notice thereof.

8. Proof of Delivery, Transport Document or Equivalent Electronic Message

A8 The seller must, at his own expense, provide the buyer without delay with the usual transport document for the agreed port of destination.

This document (for example a negotiable bill of lading, a non-negotiable sea waybill, or an inland waterway document) must cover the contract goods, be dated within the period agreed for shipment, enable the buyer to claim the goods from the carrier at the port of destination and, unless otherwise agreed, enable the buyer to sell the goods in transit by the transfer of the document to a subsequent buyer (the negotiable bill of lading) or by notification to the carrier.

When such a transport document is issued in several originals, a full set of originals must be presented to the buyer.

Where the seller and the buyer have agreed to communicate electronically, the document referred to in the preceding paragraph may be replaced by an equivalent electronic data interchange (EDI) message.

B8 The buyer must accept the transport document in accordance with A8 if it is in conformity with the contract.

9. Checking-Packaging-Marking

A9 The seller must pay the costs of those checking operations (such as checking quality, measuring, weighing, counting) which are necessary for checking for the purpose of delivering the goods in accordance with A4.

The seller must provide at his own expense packaging (it is usual for the particular trade to send the goods of contract description unpacked) which is required for the transport of the goods arranged by him. Packaging is to be marked appropriately.

B9 The buyer must pay the costs of any pre-shipment inspection except when such inspection is mandated by the authorities of the country of export.

10. Other Obligations

A10 The seller must render the buyer at the latter's request, risk and expense, every assistance in obtaining any document or equivalent electronic messages (other than those mentioned in A8) issued or transmitted in the country of dispatch and/or of origin which the buyer may require for the import of the goods and for their transit through any country.

The seller must provide the buyer, upon request, with the necessary information for procuring any additional insurance.

B10 The buyer must pay all costs and charges incurred in obtaining the documents or equivalent electronic messages mentioned in A10 and reimburse those incurred by the seller in rendering his assistance in accordance therewith.

The buyer must provide the seller, upon request, with the necessary information for procuring insurance.

1.3.7 CPT

CPT(... named place of destination)

"Carriage paid to..." means that the seller delivers the goods to the carrier nominated by him but the seller must in addition pay the cost of carriage necessary to bring the goods to the named destination. This means that the buyer bears all risks and any other costs occurring after the goods have been so delivered.

"Carrier" means any person who, in a contract of carriage, undertakes to perform or to procure the performance of transport, by rail, road, air, sea, inland waterway or by a combination of such modes. If subsequent carriers are used for the carriage to the agreed destination, the risks pass when the goods have been delivered to the first carrier.

The CPT term requires the seller to clear the goods for export.

This term may be used irrespective of the modes of transport including multimodal transport.

1. Provision of Good in Conformity with the Contract

A1 The seller must provide the goods the commercial invoice, or its equivalent electronic message, in conformity with the contract of sale and any other evidence of conformity which may be required by the contract.

B1 The buyer must pay the price as provide in the contract of sale.

2. Licenses, Authorizations and Formalities

A2 The seller must obtain at his own risk and expense any export license or other official authorization and carry out, where applicable, all customs formalities necessary for the export of goods.

B2 The buyer must obtain at his own risk and expense any export license or other official authorization and carry out, where applicable, all customs formalities for the import of the goods and for their transit through any country.

3. Contracts of Carriage and Insurance

A3 The seller must contract on usual terms at his own expense for the carriage of the good s to the agreed point at the named place of destination by a usual route and in a customary manner. If a point is not agreed or is not determined by practice, the seller may select the point at the named place of destination which best suits his purpose.

The seller has no obligation for the contract of insurance.

B3 The buyer has no obligation for the contract of carriage and the contract of insurance.

4. Delivery

A4 The seller must delivery the goods to carrier contracted in accordance with A3 or, if there are subsequent carrier, for transport to the agreed point at the named place on date within the agreed period.

B4 The buyer must accept delivery of the goods when they have been delivered in accordance with A4 and receive them from the carrier at the named place.

5. Transfer of Risks

A5 The seller must, subject to the provision of B5, bear all risks of loss of or damage to the goods until such time as they have been delivered in accordance with A4.

B5 The buyer must bear all risks of loss of damage to the goods from the time they have been delivered in accordance with A4.

The buyer must, should he fail to give notice in accordance with B7, bear all risks of the goods from the agreed date or the expiry date of the period fixed for delivery provided, however, that the goods have been duly appropriated to contract, that is to say, a clearly set aside or otherwise identified as the contract goods.

6. Division of Costs

A6 The seller must pay, subject to the provisions of B6:

a. All costs relating to the goods until such time as they have been delivered in accordance with A4 as well as the freight and all other costs resulting from A3, including the costs of loading the goods and any charges for unloading at the place of destination which were for the seller's account under the contract of carriage.

b. Where applicable, the cost of customs formalities necessary for export as well as all duties, taxes or other charges payable upon export, and for their transit through any country if were for the seller's account under contract of carriage.

B6 The buyer must pay, subject to the provisions of A3.

a. All costs relating to the goods from the time they have been delivery in accordance with A4.

b. All costs and charges relating to the goods whilst in transit until their arrival at the agreed place of destination, unless such costs and charges were for the seller's account under the contract of carriage.

c. Unloading costs unless such costs and charges were for the seller's account under the contract of carriage.

d. All additional costs incurred if he fails to give notice I accordance with B7, for the goods from the agreed date or the expiry date of the period fixed for dispatch, provided, however, that the goods have been duty appropriated to the contract, that is to say, clearly set aside or otherwise identified as the contract goods.

e. Where applicable, all duties, taxes and other charges as well as the costs of carrying out customs formalities payable upon import of the goods and for their transit through any country unless included within the cost of the contract of carriage.

7. Notice

A7 The seller must give the buyer sufficient notice that the goods have been delivered in accordance with A4 as well as any other notice required in order to allow the buyer to take measures which are normally necessary to enable him to take the goods.

B7 The buyer must, whenever he is entitled to determine the time for dispatching the goods and/or the destination, give the seller sufficient notice thereof.

8. Proof of Delivery, Transport Document or Equivalent Electronic Message

A8 The seller must provide the buyer at the seller's expense, if customary, with the usual transport document or documents (for example a negotiable bill of lading a non-negotiable sea waybill, an inland waterway document, an air waybill, a railway consignment note, a road consignment note, or a multimodal transport document) for the transport contracted in accordance with A3.

B8 The buyer must accept the transport document in accordance with A8 if it is in conformity with the contract.

9. Checking-Packaging-Marking

A9 The seller must pay the costs of those checking operations (such as checking quality, measuring, weighing, counting) which are necessary for checking for the purpose of delivering the goods in accordance with A4.

The seller must provide at his own expense packaging (it is usual for the particular trade to send the goods of contract description unpacked) which is required for the transport of the goods arranged by him. Packaging is to be marked appropriately.

B9 The buyer must pay the costs of any pre-shipment inspection except when such inspection is mandated by the authorities of the country of export.

10. Other Obligations

A10 The seller must render the buyer at the latter's request, risk and expense, every assistance in obtaining any document or equivalent electronic messages (other than those mentioned in A8) issued or transmitted in the country of dispatch and/or of origin which the buyer may require for the import of the goods and for their transit through any country.

The seller must provide the buyer, upon request, with the necessary information for procuring insurance.

B10 The buyer must pay all costs and charges incurred in obtaining the documents or equivalent electronic messages mentioned in A10 and reimburse those incurred by the seller in rendering his assistance in accordance therewith.

1.3.8 CIP

Carriage and Insurance Paid to(... named place of destination)

"Carriage and Insurance paid to …" means that the seller delivers the goods to the carrier nominated by him but the seller must in addition pay the cost of carriage necessary to bring the goods to named destination. This means that the buyer bears all risks and additional costs occurring after the goods have been so delivered. However, in CIP the seller also has to procure insurance against the buyer's risk of loss of or damage to the goods during the carriage. Consequently, the seller contracts for insurance and pays the insurance premium.

The buyer should note that under the CIP term the seller is required to obtain insurance only on minimum cover. Should the buyer wish to have the protection of greater cover, he would either need to agree as such expressly with the seller or to make his own extra insurance arrangements.

"Carrier" means any person who, in a contract of carriage, undertakes to perform or to procure the performance of transport, by rail, road, air, sea, inland waterway or by a combination of such modes.

If subsequent carriers are used for the carriage to the agreed destination, the risk passes when the goods have been delivery to the first carrier.

The CIP term requires the seller to clear the goods for export.

This term may be used irrespective of the mode of transport including multimodal transport.

1. Provision of Goods in Conformity with the Contract

A1 The seller must provide the goods and the commercial invoice, or its equivalent electronic message, in conformity with the contract of sale and any other evidence of conformity which may be required by the contract.

B1 The buyer must pay the price as provided in the contract of sale.

2. Licenses, Authorizations and Formalities

A2 The seller must obtain at his own risk and expense any export license or other official authorization and carry out, where applicable, all customs formalities necessary for the export of the goods.

B2 The buyer must obtain at his own risk and expense any import license or other official authorization and carry out, where applicable, all customs formalities for the import of the goods and for their transit through any country.

3. Contracts of Carriage and Insurance

A3 The seller must contract on usual terms at his own his expense for the carriage of the goods to the agreed point at the named place of destination by a usual route and in a customary manner. If a point is not agreed or is not determined by practice, the seller may select the point at the named place of destination which best suits his purpose.

The seller must obtain at his own expense cargo insurance as agreed in the contract, such that he buyer, or any other person having an insurable interest in the goods, shall be entitled to claim directly from the insurer and provide the buyer with the insurance policy or other evidence of insurance cover.

The insurance shall be contracted with underwriters or an insurance company of good repute and, failing express agreement to the contrary, be in accordance with minimum cover of the Institute Cargo Clauses (Institute of London Underwriters) or any similar set of clauses. The duration of insurance cover shall be in accordance with B5 and B4. When required by the buyer, the seller shall provide at the buyer's expense war, strikes, riot and civil commotion risk insurances if procurable. The minimum insurance shall cover the price provides in the contract plus ten per cent (e.g. 110%) and shall be provided in the currency of the contract.

B3 The buyer has no obligation for the contract of carriage and the contract of insurance.

4. Delivery

A4 The seller must deliver the goods to the carrier contracted in accordance with A3 or, if there are subsequent carriers to the first carrier, for transport to the agreed point at the named place on the date or within the agreed period.

B4 The buyer must accept delivery of the goods when they have been delivered in accordance with A4 and receive them from the carrier at the named place.

5. Transfer of Risk

A5 The seller must, subject to the provision of B5, bear all risk of loss of or damage to the goods until such time as they have been delivered in accordance with A4.

B5 The buyer must bear all risk of loss of or damage to the goods from the time they have been delivered in accordance with A4.

The buyer must, should he fail to give notice in accordance with B7, bear all risks of the goods from the agrees fate or the expiry date of the period fixed for delivery provided, however, that the goods have been duly appropriated to the contract, that is to say, clearly set aside or otherwise identified as the contract goods.

6. Division of Costs

A6 The seller must pay, subject to the provisions of B6.

a. All costs relating to the goods until such time as they have been delivered in accordance with A4 as well as the freight and all other costs resulting from A3, including the costs of loading the goods and any charges for unloading at the place of destination which were for the seller's account under the contract of carriage.

b. The costs of insurance resulting from A3.

c. Where applicable, the cost of customs formalities necessary for export as well as all duties, taxes or other charges payable upon export, and for their transit through any country if they were for the seller's account under the contract carriage.

B6 The buyer must pay, subject to the provisions of A3.

a. All costs relating to the goods from the time they have been delivered in accordance with A4.

b. All costs and charges relating to the goods whilst in transit until their arrival at the agreed place of destination, unless such costs and charges were for the seller's account under the contract of carriage.

c. Unloading costs unless such costs and charges were for the seller's account under the contract of carriage's.

d. All additional costs incurred if he fails to give notice in accordance with B81, for the goods from the agreed date or the expiry date of the period fixed for dispatch, provided, however, that the goods have been duly appropriated to the contract, that is to say, clearly set aside or otherwise identified as the contract goods.

e. Where applicable, all duties, taxes and other charges as well as the cost of carrying out customs formalities payable upon import of the goods and for their transit through any country unless included within the cost of the contract of carriage.

7. Notice

A7 The seller must give the buyer sufficient notice that the goods have been delivered in accordance with A4as well as any other notice required in order to allow the buyer to take measures which are normally necessary to enable him to take the goods.

B7 The buyer must, whenever he is entitled to determine the time for dispatching the goods and/or the destination, give the sufficient notice thereof.

8. Proof of Delivery, Transport Document or Equivalent Electronic Message

A8 The seller must provide the buyer at the seller's expense, if customary, with the usual transport document or documents. (for example a negotiable bill of lading, a non-negotiable sea waybill, an inland waterway document, an air waybill, a railway consignment note, a road consignment note, or a multimodal transport document) for the transport contracted in accordance with A3.

Where the seller and the buyer have agreed to communicate electronically, the document referred to in the preceding paragraph may be replaced by an equivalent electronic data interchange (EDI) message.

B8 The buyer must accept the transport document in accordance with A8 if it is in conformity with the contract.

9. Checking-Packaging-Marking

A9 The seller must pay the cost of those checking operations (such as checking quality, measuring, weighing, counting) which are necessary for the purpose of delivering the goods in accordance with A4.

The seller must provide at his own expense packing (unless it is usual for the particular trade to send the goods of the contract description unpacked) which is required for the transport of the goods arranged by him. Packaging is to be marked appropriately.

B9 The buyer must pay the costs of any pre-shipment inspection except when such inspection is mandated by the authorities of the country of export.

10. Other Obligations

A10 The seller must render the buyer at the latter's request, risk and expense, every assistance in obtaining any documents or equivalent electronic messages (other than those mentioned in A8) issued or transmitted in the country of dispatch and/or of origin which the buyer may require for the import of the goods and for their transit through any country.

The seller must provide the buyer, upon request, with the necessary in formation for procuring any additional insurance.

B10 The buyer must pay all costs and charges incurred in obtaining the documents or equivalent electronic messages mentioned in A10 and reimburse those incurred by the seller in rendering his assistance in accordance therewith.

The buyer must provide the seller, upon request, with the necessary information for procuring insurance.

1.3.9 DAF

Delivered at Frontier(... named place)

"Delivered at Frontier" means that the seller delivers when the goods are placed at the disposal of the buyer on the arriving means of transport not unloaded, cleared for export, but not cleared for import at the named point and place at the frontier, but before the customs border of the adjoining country. The term "frontier" may be used for any frontier including that of the country of export. Therefore, it is of vital importance that the frontier in question be defined precisely by always naming the point and place in the term.

However, if the parties wish the seller to be responsible for the unloading of the goods from the arriving means of transport and to bear the risks and costs of unloading, this should be made clear by adding explicit wording to this effect in the contract of sale1.

This term may be used irrespective of the mode of transport when goods are to be delivered at a land frontier. When delivery is to take place in the port of destination, on board a vessel or on the quay (wharf), the DES or DEQ terms should be used.

1. Provision of Goods in Conformity with the Contract

A1 The seller must provide the goods and the commercial invoice, or its equivalent electronic message, in conformity with the contract of sale and any other evidence of conformity which may be required by the contract.

B1 The buyer must pay the price as provided in the contract of sale.

2. Licences, Authorisations and Formalities

A2 The seller must obtain at his own risk and expense any export licence or other official authorisation or other document necessary for placing the goods at the buyer's disposal.

The seller must carry out, where applicable2, all customs formalities necessary for the export of the goods to the named place of delivery at the frontier and for their transit through any country.

B2 The buyer must obtain at his own risk and expense any import licence or other official authorisation or other documents and carry out, where applicable3, all customs formalities necessary for the import of the goods, and for their subsequent transport.

3. Contracts of Carriage and Insurance

A3 The seller must contract at his own expense for the carriage of the goods to the named point, if any, at the place of delivery at the frontier. If a point at the named place of delivery at the frontier is not agreed or is not determined by practice, the seller may select the point the named place of delivery which best suits his purpose. However, if requested by the buyer, the seller may agree to contract on usual terms at the buyer's risk and expense for the on-going carriage of the goods beyond the named place at the frontier to the final destination in the country of import named by the buyer. The seller may decline to make the contact and, if he does, shall promptly notify the buyer accordingly.

The seller has no obligation for the contract of insurance.

B3 The buyer has no obligation for the contract of carriage and the contract of insurance.

4. Delivery

A4 The seller must place the goods at the disposal of the buyer on the arriving means of transport not unloaded at the named place of delivery at the frontier on the date or within the agreed period.

B4 The buyer must take delivery of the goods when they have been delivered in accordance with A4.

5. Transfer of Risks

A5 The seller must, subject to the provisions of B5, bear all risks of loss of or damage to the goods until such time as they have been delivered in accordance with A4.

B5 The buyer must bear all risks of loss of or damage to the goods from the time they have delivered in accordance with A4.

The buyer must, should he fail to give notice in accordance with B7, bear all risks of loss of or damage to the goods from the agreed date or the expiry date of the agreed period for delivery provided, however, that the goods have been duly appropriated to the contract, that is to say, clearly set aside or otherwise identified as the contract goods.

6. Division of Costs

A6 The seller must pay, subject to the provisions of B6.

a. In addition to the costs resulting from A3, all costs relating to the goods until such time as they have been delivered in accordance with A4.

b. Where applicable, the costs of customs formalities necessary for export as well as all duties, taxes or other charges payable upon export of the goods and for their transit through any country prior to delivery in accordance with A4.

B6 The buyer must pay:

a. All cost relating to the goods from the time they have been delivered in accordance with A4 including the expenses of unloading necessary to take delivery of the goods from the arriving means of transport at the named place of delivery at the frontier.

b. All additional costs incurred if he fails to take delivery of the goods when they have been delivered in accordance with A4, or to give notice in accordance with B7, provided, however, that the goods have been appropriated to the contract, that is to say, clearly set aside or otherwise identified as the contract goods.

c. Where applicable8, the cost of customs formalities as well as all duties, taxes and other charges payable upon import of the goods and for their subsequent transport.

7. Notice

A7 The seller must give the buyer sufficient notice of the dispatch of the goods to be named place at the buyer to take measures which are normally necessary to enable him to take delivery of the goods.

B7 The buyer must, whenever he is entitled to determine the time within an agreed period and/or the point of taking delivery at the named place, give the seller sufficient notice thereof.

8. Proof of Delivery, Transport Document or Equivalent

A8 The seller must provide the buyer at the seller's expense with the usual document or other evidence of the delivery of the goods at the named place at the frontier in accordance with A3. The seller must, should the parties agree on on-going carriage beyond the frontier in accordance with A3, provide the buyer at the latter's request, risk and expense, with the through document of transport normally obtained in the country of dispatch covering on usual terms the transport of the goods from the point of dispatch in that country to the place of final destination in the country of import named by the buyer.

Where the seller and the buyer have agreed to communicate electronically, the document referred to in the preceding paragraph may be replaced by an equivalent electronic data interchange (EDI) message.

B8 The buyer must accept the transport document and/or other evidence of delivery in accordance with A8.

9. Checking-Packaging-Marking

A9 The seller must pay the costs of those checking operations (such as checking quality, measuring, weighing, counting) which are necessary for the purpose of delivering the goods in accordance with A4.

The seller must provide at his own expense packaging (unless it is agreed or usual for the particular trade to deliver the goods of the contract description unpicked) which is required for the delivery of the goods at the frontier and for the subsequent transport to the extent that the circumstances (for example modalities, destination) are made known to the seller before the contract of sale is concluded. Packaging is to be marked appropriately.

B9 The buyer must pay the costs of any pre-shipment inspection except when such inspection is mandated by the authorities of the country of export.

10. Other Obligations

A10 The seller must render the buyer at the latter's request, risk and expense, every assistance in obtaining any documents or equivalent electronic messages (other than those mentioned in A8) issued or transmitted in the county of dispatch and/or origin which the buyer may require for the import of the goods and, where necessary, for their transit through any country.

The seller must provide the buyer, upon request, with the necessary information for procuring insurance.

B10 The buyer must pay all costs and charges incurred in obtaining the documents or equivalent electronic messages mentioned in A10 and reimburse those incurred by the seller in rendering his assistance in accordance therewith.

If necessary, according to A3, the buyer must provide the seller at his request and the buyer's risk and expense with the exchange control authorization, permits, other documents or certified copies thereof, or with the address of the final destination of the goods in the country of import for the purpose of obtaining the through document of transport or any other document contemplated in A8.

1.3.10 DES

Delivered Ex Ship(... named port of destination)

"Deliver Ex Ship" means that the seller delivers when the goods are placed at the disposal of the buyer on board the ship not cleared for import at the named port of destination. The seller has to bear all the costs and risks involved in bringing the goods to the named port of destination before discharging. If the parties wish the seller to bear the costs and risks of discharging the goods, then the DQE term should be used.

This term can be used only when the goods are to be delivered by sea or inland waterway or multimodal transport on a vessel in the port of destination.

1. Provision of Goods in Conformity with the Contract

A1 The seller must provide the goods and the commercial invoice, or its equivalent electronic message, in conformity with the contract of sale and any other evidence of conformity which may be required by the contract.

B1 The buyer must pay the price as provided in the contract of sale.

2. Licenses, Authorizations and Formalities

A2 The seller must obtain at his own risk and expense any import license or other official authorization or other documents and carry out, where applicable, all customs formalities necessary for the export of the goods and for their transit through any country.

B2 The buyer must obtain at his own risk and expense any import license or other official authorization and carry out, where applicable, all customs formalities necessary for the import of the goods.

3. Contracts of Carriage and Insurance

A3 The seller must contract at his own expense for the carriage of the goods to the named point, if any, at the named port of destination. If a point is not agreed or is not determined by practice, the seller may select the point at the named port of destination which best suits his purpose.

The seller has no obligation for the contract of insurance.

B3 The buyer has no obligation for the contract of carriage and the contract of insurance.

4. Delivery

A4 The seller must place the goods at the disposal of the buyer on board the vessel at the unloading point referred to in A3, in the named port of destination on the date or within the agreed period, in such a way as to enable them to be removed from the vessel by unloading equipment appropriate to the nature of the goods.

B4 The buyer must take delivery of the goods when they have been delivered in accordance with A4.

5. Transfer of Risks

A5 The seller must, subject to the provisions of B5, bear all risks of loss of or damage to the goods until such time as they have been delivered in accordance with A4.

B5 The buyer must bear all risks of loss of or damage to the goods from the time they have been delivered in accordance with A4.

The buyer must, should he fail to give notice in accordance whit B7, bear all risks of loss of or damage to the goods from the agreed date or the expiry date of the agreed period for delivery provided, however, that the goods have been duly appropriated to the contract, that is to say, clearly set aside or otherwise identified as the contract goods.

6. Division of Costs

A6 The seller must pay, subject to the provisions of B6.

a. In addition to costs resulting from A3, all costs relating to the goods until such time as they have been delivered in accordance with A4.

b. Where applicable, the costs of customs formalities necessary for export as well as all duties, taxes or other changes payable upon export of the goods and for their transit through any country prior to delivery in accordance with A4.

B6 The buyer must pay:

a. All costs relating to the goods from the time they have been delivered in accordance with A4, including the expenses of discharge operations necessary to take delivery of the goods from the vessel.

b. All additional costs incurred if he fails to take delivery of the goods when they have been placed at his disposal in accordance with A4, or to give notice in accordance with B7, provided, however, that is to say, clearly set aside or otherwise identified as the contract goods.

c. Where applicable, the costs of customs formalities as well as all duties, taxes and other charges playable upon import of the goods.

7. Notice

A7 The seller must give the buyer sufficient notice of the estimated time of arrival of the nominated vessel in accordance with A4 as well as any other notice required in other to allow the buyer to take measures which are normally necessary to enable him to take delivery of the goods.

B7 The buyer must, whenever he is entitled to determine the within an agreed period and/or the point of taking delivery in the named port of destination, give the seller sufficient notice thereof.

8. Proof of Delivery, Transport Document or Equivalent Electronic Message

A8 The seller must provide the buyer at the seller's expense with the delivery order and/or the usual transport document (for example a negotiable bill of lading, a non-negotiable sea waybill, an inland waterway document, or a multimodal transport document) to enable the buyer to claim the goods from the carrier at the port of destination.

Where the seller and the buyer have agreed to communicate electronically, the document referred to in the preceding paragraph may be replaced by an equivalent electronic data interchange (EDI) message.

B8 The buyer must accept the delivery order or the transport document in accordance with A8.

9. Checking-Packaging-Marking

A9 The seller must pay the costs of those checking operations (such as checking quality, measuring, weighing, counting) which are necessary for the purpose of delivering the goods in accordance with A4.

The seller must provide at his own expense packaging (unless it is usual for the particular trade to deliver the goods of the contract description unpacked) which is required for the delivery of the goods. Packaging is to be marked appropriately.

B9 The buyer must pay the costs of any pre-shipment inspection except when such inspection is by the authorities of the country of export.

10. Other Obligations

A10 The seller must render the buyer at the latter's request, risk and expense, every assistance in obtaining any documents or equivalent electronic messages (other than those mentioned in A8) issued or transmitted in the country of dispatch and/or of origin which the buyer may require for the import of the goods.

The seller must provide the buyer, upon request, with the necessary information for procuring insurance.

B10 The buyer must pay all costs and charges incurred in obtaining the documents or equivalent electronic messages mentioned in A10 and reimburse those incurred by the seller in rendering his assistance in accordance therewith.

1.3.11 DEQ

Delivered Ex Quay(... named port of destination)

"Delivered Ex Quay" means that the seller delivers when the goods are placed at the disposal of the buyer not cleared for import on the quay (wharf) at the named port for destination. The seller has to bear costs and risks involved in bringing the goods to the named port for destination and discharging the goods on the quay (wharf). The DEQ term requires the buyer to clear the goods for import and to pay for all formalities, duties, taxes and other charges upon import.

This is a reversal from previous INCOTERMS versions which required the seller to arrange for import clearance.

If the parties wish to include in the seller's obligations all or part of the costs payable upon import of the goods, this should be made clear by adding explicit wording to this effect in the contract sale.

This term can be used only when the goods are to be delivered by sea or inland waterway or multimodal transport on discharging from a vessel onto the quay (wharf) in the port of destination. However if the parties wish to include in the seller's obligations the risks and costs of the handling of the goods from the quay to another place (warehouse, terminal, transport station, etc.) in or outside the port, the DDU or DDP terms should be used.

1. Provision of the Goods in Conformity with the Contract

A1 The seller must provide the goods and the commercial invoice, or its equivalent electronic message, in conformity with the contract of sale and any other evidence of conformity which may be required by the contract.

B1 The buyer must pay the price as provided in the contract of sale.

2. Licenses, Authorizations and Formalities

A2 The seller must obtain at his own risk and expense any export license or other official authorization or other documents and carry out, where applicable, all customs formalities for the export of the goods, and for their transit through any country.

B2 The buyer must obtain at his own risk and expense any import license or official authorization or other documents and carry out, where applicable, all customs formalities necessary for the import of the goods.

3. Contracts of Carriage and Insurance

A3 The seller must contract at his own expense for the carriage of the goods to the named quay (wharf) at the named port of destination. If a specific quay (wharf) is not agreed or is not determined by practice, the seller may select the quay (wharf) at the named port of destination which best suits his purpose.

The sellerhas no obligation for the contract of insurance.

B3 The buyer has no obligation for the contract of carriage and the contract of insurance.

4. Delivery

A4 The seller must place the goods at the disposal of the buyer on the quay (wharf) referred to in A3, on the date or within the agreed period.

B4 The buyer must take delivery of the goods when they have been delivered in accordance with A4.

5. Transfer of Risks

A5 The seller must, subject to the provisions of B5, bear all risks of loss of or damage to the goods until such time as they have been delivered in accordance with A4.

B5 The buyer must bear all risks of loss of or damage to the goods from the time they have been delivered in accordance with A4.

The buyer must, should he fail to give notice in accordance with B7, bear all risks of the loss of or damage to the goods from the agreed date or the expiry date of the agreed period for delivery provided, however, that the goods have been duly appropriated to the contract, that is to say, clearly set aside or otherwise identified as the contract goods.

6. Division of Costs

A6 The seller must pay subject to the provisions of B6.

a. In addition to costs resulting from A3, all costs relating to the goods until such time as they are delivered on the quay (wharf) in accordance with A4.

b. Where applicable, the costs of customs formalities necessary for export as well as all duties, taxes and other charges payable upon export of the goods and for their transit through any country prior to delivery.

B6 The buyer must pay:

a. All costs relating to the goods from the time they have been delivered in accordance with A4, including any costs of handling the goods in the port for subsequent transport or storage in warehouse or terminal.

b. All additional costs incurred if he fails to take delivery of the goods when they have been placed at his disposal in accordance with A4, or to give notice in accordance with B7, provided, however, that the goods have been appropriated to the contract, that is to say, clearly set aside or otherwise identified as the contract goods.

c. Where applicable, the cost of customs formalities as well as all duties, taxes and other charges payable upon import of the goods and for their subsequent transport.

7. Notice

A7 The seller must give the buyer sufficient notice of the estimated time of arrival of the nominated vessel in accordance with A4, as well as any other notice required in order to allow the buyer to take measures which are normally necessary to enable him to take delivery of the goods.

B7 The buyer must, whenever he is entitled to determine the time within an agreed period and/or the point of taking delivery in the named port of destination, give the seller sufficient notice thereof.

8. Transport Document or Equivalent Electronic Message

A8 The seller must provide the buyer at the seller's expense with the delivery order and/or the usual transport document (for example a negotiable bill of lading, a non-negotiable sea waybill, an inland waterway document or a multimodal transport document) to enable him to take the goods and remove them from the quay (wharf).

Where the seller and the buyer have agreed to communicate electronically, the document referred to in the preceding paragraph may be replaced by an equivalent electronic data interchange (EDI) message.

B8 The buyer must accept the delivery order or transport document in accordance with A8.

9. Checking-Packaging-Marking

A9 The seller must pay the costs of those checking operations (such as checking quality, measuring, weighing, counting) which are necessary for the purpose of delivering the goods in accordance with A4.

The seller must provide at his own expense packaging (unless it is usual for the particular trade to deliver the goods of the contract description unpacked) which is required for the delivery of the goods. Packaging is to be marked appropriately.

B9 The buyer must pay the costs of any pre—shipment inspection except when such inspection is mandated by the authorities of the country of export.

10. Other Obligations

A10 The seller must render the buyer at the latter's request, risk and expense, every assistance in obtaining any documents or equivalent electronic messages (other than those mentioned in A8) issued or transmitted in the country of dispatch and/or origin which the buyer may require for the import of the goods.

The seller must provide the buyer, upon request, whit the necessary information for procuring insurance.

B10 The buyer must pay all costs and charges incurred in obtaining the documents or equivalent electronic messages mentioned in A10 and reimburse those incurred by the seller in rendering his assistance in accordance therewith.

1.3.12 DUU

Delivered Duty Unpaid(... named place of destination)

"Delivered duty unpaid" means that the seller delivers the goods to the buyer, not cleared for import, and not unloaded from any arriving means of transport at the named place of destination. The seller has to bear the costs and risks involved in bringing the goods thereto, other than, where applicable, any "duty" (which term includes the responsibility for and the risks of the carrying out of customs formalities, and the payment of formalities, customs duties, taxes and other charges) for import in the country of destination. Such "duty" has to be borne by the buyer as well as any costs and risks caused by his failure to clear the goods for import in time.

This term may be used irrespective of the mode of transport but when delivery is to take place in the port of destination on board the vessel or on the quay (wharf), the DES or DEQ terms should be used.

1. Provision of the Goods in Conformity with the Contract

A1 The seller must provide the goods and the commercial invoice, or its equivalent electronic message, in conformity with the contract of sale and any other evidence of conformity which may be required by the contract.

B1 The buyer must pay the price as provided in the contract of sale.

2. Licenses, Authorizations and Formalities

A2 The seller must obtain at his own risk and expense any export license and other official authorization or other documents and carry out, where applicable, all customs formalities necessary for the export of the goods and for their transit through any country.

B2 The buyer must obtain at his own risk and expense any import license or other official authorization or other documents and carry out, where applicable, all customs formalities necessary for the import of the goods.

3. Contracts of Carriage and Insurance

A3 The seller must contract at his own expense for the carriage of the goods to the named place off destination. If a specific point is not agreed or is not determined by practice, the seller may select the point at the named place of destination which best suits his purpose. The seller has no obligation for the contract of insurance.

B3 The buyer has no obligation for the contract of carriage and the contract of insurance.

4. Delivery

A4 The seller must place the goods at the disposal of the buyer, or at that of another person named by the buyer, on any arriving means of transport not unloaded, at the named place of destination on the date or within the period agreed for delivery.

B4 The buyer must take delivery of the goods when they have been delivered in accordance with A4.

5. Transfer of Risks

A5 The seller must, subject to the provisions of B5, bear all risks of loss of or damage to the goods until such time as they have been delivered in accordance with A4.

B5 The buyer must bear all risks of loss of or damage to the goods from the time they have been delivered in accordance with A4.

The buyer must, should he fail to fulfill his obligations in accordance with B2, bear all additional risks of loss of or damage to the goods incurred thereby.

The buyer must, should he fail to give notice in accordance with B7, bear all risks of loss of or damage to the goods from the agreed date or the expiry date of the agreed period for delivery provided, however, that the goods have been duly appropriated to the contract, that is to say, clearly set aside or otherwise identified as the contract goods.

6. Division of costs

A6 The seller must pay, subject to the provisions of B6.

a. In addition to costs resulting from A3, all costs relating to the goods until such time as they have been delivered in accordance with A4.

b. Where applicant, the costs of customs formalities necessary for export as well as all duties, taxes and other charges payable upon export and for their transit through any country prior to delivery in accordance with A4.

B6 The buyer must pay:

a. All costs relating to the goods from the time they have been delivered in accordance with A4.

b. All additional costs incurred if he fails to fulfill his obligations in accordance with B2, or to give notice in accordance with B7, provided, however, that the goods have been duly appropriated to the contract, that is to say, clearly set aside or otherwise identified as the contract goods.

c. Where applicable, the costs of customs formalities as well as all duties, taxes and other charges payable upon import of the goods.

7. Notice

A7 The seller must give the buyer sufficient notice of the dispatch of the goods as well as any other notice required in order to allow the buyer to take measures which are normally necessary to enable him to take delivery of the goods.

B7 The buyer must, whenever he is entitled to determine the time within an agreed period and/or the point of taking delivery all the named place, give the seller sufficient notice thereof.

8. Proof of Delivery, Transport Document or Equivalent Electronic Message

A8 The seller must provide the buyer at the seller's expense the delivery order and/or the usual transport document (for example a negotiable bill of lading, a non-negotiable sea waybill, an inland waterway document, an air waybill, a railway consignment note, a road consignment note, or a multimodal transport document) which the buyer may require to take delivery of the goods in accordance with A4 or B4.

Where the seller and the buyer have agreed to communicate electronically, the document referred to in the preceding paragraph may be replaced by an equivalent electronic data interchange (EDI) message.

B8 The buyer must accept the appropriate delivery order or transport document in accordance with A8.

9. Checking-Packaging-Marking

A9 The seller must pay the costs of those checking operations (such as checking quality, measuring, weighing, counting) which are necessary for the purpose of delivering the goods in accordance with A4.

The seller must provide at his own expense packaging (unless it is usual for the particular trade to deliver the goods of the contract description unpacked) which is required for the delivery of the goods. Packaging is to be marked appropriately.

B9 The buyer must pay the costs of any pre-shipment inspection expect when such inspection is mandated by the authorities of the country of export.

10. Other Obligations

A10 The seller must render the buyer at the latter's request, risk and expense, every assistance in obtaining any documents or equivalent electronic message (other than those mentioned in A8) issued or transmitted in the country of dispatch and/or of origin which the buyer may require for the import of the goods.

The seller must provide the buyer, upon request, with the necessary information for procuring insurance.

B10 The buyer must pay all costs and charges incurred in obtaining the documents or equivalent electronic message mentioned in A10 and reimburse those incurred by the seller in rendering this assistance in accordance therewith.

3.3.13 DDP

Delivered Duty Paid(... named place of destination)

"Delivered duty paid" means that the seller delivers the goods to the buyer, cleared for import, and not unloaded from any arriving means of transport at the named place of destination. The seller has to bear all the costs and risks involved in bringing the goods thereto including, where applicable, any "duty" (which term includes the responsibility for and the risk of the carrying out of customs formalities and the payment of formalities, customs duties, taxes and other charges) for import in the country of destination.

Whilst the EXW term represents the minimum obligation for the seller, DDP represents the maximum obligation.

This term should not be used if the seller is unable directly or indirectly to obtain the import license.

However, if the parties wish to exclude from the seller's obligations some of the costs payable upon import of the goods (such as value-added tax: VAT), this should be made clear by adding explicit wording to this effect in the contract of sale.

If the parties wish the buyer to bear all risks and costs of the import, the DDU term should be used.

This term may be used irrespective of the mode of transport but when delivery is to take place in the port of destination on board the vessel or on the quay (wharf), the DES or DEQ terms should be used.

1. Provision of the Goods in Conformity with the Contract

A1 The seller must provide the goods and the commercial invoice, or its equivalent electronic message, in conformity with the contract of sale and any other evidence of conformity which may be required by the contract.

B1 The buyer must pay the price as provided in the contract of sale.

2. Licenses, Authorizations and Formalities

A2 The seller must obtain at his own risk and expense any import license and other official authorization or other documents and carry out, where applicable, all customs formalities necessary for the export of the goods, for their transit through any country and for their import.

B2 The buyer must render the seller at the latter's request, risk and expense, every assistance in obtaining, where applicable, any import license or other official authorization necessary for the import of the goods.

3. Contract of Carriage and Insurance

A3 The seller must contract at his own expense for the carriage of the goods to the named place of destination. If a specific point is not agreed or is not determined by practice, the seller may select the point at the named place of destination which best suits his purpose. The seller has no obligation for the contract of insurance.

B3 The buyer has no obligation for the contract of carriage and the contract of insurance.

4. Delivery

A4 The seller must place the goods at the disposal of the buyer, or at that of another person named by the buyer, on any arriving means of transport not unloaded at the named place of destination on the date or within the period agreed for delivery.

B4 The buyer must take delivery of the goods when they have been delivered in accordance with A4.

5. Transfer of Risk

A5 The seller must, subject to the provisions of B5, bear all risks of loss of or damage to the goods until such time as they have been delivered in accordance with A4.

B5 The buyer must bear all risks of loss of or damage to the goods from the time they have been delivered in accordance with A4.

The buyer must, should he fail to fulfill his obligations in accordance with B2, bear all additional risks of loss of or damage to the goods incurred thereby.

The buyer must, should he fail to give notice in accordance with B7, bear all risks of loss of or damage to the goods from the agreed date or the expiry date of the agreed period for delivery provided, however, that the goods have been duly appropriated to the contract, that is to say, clearly set aside or otherwise identified as the contract goods.

6. Division of Costs

A6 The seller must pay, subject to the precisions of B6.

a. In addition to costs resulting from A3, all costs relating to the goods until such times as they have been delivered in accordance with A4.

b. Where applicable, the costs of customs formalities necessary for export and import as well as all duties, taxes and other charges payable upon export and import of the goods, and for their transit through any country prior to delivery in accordance with A4.

B6 The buyer must pay:

a. All costs relating to the goods from the time they have been delivered in accordance with A4.

b. All additional costs incurred if he fails to fulfill his obligations in accordance with B2, or to give notice in accordance with B7, provided, however, that the goods have been duly appropriated to the contract, that is to say, clearly set aside or otherwise identified as the contract goods.

7. Notice

A7 The seller must give the buyer sufficient notice of the dispatch of the goods as well as any other notice required in order to allow the buyer to take measures which are normally necessary to enable him to take delivery of the goods.

B7 The buyer must, whenever he is entitled to determine the time within an agreed period and/or the point of the point of taking delivery at the named place, give the seller sufficient notice thereof.

8. Proof of Delivery, Transport Document or Equivalent Electronic Message

A8 The seller must provide the buyer at the seller's expense with the delivery order and/or the usual transport document (for example a negotiable bill of lading, a non-negotiable sea waybill, an inland waterway document, an air waybill, a railway consignment note, a road consignment note, or a multimodal transport document) which the buyer may require to take delivery of the goods in accordance with A4 or B4.

Where the seller and the buyer have agreed to communicate electronically, the document referred to in the preceding paragraph may be replaced by an equivalent electronic date interchange (EDI) message.

B8 The buyer must accept the appropriate delivery order or transport document in accordance with A8.

9. Checking-Packaging-Marking

A9 The seller must pay the costs of those checking operations (such as checking quality, measuring, weighing, counting) which are necessary for the purpose of delivering the goods in accordance with A4.

The seller must provide at his own expense packaging (unless it is usual for the particular trade to deliver the goods of the contract description unpacked) which is required for the delivery of the goods. Packaging is to be marked appropriately.

B9 The buyer must pay the costs of any pre-shipment inspection except when such inspection is mandated by the authorities of the country of export.

10. Other Obligations

A10 The seller must pay all costs and charges incurred in obtaining the documents or equivalent electronic messages mentioned in B10 and reimburse those incurred by the buyer, upon request, with the necessary information for pro procuring insurance.

B10 The buyer must render the seller, at the latter's request, risk and expense, every assistance in obtaining any documents or equivalent electronic messages issued or transmitted in the country of import which the seller may require for the purpose of making the goods available to the buyer in accordance therewith.

Chapter 2 Basic Articles on Contracts for International Sales of Goods

2.1 Name and Quality of Commodity

2.1.1 Name of Commodity

Usually, the parties to a contract specify the name of the product under the subject "Name of Commodity". This clause is a main component of the Description of Goods. As the basis of a transaction, it concerns the rights and obligations of the buyer and the seller. If the goods delivered by the seller are not in accordance with the agreed name of commodity, the buyer reserves the right to lodge a claim, reject the goods or even cancel the contract. Therefore, as a main clause of a sales contract, the name of commodity should be clearly stipulated. When giving the name, try to be specific and adopt the widely accepted name agreed by both parties. To some products, we should be cautious in selecting suitable names, either reducing customs duties, or saving freight.

2.1.2 Quality of Commodity

Quality is the most important factor in the sale of goods. According to UN Convention, the seller must deliver the goods as required by the contract. Otherwise, the buyer may claim damages, require delivery of substitute goods, or require the seller to remedy, or even reject the goods and cancel the contract. The quality agreed upon in the contract is the basis of the seller's delivery. In international transactions, there are different ways of describing the quality of goods in a contract.

1. Sale by Actual Quality

Products are showed to buyers in factory, then business will be done after buyer's inspection on spot. Through this method, the quality of the product must be based on the inspection result. If the seller delivers the inspected products to buyer, he has no right to refuse them. In general, such practice is suitable to the situation, which the quantity of these products is not so large that buyer can inspect them on spot. Therefore, expensive goods such as arts and crafts can adopt this kind of way.

2. Sale by Sample

Samples are either offered by the seller or the buyer. They are described as sale by seller's sample, and the sale by buyer's sample respectively.

a. Counter sample: When sale is made by buyer's the goods delivered by the seller, may sometimes not be in conformity with the buyer's sample and thus the buyer may refuse to accept the goods. In order to avoid disputes over the quality of goods in the days to come, a wise seller should first send a copied piece of product for confirmation before putting into production. This copied product is called "counter sample" or "confirming sample", on which the seller's delivery will be based.

b. Sealed sample: Before sending samples or delivering the goods to the buyer, the seller may select some samples and seal them in the presence of the buyer on notary. This sealed sample is for checking the quality of the shipments in the future.

c. Safeguard clauses: When sale by buyer's sample, to prevent disputes upon the third party's intellectual properties, safeguard clauses are usually stipulated in the contract. The following is an example:

"It is the buyer rather from the infringement of the third party's intellectual properties."

d. Reference sample: When sale is made by description, either the seller or the seller or the buyer may send a physical sample to the other party to let him know more clearly about the products. This sample is often marked "for reference only". It is not the basis of delivery.

3. Sale by Description

a. Sale by specification, grade or standard: some indices such as chemical composition, contents, length, sizes, etc. can reflect the quality of the goods sufficiently. Describing quality by specification is simple as well as accurate. That's why it is most widely used. Some products can be divided into different grades based on different specifications.

Standards are formulated either by government or commercial organizations. Some of them are national, others are international. Many countries have their own standards, for example, BS in Britain, ANSI in the USA and Japan. The typical international standard is ISO standard. When sale is made by standard, it is important to mark the publication year of the standard.

b. Sale by trademark or brand: some products may have been sold in the market for many years and enjoy high popularity. Their quality can be represented by their trademarks and brands. However, some well-known brand products cannot be traded only by their marks and brands owing to their varieties and complexities.

c. Sale by descriptions and illustrations: Some products like machinery, instruments, equipments, and transportation tools are complicated in structure. It is difficult to describe the full aspects of their quality, thus sale by descriptions and illustrations is applicable. In the contract, the clause of quality contains not only the name of commodity, the brand but also the instructions to illustrate the structure and functions of the product. Clauses like "quality and technical data to be strictly in conformity with the description submitted by the seller" are to be stipulated.

d. Sale by name of origin: this method is limited only for native products with traditional arts or special local flavor. It is usually used together with brands or specifications. e. g. Shichuan Preserved.

4. Quality Clause in Contract

In quality clause, the name and specification, grade, or the serial number and data of the sample, etc, should be clearly stated. We may use description or sample separately or together to describe quality, depending on the product features.

We may stipulate in the contract some flexible quality range as follows.

a. When sale is made by sample, sometimes it is not easy for the goods shipped to be in complete conformity with the sample, or we are not quite sure of the quality. In this case, clauses like "the quality of the shipped to be about equal to the sample" may be stipulated.

b. *Flexible quality range for some primary products including range and allowing more or less.*

c. Quality Tolerance. It is very unavoidable for some industrial products such as instruments, mechanical products to have some tolerance. e. g. Soybean, if the oil content of the goods shipped is 1% higher, the price will be accordingly increased by 2%.

2.2 Quantity of Commodity

2.2.1 Metrical Units

In international trade, as different products have different characteristics and different countries may adopt different systems of weights and measures, units and ways of quantity calculation are varied. There are International System of Units, Metric System, British System and U. S. System. While the British system's long ton, L/T equals to 2200 pounds, the U. S. system's short ton, S/T equals to 2000 pounds. Besides, some capacity units like gallon and bushel are of the same names under the Britain system and the U. S. system, but the actual capacities are different. There are two categories of metric units which are used to show the quantity of commodity in international trade One is metrical units, including weight, length, area, volume and capacity; the other is numbers, including some customary units such as. dozen, gross, great gross, ream, and some packing units like barrel (petroleum, oil), bale (cotton), etc.

2.2.2 Calculation Methods

In international trade, a lot of products are measured by weight according to general commercial practices and rules, the following are the methods of calculating weight.

1. Gross Weight

Gross weight refers to the weight of the product itself plus the package of this product, such method is suitable for calculating low value goods.

2. Net Weight

Net weight means the weight of the product itself. According to international rules and practices, weight is calculated by net weight unless otherwise stated in the contract. Some products can be weighted only when they are packed, and this weight including package is called gross weight. For some less valued products, we may stipulate in called gross for net. If net weight has to be used, we must deduct the weight of package, i. e. the weight of tare. The following are some methods of calculating tare:

a. Real tare. The package is actually weighted.

b. Average tare. When the package is in the same sizes, we may select some of them to weight in the balance, and calculate the average weight.

c. Customary tare. This is suitable for standardized package is known to everyone and it is unnecessary to weight.

d. Computed tare: the weight of the package is agreed upon by both sides.

3. Conditioned Weight

Some products like wool, cotton, raw silk have unstable moisture contents. In order to determine the moisture contents accurately, the universal conditioned weight is used. Conditioned weight equals to dry weight plus standard moisture content.

4. Theoretical Weight

Some products are of uniform sizes and/or specifications, so the weight of each unit is almost the same. We can get the total weight by multiplying the total number and the weight of each unit.

2.2.3 Quantity Clause in Contract

1. Importance of Quantity Clause

The quantity of commodity is a major indispensable clause in a contract. The CISG states that the seller must deliver goods which are of the quantity required by the contract. If the seller delivers a quantity of goods greater than that provided for in the contract, the buyer may take delivery or refuse to take delivery of the excess quantity. If the buyer takes delivery of all or part of the excess quantity, he must pay for it at the contract rate. if the quantity of goods delivered is less.

2. More or Less Clause

In practice, it is sometimes hard to control strictly the quantity of some bulk cargoes like farm products, mineral products. Besides, owing to changer to supplies and limitation to processing conditions, the actual quantity may bi somewhat more or less than the contracted quantity. Under such circumstances, more or less clause is usually stipulated in the contract so that the seller can fulfill the contract more smoothly. The more or less clause is a clause which stipulates the quantity delivered can be more or less within certain extent. The most commonly used way is allowing some percentage more or less. For example, 2000 M/T, 5% more or less at seller's option. However, if the quantity is related with transportation, we may stipulate as "at carrier's option", or "at buyer's option" when the ship is arranged by the buyer. Settlement for the more or less part is usually based on the contract price. If the parties are concerned about the great changes in price at the time when delivery is made, they may stipulate that settlement or this part is based on the market price at the time when the goods are shipped on board the vessel.

2.3 Packing of Commodity

Commodity is usually connected with certain kinds of packing. Some packing is a constitutional part of a product. In international trade, packing is especially is especially significant. Packing clause is often one of the major trade clauses in a contract. Packing can be divided in to selling packing and transport packing according to their different functions in commodity circulation. Selling packing is also called small or inner or immediate packing. It is mainly used to protect products, make the products convenient to use, and to promote sales. Inner packing should be in conformity with the laws and regulations of the purchase countries. Transport packing is also called big or outer packing. Its main functions are to protect goods, and make the goods easy to store and ship. In this section, we shall mainly discuss transport packing.

2.3.1 Types of Transport Packing

In transit, not all goods are necessarily packed. With the development of transportation, more and more small and roundish cargoes like grain, cement and liquid cargoes like petroleum are in bulk, i. e. they can bi loaded directly into the transportation vehicles with mechanical operation. In this way, the costs of carriage are saved, and he carriage is speeded up. Some cargoes like steel, timber, etc. need only to be bundled up. Which are described as goods in naked packing. But for most cargoes, packing is essential in transportation. There are two kinds of transportation packing.

1. Unit Packing

The goods are packed in unit. The common unit packing is as follows.

a. Bale: Bale is a heap of material pressed together and tied with rope or metal wire, suitable for paper, wool, cotton, and carpets, etc. Bag: Bag is made of cotton, plastic, paper or jute, ideal for cement, fertilizer, flour, chemicals, etc. Barrel/drum: Barrel/drum is made of wood, plastic or metal used for liquid or greasy cargoes. Box/case: Box/case is wooden in structure and of various sizes, and some airtight, providing strong protection for cargoes as equipment and car accessories.

b. Glass container: Glass container is used for dangerous liquid cargoes such as acid which needs careful handling. Carton: Carton is a very common form of packing particularly for consumer-type of products. It can promote sales to some extent as words can be printed on them. Crate/skeleton case: Wooden structure between a bale and a case used for light weight goods of large cubic capacity as machinery.

2. Unionization (or Combined) Packing

When we put the individual packing together and place them into a lager container, it is called unionization packing. Pallet, flexible container and container all are combined packing. The combined packing has such advantages as to protect goods effectively, improve efficiency, and to save packing costs as well as freight.

2.3.2 Marks on Transport Packing

Marks on transport packing help to identify goods, and facilitate correct operation. According to their functions, marks on transport packing can be divided into shipping mark, indicative mark, warning mark, weight/volume mark, and origin mark.

1. Shipping Mark

Shipping mark facilitates the identification and count of the goods in the process of loading and unloading, shipping and storing. Shipping marks can also prevent the goods from being wrongly delivered or shipped. Shipping marks are usually composed of numbers, alphabets, and simple words. The UN has recommended a type of standard shipping mark to all countries, which cover four parts: the English abbreviation of the receiver; reference number, such as order number, invoice number; destination; serial number.

Shipping mark is usually indicated in export documents like invoice, bill of landing. and insurance policy.

2. Indicative Mark

It is a caution mark, which reminds people of carefulness in handling or carrying goods. It is composed of graphs and words, such as HANDLE WITH CARE, THIS WAY UP, KEEP DRY.

3. Warning Mark

It is also called dangerous mark and is used to indicate explosive, poisonous, inflammable goods. It is also composed of graphs or pictures and words.

2.3.3 Neutral Packing

Neutral packing is a special type of packing, which means the origin of the product is not shown on the inner and outer packages. Chinese export product are usually marked with words like "Made in the People's Republic of China", "Made in China". But sometimes, at the request of the buyer, the seller would accept neutral packing. Neutral packing is divided into neutral packing with designated brand and neutral packing without designated brand. Neutral packing with designated brand means the brand and/or trade mark designed by the buyer are marked out on the product and/or package, but with no indication of the country of origin. Neutral packing without designated brand means neither brand and/or trademark nor country of the origin are marked out on the product and/or package. Neutral packing is a usual practice in international trade, but in recent years it has been restricted by some countries. Exporters should be cautions in adopting it.

2.3.4 Packing Clause in Contract

Ambiguous terms like "seaworthy packing" or "customary packing" are not applicable, since disputes may arise. Usually, there is no need to stipulate packing marks in the contract, as they are usually decided by the seller. But on condition that the buyer nominates it, it is necessary to stipulate the details of the shipping mark. Packing charges are usually included in price. But if the buyer asks for special packing, we should make it clear as to who shall bear the additional charges. The time and methods of payment should also be stated.

2.4 Price of Commodity

Pricing is one of the most important and complex tasks in business, and even more of a problem when linked with exporting. An exporter should sell his products at a price acceptable to the customers and, at the same time, generate enough revenue to cover all its costs. Appropriate pricing is not easy, which requires much skill and must be treated seriously and carefully.

2.4.1 Choice of Currency for Payment

Currency for account is the currency used for price calculation. Currency for payment is the currency for settlement. Normally, the currency for account is the currency for payment if no otherwise is stipulate in contract. Currency for account and payment can be the home currency of the exporter the importer's currency or a third currency if only these currencies are convertible. When choosing the currency, the exporter and importer should take foreign exchanges rates into consideration, and the fluctuations of exchange rates may influence their interests. Theoretically, use of hard currency (currency that is reliable and stable and more in demand) as payment currency is more favorable to the exporter, while the importer prefers to pay in soft currency (currency that is not readily convertible to gold, or into other currencies which are more in demand and that is unstable in value). Which currency is to be used depends on the consultation between the buyer and the seller. If one seller has to adopt an unfavorable currency as payment currency, he should take some measures to offset the foreign exchange exposures.

a. Try to reduce the import price and raise the export price. When sign the contract, take the trend of currency into consideration. If you are an importer, while the currency used is likely to float upward, you should try to press the seller to reduce the price. If you are an exporter, while the currency is likely to float downward, you should try to raise the price.

b. Stipulate exchange proviso clause. In the case that the currency for account and amount are the same soft currency, i. e. the change of the exchange rate between the present date and the settlement date might be for the seller. To product its firm from suffering loss, the seller should define in the contract its firm from suffering loss, the seller should define in the contract the equivalent contractual amount in another strong currency according to the rate between this soft currency and another strong currency on the day of concluding the contract. On the date of payment, the amount in hard currency shall be converted into soft currency at the rate of that date accordingly. This converted amount of soft currency is what the buyer should pay to the seller.

2.4.2 Commission and Discount

In price clause, sometimes commission or discount is involved.

1. Commission

Commission will be specifically stipulated when an intermediary is involved in the deal. It refers to the money received by an agent for his intermediary service. Commission may or may not be include in the price, which may be expressed in different ways, such as USD 1000 per M/T CFR Seattle, including 2% commission, or USD 1000 per M/T CFRC 2% Seattle, or USD 1000 per M/T CFRC 2% Seattle, or USD 1000 per M/T CFRC2 Seattle. The commission included in a price is called plain commission, otherwise it's called secret commission. Chinese foreign trade enter prices usually make quotations with commissioners, while collecting secret commission when they act as agents of domestic enterprises in import and export, that is, the amount of commission is not shown in the quotation. Contract price with commission is called commission-included price.

2. Discount

Discount is a certain percentage of price reduction, a special favor given by the exporter to the importer. There are different types of discount such as "quantity discount", "cash discount", and "special discount" for some special purposes. Discount is also specified in the price clause, such as "US $ 200 per metric ton CIF London less 3% discount". Discount is usually used as a means of promoting and expanding sales.

2.4.3 Clause of Price in Contract

Price clause includes unit price and total amount. A unit price is composed of four parts; currency unit, unit price figure, measurement unit and delivery term.

2.5 Transport of Commodity

International cargo transport is an important link in international trade. Shipping documents are one of the essential documents in international settlement. Clause of shipment is one of the major clauses of the contract. Transport allows goods to be conveyed from one place to another. Without transport, international trade would not be possible. Carriage of goods can take place by sea, rail, air, road, inland waterway, parcel post, container and multimodal transportation.

2.5.1 Sea Transportation (Ocean Transportation)

Ocean transport is the most widely used mode of transport in international trade. It accounts for 90% of international transport, In China, ocean transport is in the overwhelmingly majority. The advantages of ocean transport are easy passage, large capacity and low cost. However, ocean transport is slow, vulnerable to bad weather and less punctual if compared with road or air transport. According to ways of operation, ocean transport can be divided into liner transport and charter transport.

1. Liner Transport

a. Characteristics of liner transport

(**a**) Fixed sailing date (an advertised schedule), fixed route (operating on a regular route), making calls at scheduled ports and relatively fixed freight rate.

(b) Liner freight covers loading and unloading charges, so the carrier is responsible for the loading and unloading.

Liner transport is suitable for cargo of small quantity.

b. Freight rate

Freight rate is stipulated in the tariff. It contains basic freight rate and various kinds of surcharges.

(a) Standards of collecting freight.

(i) Weight: For items marked with "W" in the tariff, the freight thereon is to be calculated per metric ton on weight (weight ton).

(ii) Measurement: For items marked with "M", the freight is to be calculated per cubic meter on measurement of the cargo (measurement ton).

(iii) Weight or measurement: For items marked with "W/M", the freight is to be calculated on basis of either weight or measurement ton, subject to the higher one.

(iV) "Ad Val.": For items marked with "Ad Val.", the freight is to be calculated on the basis of the price or value of the cargo concerned. For some valuable goods like gold, platinum, silver, precision instrument, expensive fur, usually 1%-5% of the price.

(V) "W/M or Ad Val.": For items marked "W/M, or Ad Val." The highest rate is adopted.

(b) Various kinds of surcharges

In addition to be the basic freight rates, there are many kinds of surcharges that can not be ignored: bunker adjustment factor, port surcharges, transshipment surcharges, heavy lift and long length additional and the following is an example of calculation of freight.

2. Charter Transport

Charter here refers to the practice of paying money to a shipping company to use their boats. Charter rate is much cheaper than that of the liner. Shippers may choose direct route. There are two types of charter transport, i. e. voyage charter transport and time charter transport.

a. Voyage charter transport. A voyage charter is the hire of a ship for a particular voyage. It can be further divided into single voyage charter, consecutive voyage charter and so on. The ship owner is responsible for fulfilling transportation according to the stipulated voyage, and for the operation and management of the ship, and should bear all costs in transit. The freight rate is usually charged by quantities of the goods carried, or a fixed rate, no matter how much is the quantity.

A charterparty is a contract for the hire of an entire ship for a particular voyage or a set period of time. It provides the rights and obligations of the two sides. It should be made clear as to who will bear the loading and unloading charges. If the ship owner is not prepared to bear these charges, the deadline or rate of loading and unloading should be set down.

Stipulation of loading and unloading charges. This stipulation should be in correspondence with the derived trade terms.

(**a**) Liner terms: The freight includes loading and unloading charges. The ship owner shall be responsible for loading and unloading.

(**b**) Free out: The freight includes loading charges.

(**c**) Free in: The freight includes unloading charges.

(**d**) Free in and out: If the ship owner is neither responsible for loading and unloading nor for stowed and trimmed charges, "F. I. O. S. T." is applicable.

b. Time charter transport. A time charter is the charter of a ship for a definite period of time. The ship owner is responsible for providing seaworthy ship and the related charges. The renter has the right to dispatch the ship, but should bear all expenditures in transit, such as charges for fuels, port and loading and unloading.

2.5.2 Rail Transport

Rail transport is a major mode of transport in terms of capacity, only second to ocean transport. It is capable of achieving relatively high speed and is very economical especially if it provides the complete trainload for a shipper on a regular basis. Besides, it is less prone to interruption by poor weather. But it is confined to railroads and therefore less flexible. Rail transport can be divided into international combined rail transport and domestic rail transport.

2.5.3 Air Transport

1. The Features of Air Transport

Air transport is one of the youngest forms of distribution. The most obvious advantage of air freight is quick transit. The following are its pros and cons:

a. Quick, reliable transits: This eliminates the need of extensive warehouse accommodation and reduces the risk of stockpiling, obsolescence, deterioration and capital tied up in warehouse and stock provision.

b. Low risk of damage and pilferage, competitive insurance premium.

c. Ideal mode for consumer-type cargoes such as fresh flowers and fruits which deteriorate easily, fashionable articles that have a short selling lie, seasonal goods or merchandise of high value to low weight ratio.

d. High operating cost and initial cost of air when compared to overall capacity. Average aircraft capacity is only 2,000-25,000kg.

2. Types of Air Transport

Air transport services are divided into three categories: scheduled airlines, chartered carriers, and consolidated consignments by freight forwarders.

a. Scheduled airlines: scheduled airlines operate on a scheduled service, over a fixed airline and between fixed airports. They are suit-able for conveying fresh, emergent and seasonal goods.

b. Chartered carriers: Chartered carriers are the hire of an air craft by a shipper or several shippers to deliver cargoes. They are ideal for carrying cargoes o large quantities or carrying cargoes of different shippers to the same destination.

c. Consolidate consignments: Consolidated consignments mean that the air freight forwarder usually assembles a number of individual shipments into one consignment and dispatches them on one air way bill. A consolidated shipment made up by several shipments can be dispatched to one common destination. Many shippers prefer this kind of shipment as the freight rate is 7%-10% lower than that of a scheduled airline published by IATA.

Airline rates are normally based on actual weight for heavy cargo or measurement weight for large volume cargo. The shipper of air freight will encounter several different types of freight classification, such as General Cargo Rates, Classified Rates, Specified Commodity Rates and so on.

2.5.4 Container Transport

Container transport is a method of distributing merchandise in a unitized form, suitable for ocean, rail and multi-modal transport. It is the most modern form of physical international distribution and overall is highly efficient in terms of reliability, cost, quality of service, advanced technology and so on.

a. It can be handled quickly and easily by standardized equipment and can thus save labors and loading and unloading charges.

b. The low risk of cargo damage and pilferage enables more favorable cargo premium to be obtained, compared with break-bulk cargo shipments.

c. Less packing is required for containerized consignments, in some caser, particularly with specialized ISO containers such as refrigerated ones or tanks, no packing is required. This produces substantial cost savings in the international transit and raises service quality.

d. Faster transit, coupled with more reliable maritime schedules, and ultimately increased service frequency, produces savings in warehouse accommodation needs, lessens risks of obsolescent stock and speeds up capital turnover.

2.5.5 International Multi-modal Transport

Following the containerization of international transport, a brand new mode of transport "international multi-modal transport" has been introduced in the transport industry. International multi-modal transport means the carriage of cargo by at least two modes of transport on the basis of a multi-modal transport contract from a place at which the cargoes are collected in one country to a place designed for delivery in another country. Although different models of transport (sea, air, rail, etc.) are combined, only one multi-modal transport operator is responsible for taking the cargo from the consignor and delivering them to the consignee. The use of containers in multi-modal transport means high efficiency. Better quality of transport, lower cost and less time required for cargo movement between the point of origin and place of delivery. Multi-model transport document is the only document to use, which also adds to the economy and simplicity of the documentation process.

2.5.6 Transport document

1. Bill of Lading (B/L)

A bill of lading is a transportation document which is issued by an ocean carries to a shipper with whom the carrier has entered into a contract for the carriage of goods.

A bill of lading serves there purpose : it is a carrier's receipt for goods. Second, it's evidence of a contract of carriage. finally it's a document of title, that is, the person rightfully in possession of the bill is entitled to possess, use, and dispose of the goods the bill represents. The B/L is a receipt for goods shipped on board a vessel, signed by the person (or his agent) who contract to carry them, and stating the conditions in which the goods were delivered to (and received by) the ship.

a. Receipt for the goods. A bill of lading describes the goods put on board a carrier, states the quality, and their condition. The form itself is normally filled out in advance by the shipper; then, as the goods loaded comply with the goods listed. The carrier, however, is responsible only to check for out ward compliance—that is, that the labels comply and that the packages are not damaged. If all appears proper, the appropriate agent of the carrier will sign the bill and return it to the shipper.

b. Evidence of the contract of carriage. Between the shipper and the carrier the bill of lading is evidence of their contract of carriage. The bill becomes conclusive evidence of their contract of carriage once it is negotiated to a good-faith third party.

c. Document of title to the goods. The named consignee of the holder of a bill of lading, provided he has received it in good faith through due negotiation, has a claim to title and, by surrendering the bill, to delivery of the goods.

2. Types of Bill of Lading

There are a number of different types of bill of lading. The following lists those encountered the most often.

a. Shipped (on board) bill of lading and received for shipment bill of lading. Shipped B/L is issued by the shipping company after the goods are actually shipped on board the designed vessel and the date of issue of the B/L are indicated on the shipped B/L. And the date of issue is the date of shipment. Since shipped bill of lading provides better guarantee for the consignee to receive the cargo at the destination, the importer will normally required exporter to produce shipped B/L and most bill of lading forms are preprinted as "Shipped Bill". Receive for Shipment B/L arises where the word "shipped" does not appear on bill of lading. It merely confirms that the goods have been over to. and are in the custody of the ship owner.

b. Clean bill of lading and unclean bill of lading (four bill of lading or bill of lading). A clean bill of lading is the one issued by a carrier for goods which were received in good condition. A clean bill of lading provides proof that up until the time goods were transferred to the carrier, no damage has occurred. This assists in placing responsibility if in fact goods are eventually in other than undamaged condition.

When goods are received in damaged condition for shipment on a vessel, the master of the ship will note the damage on the bill of lading. A bill of lading with such a notation is referred to as an unclean bill of lading. Unclean B/L is usually not acceptable to the buyer and bank.

c. Straight blank and order B/L. Straight bill of lading has designed consignee. Under this bill, only the consignee at the destination is entitled to take delivery of the cargo. As it is not transferable, it is not commonly used in international trade and normally applies to high-value shipments or goods for special purposes.

Blank B/L also called Open B/L or bear B/L, means that there is no definite consignee of the goods. There usually appear in the box of consignee word like "to bear". Anyone who holds the bill is entitled to the goods the bill represents. NO endorsement is needed for the transfer of the blank bill. Due to the exceedingly high risk involved, this bill is rarely used.

Order B/L is widely used in international trade. It means that the goods are consigned or destined to the order of a named person. In the box of consignee," to order"," to order the shipper", or "To order of the consignee" is marked. this type of bill of lading is a negotiable instrument. that is it may be used to transfer title to goods being shipped to another party. The transfer may occur at any time during the transit process simply by conveying the order bill to another party. Order B/ L can be transferred only after endorsement is made. if it is made out "to order of the consignee", the consignee will endorse the bill to transfer it. A blank endorsement, i. e. only the endorse ' name is usually required for a "to order" bill.

Order B/L blank endorsed is widely used in international trade

d. Direct transshipment through bill of lading. Direct B/L means the goods are shipped from the port of lading direct to the port of destination without involving transshipment. It is something necessary to employ two or more carriers to get the goods to their final destination. in this case, usually the fast carrier will sign and issued a through bill of ;lading the on -carriage may be either by a second vessel or by a different form of transport.

Lined bill of lading, charter party bill of lading, container bill of lading. Lined bill of lading is issued by a lined company for shipment on scheduled port calls through schedule routes. Charter party bill of lading is issued by the carrier (or is agent) based on the charter party. this bill of lading is subject the clauses of charter party. That is why when charter bill of lading is accepted by the bank or other buyer, the copy charter party is required. Container bill of lading is issued when the goods are conveyed by container.

e. Long form bill of lading and short form bill of lading. Long form bill of lading is more detailed with shipping contract clauses printed on the back of the page. Short form B/L, as the name implied, is an abbreviated type of document, not containing the long list of detailed clauses that generally appear on bills of lading.

All the above mentioned bills are not independent of each other. Several types may be combined into one like "clean on board, to order, blank endorsed B/L". A receipt shipment bill may also be a straight and clean bill. Bills of lading are made out in sets, consisting of a number of originals (usually three) and a number of copies and marked "original" and "copy" respectively. Only the original signed by the carrier enable the consignee to take delivery of the goods. The copies are just for reference.

2.5.7 Transport Clause in Contract

Shipment clause includes time of delivery, port (place) of shipment and destination, etc.

1. Time of Shipment and Delivery

INCOTERMS 2000 provides that in FOB, CFR, CIF, FCA, CPT, CIP contract, the seller fulfills his obligation of delivery when the goods are shipped on board the vessel or delivered to the carrier. All these contracts are shipment contracts. The time of delivery in the contract is the time of shipment is a very important clause in a contract. Any delay or advance of delivery constitutes violation of contract. There are several ways of stipulating time of delivery in contract.

a. time of shipment definitely stated. for example: shipment during December, 1997; shipment not later than 31 st december, 1997.

b. shipment within XXX days after receipt of L/C. For a contract in which payment is made by L/C, in order to avoid the risks of losses resulted from the buyer's failure in opening L/C, or for taking use of L/C as a means of delivery this way. Under this circumstance, the seller would wait for the arrival of the L/C before getting the goods ready. Therefore the time of delivery is related with the time of receipt of L/C. Stipulating "prompt shipment" similar expressions like "shipment immediately", "shipment as soon as possible", shipment is to be effected by the first available ship". Since there are no definite explanations to these expressions, confusion or dispute may occur. Thus in practice, we'd better avoid words like "immediately", "promptly", "as soon as possible" should not be used, otherwise the bank shall ignore these words.

2. Partial Shipment and Transshipment

a. Partial shipment, also described as shipment by installments, means the goods in one contract are to be shipped in lots. In international trade, sometimes partial shipment has to be made because of large quantity of the transaction, or the limitation of supplies and transportation. If no such clause is stated in the contract, it is regarded as "partial shipment is not allowed". But some international rules stipulate oppositely, for example, article 40 of UCP500 stipulates that partial drawings and/or shipments are allowed unless the credit stipulates otherwise. In view of the above differences, we should make it clear in the contract as to whether partial shipment is allowed to avoid misunderstandings. Stipulate allowing partial shipment only. The exact time of delivery and the quantities of each lot and the total lots are not stipulated in the contract. This way of stipulating is favorable to the seller since he can decide how much and when the goods are to be shipped based on the supplies of goods an the transportation conditions. State in detail the time of delivery and quantity of each lot. This way is usually adopted when the buyer need to resell the goods or has some special requirements in use. This way strictly limits the seller. If he fails to carry out any one lot, he shall be responsible for breaking the contract. According to UCP 500, transportation documents which appear on their face to indicate that shipment has been made on the same means of conveyance and for the same journey, provided they indicate the same destination, will not be regarded as covering partial shipments, even the transport documents indicate different dates of shipment and/or different ports of loading.

b. According to UCP500, transshipment means a transfer and reloading during the course of carriage from one conveyance or vessel to another conveyance or vessel, within the same mode of transport or from one mode of transport to another mode of transportation. Unless transshipment is prohibited by the terms of the credit, it is allowed. However, in the absence of terms as to whether transshipment is allowed or not in the contract, transshipment is to be construed as not allowed.

2.6 Insurance of Commodity

2.6.1 Perils of the Sea

Perils of the sea are some of the causes of losses of losses which may affect property on an ocean voyage. Generally speaking, perils of the sea are those causes over which the captain of a vessel has no control. Thus if a peril of the sea causes damage to cargo, whether the carrier may be responsible depends upon the nature of the loss. If there was no negligence on the part of the captain of the ship, the carrier could probably not be held responsible for compensating cargo owners for loss or damage. Cargo insurance coverage is available to cover for such losses for the benefit of the cargo owner. Perils of the sea include:

a. Natural calamities: Natural calamities cover bad weather, thunder and lightening, flood, floating, drift ice, earthquake, tsunami and other irresistible disasters.

b. Fortuitous accident: Fortuitous accidents mainly include stranded (get aground), striking a rock, sunk, collide, fire, exploding and missing and other accidents with sea characteristics.

c. Extraneous risks: Extraneous risks refer to risks outside perils of the sea. General extraneous risks include theft, breakage, leakage, contamination, sweat and heating, taint of odor, hook damage, shortage, and rust. Special extraneous risks refer to risks resulting from military affairs, political and administrative rules such as war, strike, failure to deliver, rejection, etc.

2.6.2 Ocean Average

1. Average

Average means loss sustained in sea transportation. According to the extent of the loss, it is divided into total loss and partial loss.

a. Total loss. Total loss means all the goods insured suffered loss.

b. Actual total loss. Where the subject matter insured is destroyed, or so damaged as to cease to be a thing of the kind insured, or where the assured is irretrievably deprived thereof, there is an actual total loss. Furthermore, actual total loss, within the meaning of the definition, may be construed in three distinct ways, namely:

(**a**) When the subject matter is totally destroyed.

(**b**) When the subject matter is so damaged as to cease to be a thing of the kind insured.

(**c**) When the assured is irretrievably deprived thereof.

c. Constructive total loss. The concept of constructive total loss, whereby the subject matter insured is effectively lost to the assured, but is not actually destroyed, is unique to marine insurance. There is a constructive total loss where the subject matter insured is reasonably abandoned on account of its actual total loss appearing to be unavoidable, or because it could not be preserved from actual loss without an expenditure which would exceed its value when the expenditure had been incurred.

Where there is a constructive total loss, the assured may either treat the loss as a partial loss, or abandon the subject matter insured to the insurer and treat the loss as if it were an actual total loss. Where the assured elects to abandon the subject matter insured to the insurer, he must give notice of abandonment. If he fails to do so, the loss can only be treated as a partial loss.

2. Partial Loss

A partial loss is any loss other than a total loss. A partial loss may include a particular average loss, a general average loss and particular charges. Thus there are two distinct types of partial loss.

a. A particular average loss. If the average (damage) is accidently occasioned by some perils insured against, and not by the deliberate act of a person for the common benefit, that loss must be sustained exclusively by the person upon whom the damage falls and is termed a particular average. Or we may say it is the accidental damage to part of the cargo. For instance, ten per cent of the cotton yarn cargo was burned when the ship caught fire.

b. General average loss. A general average loss is a loss caused by or directly consequential on a general average act. It includes a general average expenditure as well as a general average sacrifice. There is a general average act where any extraordinary sacrifice or expenditure is voluntarily and reasonably made or incurred in time of peril for the purpose of preserving the property imperiled in the common adventure. Thus, for there to be a general average act, certain criteria must be met.

2.6.3 Insurance Clause in Contract

Ocean Marine Cargo Clause of the People's Insurance Company of China was constituted in 1972 and revised in 1976 and 1981. There are mainly two types of insurance coverage: basic coverage and additional coverage includes general additional coverage and special additional coverage.

1. FPA (free from particular average)

FPA is a limited form of cargo insurance cover under which partial loss or damage resulted from natural calamities is not recoverable, unless these natural calamities occur before or after fortuitous accidents. It provides coverage for total losses and general average.

2. WPA or WA (with particular average, with average)

WPA is a wider cover than FPA. It provides cover against all loss or damage due to marine perils throughout the duration lf the policy, including partial loss or damage which may bi attributed to natural calamities like heavy weather.

3. All Risks

All Risks is the most comprehensive of the three basic coverage under which the insurer is responsible for all total or partial loss of, or damage to the goods insured either arising from sea perils or general external causes, However, it does not cover loss, damage or expense caused by delay, inherent vice or nature of the goods, or special external risks of war, strike, etc.

4. Additional risks

a. General additional risks. The following general extraneous risks are to be covered subject to additional premium.

(**a**) Risk of theft, pilferage and non-delivery (TPND), Risk of theft and pilferage refers to the risk against the cargo's being stolen in transit of voyage. Risk of non-delivery refers to the risk against loss f complete packages (including box, case, drum etc.) due to improper unloading or for some unknown reason.

(**b**) Risk of fresh water and/or rain damages (FWRD). The risk of damage to the goods by fresh water and /or rain is covered by this coverage.

(**c**) Risk of clean and breakage. Under this coverage is the risk of breakage of the fragile goods by vibration, clash or pressing.

(**d**) Risk of leakage. It covers the risk of seepage and leakage of the liquid goods caused by the damaged container.

(**e**) Risk of shortage. This risk covers the shortage of weight for the goods due to the external packing broken. However, normal short age of weight in transit is covered.

(**f**) Risk of intermixture and contamination. Damage to the goods caused by its being intermixed or contaminated with each other is covered by this risk.

(**g**) Risk of taint of odor. Edibles, herbal medicine, cosmetics or raw materials may sometimes be tainted by odor of their own. Such a risk is under this coverage.

(**h**) Risk of sweating and heating. Under this coverage is the risk of damage of the goods by sweat and heating as a result of the sudden change of temperature or the ventilation on the vessel being out of order, etc.

(**i**) Risk of rust. It covers the risk of damage to the goods by rust caused by contamination with sea water. But goods getting rusty by itself or due to its own flaw are exclude.

(j) Risk of breakage of packing. Damage to the goods caused by rough handling is covered by this risk.

Hook damage. It covers damage to the goods caused by hooks in the process of loading and unloading, such as the losses of cereals due to the damage of packing bags by hooks.

General additional risks cannot be covered independently and should go with FPA or WPA. They are included in All Risks coverage.

Special additional risks cover the damage or losses arising from special additional reason such as political event, military affairs, national policies and acts, and administrative measures. The special additional risks include war risk strike risk failure to delivery risk import duty risk on deck risk rejections risk aflat0xin risk fire risk extension clause (FREC)

These additional coverage are usually taken out together with FPA, WPA and All Risks.

2.7 Inspection, Claim, Force Majeure and Arbitration of Commodity

In international trade, inspection is an absolutely necessary step in the transfer of the goods form the seller to the buyer. United Nations Convention on Contracts for the International Sale of Goods (hereinafter called CISG) and the laws of various countries have made similar stipulations on the buyer right of inspection. In actuality, in order to clarify the responsibilities, clauses regarding inspection are ally stipulated in the contract, which cover the place and time of inspection, basis for inspection, inspection organization, and so on. In order to solve disputes arising from breach of contract by any party, claim clauses regarding validity of claim, basis for claim, and even the amount for claim are included in the contract. If, however, the, breach of contract by any party is due to force majeure, the party concerned shall hold no liability. in order to ascertain whether an event is force majeure, we may stipulate the scope of majeure in the advance. In the event that both parties have different interpretation on some facts or clauses or any party shirks liabilities intentionally, mediation and arbitration are usually required. Sometimes a law suit may be taken. Among the ways of settling international trade disputes, arbitration is favored by most businessmen.

2.7.1 Commodity Inspection

1. Purpose of Commodity Inspection

In international trade, the quality and quantity of the goods delivered by the seller should be in the manner requires by the contract. In this sense, inspection of commodity and the issuance of certificate of inspection are necessary steps in the transfer of goods. Inspection may be made by the seller and the buyer themselves. But on most occasions, the seller dose not transfer the goods to the buyer face to face. In addition, during the long-distance transit, loading and unloading operation, losses of or damage to the goods may occur owing to the various kinds of risks or the carriers' fault. For the purpose of identifying liabilities and ascertaining facts, inspection by authoritative, impartial inspection bodies is required, by whom the certificates of inspection are issued. There certificates have been the major basis for transferring the goods, making payments, lodging and settling claims in international trade. Besides, CISG and the laws of various countries have made similar stipulations on buyer's right of inspection.

2. Time and Places of Inspection

CISG provides that except where the parties have agreed otherwise, the buyer has the right to inspect the goods. And the time and place of inspection have been stipulate in detail. CISG Article 38 states:

a. The buyer must examine the goods, or cause them to be examined, which as short a period as in practicable in the circumstances.

b. If the contract involves carriage of the goods, examination may be deferred until after the goods have arrived at their destination.

c. If the goods are redirected in transit or re-dispatched by the buyer without a reasonable opportunity for examination by him and at the of the conclusion of the contract the seller knew or ought to have known of possibility of such redirection or re-dispatch, examination may be deferred until after the goods have arrived at new destination.

There are three ways of stipulating the and time of inspection in the contract.

a. Shipping quality and weight. This means that inspection at the seller's factory or the port of shipping is final. Buyers can re-inspect the goods at the port destination, but normally he cannot claim for compensation. Thus it is favorable to the seller.

b. Landed quality and weight. This means inspection carried out at the port of destination is final. This arrangement is favorable to the buyer.

c. Inspection at the port of shipment and re-inspection at the port of destination. It means after inspection at port of shipment, the buyer retains the right to re-inspect and claim for compensation if the merchandise doesn't comply with the contract. This method is favorable to both sides and therefore is widely used in international trade.

3. Inspection Body

According to the Law of the of People's Republic of China on Import (hereinafter referred to as This law) and Export Commodity Inspection and the Regulations for the Implementation of the law of the people's Republic of China on Import and Export Inspection (hereinafter referred to as the Regulations), the State Commodity Inspection Authorities are in charge of the inspection of import and export commodities throughout the country. Their basic tasks are as follows:

a. Statutory inspection on import and export. Import and export commodity inspection can be divided into two types: statutory inspection and non-statutory inspection. In the light the need in the development of foreign trade, the state inspection agency formulates, adjust and publishes a List of Import and Export Commodities Subject to Inspection Enforced by the Commodities Inspection Authorities (hereinafter referred to as the List of Commodities) for those commodities which involve social and public interests. The list of Commodities varies with the development of foreign trade. For example, the list adopted on July 1, 1995, involves 18 categories, covering 2012 commodity codes widely used in Harmonized Description and Coding System. The statutory inspection on imports and exports includes the following items:

(**a**) inspection of import and export commodities included in the List of Commodities;

(**b**) hygiene inspection on the foods for export;

(**c**) testing and inspection on the performance and employment of the packages and containers for dangerous export goods;

(**d**) cargo worthiness inspection on such means of transportation as vessels' holds and containers for carrying perishable foods and frozen goods for export ;

(**e**) inspection of imports and exports to be conducted by the commodity inspection authorities according to relevant international treaties.

(**f**) inspection of import and exports to be carried out by the commodity inspection regulations.

b. Survey of import and export commodities. The State Inspection Authorities and their designated or the international trade interested parties, relevant units in china, and export commodities within the specified scope may issue certificates of survey. The commonly issued inspection certificates are Inspection Certificate of Quality, Weight, Health, Inspection Certificate Damaged Cargo, and Disinfection Inspection Certificate.

c. Supervision and control. This Law and the Regulations hold that the State commodity Inspection Authorities exercise supervision and control over the inspection conducted by the inspection agencies and personnel designated or accredited by the consignees, consignors, manufacturers, trading units, storage and transport units of import and export commodities. The principal measures of supervision and control include the following items.

(**a**) System of import safety license and export quality license. No import commodities subject to the import safety license system shall be allowed for import unless they have been granted an import safety license by the State Commodity Inspection Authorities. No export commodities subject to the export quality license system shall be allowed for export unless they have been granted an export license.

(**b**) Hygiene registration system. Manufacturers of foods for export which are subject to a hygiene registration system shall apply to the commodity inspection authorities for hygiene registration ; they shall not be allowed to produce, process or store foods for export unless they have obtained the approval from the State Commodity Inspection Authorities.

(**c**) Quality certification marks. The State Commodity Inspection Authorities shall conclude quality certification agreement on import and export commodities with relevant foreign bodies and shall conduct quality certification for import and export commodities according to the relevant agreements or upon entrustment by relevant foreign bodies. For those import and export commodities and their manufacturers which are found qualified through certification, due certificates shall be issued, and the use or quality certification marks for import and export commodities shall be allowed.

(**d**) Commodity inspection marks. The commodity inspection authorities may affix commodity inspection marks on the import and export commodities found up to standard through inspection; and carry out the sealing for the import and export commodities found up to the standard or those that must be sealed.

4. Inspection Methods and Inspection Standards

Inspection on import and export commodities performed by the commodity inspection authorities shall cover quality, specifications, quantity, weight, packing and the requirements for safety and hygiene. The commodity inspection authorities shall conduct inspection according to the following standards.

a. If the compulsory standards or other inspection standards which must be complied with are specified by laws or administrative regulations, the inspection shall be performed according to the standards as specified by laws and administrative regulations.

b. In the absence of the compulsory standards or other inspection standards which must be complied with as specified by laws or administrative regulations, the inspection shall be performed according to the standards agreed upon in the international trade contracts. If the trade is conducted against the sample, the inspection shall be performed simultaneously according to the sample provided.

c. In case the compulsory standards or other inspection standards which must be complied with as specified by laws or administrative regulations are lower than the standards agreed upon in the international trade contract, the inspection shall be according to the standards agreed upon in the international trade contracts. If the trade is conducted against the sample, the inspection shall be performed simultaneously according to the sample provided.

d. In the absence of the compulsory standards or other inspection standards which must be complied with as specified by laws or administrative regulations, and in case the compulsory standards are either not agreed upon or agreed upon unclearly in the contract, the inspection shall be conducted according to the standards of the manufacturing country, or relevant international standards or the standards designated by the state inspection age

2.7.2 Claim

There are generally three types of claim; claim regarding selling and buying, claim regarding transportation, claim regarding insurance. In the section, only the claim regarding selling and buying is discussed.

1. Definition of Claim

a. Breach of contract committed by the seller mainly covers: The seller fails to deliver the goods; The documents relating to goods are incomplete; The goods do not conform with the contract, etc.

b. Breach of contract committed by the buyer mainly covers: The buyer fails to pay the price; The buyer fails to take delivery of the goods, etc.

A breach of contract committed by one of the parties is fundamental if it results in such detriment to the other party as substantially to deprive him of what he is entitled to expect under the contract, unless the party in breach did not foresee and a reasonable person of the same kind circumstances would not have foreseen such a result." The injured party may declare the contract avoided and claim damages. If, however, the breach of contract is non-fundamental, the injured party can only claim damages but cannot declare the contract avoided. The British law divides the breach of contract into Breach of Condition and Breach of Warranty. Breach of Condition refers to the breach of the major terns of the contract, the injured party may declare the contract avoided and claim damages. Breach of Warranty means breach of the minor terns of the contract, the breach of which gives rise to claim for damages, but not to a right to reject the goods and treat the contract as repudiated.

2. Claim Clause in Contract

a. Discrepancy and claim clause. This is the commonly adopted claim clause in a sales contract.

The cause includes: Basis for claim, evidences to be provided; Term of validity of claim.

The following is an example of claim clause in a sales contract.

"Claim: any claim by the buyers regarding the goods shipped shall be filed within 30 days after arrival of the goods at the port of destination specified in the relative Bill of Lading and reported by survey a report issued by a surveyor approved by the Sellers."

b. Penalty clause in contract. Sometimes a penalty clause should be included in the contract in case the buyer fails to delay in opening of L\C, or the seller fails to deliver the goods on time. Under this clause, the party who fails to fulfill the contract must pay a fine, a certain percentage of total contractual value.

The following are two example of penalty clause.

(**a**) Penalty clause regarding the seller's delay in delivery. "should the sellers fail to make delivery on time as stipulated in the contract, the Buyers shall agree to postpone the delivery on condition that the Sellers agree to pay a penalty which shall be deducted by the paying bank from the payment under negotiation, or by the Buyers direct at the time of payment. The rate of penalty is charged at 0.5% of the total value of the goods whose delivery has been delayed for every seven days, odd days less than seven days should be counted as seven days. But the total amount of penalty, however, shall not exceed 5% of the total value of the goods involved in the late delivery. In case the sellers fail to make delivery ten weeks later than the time of shipment stipulated in the contract, the buyers shall have the right to cancel the contract and the sellers, in spite of the cancellation, shall still pay the aforesaid penalty to the buyers without delay."

(**b**) penalty clause regarding the buyer's delay in opening of L/C. "should the buyers for its own sake fail to open the letter of credit on time stipulated in the contract, the buyers shall pay a penalty to the sellers. The penalty shall be charged at the rate of 0.5% of the amount of the letter of credit for every ten days of delay in opening the letter of credit. However, the penalty shall not exceed 5% of the total value of the credit which the buyers should have opened. Any fractional days less than ten days for the calculation of penalty. The penalty shall be the sole compensation for the damage caused by such delay."

2.7.3 Force Majeure

1. Definition of Force Majeure

Force majeure (french: "superior force") is an event or effect that cannot be reasonably anticipated nor controlled. a party is not liable for any damage resulting from his failure to perform the contract if he can show: that his failure was "due to an impediment beyond his control"; that the impediment was not something he could have reasonably taken into account at the time of contracting; that he remains unable to overcome the impediment or its consequences. Force majeure is not only narrowly defined, but also limited in its application. it applies to situations—

such as natural disasters, war, embargoes, strikes, break downs, and the bankruptcy of a supplier—that frustrate both the party attempting to perform and the party expecting performance. because neither party is really at fault, the breaching party is excused from paying damages. he is not, however, exempted from the application of any other appropriate remedy (such as suspension of performance of avoidance).

There are usually two consequences of force majeure: termination of the contract and postponement of the contract. whether terminating the contract or postponing the performance of the contract depends on what degree the force majeure event has affected the performance of the contract, or on the detailed stipulations in the contract. generally speaking, the contract can be avoided only if the occurrence of the force majeure event makes it impossible to perform the contract such as the loss of or damage to specifically designated goods, or the event is so serious that it is impossible to recover within a short period of time. Otherwise, the suffering party can only make amendments to the contract to reduce the possible losses to the other party.

2. Force Majeure Clause in Contract

The force majure clause usually contains:

a. The scope of force majeure events: since there is still no definite explanation as to which events should be regarded as force majeure, the seller and the buyer usually stipulate in their contract the scope of force majeure events. force majeure events include certain natural disasters such as fire, flood, storm, heavy snow, earthquake, etc. and social disturbances like war, strikes, sanction, etc.

b. Time limit of notifying the other party: in case of a force majeure event, the party seeking to use the clause of farce majeure has a duty to promptly notify the other party of the impediment and its effect on his ability of perform.

c. The issuer of the certificate: a force majeure event should be verified by a certificate that attests such an event. the issuer of the certificate should be mentioned in the clause.

The following is an example of force majeure clause.

Force majeure: if the shipment of the contracted good s is prevent or delayed in whole or in part by reason of war, earthquake, flood, fire, storm, heavy snow, or other causes of force majeure, the seller shall not be liable for non-shipment or late shipment of the goods or non-performance of this contact. However, the seller shall notify the buyer by cable or telex and furnish the latter by registered airmail with a certificate issued by the china council for the promotion of international trade attesting such event or events.

2.7.4 Arbitration

1. the Ways of Disputes Settlement

When disputes arise between exporter and importer, they can be settled though friendly consultation, arbitration, or litigation. Friendly negotiation is an important tool in the process of dispute settlement, and undoubtedly the one most commonly relied on. The majority of the disputes are settled this way and friendly business relations are thus maintained between exporters. Arbitration is the next best alternative. It is a means of settled between two parties though the medium of a third party to compel anther to do him justice. It is usually costly and time-consuming. This section will focus on arbitration. Arbitration means a method of resolving disputes arising from the two-side of parties who voluntarily render their disputes to a third party agreed by themselves to deal with in accordance with certain arbitration rules and make a final decision binding each of the parties based on the arbitration clause concluded previously by them or based on the arbitration agreement the parties have reached after the disputes arose.

a. voluntarily: the litigants submit themselves voluntarily to an arbitrator. The arbitrator is a private, disinterested person, or nonofficial government organization chosen by the parties to a disputed question.

b. an arbitration agreement in written form between the parties concerned is prerequisite for arbitration. An arbitration agreement is a contract between two or more parties whereby they agree to refer the subject in dispute to others and to be bound by their award.

c. more simple in procedures, less costly and time-consuming than litigation

d. the award is final and binding on both parties.

Neither party may bring a suit before a law court or make a request to any other organization for revising the arbitral award. The characteristic of finality of arbitral awards is the basic element of the modern commercial arbitration recognized all over the world.

2. Arbitration Procedures

Pursuant to the current arbitration rules of CIETAC which took effect on Oct. 1, 2000, the general arbitration procedures are application for arbitration.

a. procedure of applying for arbitration; when applying for arbitration, the claimant must submit to the secretariat of the arbitration commission an arbitration agreement, an application for arbitration in writing and the facts and evidence on which his claim is based, and the claimant shall pay an arbitration fee in advance to the arbitration commission according to the arbitration fee schedule of the arbitration commission.

b. The application for arbitration; The Application for arbitration and relevant documentary evidence should be submitted in the same copies as the total number of the respondent and arbitrators plus the secretariat as a separate party.

c. Arbitration costs. when applying for arbitration, the parties shall pay certain fees in advance.

The arbitration tribunal shall decide which party shall pay the deposit for making investigations and collecting evidence, and those for engaging expert to make appraisal; and the actual expenses for the arbitrator outside Beijing or foreign arbitrator to attend the hearing shall be paid in advance by the party who appoints the arbitrator. The arbitration tribunal shall decide in the arbitral award which party should bear those actual fees and expenses, and how much each party should bear. The arbitration tribunal has the power to decide in the arbitral award that the losing party shall pay the winning party as compensation a proportion of the expenses reasonably incurred by the winning party in dealing with the case. The amount of such compensation shall not in any case exceed 10% of the total amount awarded to the winning party.

Apart from charging arbitration fee according to this arbitration fee schedule, the arbitration commission may collect other extra, reasonable and actual expenses pursuant to the relevant provisions of the arbitration rules.

An arbitration agreement must provide the rule of arbitration procedure. It is of vital importance to provide the rule of arbitration procedure in the arbitration agreement or arbitration clause, because the rule of arbitration procedure governs the whole process of the arbitration case from the beginning of accepting the case to the end of making an award. Different rule of arbitration procedure will more or less have some influence on the arbitration case. According to international practice, in principle, the rule of the arbitration agency is applied. But the parties to an arbitration agreement are also allowed to make an agreement that the arbitration rule s of other arbitration agencies are applied. Since 1998 in CIETAC arbitration, parties can choose another arbitration rule under the condition that Arbitration Commission also agrees.

3. Arbitration Place

The arbitration place can be anywhere in the seller's country, the buyer's country or a third country. The status of arbitration place is as important as that of arbitration body in an arbitration agreement. The country where an arbitration place is or an arbitral award is made is the country of the nationality of a foreign arbitral awards, therefore, it is the arbitration place that is in the first important place in recognition and enforcement of an arbitral award. In accordance with the provision of the New York Convention on Recognition and Enforcement of Foreign Arbitration Awards, 1958, the foreign arbitration awards that have been made out of the country where the recognition and enforcement are required are the foreign arbitration awards. It shows the important position of arbitration place in international trade arbitration, since the Convention does not provide that arbitration body is the criterion of basis on which foreign arbitral awards are divided. On the other hand, to provide an arbitration place is equal to provide an arbitration procedure law which shall be applied to the arbitration case. The procedure law of the place usually applies to Arbitration procedure where the arbitration undertakes with the exception of which the parties have explicitly selected the procedure law of a certain country or the arbitration rules of a certain arbitration body in their arbitration clause be their arbitration procedure law.

4. Arbitration Bodies

There are two forms of arbitration: institutional arbitration and ad hoc arbitration. What the major difference between an ad hoc arbitration and an institutional arbitration falls on the fact that it is unnecessary for an ad hoc arbitration to have an institutional arbitration body to administrate a case. That is to say, arbitration body is not the element that all forms of arbitration or arbitration clause must have. Generally it is not essential to stipulate an arbitration body in an arbitration clause for an ad hoc arbitration. But things are different in China, there is no ad hoc arbitration in China at present. So in China, it is necessary to indicate an arbitration body (an arbitration commission), otherwise the arbitration clause may be considered as an invalid clause. The China International Economic and Trade Arbitration Commission (CIETAC) in Beijing, and its chapters in Shenzhen and Shanghai, and liaison offices in Dalian, Fuzhou, Changsha, Chengdu and Chongqing accept arbitration cases according to arbitration rules and regulations, and use the unified Arbitration Rules and Panel of Arbitrators.

The mane of the arbitration body should be written correctly otherwise it will have a bad result. For example, when an arbitration clause provides an arbitration body never existed, the desire for arbitration will be frustrated.

5. Arbitration Clause in Contract

In international arbitration contract, there are arbitration place, arbitration body, arbitration procedure, arbitration effect and arbitration fees, etc. The foreign trade contract of our country includes the following three arbitration clauses.

a. Arbitration clause in our country. All disputes arising from the execution of, or in connection with this contract, shall then be settled amicably through negotiation. In case no settlement can breached through negotiation, the case shall then be submitted to the Foreign Economic and Trade Arbitration commission of the China Council for the Promotion of International Trade, Beijing for arbitration in accordance with its Provisional Rules of Procedure. The arbitral award is final and binding upon both parties.

b. Arbitration clause in counterparty's country. All disputes arising from the execution of, or in connection with this contract, shall be settled amicably through negotiation. In case no settlement can be reached through negotiation, the case shall then be submitted for arbitration. The location of arbitration shall be in the country of the domicile of the sued party.

c. Arbitration clause in the third country. All disputes arising from the execution of, or in connection with this contract, shall be settled amicably through negotiation, incase no settlement can be reached through negotiation, the case shall then be submitted to in accordance with its arbitral rules of procedure, The arbitral award is final and binding upon both parties.

Chapter 3 International Trade Payment

3.1 Instruments of Payment

In international trade, it is hardly possible for the seller to deliver the goods and the buyer to make the payment face to face. Usually, the seller delivers the goods and hands over the documents. Bands are intermediaries. Bills are instruments of payment. These are the features of modern international trade payment. Nowadays non-cash payment is universally adopted all over the world. Under non-cash payment, negotiable instruments to be commonly used as payment instruments are bills of exchange, promissory notes and cheques, among which bills of exchange are the most widely used ones. No export transaction can be said to be successful until payment has been received for the goods delivered overseas, and the proceeds have been safely credited to the exporter's account. Compared with payment arrangements for domestic transactions, international payment arrangements are much more complicated and difficult. This chapter will focus on instruments of payment, methods and terms of payment in international trade of goods.

3.1.1 Bills of Exchange (Draft)

1. Definition of Bills of Exchange

A bill of exchange is a written, dated and signed instrument that contains an unconditional order from the drawer that directs the drawer to pay a definite sun of money to a payee on demand or at a specified future date. It is a useful instrument because it allows one party to direct another to pay money either to himself, to his agent, or to a third party. Of course, the order is valid only if the drawer has an underlying obligation to pay money to the drawer. This can arise in situations where the drawer is holding money on account of the drawer, where the drawer lent money to a drawee, or where the drawer has sold goods to the drawee and the drawee owes the sale price to the drawer.

2. Contents of Bills of Exchange

a. Parties related to Draft

(**a**) Drawer—person who issues the draft, in international trade, the person is usually the exporter.

(**b**) Drawee—the payer of the draft, in international trade, the person is usually the importer.

(**c**) Payee—person who accepts the draft, in international trade, the person is usually the exporter or his or her nominated person.

b. Amount and Monetary

It specifies definitely the amount drawee should pay, and the monetary be used. In international trade, the amount of draft ahould be within the range that of contract or L/C, if there is no special condition, the amount and monetary should be as same as that of invoice, otherwise, the drawee have right to refuse it.

c. Payment Time

It specifies definitely the payment time, such as "payment at sight", "payment in 30 days", etc.

d. Place of Issue and Payment

It specifies the place of issue and payment. Usually it marks by the place in which drawer and drawee living.

e. Signature of drawer

3. Types of Bills of Exchange

Draft can be classified as the follows according to different views.

a. Commercial draft: It is a bill issued by a trader on another trader or on a bank.

Banker's draft: It is a draft drawn by a bank on another bank. Both the payer and payee are banks.

b. Clean draft: It is a bill without shipping documents attached thereto.

Documentary draft: It is a bill with shipping documents attached thereto.

c. Sight draft or demand draft: It is a bill payable on demand or at sight or on presentation.

Time draft or usance draft: It is a bill payable at a fixed or determinable future time. The time may be expressed in the following three ways:

(**a**) at . . . days after sight.

(**b**) at . . . days after date.

(**c**) at a fixed date.

4. Application of Bills of Exchange

In international trade, the drawer draws and signs and delivers it to the payee. Upon issuance, the drawer has the responsibility to ensure the draft be accepted and paid. If the draft is dishonored, the drawer shall be recoursed by the bearer and reimburse the amount, interest and the relevant charges. Acceptance means the drawee of the bill writes down the word "accept", marks the date and signs his name across the face of the bill. This action means the payer promise to pay at the date of payment. In doing so, the drawee (acceptor) commits himself to pay the bill upon presentation at maturity. After accepting the bill, the drawee should return it to the holder who will present it for payment at maturity. On the expiry date of draft, the payer makes sufficient payment to the legal bearer, the latter then writes off the draft and return it to the payer as a receipt. The act of a payee, drawee, or holder of a draft in signing the back of the draft to transfer rights in the draft to another. In financial market, the typical endorsement is discount of draft, i. e. , the bearer transfers a time and accepted draft to a bank or a discounting company, who, as transferee, will deduct the interest as discount rate and pay the remaining sum to the bearer. Dishonor means the payer refuses or fails to pay or accept the bill when the holder makes presentment to him. When dishonored, the holder shall pursue the right of recourse by giving notice of dishonor to the drawer and each endorser. Protest is a written statement under seal drawn up and signed by a Notary Public or other authorized person for the purpose of giving evidence that a bill of exchange has been presented by him for payment but dishonored. After a bill is dishonored by non-acceptance or by non-payment, and a notice of dishonor is sent, the holder may hand the bill to a Notary Public who will present it again for acceptance or for payment as the case may be, so as to obtain a legal proof of the act of dishonor. As it is dishonored again, the Notary Public then draws up a protest, i. e. , an official certificate evidencing the act of dishonor and stating the reason for the protest, demands made on the drawee (or the acceptor) and the response received.

3.1.2 Promissory Note

A written promise to pay a determinate sum of money made between two parties is a promissory note, or simply a note. The party who promises to pay is called the maker; the party who is to be paid is the payee.

3.1.3 Cheque

A cheque is a special type of draft, the drawer is the person signing the cheque, the drawee is the bank where the drawer has an account, and the payee is the beneficiary, that is, the person in whose favor the cheque is made out. thus, a cheque is an unconditional order by the drawer or maker. asking his bank to pay a certain amount of money to a third party on demand. in simple terms, a cheque is a demand draft drawn in a bank. When the drawer signs a cheque, he should see to it that his deposit in the bank is not lower than the amount of the cheque if the drawer has not enough deposit in the bank for the cheque amount, the cheque will bi dishonored, and this kind as cheque is called "bounced cheque", which in not allowed.

3.2 Methods of Payment

3.2.1 Remittance

Remittance refers to the transfer of funds from one party to another among different countries, that is, a bank (the remitting bank), at the request of its customer, transfers a certain sum of money to its overseas branch to correspondent bank (the paying bank) instructing them to pay to a named person to corporation (the payee to beneficiary) domiciled in that country. There are three basic ways for a bank to transfer founds for its client from home country to abroad. they are remittance by remittance by airmail remittance by cable. and remittance by demand draft.

1. Remittance by Airmail (M/T)

Remittance by airmail is more generally knows as mail transfer, i. e. M/T. A mail transfer is to transfer funds by means of a payment order or a mail advice to sometimes a debit advice issued by a remitting bank, at the request of the remitter. A payment order, mail advice or debit advice is an authenticated order in writing addressed by one bank to another instructing the latter to pay a sum certain in money to a specified person or a beneficiary named thereon.

2. Remittance by Cable/Telex/SWIFT (T/T)

Remittance by cable/telex/SWIFT is often referred to as cable transfer or telegraphic transfer, namely T/T. It is exactly the same as a mail transfer, except that instructions from the remitting bank to the paying bank are transmitted by cable instead of by air mail. It is therefore faster, but more expensive than the mail transfer. It is often used when the remittance amount is large and the transfer of founds is subject to a time limit. The only means of authenticating a cable transfer is the test key. However, remittance by SWIFT should be authenticated by SWIFT authentic key.

3. Remittance by Banker's Demand Draft (D/D)

Remittance by banker's demand draft is often referred to as D/D. A banker's draft is a negotiable instrument drawn by a bank on its overseas bank.

In our foreign trade practice, remittance is only adopted in making down payments, commissions, etc. It is not the major method of payment. But it is a major method in developed countries, because of the substantial internal transactions of transnational companies and reliable trade partners and sales network. With the development of China's foreign trade, Chinese foreign trade enterprises have established relatively stable relationship with trade partners abroad. And with more and more fierce competition in the world market, foreign importers often ask for payment against delivery to reduce import cost. At present, in our export, especially in trade with developed countries, the use of remittance is growing. In transactions with partial or deferred payment, remittance is used together with banker's letter of guarantee or standby L/C.

3.2.2 Collection

1. Definition of Collection

After he has shipped the goods to his customers abroad, the exporter draws a bill of exchange on the latter with or without shipping documents attached thereto and then gives the draft to his bank together with his appropriate collection instructions. In simple terms, a collection means that the creditor (the exporter) entrusts the bank to collect payment from the debtor (importer). The bank acts as the intermediary.

2. Parties related to Collection

Usually there are four parties related to collection, that is principal (exporter), remitting bank, collecting bank and drawee.

a. drawer or principal. It is the exporter or the seller who entrusts the collection items to his bank

b. drawee. It is the buyer or the important to whom the collection items are to be presented for acceptance or payment

c. remitting bank. It is the bank to which the drawer entrusts the collection items. upon receipt of the collection items from the exporter, the bank for wards them to the collection bank, in accordance with the collection instruction given by the principal

d. collecting bank. It is the bank entrusted by the remitting bank to present the collection items to the drawer. the collecting items of drawer, the collection bank is generally a branch of a correspondent or an agent of the remitting bank

3. Types of Collection

a. clean collections. Clean collections are collections on financial instruments without being accompanied by commercial documents. Such as invoice, bill of lading, insurance policy etc.

b. documentary collections. Documentary collection nay be described as collection financial instruments accompanied by commercial documents without being accompanied by financial instruments that is, commercial documents alone without a bill if exchange.

(a) documents against payment (D/P)

When entrusting the bank to collect, the principal instructs the bank to deliver the document when payment has been made. according to the different time of payment, it is divided into D/P at sight and D/P after sight.

(i) D/P at sight. The draft issued is demand draft. when the collecting. bank make presentation to the drawer (the important), the latter should make payment upon presentation. the collecting bank will then deliver the documents to him

(ii) D/P after sight. Time draft is used in D/P after sight. when the collecting bank makes presentation, the buyer shall first make acceptance after checking the documents and will make payment in the date of expiry of payment

(b) document against acceptance (D/A)

But there are some differences between D/A and cash on delivery: In cash on delivery, the seller can only sue the buyer on basis contract but also on draft accepted by the buyer. The relationship between the creditor and the debtor defined by the draft is simple and stable, and the seller is relatively in favorable position.

3.2.3 Letter of Credit

1. Definition of Letter of Credit

In international sales transaction, the seller, undoubtedly, would prefer to be paid in advance. The buyer, on the other hand, would like to make sure, before paying, that (a) the goods are actually shipped and that (b) the goods shipped meet his contractual specifications; and, in actuality, he would prefer(c) to take delivery before paying. Depending on the relative bargaining power of the buyer and seller, any of these possible arrangements can be included as a term in the sales contract, If the seller is unable to determine the buyer's creditworthiness, he may insist upon "cash in advance". If the buyer wants to confirm that the goods have been shipped, the term documents against payment can be used. If the buyer insists upon taking delivery before making payment, a document against acceptance term can be used. None of these terms are used very often. In part, this is because they imply that both sides distrust each other, To avoid this, contracting parties use a "letter of credit" (or "documentary credit", or "banker's credit" or, simply, a "credit") A letter of credit or L/C is a conditional undertaking of payments by a bank.

2. Parties to Letter of Credit

Probably the parties related to L/C include opening bank, applicant, advising bank, negotiating bank and paying bank.

a. The applicant or the opener is always an importer or a buyer, who fills out and signs an application form, requesting the bank to issue a letter of credit in favor of an exporter or a seller abroad.

b. The issuing bank is one which issues a letter of credit at the request of an applicant. It undertakes to pay to the beneficiary. If the applicant fails to pay after the issuing bank makes payment, the latter has the right to sell the goods and claim from the applicant if the proceeds are not sufficient.

c. The advising bank is one which advises the credit to the beneficiary in accordance with stipulations on the credit. It is located in the place of the beneficiary, which is usually the issuing bank's branch or correspondent acting as an agent of the opening bank in accordance with the instructions given.

d. The beneficiary is the exporter or the seller in whose favor the credit is issued. If there is a discrepancy between the credit opened and the sales contract, the beneficiary may have the option to accept it as it stands or persuade the opener to have it amended so as to be in line with the contract.

e. Negotiating means the giving value for draft and/or documents by the bank authorized to negotiate.

f. The paying bank is always the drawee of a draft stipulated in the credit. Or we may say it is a bank nominated by the issuing bank to make payment under the credit. Sometimes the paying bank is the issuing bank itself.

3. Procedures of Letter of Credit Operations

The documentary credit procedure involves the following steps:

a. The buyer and seller agree on the terms of sale: specifying a documentary credit as the means of payment, naming an advising bank (usually the seller's bank) and listing required documents.

b. The buyer applies to his bank (issuing bank) to open a documentary credit naming the seller as the beneficiary based on specific terms and conditions that are listed in the credit.

c. After accepting the application, the opening bank shall stipulate L/C clauses strictly conforming to the instructions of application form and mail or send by SWIFT to the advising bank named in the credit.

d. After verifying the authenticity of the credit, the advising bank shall advise the beneficiary of L/C or just transferring the L/C to him. And a copy is usually kept for file. There are two ways of advising: one is to deliver the L/C directly to the beneficiary, attached with a signed advice note. Another one is when the addressee of the L/C is the advising bank, the advising bank shall copy word by word in its own advice note, sign, and deliver it to the beneficiary.

e. The seller (beneficiary) ships the goods to the buyer and obtains a negotiable transport document (negotiable bill of lading) from the shipping firm/agent.

f. The seller prepares and presents a document package to the advising bank consisting of documents such as negotiable transport document, commercial invoice, insurance document inspection certificate, etc.

g. The advising bank reviews the document package making certain the document are in conformity with the terms of the credit and pays the seller. In the case of a credit available by negotiation, the negotiating bank (usually be the advising bank) negotiates the documents with recourse to the beneficiary. After negotiation, the negotiating bank will claim reimbursement from the issuing bank or the reimbursing bank in accordance with the reimbursement terms indicated in the credit and documents will be sent to the issuing bank. The advising bank sends the document package by mail or by courier to the issuing bank. The issuing bank reviews the document package making certain the documents are in conformity with the terms of the credit, pays the advising bank and advising the buyer that the documents have arrived. The buyer reviews the document package making certain the documents are in conformity with the terms of credit, and makes a cash payment (with a sight draft) to the issuing bank, or signs an acceptance (promising to pay at a future date). The issuing bank sends the document package by mail or courier to the buyer who then takes possession of the shipment. At present, most L/Cs are opened by telecommunication. Although the forms are different their contents are, in the main, the same. The following details are to be found on all credits.

4. Characteristics of Letter of Credit Business

a. A banker's credit. The issuing bank undertakes to effect payment, provided the documents presented are in compliance with the terms and conditions of the letter of credit. Thus the bank assumes a primary liability rather than a secondary liability for payment.

b. Banks deal with documents. In letter of credit business, banks deal with documents and not with goods, services and/or other performances to which the documents may relate. They examine exclusively on the basis of the credit are fulfilled. They are not in a position to verify whether the goods supplied actually conform with those specified in the credit. They are not to be held liable for a discrepancy between the goods invoiced and those actually delivered. If the documents presented are not in compliance with the terms and conditions of the credit, the bank will refuse to pay no matter whether the goods shipped are agreed with those mentioned in the contract.

c. A letter of credit is a self-sufficient instrument Although the credit is issued on the basis of the sales contract, banks are in no way concerned with or bound by such contract, even if any reference whatsoever to such contract is included in the credits. The bank, when issuing the credit has no regard for the sales contract but follows an application handed in by the buyer.

5. Classification of Letters of Credit

a. According to the revocability of credit. A credit may be either revocable or irrevocable.

Every credit should clearly indicate whether it is revocable or irrevocable. In the absence of such indication the credit shall be deemed to be irrevocable.

(a) Irrevocable credit. An irrevocable credit is a credit which constitutes a definite undertaking of the issuing bank and can be amended or cancelled by the issuing bank only on condition that all parties concerned, that is, the issuing bank, the beneficiary and the confirming bank, if any, do agree. This credit gives the beneficiary greater assurance of payment.

(b) A revocable credit is a credit which can be amended or cancelled at any moment by the issuing bank without prior notice to the beneficiary. However, under such a credit, if the payment, acceptance, or negotiation has been effected by the banks concerned prior to their receipt of notice of amendment or cancellation, the issuing bank will still have to reimburse them.

b. According to the method of payment. All credits must clearly indicate whether they are available by payment, by acceptance or by negotiation.

(a) payment L/C. A payment credit is a credit available by payment, under which a bank specifically nominated there in is authorized to pay against the shipping documents with or without a draft presented in conformity with the terms of the credit.

(b) Acceptance credit. An acceptance credit is a credit available by acceptance, under which a bank specifically nominated therein is authorized to accept.

(c) Negotiation credit. A negotiation credit is a credit under which a bank specifically nominated there in is authorized to negotiate or a credit which is freely negotiable by any bank.

c. Special credits

(a) Revolving credit. This is a type of credit that renews itself after amount is drawn. To define it more clearly, it is a credit where, under the terms and conditions thereof, its amount is renewed or reinstated without any specific amendment made thereto.

(b) Back-to-back credit. This is a new credit opened on the basis of an already existing nontransferable credit. It is used by traders to make payment to the ultimate supplier. A trader receives a little of credit from the buyer and then opens another letter of credit in favor of the supplier.

6. Letter of Credit Clause in Contract

a. Sight L/C. The buyers shall arrange with XX bank for opening an irrevocable (transferable divisible) letter of credit (confirmed by XX bank) in favor of the Sellers before-(or within— days after receipt of the Sellers' advice or within—days after signing of this contract). The said letter of credit shall be available by sight draft for full invoice value and remain valid for negotiation in China until the 15th day after date of shipment.

b. Draft L/C. The letter of credit must stipulate that reimbursement is to be made telegraphically upon receipt of the cable advice of negotiation. The buyers shall arrange with XX bank for opening an irrevocable(transferable) banker's acceptance letter of credit in favor of the sellers before-(or within—days after receipt of Sellers advice, or within—days after signing of this Contract). The said letter of credit shall be available by draft at—sight(or after shipment) and remain valid for negotiation in China until the 15th day after the aforesaid time of shipment.

3.2.4 Banker's Letter of Guarantee

In international trade, each party of the contract wants to be ensured that the other party is in a position to honor its commitment as contracted. Such security may be obtained through banks in the form of letter of guarantee. A Banker's Letter of guarantee (L/G) or bond is a contract by which a bank (the guarantor) agrees to pay another's debt or to perform another's obligation only if that other individual or legal entity fails to pay or perform. A banker's letter of guarantee is usually a separate contract from the principal agreement, and therefore the letter of guarantee is secondarily liable to the third person. Parties to a letter of guarantee include.

Chapter 4 Negotiation on Contracts for International Sales of Goods

4.1 Negotiation Procedure

Contracts are formed through negotiations between the buyer and the seller. The process of negotiation usually includes enquiry, offer, counter-offer and acceptance, among which offer and acceptance are the two integral steps in forming a contract. In this chapter, the formation of a contract will be discussed based on CISG. International trade negotiations may be conducted through letters, faxes, e-mails, etc. Negotiations may also be carried out face-to-face. Whatever is chosen for the negotiation, four procedures are generally involved:

4.1.1 Enquiry

Enquiry is also known as invitation to offer. Both importers and exporters can make use of this step to initiate a potential transaction. By making an enquiry, the exporter may aim find out certain terms for a desired transaction.

The seller should attach much importance to the enquiries sent by the buyer, who might by a potential customer of the seller. Each enquiry stands for a sales opportunity, an opportunity to foster a potential long-term relationship. An enquiry may be made in a way like:

e. g. By cable: INTERESTED IN BUTTERFLY BRAND SEWING MACHINE PLEASE QUOTE.

4.1.2 Offer

An offer is a proposal that is made to a certain individual or legal entity to enter into a contract, which is definite in its terms, and which indicates the offer's intent to be bound.

An offer may be made by the seller or the buyer. The former is called "selling offer"; whereas the latter is called "buying offer" which usually described as a "bid". Terms like "offer", "offer firm", "quote", "book", "bid", etc. are usually adopted in making offers.

The following is an example of an offer by cable: OFFER 2000 DOZEN SPORT SHIRTS SAMPLED MARCH 15TH USD90 PER DOZEN CIF NEW YORK EXPORT STANDARD PACKING MAY/JUNE SHIPMENT IRREVOCABLE SIGHT L/C SUBJECT REPLY HERE 20TH

4.1.3 Counter-offer

A counter-offer is a reply to an offer that adds to, limits, r modifies materially the terms of the offer. A seller, for example, who accepts a buyer' offer but informs the buyer that goods will be a different color, has made a counter-offer.

Virtually, a counter-offer is a new offer made by the offer. The original offer or is the offer of the new offer. The original offer becomes null and void and its original offer or is not bound any more. Counter-offers may be made repeatedly between the buyer and the seller. The following are two examples of counter-offers made by telegram.

Outgoing telegram: YOURTLX THIRD REGRET UNABLE ACCERT COMPETITORS QUOTING SIMILAR QUALITY USD55 PLEASE REPLY IMMEDIATELY.

Incoming telegram: OURS THIRD RENEW OFFER SUBJECT REPLY TENTH OUR TIME.

4.1.4 Acceptance

AN acceptance is an unconditional assent to an offer or an assent to 356 an offer conditioned on only minor changes that do not affect any material terms of offer. For example, a cable reading "YOURS FOURTEENTH WE ACCEPT" is a typical acceptance.

4.2 Formation of the Contract

A contract is formed, and the parties are bound by its provisions, when an offer to buy or sell a good is accepted, we shall discuss offer and acceptance on the basis of CISG.

4.2.1 Offer

An offer is a proposal addressed to specific persons indicating an intention by the offeror to be bound to the sale or purchase of particular goods for a price, According to Article 14 of CISG, a proposal for concluding a contract addressed to one or more specific persons constitutes an offer if it is sufficiently definite and indicates the intention of the offeror to be bound in case of acceptance. A proposal is sufficiently definite if it indicates the goods and expressly or implicitly fixes or makes provision for determining the quantity.

1. Constitution of an Offer

a. To one or more specific persons. For a proposal to be an offer, it must be addressed to "one or more specific persons." Proposals made to the public are ordinarily intended to be nothing more than invitations to negotiate. For example, an advertisement in a newspaper for the sale of goods at a particular price might put the advertiser in the awkward position of having to deliver more goods than he has on hand because of heavier than expected demand, or of absorbing a substantial loss because of an increase in the cost of the goods between the advertisement was placed and the time it appeared. CISG, accordingly, adopts the rule that public offers are only invitations to negotiate "unless the contrary is clearly indicated."

b. Sufficiently definite. A proposal is sufficiently definite if it indicates the goods and expressly or implicitly fixes or makes provision for determining the quantity and the price.

Other terms and conditions, if not definitely stipulated in the contract, should be added

Either on the basis of usual practices between both sides or on the basis of part III of CISG.

In inter national trade practice, the contents of an offer should be

2. Term of Validity

There is a term of validity for each offer, a period within which the offeree can make acceptance, and the offeror is only bound. the offeror may clearly define it in the offer, otherwise a reasonable time should be regarded as the term of validity. But it is hard to tell what a reasonable time is. So we'd better state it clearly in the offer. The ways of stipulating term of validity are:

a. The latest time: e. g. REPLY REACHING HERE BEFORE 15th.

b. A period of time: e. g. This offer is valid for 3 days.

3. Withdrawal and Revocation of an Offer

a. Withdrawal. An offer becomes effective only after it reaches the offeree. Thus; offers-including offers that promise they are irrevocable—can be withdrawn prior to their reaching the offeree.

b. Revocation. Article 16 of CISG states that:

(**a**) "Until a contract is concluded an offer may be revoked if the revocation reaches the offeree before he has dispatched an acceptance.

(**b**) However, an offer cannot be revoked:

(**i**) If it indicates, whether by stating a fixed time for acceptance or otherwise, that it is irrevocable; or

(**ii**) If it was reasonable for the offeree to rely on the offer as being irrevocable and the offeree has acted in reliance on the offer."

Illustration is given by this example: Constructor A made an enquiry with B for 10, 000 M/T Steel. A told B that this enquiry was made for the purpose of calculating price for his submission of a tender, which was due to begin on June 1 and the result should be announced on June 15th. On May 20th, B made an offer to A with neither term of validity, nor indication of irrevocable. On June 10, B informed A that his offer was revoked. But on June 15, A was advised that he won the tender. In this case, B was not allowed to revoke his offer.

4. Termination

An offer is terminated when it is over the term of validity; it is rejected or declined; it is legally revoked.

4.2.2 Acceptance

A contract comes into existence at the point in time an offer is accepted. Acceptance is a statement or conduct by the offeree indicating assent that is communicated to the offeror.

1. Constitution of an Acceptance

a. The acceptance must be made by the offeree. Any acceptance made by others is not effective.

b. The contents of an acceptance must conform to that of an offer. As a rule, only the complete conformity indicates that the two parties of a transaction reached an agreement, i. e. the meeting of minds.

Article 19 of CISG states that:

"A reply to an offer which purports to be an acceptance but contains additions, limitations or other modifications is a rejection of the offer and constitutes a counter-offer." This provision, however, does not mean that the offeree is not allowed to make any additions, limitations or other modifications when making an acceptance. The question is whether the alteration is fundamental or not.

"However, a reply to an offer which purports to be an acceptance but contains additional or different term which do not materially alter the terms of the offer constitutes an acceptance, unless the offeror, without undue delay, object orally to the discrepancy or dispatches a notice to effect, If he does not so object, the terms of the contract are the terms of the offer with the modifications contained in the acceptance."

"Additional or different terms relating, among other things, to the price, payment, quality and quantity of the goods, place and time of delivery, extent of one party's liability to the other materially."

c. The acceptance must be made within the period of time for acceptance. An offer usually contains the term of validity, implying the offer or is bound within this term. He can not wantonly revoke or effective on condition that it is made within the term of validity. If the term is not contained in an offer, the offer is valid within a reasonable time.

An acceptance which is made after the period of time for acceptance is late acceptance. A late acceptance is not effective as an acceptance. But there are two exceptions.

Article 21 of CISG states that:

"Alate acceptance is nevertheless effective as an acceptance if without delay the offeror orally so informs the offer or dispatches a notice to that effect. If a letter or other writing containing a late acceptance shows that it has been sent in such circumstances that if its transmission had been normal it would have reached the offeror in due time, the late offeror orally informs the offeree that he considers his offer as having lapsed or dispatches a notice to that effect."

All in all, it depends on the offeror as to whether a late acceptance is effective or not.

d. An acceptance must be indicated. Silence or inactivity does not, in and of itself constitute acceptance. For example, if the seller sends a buyer an offer that says, "I know that this is such a good deal that I will assume that you have accepted will not create a contract. A different result would occur, however, if the seller were to send the buyer an invitation to negotiate that says, "Unless you hear otherwise from me within 3 days after I receive you order, I will deliver the widgets you need at $100 each."

2. Moment When an Acceptance Becomes Effective

Article 18 of CISG state that "An acceptance of an offer becomes effective at the moment the indication of assent reaches the offer. An acceptance is not effective if the indication of assent reaches the offer within the time he has fixed or, if no time is fixed, within a reasonable time, due account being taken of the circumstances of transaction, including the rapidity of the means of communication employed by the offeror. An offer must be accepted immediately unless the circumstances indicate otherwise."

3. Forms and Content of Written Contact

a. There is no specific requirements about the forms of contact in international trade. The commonly used forms are: Contract, Confirmation, Agreement, Memorandum, etc. The first two are more commonly used in Chinese foreign trade enterprises which generally have their own printed set format of contract or confirmation.

Once a deal is made, traders may sign two copies of contract face to face. Or the seller may send two copies signed by him to the buyer for counter-signature and the buyer should return one copy to the seller for file.

b. A sales contract usually covers: Name and address of the seller and buyer; The willingness and guarantee of both sides to carry out the contract ; Name, model, quality, packing etc. of the goods; Price; Terms of payment; Shipment; Insurance; General terms and conditions, such as claim, arbitration, and force majeure; Remarks; Signature.

4.3 Implementation of the Contract

Once a contract is concluded, both the seller and the buyer should perform their obligations.

The seller must deliver the goods, hand over any documents relating to them and transfer the property in the goods, as required by the contract. The buyer must pay the price for the goods and take delivery of them as required by the contract. The specific procedures of implementing the contract may be different since the terms and conditions included in each contract vary. This chapter is to illustrate the procedures in carrying out a Sales Contract based on CIF and payment by L/C.

4.3.1 Cargo Readiness

When the sale is by description, the goods should comply with the description; when the sale is by sample, the goods should be in accordance to the sample in terms of quality; when the sale is by sample as well as by description, the goods will correspond with both the sample and the description.

4.3.2 Examination and Amendment to L/C

After receiving the L/C, the exporter must examine the L/C against the sales contract. The examining points cover:

a. The political background and financial standing of the issuing bank. If the issuing bank is domiciled in a country which has friendly relations with China, but its nationality is not acceptable, this credit is not acceptable. If the issuing bank is a very small bank with a very poor financial standing, this credit is unacceptable too.

b. The nature of the credit and the liabilities of opening bank. Credit with a word like "revocable" is not acceptable. The undertaking clause of the issuing bank should be included. Sometimes although there is the word "irrevocable" in the L/C, some "limitation clauses" regarding the undertaking of the issuing bank also include such clauses as "This credit is not effective until we receive the notification of import licenses."

The above two points are also the examining focuses of the notifying bank.

c. The amount and currency in the credit should conform to the contract. If there is a more or less clause in the contract, the amount of the L/C should cover the more or less part. The unit price and the total price should be correct.

d. The quality, quantity, packing clauses.

e. The date of shipment, the date and place of validity. There is usually a reasonable interval between the date of shipment and the date of validity. In this way, the seller has sufficient time to prepare documents and make settlement.

f. The types, copies of documents are required as well as the methods of filling them out.

g. Other special clauses are also required to designate the shipping company, the nationality, age and class of the ship, etc.

Upon receipt of a letter of credit, the beneficiary finds that the terms stipulated in the credit are not in line with those mentioned in the contract, he must immediately notify the applicant in the shortest possible time. But he should also bear in mind that before receipt of the advice of L/C amendment from the opening bank, he had better not start to make shipment, otherwise he is liable to some very unfavorable stimulation.

For example, one of our export corporations prepared to sell certain products to an oversea buyer. Transshipment had been agreed upon in the contract of sales but was prohibited later in the credit. Since this consignment of goods had to be transshipped, he exporter cabled the applicant twice for prompt amendment to that clause. The applicant notified him that he was processing with the amendment. Thinking that there would not be any problem with the amendment, the exporter finally decided to dispatch the goods before receipt of the amendment to the Credit. So the goods were transshipped at Hong Kong. At that moment, the price of the goods began to decline in international market, so the buyer refused to confirm amendment. The validity of the credit expired and the exporter had to sell the goods under collection. The buyer still refused to take the documents until the seller made substantial reduction of the price of the goods.

It is true that conformity between credit terms and those of the contract constitutes the prerequisite for the smooth execution of the business transactions, but this principle does not mean that whatever discrepancies exist, no matter whether they are minor or material in nature, the beneficiary must demand amendment. In fact, there is quite a lot of flexibility in judging whether the amendment is necessary or not. In the practice of our export documentation, if the discrepancy is not of material nature, i. e. it is not so serious to effect the execution of the contract and our getting payment, it will not be necessary to ask the applicant to make amendment.

If the beneficiary is not prepared to accept the amendment, he should inform the issuing bank through the advising bank of his refusal. Partial acceptance of amendments contained in one and the same advise of amendment is not allowed and consequently will not be given any effect.

4.3.3 Shipment

Shipment must be made according to the contract terms. Usually, the exporter shall fill in the Shipping Note to book the shipping space or ship. After receiving the Shipping Order from the carrier, the exporter may start to ensure the loading of the goods. The exporter should supervise the loading process. After the goods being loaded on board the vessel, the Captain or the Mate will issue a receipt, i. e. the Mate's Receipt. The shipper shall exchange it for the Bills of Lading from the Shipping Agency after making payment of the freight.

Exporters should declare the export goods to the customs by filling in certain customs forms and submitting appropriate documents such as commercial invoice, export license, copy of sales contract, and inspection certificates etc. The customs will inspect the export goods and decide if the shipment can be cleared through. Once the goods are cleared, shipment can be made anytime.

The exporter should obtain at his own expense cargo insurance as agreed in the contract.

4.3.4 Documentation

Presentation of documents plays a very important part in the process of documentary credit operation because it will lead to the final settlement of the credit. Whether the beneficiary can get paid after he presents the credit has been prepared.

Chapter 5 Uniform Customs and Practice for Documentary Credits

5.1 UCP 600

Article 1 Application of UCP

The Uniform Customs and Practice for Documentary Credits, 2007 Revision, ICC Publication no. 600 ("UCP") are rules that apply to any documentary credit ("credit") (including, to the extent to which they may be applicable, at it is subject to these rules. They are binding on all parties thereto unless expressly modified or excluded by the credit.

Article 2 Definitions

For the purpose of these rules.

Advising bank means the bank that advises the credit at the request of the issuing bank.

Applicant means the party on whose request the credit is issued.

Banking day means a day on which a bank is regularly open at the place at which an act subject to these rules is to be performed.

Beneficiary means the party in whose favor a credit is issued.

Complying presentation means a presentation that is in accordance with the terms and conditions of the credit, the applicable provisions of these rules and international standard banking practice.

Confirmation means a definite undertaking of the confirming bank, in addition to that of the issuing bank, to honor or negotiate a complying presentation.

Confirming bank means the bank that adds its confirmation to a credit upon the issuing bank's authorization or request.

Credit means any arrangement, however named or described, that is irrevocable an thereby constitutes a definite undertaking of the issuing bank to honor a complying presentation.

Honor means:

a. To pay at sight if the credit is available by sight payment.

b. to incur a deferred payment undertaking and pay at maturity if the credit is available by deferred payment.

c. to accept a bill of exchange ("draft") drawn by the beneficiary and pay at maturity if the credit is available by acceptance.

Issuing bank means the bank that issues a credit at the request of an applicant or on its own behalf.

Negotiation means the purchase by the nominated bank of drafts (drawn on a bank other than the nominated bank) and/or documents under a complying presentation by advancing or agreeing to advance funds to the beneficiary on or before the banking day on which reimbursement is due to the nominated bank.

Nominated bank means the bank with which the credit is available or any bank in the case of a credit available with any bank.

Presentation means either the delivery of documents under a credit to the issuing bank or nominated bank or the documents so delivered.

Presenter means a beneficiary, bank or other party that makes a presentation.

Article 3 Interpretations

For the purpose of these rules:

Where applicable, words in the singular include the plural and in the plural include the singular.

A credit is irrevocable even if there is no indication to that effect.

A document may be signed by handwriting, facsimile signature, perforated signature, stamp, symbol or any other mechanical or electronic method of authentication.

A requirement for a document to be legalized, certified or similar will be satisfied by any signature, mark, stamp or label on the document which appears to satisfy that requirement.

Branches of a bank in different countries are considered to be separate banks.

Terms such as "first class", "well known", "qualified", "independent", "official", "competent" or "local" used to describe the issue that document.

Unless required to be used in a document, words such as "prompt", "immediately" or "as soon as possible" will be disregarded.

The expression "on or about" or similar will be interpreted as a stipulation that an event is to occur during a period of five calendar days before until five calendar days after days the specified date, both start and end dates include.

The words "to", "until", "from" and "between" when used to determine a period of shipment include the date or dates mentioned, and the words "before" and "after" exclude the date mentioned.

The words "from" and "after" when used to determine a maturity date exclude the date mentioned.

The terms "first half" and "second half" of a month shall be construed respectively as the 1st to the 15th and the 16th to the last day of the month, all dates inclusive.

The terms "beginning", "middle" and "end" of a month shall be construed respectively as the 1st to the 10th, the 11th to the 20th and the 21st to the last day of the month, all dates inclusive.

Article 4 Credits v. s. Contracts

a. A credit by its nature is a separate transaction from the sale or other contract on which it may be based. Banks are in no way concerned with or bound by such contract, even if any reference whatsoever to it is include in the credit. Consequently, the undertaking of a bank to honor, to negotiate or to fulfill any other obligation under the credit is not subject to claims or defenses by the applicant resulting from its relationships with the issuing bank or the beneficiary.

A beneficiary can in no case avail itself of the contractual relationships existing between banks or between the applicant and the issuing bank.

b. An issuing bank should discourage any attempt by the applicant to include, as an integral part of the credit, copies of the underlying contract, pro forma invoice and the like.

Article 5 Documents v. s. Goods, Services or Performance

Banks deal with documents and not with goods, services or performance to which the documents may relate.

Article 6 Availability, Expiry Date and Place for Presentation

a. A credit must state the bank with which it is available or whether it is available with any bank. A credit available with a nominated bank is also available with the issuing bank.

b. A credit must state whether it is available by sight payment, deferred payment, acceptance or negotiation.

c. A credit must not be issued available by a draft drawn on the applicant.

d. A credit must state an expiry date for presentation. An expiry date stated for honor or negotiation will be deemed to be an expiry date for presentation.

The place of the bank with which the credit is available is the place for presentation. The place for presentation under a credit available with any bank is that of any bank. A place for presentation other than that of the issuing bank is in addition to the place of the issuing bank.

e. Except as provided in sub-Article 29**a**, a presentation by or on behalf of the beneficiary must be on or before the expiry date.

Article 7 Issuing Bank Undertaking

a. Provided that the stipulated documents are presented to the nominated bank or to the issuing bank and that they constitute a complying presentation, the issuing bank must honor if the credit is available by.

(**a**) sight payment, deferred payment to acceptance with the issuing bank;

(**b**) sight payment with a nominated bank and that nominated bank does not pay;

(**c**) acceptance with a nominated bank and that nominated bank does not incur its deferred payment undertaking or, having incurred its deferred payment undertaking, does not pay a maturity;

(**d**) acceptance with a nominated bank and that nominated bank does not accept a draft drawn on it or, having accept a draft drawn on it, does not pay a maturity;

(**e**) negotiation with a nominated bank and that nominated bank does not negotiate.

(**f**) An issuing bank is irrevocably bound to honor as of the time it issues the credit.

(**g**) An issuing bank undertakes to reimburse a nominated bank that has honored or negotiated a complying presentation and forwarded the documents to the issuing bank. Reimbursement for the amount of a complying presentation under a credit available by acceptance or deferred payment is due at maturity, whether or not the nominated bank prepaid or purchased before maturity. An issuing bank's undertaking to reimburse a nominated bank is independent of the issuing bank's undertaking to the beneficiary.

Article 8 Confirming Bank Undertaking

a. Provided that the stipulated documents are presented to the confirming bank or to any other nominated bank and that they constitute a complying presentation, the confirming bank must:

(**a**) honor, if the credit is available by:

(**i**) sight payment, deferred payment or acceptance with the confirming bank;

(**ii**) sight payment with another nominated bank and that nominated bank does not pay;

(**iii**) deferred payment with another nominated bank and that nominated bank does not incur its deferred payment undertaking or, having incurred its deferred payment undertaking, does not pay at maturity;

(**iV**) acceptance with another nominated bank and that nominated bank does not accept a draft drawn on it or, having accepted a draft drawn on it, does not pay at maturity;

(**V**) negotiation with another nominated bank and that nominated bank does not negotiate.

b. negotiate, without recourse, if the credit is available by negotiation with the confirming bank.

(**i**) A confirming bank is irrevocably bound to honor or negotiate as of the time it adds its confirmation to the credit.

(**ii**) A confirming bank undertakes to reimburse another nominated bank that has honored or negotiated a complying presentation and forwarded the documents to the confirming bank. Reimbursement for the amount of a complying presentation under a credit available by acceptance or deferred payment is due at maturity, whether or not another nominated bank prepaid or purchased before maturity. A confirming bank's undertaking to reimburse another nominated bank is independent of the confirming bank's undertaking to the beneficiary.

(iii) If a bank is authorized or requested by the issuing bank to confirm a credit but is not prepared to do so, it must inform the issuing bank without delay and may advise the credit without confirmation.

Article 9 Advising of Credits and Amendments

a. A credit and any amendment may be advised to a beneficiary through an advising bank. An advising bank that is not a confirming bank advises the credit and any amendment without any undertaking to honor or negotiate.

b. By advising the credit or amendment, the advising bank signifies that it has satisfied itself as to the apparent authenticity of the credit or amendment and that the advice accurately reflects the terms and conditions of the credit or amendment received.

c. An advising bank may utilize the services of another bank ("second advising bank") to advise the credit and any amendment to the beneficiary. By advising the credit or amendment, the second advising bank signifies that it has satisfied itself as to the apparent authenticity of the advice it has received and that the advice accurately reflects the terms and conditions of the credit or amendment received.

d. A bank utilizing the services of an advising bank or second advising bank to advise a credit must use the same bank to advise any amendment thereto

e. If a bank is requested to advise a credit or amendment but elects not to do so, it must so inform, without delay, the bank from which the credit, amendment or advice has been received.

f. if a bank is requested to advise a credit or amendment but cannot satisfy itself as to the apparent authenticity of the credit, the amendment or the advice, it must so inform, without delay, the bank from which the instructions appear to have been received. If the advising bank or second advising bank elects nonetheless to advise the credit or amendment, it must inform the beneficiary or second advising bank that it has not been able to satisfy itself as to the apparent authenticity of the credit, the amendment or the advice.

Article 10 Amendments

a. Except as otherwise provided by article 38, a credit can neither be amended nor cancelled without the agreement of the issuing bank, the confirming bank, if any, and the beneficiary.

b. An issuing bank is irrevocably bound by an amendment as of the time it issues amendment. A confirming bank may extend its confirmation to an amendment and will be irrevocably bound as of the time it advises the amendment. A confirming bank may, however, choose to advise an amendment without extending its confirmation and, if so, it must inform the issuing bank without delay and inform the beneficiary in its advice.

c. The terms and conditions of the original credit (or a credit incorporating previously acceptance amendment) will remain in force for the beneficiary until the beneficiary communicates its acceptance of the amendment to the bank that advised such amendment. The beneficiary should give notification of acceptance or rejection of an amendment. If the beneficiary fails to give such notification, a presentation that complies with the credit and to any not yet accepted amendment will be deemed to be notification of acceptance by the beneficiary of such amendment. As of that moment the credit will be amended.

d. A bank that advises an amendment should inform the bank from which it received the amendment of any notification of acceptance or rejection.

e. Partial acceptance of an amendment is not allowed and will be deemed to be notification of rejection of the amendment.

f. A provision in an amendment to the effect that the amendment shall enter into force unless rejection by the beneficiary within a certain time shall be disregarded.

Article 11 Teletransmitted and Pre-Advised Credits and Amendments

a. An authenticated teletransmission of a credit or amendment will be deemed to be the operative credit or amendment, and any subsequent mail confirmation shall be disregarded.

If a teletransmission states"full details to follow"(or words of similar effect), or states that the mail confirmation is to be the operative credit or amendment, then the teletransmission will not be deemed to be the operative credit or amendment. The issuing bank must then issue the operative credit or amendment without delay in terms not in consistent with the teletransmission.

b. A preliminary advice of the issuance of a credit or amendment ("pre-advice") shall only be sent if the issuing bank is prepared to issue the operative credit or amendment. An issuing bank that sends a pre-advice is irrevocably committed to issue the operative credit or amendment, without delay, in terms not inconsistent with the pre-advice.

Article 12 Nomination

a. Unless a nominated bank is confirming bank, an authorization to honor or negotiate does not impose any obligation on that nominated bank to honor or negotiate, except when expressly agreed to by that nominated bank and so communicated to the beneficiary.

b. By nominating a bank to accept a draft or incur a deferred payment undertaking, an issuing bank authorizes that nominated bank to prepay or purchase a drafty accepted.

c. Receipt or examination and forwarding of documents by a nominated bank that is not a confirming bank does not make that nominated bank liable to honor or negotiate, nor does it constitute honor or negotiation.

Article 13 Bank-to-Bank Reimbursement Arrangements

a. If a credit states that reimbursement is to be obtained by a nominated bank ("claiming bank") claiming on another party ("reimbursing bank"), the credit must state if the reimbursement is subject to the ICC rules for bank-to-bank reimbursements in effect on the date of issuance of the credit.

b. If a credit does not state that reimbursement is subject to the ICC rules for bank-to-bank reimbursements, the following apply:

(**a**) An issuing bank must provide a reimbursing bank with a reimbursement authorization that conforms with the availability stated in the credit. The reimbursement authorization should not be subject to an expiry date.

(**b**) A claiming bank shall not be required to supply a reimbursing bank with a certificate of compliance with the terms and conditions of the credit.

(**c**) An issuing bank will be responsible for any loss of interest, together with any expenses incurred, if reimbursement is not provided on first demand by a reimbursing bank in accordance with the terms and conditions of the credit.

(**d**) A reimbursing bank's charges are for the account of the issuing bank. However, if the charges are for the account of the beneficiary, it is the responsibility of an issuing bank to so indicate in the credit and in the reimbursement authorization. If a reimbursing bank's charges are for the account of the beneficiary, they shall be deducted from the amount due to a claiming bank when reimbursement is made. If no reimbursement is made, the reimbursing bank's charges remain the obligation of the issuing bank.

c. An issuing bank is not relieved of any of its obligations to provide reimbursement if reimbursement is not made by a reimbursing bank on first demand.

Article 14 Standard for Examination of Documents

a. A nominated bank acting on its nomination, a confirming bank, if any, and the issuing bank must examine a presentation to determine, on the basis of the documents alone, whether or not the documents appear on their face to constitute a complying presentation.

b. A nominated bank acting on its nomination, a confirming bank, if any, and the issuing bank shall each have a maximum of five banking days following the day of presentation to determine if a presentation is complying. This period is not curtailed or otherwise affected by the occurrence on or after the date of presentation of any expiry date or last day for presentation.

c. A presentation including one or more original transport documents subject to articles 19,

20, 21, 22, 23, 24 or 25 must be made by or on behalf of the beneficiary not later than 21 calender days after the date of shipment as described in these rules, but in any event not later than the expiry date of the credit.

d. Data in a document, when read in context with the credit, the document itself and international standard banking practice, need not be identical to, but must not conflict with, data in that document, any other stipulated document or the credit.

e. In documents other than the commercial invoice, the description of the goods, services or performance, if stated, may be in general terms not conflicting with their description in the credit.

f. If a credit requires presentation of a document other than a transport document, insurance document or commercial invoice, without stipulating by whom the document is to be issued or its content, banks will accept the document as presented if its content appears to fulfill the function of the required document and otherwise complies with sub-article 14 (d).

g. A document presented but not required by the credit will be disregarded and may be returned to the presenter.

h. If a credit contains a condition without stipulating the document to indicate compliance with the condition, banks will deem such condition as not stated and will disregard it.

i. A document may be dated prior to the issuance date of the credit, but must not be dated later than its date of presentation.

j. When the addresses of the beneficiary and the applicant appear in any stipulated document, they need to be the same as those stated in the credit or in any other stipulated document, but must be within the same country as the respective addresses mentioned in the credit. Contact details (telefax, telephone, email and the like) stated as part of the beneficiary's and the applicant's address will be disregarded. However, when the address and contact details of the applicant appear as part of the consignee or notify party details on a transport document subject to articles 19, 20, 21, 22, 23, 24 or 25, they must be as stated in the credit.

k. The shipper or consignor of the goods indicated on any document need not be the beneficiary of the credit.

l. A transport document may be issued by any party other than a carrier, owner, master or charterer provided that the transport document meets the requirements of articles 19, 20, 21, 22, 23or24 of these rules.

Article 15 Complying Presentation

a. When an issuing bank determines that a presentation is complying, it must honor.

b. When a confirming bank determines that a presentation is complying, it must honor or negotiate and forward the documents to the issuing bank.

c. When a nominated bank determines that a presentation is complying and honors or negotiates, it must forward the documents to the confirming bank or issuing bank.

Article 16 Discrepant Documents, Waiver and Notice

a. When a nominated bank acting on its nomination, a confirming bank, if any, or the issuing bank determines that a presentation does not comply, it may refuse to honor or negotiate.

b. When an issuing bank determines that a presentation does not comply, it may in its sole judgment approach the applicant for the discrepancies. This does not, however, extend the period mentioned in sub-article14 **b**.

c. When a nominated bank acting on its nomination, a confirming bank, if any, or the issuing bank decides to refuse to honor or negotiate, it must give a single notice to that effect to the presenter.

The notice must state:

(**a**) that the bank is refusing to honor or negotiate.

(**b**) each discrepancy in respect of which the bank refuse to honor or negotiate.

(**c**) that the bank is holding the documents pending further instructions from the presenter; or that the issuing bank is holding the documents until it receives a waiver from the applicant and agrees to accept it, or receives further instructions from the presenter prior to agreeing to accept a waiver; or that the bank is returning the documents; or that the bank is acting in accordance with instructions previously received from the presenter.

d. The notice required in sub-article 16 **c** must be given by telecommunication or, if that is not possible, by other expeditious means no later than the close of the fifth banking day following the day of presentation.

e. A nominated bank acting on its nomination, a confirming bank, if any, or the issuing bank may, after providing notice required by sub-article 16**c**, **a** or **b**, return the documents to the presenter at any time.

f. If an issuing bank or a confirming bank fails to act in accordance with the provisions of this article, it shall be precluded from claiming that the documents do not constitute a complying presentation.

g. When an issuing bank refuses to honor or a confirming bank refuses to honor or negotiate and has given notice to that effect in accordance with this article, it shall then be entitled to claim a refund, with interest, of any reimbursement made.

Article 17 Original Documents and Copies

a. At least one original of each document stipulated in the credit must be presented.

b. A bank shall treat as an original any document bearing an apparently original signature, mark, stamp, or label of the issuer of the document, unless the document itself indicates that it is not an original.

c. Unless a document indicates otherwise, a bank will also accept a document as original if it. appears to be written, typed, perforated or stamped by the document issuer's hand; or appear to be on the document issuer's original stationery; or states that it is original, unless the statement appears not to the document presented.

d. if a credit requires presentation of copies of documents, presentation of either originals or copies is permitted.

e. if a credit requires presentation of multiple documents by using terms such as "in duplicate", "in two fold" or "in two copies", this will be satisfied by the presentation of at least one original and the remaining number in copies, except when the document itself indicates otherwise.

Article 18 Commercial Invoice

a. A commercial invoice: must appear to have been issued by the beneficiary (except as provided in article 38); must be made out in the name lf the applicant (except as provided in sub-article 38 **g**; must be made out in the same currency as the credit. Need not be signed.

b. A nominated bank acting on its nomination, a confirming bank, if any, or the issuing bank may accept a commercial invoice issued for an amount in excess of the amount permitted by the credit, and its decision will be binding upon all parties, provided the bank in question has not honored or negotiated for an amount in excess of that permitted by the credit.

c. The description of the goods, services or performance in a commercial invoice must correspond with that appearing in the credit.

Article 19 Transport Document Covering at least Two Different Modes

a. A transport document covering at least two different modes of transport (multimodal or combined transport document), however named, must appear to:

(**a**) indicate the name of the carrier and be signed by the carrier or a named agent for or on behalf of the carrier, or the master or a named agent for or on behalf of the master.

Any signature by the carrier, master or agent must identified as that of the carrier, master or agent.

Any signature by an agent must indicate whether the agent has signed for or on behalf of the carrier or for or on behalf of the master.

(**b**) indicate that the goods have been dispatched, taken in charge or shipped on board at the place stated in the credit by pre-printed wording, or a stamp or notation indicating the date on which the goods have been dispatched, taken in charge or shipped on board. The date of issuance of the transport document will be deemed to be the date of dispatch, taking in charge or shipped on board, and the date of shipment. However, if the transport document indicates, by stamp or notation, a date of dispatch, taking in charge or shipped on board, this date will be deemed to be the date of shipment.

(**c**) indicate the place of dispatch, taking in charge or shipment and the place of final destination stated in the credit, even if the transport document states, in addition, a different place of dispatch, taking in charge or shipment or place of final destination, or the transport document contains the indication "intended" or similar qualification in relation to the vessel, port of loading or port of discharge.

(**d**) be the sole original transport document or, if issued in more than one original, be the full set as indicated on the transport document.

(**e**) contain terms and conditions of carriage or make reference to another source containing the terms and conditions of carriage (short form or blank back transport document). Contents of terms and conditions of carriage will not be examined.

(**f**) contain no indication that it is subject to a charter party.

b. For the purpose of this article, transhipment means unloading from one means of conveyance and reloading to another means of conveyance (whether or not in difference modes of transport) during the carriage from the place of dispatch, taking in charge or shipment to the place of final destination stated in the credit.

c. A transport document may indicate that the goods will or may be transshipped provided that the entire carriage is covered by one and the same transport document.

A transport document indicating that transhipment will or may take place is acceptable, even if the credit prohibits transshipment.

Article 20 Bill of Lading

a. A bill of lading, however named, must appear to:

(**a**) indicate the name of the carrier and be signed by the carrier or a named agent for or on behalf of the carrier, or the master or a named agent for or on behalf of the master.

Any signature by the carrier, master or agent must be identified as that of the carrier, master or agent.

Any signature by an agent must indicate whether the agent has signed for or on behalf of the carrier or for or on behalf of he master.

(**b**) indicate that the goods have been shipped on board a named vessel at the port of loading stated in the credit by pre-printed wording, or an on board notation indicating the date on which the goods have been shipped on board.

The date of shipment unless the bill of lading contains an on board notation indicating the date of shipment, in which case the date stated in the on board notation will be deemed to be the date of shipment.

If the bill of lading contains the indication "intended vessel" or similar qualification in relation to the name of the vessel, an on board notation indicating the date of shipment and the name of the actual vessel is required.

(c) indicate shipment from the port of loading to the port of discharge stated in the credit.

If the bill of lading does not indicate the port of loading stated in the credit as the port of loading, or if it contains the indication "intended" or similar qualification in relation to the port of loading, an on board notation indicating the port of loading as stated in the credit, the date of shipment and the name of the vessel is required. This provision applies even when loading on board or shipment on a named vessel is indicated by pre-printed wording on the bill of lading.

(d) be the sole original bill of lading or, if issued in more than one original, be the full set as indicated on the bill of loading.

(e) contain terms and conditions of carriage or make reference to another source containing the terms and conditions of carriage (short form or blank back bill of loading). Contents of terms and conditions of carriage will not be examined.

(f) contain no indication that it is subject to a charter party.

b. For the purpose of this article, transshipment means unloading from one vessel and reloading to another vessel during the carriage from the port of discharge stated in the credit.

c. A bill of lading may indicate that the goods will or may be transshipped provided that the entire carriage is covered by one and the same bill lading.

A bill of lading indicating that transshipment, if the goods have been shipped in a container, trailer or LASH barge as evidenced by the bill of lading.

d. Clauses in a bill of lading stating that the carrier reserves the right to transship will be disregarded.

Article 21 Non-negotiable Sea Waybill

a. A non-negotiable sea waybill, however named, must appear to:

(a) indicate the name of the carrier and be signed by the carrier, or a named agent for or on behalf of the carrier, or the master or a named agent for or on behalf of the master.

Any signature by the carrier, master or agent must be identified as that of the carrier, master or agent.

Any signature by an agent must indicate whether the agent has signed for or on behalf of the carrier or for or on behalf of the master.

(**b**) indicate that the goods have been shipped on board a named vessel at the port of loading stated in the credit by pre-printed wording, or an on board notation indicating the date on which the goods have been shipped on board.

The date of issuance of the non-negotiable sea waybill will be deemed to be the date of shipment unless the non-negotiable sea waybill contains an on board notation indicating the date of shipment, in which case the date stated in the on board notation will be deemed to be the date of shipment.

If the non-negotiable sea waybill contains the indication "intended vessel" or similar qualification in relation to the name of the vessel, an on board notation indicating the date of shipment and the name of the actual vessel is required.

(**c**) Indicate shipment from the port of loading to the port of discharge stated in the credit.

If the non-negotiable sea waybill does not indicate the port of loading stated in the credit as the port of loading, or if it contains the indication "intended" or similar qualification in relation to the port of loading, an on board notation indicating the port of loading as stated in the credit, the date of shipment and the name of the vessel is required. This provision applies even when loading on board or shipment on a named vessel is indicated by pre-printed wording on the non-negotiable sea waybill.

(**d**) be the sole original non-negotiable sea waybill or, if issued in more than one original, be the full set as indicated on the non-negotiable sea waybill.

(**e**) contain terms and conditions of carriage or make reference to another source containing the terms and conditions of carriage (short form or blank back non-negotiable sea waybill), Contents of terms and conditions of carriage will not be examined.

(**f**) contain no indication that it is subject to a charter party.

b. For the purpose of this article, transshipment means unloading from one vessel and reloading to another vessel during the carriage from the port of loading to the port of discharge stated in the credit.

c. A non-negotiable sea waybill may indicate that the goods will or may be transhipped provided that the entire carriage is covered by one and the same non-negotiable sea waybill

A non-negotiable sea waybill indicating that transshipment will or may take place is acceptable, even if the credit prohibits transshipment, if the goods have been shipped in a container, trailer or LASH barge as evidenced by the non-negotiable sea waybill.

d. Clauses in a non-negotiable sea waybill stating that the carrier reserves the right to transship will be disregarded.

Article 22 Charter Party Bill of Lading

a. A bill of lading, however named, containing an indication that it is subject to a charter party (charter party bill of lading), must appear to:

(**a**) be signed by the master or a named agent for or on behalf of the master, or the owner or a named agent for or on behalf of the Owner, or the charaterer or a named agent for on behalf of the charterer.

Any signature by the master, owner, charterer or agent must be identified as that of the master, owner, charterer or agent.

Any signature by an agent must indicate whether the agent has signed for or on behalf of the master, owner or charterer.

An agent signing for or on behalf of the owner or charterer must indicate the name of the owner or charterer.

(**b**) indicate that the goods have been shipped on board a named vessel at the port of loading stated in the credit by pre-printed wording, or an on board notation indicatng the date on which the goods have been shipped on board.

The date of issuance of the charter party bill of lading will be deemed to be the date of shipment unless the charter party bill of lading contains an on board notation indicating the date of shipment, in which case the date stated in the on board notation will be deemed to be the date of shipment.

(**c**) indicate shipment from the port of loading to the port of discharge state in the credit. The port of discharge may also be shown as a range or a geographical area, as stated in the credit.

(**d**) be the sole original charter party bill of lading or, if issued in more than-one original, be the full set as indicated on the charter party bill of lading.

b. A bank will not examine charter party contracts, even if they are required to be presented by the terms of the credit.

Article 23 Air Transport Document

a. An air transport document, however named, must appear to:

(**a**) indicate the name of the carrier and be signed by: the carrier, or a named agent for or on behalf of the carrier.

Any signature by the carrier or agent must be identified as that of the carrier or agent.

Any signature by an agent must indicate that the agent has signed for or on behalf of the carrier.

(**b**) indicate that the goods have been accepted for carriage.

(**c**) Indicate the date of issuance. this date will be deemed to be the date of shipment unless the air transport document contains a specific notation of the actual date of shipment, in which case the date stated in the notation will be deemed to be the date of shipment.

Any other information appearing on the air transport document relative to the flight number and date will not be considered in determining the date of shipment.

(**d**) indicate the airport of departure and the airport of destination stated in the credit.

(**e**) be the original for consignor or shipper, even if the credit stipulates a full set of originals.

(**f**) contain terms and conditions of carriage or make reference to another source containing the terms and conditions of carriage. Contents of terms and conditions of carriage will not be examined.

b. For the purpose of this article, transshipment means unloading form one aircraft and reloading to another aircraft during the carriage form the airport of departure to the airport of destination stated in the credit.

c. An air transport document may indicate that the goods will or may be transshipped, provided that the entire carriage is covered by one and the same air transport document.

An air transport document indicating that transshipment will or may take place is acceptable, even if the credit prohibits transshipment.

Article 24 Road, Rail or Inland Waterway Transport Documents

a. A road, rail or inland waterway transport document, however named, must appear to:

(**a**) indicate the name of the carrier and Be signed by the carrier or a named agent for or on behalf of the carrier, or indicated receipt of the goods by signature, stamp or notation by the carrier.

Any signature, stamp or notation of receipt of the goods by the agent must indicate that the agent has signed or acted for on behalf of the carrier.

If a rail transport document does not identify the carrier, any signature or stamp of the railway company will be accepted as evidence of the document being signed by the carrier.

(**b**) indicate the date of shipment or the date the goods have been received for shipment, dispatch or carriage at the place stated in the credit. Unless the transport document contains a dated reception stamp, an indication of the date of receipt or a date of shipment, the date of issuance of the transport document will be deemed to be the date of shipment.

(**c**) indicate the place of shipment and the place of destination stated in the credit.

b. A road transport document must appear to be the original for consignor or shipper or bear no marking indicating for whom the document has been prepared.

A real transport document marked "duplicate" will be accepted as an original.

c. In the absence of an indication on the transport document as to the number of originals issued, the number presented will be deemed to constitute a full set.

d. For the purpose of this article, transshipment means unloading from one means of conveyance and reloading to another means of conveyance, within the same mode of transport, during the carriage from the place of shipment, dispatch or carriage to the place of destination stated in the credit.

e. A road, rail or inland waterway transport document may indicate that the goods will or may be transshipped provided that the entire carriage is covered by one and the same transport document.

A road, rail or inland waterway transport document indicating that transshipment will or may take place is acceptable, even if the credit prohibits transshipment.

Article 25 Courier Receipt, Post Receipt or Certificate of Posting

a. A courier receipt, however named, evidencing receipt of goods for transport, must appear to: indicate the name of the courier service and be stamped or signed by the named courier service at the place from which the credit states the goods are to be shipped, and indicate a date of pick-up or of receipt or wording to this effect. this date will be deemed to be the date of shipment.

b. A requirement that courier charges are to be paid or prepaid may be satisfied by a transport document issued by a courier service evidencing that courier charges are for the account of a party other than the consignee.

c. A post receipt or certificate of posting, however named, evidencing receipt of goods for transport, must appear to be stamped or signed and dated at the place from which the credit states the goods are to be shipped. This date will be deemed to be the date of shipment.

Article 26 "On Deck", "Shipper's Load and Count", "Said by shipper to Contain"

a. A transport document must not indicate that the goods are or will be loaded on deck. A clause on a transport document stating that the goods may be loaded on deck is acceptable.

b. A transport document bearing a clause such as "shipper's load and count" and "said by shipper to contain" is acceptable.

c. A transport document may bear a reference, by stamp or otherwise, to charges additional to the freight.

Article 27 Clean Transport Document

A bank will only accept a clean transport document. A clean transport document is one bearing no clause or notation expressly declaring a defective condition of the goods or their packaging. The word "clean" need not appear on a transport document, even if a credit has a requirement for that transport document to be "clean on board".

Article 28 Insurance Document and Coverage

a. An insurance document, such as an insurance policy, an insurance certificate or a declaration under an open cover, must appear to be issued and signed by an insurance company, an underwriter or their agents or their proxies.

Any signature by an agent or proxy must indicate whether the agent or proxy has signed for or on behalf of the insurance company or underwriter.

b. When the insurance document indicates that it has been issued in more than one original, all originals must be presented.

c. Cover notes will not be accepted.

d. An insurance policy is acceptable in lieu of an insurance certificate or a declaration under an open cover.

e. The date of the insurance document must be no later than the date of shipment, unless it appears from the insurance document that the cover is effective from a date not later than the date of shipment.

f. The insurance document must indicate the amount of insurance coverage and be in the same currency as the credit.

A requirement in the credit for insurance coverage to be for a percentage of the value of the goods, of the invoice value or similar is deemed to be the minimum amount of coverage required.

If there is no indication in the credit of the insurance coverage required, the amount of insurance coverage must be at least 110% of the CIF or CIP value of the goods.

When the CIE or CIP value cannot be determined from the documents, the amount of insurance coverage must be calculated on the basis of the amount for which honor or negotiation is requested or the gross value of the goods as shown on the invoice, whichever is greater.

The insurance document must indicate that risks are covered at least between the place of taking in charge or shipment and the place of discharge or final destination as stated in the credit.

g. A credit should state the type of insurance required and, if any, the additional risks to be covered. An insurance document will be accepted without regard to any risks that are not covered if the credit uses imprecise terms such as "usual risks" or "customary risks".

h. When a credit requires insurance against "all risks" and an insurance document is presented containing any "all risks" notation or clause, whether or not bearing the heading "all risks", the insurance document will be accepted without regard to any risks stated to be excluded.

i. An insurance document may contain reference to any exclusion clause.

j. An insurance document may indicate that the cover is subject to a franchise or express

Article 29 Extension of Expiry Date or Last Day for Presentation

a. If the expiry date of a credit or the last day for presentation falls on a day when the bank to which presentation is to be made is closed for reasons other than those referred to in article 36, the expiry date or the last day for presentation, as the case may be, will be extended to the first following banking day.

b. If presentation is made on the first following banking day, a nominated bank must provide the issuing bank or confirming bank with a statement on its covering schedule that the presentation was made within the time limits extended in accordance with sub-article 29 **a.**

c. The latest date for shipment will not be extended as a result of sub-article 29 **b.**

Article 30 Tolerance in Credit Amount, Quantity and Unit Prices

a. The words "about" or "approximately" used in connection with the amount of the credit or the quantity or the unit price stated in the credit are to be construed as allowing a tolerance not to exceed 10% more or 10% less than the amount, the quantity or the unit price to which they refer.

b. A tolerance not to exceed 5% more or 5% less than the quantity of the goods is allowed, provided the credit does not state the quantity in terms of a stipulated number of packing units or individual items and the total amount of the drawings does not exceed the amount of the credit.

c. Even when partial shipments are not allowed, a tolerance not to exceed 5% less than the amount of the credit is allowed, provided that the quantity of the goods, if stated in the credit, is shipped in full and a unit price, if stated in the credit, is not reduced or that sub-article 30 **b** is not applicable. This tolerance does not apply when the credit stipulates a specific tolerance or uses the expressions referred to in sub-article 30 **a.**

Article 31 Partial Drawings or Shipments

a. Partial drawings or shipments are allowed.

b. A presentation consisting of more than one set of transport documents evidencing shipment commencing on the same means of conveyance and for the same journey, provided they indicate the same destination, will not be regarded as covering a partial shipment, even if they indicate different dates of shipment or different ports of loading, places of taking in charge or dispatch. If the presentation consists of more than one set of transport documents, the latest date of shipment as evidenced on any of the sets of transport documents will be regarded as the date of shipment

A presentation consisting of one of more sets of transport documents evidencing shipment on more than one means of conveyance within the same mode of transport will be regarded as covering a partial shipment, even if the means of conveyance leave on the same day for the same destination

c. a presentation consisting of more than one courier receipt, post receipt of certificate of posting will not be regarded as a partial shipment if the courier receipts, post receipts or certificates of posting appear to have been stamped or signed by the same courier or postal service at the same place and date and for the same destination

Article 32 Installment drawings or Shipments

If a drawing or shipment by installments within given periods is stipulated in the credit and any installment is not drawn or shipped within the period allowed for that installment, the credit ceases to be available for that and any subsequent installment

Article 33 Hours of Presentation

A bank has no obligation to accept a presentation outside of its banking hours.

Article 34 Disclaimer on Effectiveness of Documents

A bank assumes no liability or responsibility for the form lated in a document or superimposed thereon; nor does it assume any liability or responsibility for the description, quantity, weight, quality, condition, packing, delivery, value or existence of the goods, services or other performance represented by any document, or for the good faith or acts or omissions, solvency, performance or standing of the consignor, the carrier, the forwarder, the consignee or the insurer of the goods or any other person.

Article 35 Disclaimer on Transmission and Translation

A bank assumes no liability or responsibility for the consequences arising out of delay, loss in transit, mutilation or other errors arising in the transmission of any messages or delivery of letters or documents, when such messages, letters or documents are transmitted or sent according to the requirements stated in the credit, or when the bank may have taken the initiative in the choice of the delivery service in the absence of such instructions in the credit.

If a nominated bank determines that a presentation is complying and forwards the documents to the issuing bank or confirming bank, whether or not the nominated bank has honored or negotiated, an issuing bank or confirming bank must honor or negotiate, or reimburse that nominated bank, even when the documents have been lost in transit between the nominated bank and the issuing bank or confirming bank, or between the confirming bank and the issuing bank.

A bank assumes no liability or responsibility for errors in translation or interpretation of technical terms and may transmit credit terms without translating them.

Article 36 Force Majeure

A bank assumes no liability or responsibility for the consequences arising out of the interruption of its business by Acts of God, riots, civil commotions, insurrections, wars, acts of terrorism, or by any strikes or lockouts or any other causes beyond its control.

A bank will not, upon resumption of its business, honor or negotiate under a credit that expired during such interruption of its business.

Article 37 Disclaimer for Acts of an Instructed Party

a. A bank utilizing the services of another bank for the purpose of giving effect to the instructions of the applicant does so for the account and at the risk of the applicant.

b. An issuing bank or advising bank assumes no liability or responsibility should the instructions it transmits to another bank not be carried out, even if it has taken the initiative in the choice of that other bank.

c. A bank instructing another bank to perform services is liable for any commissions, fees, costs or expenses incurred by that bank in connection with its instructions.

If a credit states that charges are for the account of the beneficiary and charges cannot be collected from proceeds, the issuing bank remains liable for payment of charges.

A credit or amendment should not stipulate that the advising to a beneficiary is conditional upon the receipt by the advising bank or second advising bank of its charges.

d. The applicant shall be bound by and liable to indemnify a bank against all obligations and responsibilities imposed by foreign laws and usages.

Article 38 Transferable Credits

a. A bank is under no obligation to transfer a credit except to the extent and in the manner expressly consented to by that bank.

b. For the purpose of this article:

Transferable credit means a credit that specifically states it is "transferable". A transferable credit may be made available in whole or in part to another beneficiary ("second beneficiary") at the request of the beneficiary ("first beneficiary").

Transferring bank means a nominated bank that transfers the credit or, in a credit available with any bank, a bank that is specifically authorized by the issuing bank to transfer and that transfer the credit. An issuing bank may be a transferring bank.

Transferred credit means a credit that has been made available by the transferring bank to a second beneficiary.

c. Unless otherwise agreed at the time of transfer, all charges (such as commissions, fees, costs or expenses) incurred in.

d. A credit may be transferred in part to more than one second beneficiary provided partial drawings or shipments are allowed.

A transferred credit cannot be transferred at the request of a second beneficiary to any subsequent beneficiary. The first beneficiary is not considered to be a subsequent beneficiary.

e. Any request for transfer must indicate if and under what conditions amendments may be advised to the second beneficiary. The transferred credit must clearly indicate those conditions.

f. If a credit is transferred to more than one second beneficiary, rejection of an amendment by one or more second beneficiary, does not invalidate the acceptance by any other second beneficiary, with respect to which the transferred credit will be amended accordingly. For any second beneficiary that rejected the amendment, the transferred credit will remain.

g. The transferred credit must accurately reflect the terms and conditions of the credit, including confirmation, if any, with the exception of.

the amount of the credit, any unit price stated therein, The expiry date, The period for presentation, or The latest shipment date or given period for shipment. Any or all of which may be reduced or curtailed.

The percentage for which insurance cover must be effected may be increased to provide the amount of cover stipulated in the credit or these articles.

The name of the first beneficiary may be substituted for that of the applicant in the credit.

If the name of the applicant is specifically required by the credit to appear in any document other the invoice, such requirement must be reflected in the transferred credit.

h. The first beneficiary has the right to substitute its own invoice and draft, if any, for those of a second beneficiary for an amount not in excess of that stipulated in the credit, and upon such substitution the first beneficiary can draw under the credit for the difference, if any, between its invoice and the invoice of a second beneficiary.

i. If the first beneficiary is to present its own invoice and draft, if any, but fails to do so on first demand, or if the invoices presented by the first beneficiary create discrepancies that did not exist in the presentation made by the second beneficiary and the first beneficiary fails to correct them on first demand, the transferring bank has the right to present the documents as received from the second beneficiary to the issuing bank, without further responsibility to the first beneficiary.

j. The first beneficiary may, in its request for transfer, indicate that honor or negotiation is to be effected to a second beneficiary at the place to which the credit. This is without prejudice to the right of the beneficiary in accordance with sub-article 38 **h**.

k. Presentation of documents by or on behalf of a second beneficiary must be made to the transferring bank.

Article 39 Assignment of Proceeds

The fact that a credit is not to be transferable shall not affect the right of the beneficiary to assign any proceeds to which it may be or may become entitled under the credit, in accordance with the provisions of applicable law. This article relates only to the assignments of proceeds and not to the assignment of the right to perform under the credit.

5.2 Supplement to UCP for Electronic Presentation

Article e1 eUCP

a. supplements the Uniform Customs and Practice for Documentary Credits (2007Revision ICC Publication No. 600) ("UCP") in order to accommodate presentation of electronic records alone or in combination with paper documents.

b. The eUCP shall apply as a supplement to the UCP where the credit indicates that it is subject to eUCP.

c. This version is Version 1.1. A credit must indicate the applicable version of the eUCP. If it does not do so, it is subject to the version in effect on the date the credit is issued or, if made subject to eUCP by an amendment accepted by the beneficiary, on the date or that amendment.

Article e2 Relationship of the eUCP to the UCP

a. A credit subject to the eUCP ("eUCP credit") is also subject to the UCP without express incorporation of the UCP.

b. Where the eUCP applies, its provisions shall prevail to the extent that they would produce a result different from the application of the UCP.

c. If an eUCP credit allows the beneficiary to choose between presentation of paper documents or electronic records and it chooses to present only paper documents, the UCP alone shall apply to that presentation. If only paper documents are permitted under an eUCP credit, the UCP alone shall apply.

Article e3 Definitions

a. Where the following terms are used in the UCP, for the purposes of applying the UCP to an electronic record presented under an eUCP credit the term:

(**a**) ppear on their face "and the like shall apply to examination of the data content of an electronic record.

(**b**) "document" shall include an electronic record.

(**c**) "place for presentation" of electronic records means an electronic address.

(**d**) "sign" and the like shall include an electronic signature.

(**e**) "superimposed", "notation" or "stamped" means data content whose supplementary character is apparent in an electronic record.

b. the following terms used in the eUCP shall have the following meanings:

(a) "electronic record " means data created, generated, sent, communicated, received or stored by electronic means that is capable of being authenticated as to the apparent identity of a sender and the apparent source of the data contained in it, and as to whether it has remained complete and unaltered, and is capable of being examined with the terms and conditions of the eUCP credit.

(b) "electronic signature" means a data process attached to or logically associated with an electronic record and executed or adopted by a person in order to identify that person and to indicate that person's authentication of the electronic record.

(c) "format" means the data organization in which the electronic record is expressed or to which it refers.

(d) "paper document" means a document in a traditional paper form.

(e) "receive" means the time when an electronic record enters the information system of the applicable recipient in a form capable of being accepted by that system. Any acknowledgement of receipt does not imply acceptance or refusal of the electronic record under an eUCP credit.

Article e4 Format

An eUCP credit must specify the formats in which electronic records are to be presented. If the format If the electronic record is not so specified, it may be presented in any format.

Article e5 Presentation

a. An eUCP credit allowing presentation if:

(a) Electronic records must state a place for presentation of the electronic records.

(b) Both electronic records and paper documents must also state a place for presentation of the paper documents.

b. Electronic records may be presented separately and need not be presented at the same time.

c. If an eUCP credit allows for presentation of one or more electronic records, the beneficiary is responsible for providing a notice to the bank to which presentation is made signifying when the presentation is complete. The notice of completeness may be given as an electronic record or paper document and must identify the eUCP credit to which it relates. Presentation is deemed not to have been made if the beneficiary's notice is not received.

d. Each presentation of an electronic record and the presentation of paper documents under an eUCP credit must identify the eUCP credit under which it is presented. A presentation not so identified may be treated as not received.

e. If the bank to which presentation is to be made is open but its system is unable to receive s transmitted electronic record on the stipulated expiry date and/or the last day of the period of time after the date of shipment for the presentation, as the case may be, the bank will be deemed to be closed and the date for presentation and/or the expiry date shall be extended to the first following banking day on which such bank is able to receive an electronic record, If the only electronic record remaining to be presented is the notice of completeness, it may be given by telecommunications or by paper document and will be deemed timely, provided that it is sent before the bank is able to receive an electronic record.

f. An electronic record that cannot be authenticated is deemed not to have been presented.

Article e6 Examination

a. If an electronic record contains a hyperlink to an external system or a presentation indicates that the electronic record may be examined by reference to an external system, the electronic record at the hyperlink or the referenced system shall bi deemed to be the electronic record to be examined. The failure of the indicated system to provide access to the required electronic record at the time of examination shall constitute a discrepancy.

b. The forwarding of electronic records by a nominated bank pursuant to its nomination signifies that it has satisfied itself as to the apparent authenticity of the electronic records.

c. The inability of the issuing bank, or confirming bank, if any, to examine an electronic record in a format required by the eUCP credit or, if no format is required, to examine it in the format presented is not a basis for refusal.

Article e7 Notice of Refusal

a. The time period for the examination of documents commences on the banking day following the banking day on which the beneficiary's notice of completeness is received.

If the time for presentation of documents or the notice of completeness is extended, the time for the examination of documents commences on the first following banking day on which such bank is able to receive the notice of completeness.

b. If an issuing bank, the confirming bank, if any, or a nominated bank acting on its nomination, provides a notice of refusal of a presentation which includes electronic records and does not receive instructions from the party to which notice of refusal is given within 30 calendar days from the date the notice of refusal is given for the disposition of the electronic records, the bank shall return any paper documents not previously returned to the presenter but may dispose of the electronic records in any manner deemed appropriate without any responsibility.

Article e8 Originals and Copies

Any requirement of the UCP or an eUCP credit for presentation of one or more originals or copies of an electronic record is satisfied by the presentation of one electronic record.

Article e9 Date of Issuance

Unless an electronic record contains a specific date of issuance, the date on which it appear to have been sent by the issuer is deemed to be the date of issuance. The date of receipt will be deemed to be the date it was sent if no other date is apparent.

Article e10 Transport

If an electronic record evidencing transport does not indicate a date of shipment or dispatch, the date of issuance of the electronic record will be deemed to be the date of shipment or dispatch, however, if the electronic record bears a notation that evidences the date of shipment or dispatch. A notation showing additional data content need not be separately signed or otherwise authenticated.

Article e11 Corruption of an Electronic Record After Presentation

a. If an electronic record that has been received by the issuing bank, confirming bank, or another nominated bank appears to have been corrupted, the bank may inform the presenter and may request that electronic record be re-presented.

b. If the bank requests that an electronic record be re presentedthe time for examination is suspended and resumes when the presenter re-presents the electronic record. if the nominated bank is not the confirming bank, it must provide the issuing bank and any confirming bank with notice of the request for re-presentation and inform it of the suspension; butif the same electronic record is not re-presented within thirty calendar days, the bank may treat the electronic record as not presented, and

Article e12 Additional Disclaimer of Liability for Presentation of Electronic Records under eUCP

By satisfying itself as to the apparent authenticity of an electronic record, banks assume no liability for the identity of the sender, source of the information, or its complete and unaltered character other than that which is apparent in the electronic record received by the use of a commercially acceptable data process for the receipt, authentication, and identification of electronic record.

中文部分

第一章 国际贸易术语

第一节 国际贸易术语概述

一、贸易术语的作用

贸易术语是指一个简短的概念或英文缩写字母来说明商品的价格构成、买卖双方有关手续、费用及风险责任的划分和物权转移的界限。例如:Free On Board 可以缩写为 FOB,即“船上交货”。Cost, Insurance and Freight,缩写为 CIF,即“成本加保险费、运费”。在国际贸易中,将货物从一个国家运至另一个国家,作为商业交易中的一个环节,可能是要冒风险的。如果货物损坏,或者由于其他原因未能交货,当事人之间的信任感可能下降,甚至引起诉讼。因此人们采用贸易术语表明买卖双方各自承担不同的责任、费用和风险,而这些因素又会影响成交商品的价格,所以,有些人便把它当作单纯表示价格的用语,称为“价格术语”。贸易术语大大简化了买卖双方之间洽谈业务的内容,缩短了成交的过程,减少了误解和争议,节省了交易时间和费用,对国际经济贸易的发展起到了促进作用。

二、有关贸易术语的国际惯例

在国际贸易业务实践中,由于各国法律制度、贸易惯例与习惯做法不同,所以国际上对同一贸易术语的理解与运用也互有差异,容易引起贸易纠纷。为了减少纠纷和避免争议,有些国际商业团体制定了一些统一解释贸易术语的规则,现介绍如下。

1.《1932 年华沙 - 牛津规则》

《1932 年华沙 - 牛津规则》,它起源于 1928 年国际法协会在波兰华沙制订的《1928 年华沙规则》,此后几经修订,最后将此规则确定为《1932 年华沙 - 牛津规则》(Warsaw-Oxford Rules,1932)。

2.《1941 年美国对外贸易定义修订本》

1941 年,由美国商会、美国进口商全国理事会和美国对外贸易理事会所组成的联合委员会正式通过《1941 年美国对外贸易定义修订本》(Revised American Foreign Trade Definitions,1941),迄今为止,它在美洲大陆都具有相当大的影响。在该文本中,把 FOB 分为 6 种类型。

3.《2000 年国际贸易术语解释通则》

早在 1936 年,国际商会就制定了《国际贸易术语解释通则》(International Rules for the Interpretation of Trade Terms,简称 INCOTERMS)。随着国际贸易的发展和国际形势的变化,几经修订后,现行的《2000 年国际贸易术语解释通则》(简称“2000 通则”)于 2000 年 1 月 1

日起生效。该惯例共解释了 13 种贸易术语，并将其分成 4 个不同的基本类型。

(1)E 组(EXW)，卖方在其自己的所在地把货物交给买方。

(2)F 组(FCA,FAS 和 FOB)，卖方必须将货物交至买方指定的承运人。

(3)C 组(CFR,CIF,CPT 和 CIP)，卖方必须签订运输合同，但装船和启运后货物灭失或损坏的风险或其他费用，卖方不承担责任。

(4)D 组(DAF,DES,DEQ,DDU 和 DDP)，卖方必须承担把货物运至目的地国家所需的全部费用和风险。

第二节　国际惯例

一、《国际贸易术语解释通则》的宗旨和范围

《国际贸易术语解释通则》(以下称 INCOTERMS)的宗旨是为国际贸易中最普遍使用的贸易术语提供一套正确解释的国际规则，以避免因各国解释不同而出现的不确定性，或至少在相当程度上减少这种不确定性。

合同双方当事人之间互不了解对方国家的贸易习惯的情况时常出现，这就会引起误解、争议和诉讼，从而浪费时间和费用。为了解决这些问题，国际商会(ICC)先后于 1936 年，1953 年、1967 年、1976 年、1980 年、1990 年和 2000 年对 INCOTERMS 进行修订。现在通用的是在 2000 年版本基础上作出补充和修订的版本，以便使这些规则更适应当前国际贸易实践的发展。

需要强调的是，INCOTERMS 涵盖的范围只限于销售合同当事人的权利义务中与已售货物(指“有形的”货物，不包括“无形的”货物，如电脑软件)交货有关的事项。

关于 INCOTERMS，有两个非常普遍的误解。一个是常常认为 INCOTERMS 是用于运输的合同而不是销售合同；另一个是人们有时错误地认为它规定了当事人可能希望包含在销售合同中的所有责任。

对于 INCOTERMS 有以下正确的表达方法。

首先，正如 ICC 一贯强调的条文，INCOTERMS 只涉及销售合同中买卖双方的关系，并且只限于一些非常明确的条文。

对于进口商和出口商来讲，考虑那些为完成国际销售所需要的各种合同之间的实际关系是非常必要的。完成一笔国际贸易不仅需要销售合同，而且需要运输合同、保险合同和融资合同，而 INCOTERMS 只涉及其中的一项合同，即销售合同。

虽然如此，当合同双方当事人统一使用某一具体的贸易术语时，将不可避免地对其他合同产生影响。举例说明，卖方同意在合同中使用 CFR 和 CIF 术语时，他就只能以海运方式履行合同，因为在这两个术语下它必须向买方提供提单或其他海运单据，使用其他运输方式此要求就无法满足。并且，跟单信用证要求的单据也将取决于准备使用的运输方式。

其次，INCOTERMS 涉及货物进口和出口清关、货物包装的义务，买方受领货物的义务，以及提供证明各项义务得到完整履行的义务。尽管 INCOTERMS 对于销售合同的执行有着极为重要的意义，但对于销售合同中可能引起的许多问题却并未涉及，如货物所有权和其他产权的转移、违约、违约行为的后果以及某些情况下的免责等。需要强调的是，INCOTERMS 不能取代完整的销售合同中需要的标准条款或商定条款。

通常，INCOTERMS 不涉及违约的后果或由于各种法律阻碍导致的免责事项，这些问题必须通过销售合同中的其他条款和适用的法律来解决。

INCOTERMS 一直主要用于跨国境的货物销售交付，因此它是一套国际商业术语。有时 INCOTERMS 也被用于纯粹国内市场的货物销售合同中，在此情况下 INCOTERMS 中的 A2、B2 以及任何与进口有关的条款就变成多余的了。

二、《国际贸易术语解释通则》修订的原因

连续修订 INCOTERMS 的主要原因是要使其适应当代商业实践。1980 年修订本引入了货交承运人（现在为 FCA）术语，其目的是为了适应在海上运输中经常出现的情况，即交货点不再是传统的 FOB 点（货物越过船舷），而是在将货物装船之前运到陆地上的某一点，在那里将货物装入集装箱，以便经由海运或其他运输方式（即所谓的联合或多式运输）继续运输。

在 1990 年的 INCOTERMS 修订本中，涉及卖方提供交货凭证义务的条款在当事方同意使用电子方式通信时，允许用电子数据交换（EDI）信息替代纸面单据。毫无疑问，为了使 INCOTERMS 更利于实务操作，其草拟和表述一直都在改进。

三、INCOTERMS 2000

在为期两年的修订过程中，ICC 尽其最大努力通过 ICC 各国家委员会吸取了各行业国际贸易从业者的意见和建议，完成了修订稿的多次修改。令人高兴的是，INCOTERMS 2000 这个版本与 INCOTERMS 1990 相比变化很小。原因很明显，即 INCOTERMS 当前已得到世界承认，所以 ICC 决定巩固 INCOTERMS 在世界范围内得到的承认，并避免为了变化而变化。另一方面，在修订过程中，ICC 尽量保证 INCOTERMS 2000 中的语言清楚准确地反映出国际贸易实务。新的版本在两个方面作出了实质性改变：在 FAS 和 DEQ 术语下，办理清关手续和交纳关税的义务；在 FCA 术语下装货和卸货的义务。

无论是内容的变化还是形式的变化都是在对 INCOTERMS 的使用者广泛调查的基础上作出的，而且对 1990 年以来 INCOTERMS 专家小组收到的咨询意见给予了充分考虑。

四、在销售合同中订入 INCOTERMS

鉴于 INCOTERMS 不断修订，所以，当合同当事方意图在销售合同中订入 INCOTERMS

时，清楚地指明所引用的 INCOTERMS 版本是很重要的。这一点很容易被忽略，例如当在标准合同或订货单中引用了早期版本，未能引用最新版本，可能会对当事方的意图是在合同中引用新版本还是早期版本引起纠纷。希望使用 INCOTERMS 2000 时，应在合同中明确规定该合同受 INCOTERMS 2000 的约束。

五、INCOTERMS 的结构

1990 年，为了便于理解，INCOTERMS 将所有的术语分为 4 个基本不同的类型。第一组为"E 组"(EX WORKS)，指卖方仅在自己的地点为买方备妥货物；第二组为"F 组"(FCA、FAS 和 FOB)，指卖方须将货物交至买方指定的承运人；第三组为"C 组"(CFR、CIF、CPT 和 CIP)，指卖方须订立运输合同，但对货物灭失或损坏的风险以及装船和启运后发生意外所发生的额外费用，卖方不承担责任；第四组为"D 组"(DAF、DES、DEQ、DDU 和 DDP)，指卖方须承担把货物交至目的地国所需的全部费用和风险。下表反映了这种分类方法。

表 1-1　2000 年国际贸易术语解释通则

E 组(发货)		
	EXW	工厂交货(……指定地点)
F 组(主要运费未付)		
	FCA	货交承运人(……指定地点)
	FAS	船边交货(……指定装运港)
	FOB	船上交货(……指定装运港)
C 组(主要运费已付)		
	CFR	成本加运费(……指定目的港)
	CIF	成本、保险费加运费(……指定目的港)
	CPT	运费付至(……指定目的地)
	CIP	运费、保险费付至(……指定目的地)
D 组(到达)		
	DAF	边境交货(……指定地点)
	DES	目的港船上交货(……指定目的港)
	DEQ	目的港码头交货(……指定目的港)
	DDU	未完税交货(……指定目的地)
	DDP	完税后交货(……指定目的地)

与 INCOTERMS 1990 相同，在 INCOTERMS 2000 中，所有术语下当事人各自的义务均用 10 个项目列出，卖方在每一项目中的地位"对应"了买方在同一项目中相应的地位。

六、用于说明

在起草 INCOTERMS 2000 过程中，工作小组力求使这 13 个术语中的不同表达尽可能做到连贯一致,这样就避免了用不同表述方法表达相同的意义。而且,只要可能,均使用了1980年《联合国国际货物销售合同公约》中的表述。

1.“托运人”(shipper)

在一些情况下,需要用同一个词表示两个不同的意思,因为无法找到合适的代替词,商人们在销售合同和运输合同中经常遇到这种困难。例如,“托运人”一词既可以表示将货物交付运输的人,又表示与承运人订立合同的人,而这两个“托运人”可能是不同的人,如在FOB合同中,卖方将货物交付运输,而买方则与承运人订立运输合同。

2.“交货”(delivery)

需要特别注意的是,“交货”这个词在INCOTERMS中有两种不同含义。首先,“交货”一词被用来判断卖方何时完成了其交货义务,这一规定在所有INCOTERMS的A4条款中。其次,“交货”也被用于买方受领或接受货物的义务,这一规定在所有INCOTERMS的B4条款中。用于第二种含义时,“交货”首先意味着买方“接受”C组术语的基本宗旨,即卖方在将货物交运时即完成其义务;其次,“交货”一词还意味着买方有受领货物的义务。为避免因买方提取货物前支付不必要的储藏费,后一种义务是很重要的。例如,在CFR和CIF术语的合同中,买方有义务接受货物并从承运人处领取货物,若买方未履行该义务,就可能使与承运人订立运输合同的卖方损失承担赔偿责任,或者向承运人支付货物滞期费以使承运人放货。在这方面,说买方必须“受领货物”并不表示买方将为符合销售合同而接受货物,而只是指买方接受这一事实,即卖方按C组术语A3款订立运输合同,完成了将货物交付运输的义务。如果买方在目的地收到货物后,发现货物与销售合同规定不符,买方可使用销售合同和适用的法律给予的任何一种补救办法向卖方寻求补偿。如上所述,此项事宜已完全超出INCOTERMS的使用范围。

当货物在某一特定地点可交给买方时,INCOTERMS 2000在适当处使用了“将货物交给买方处置”的表达,这种表达与《联合国国际货物销售合同公约》中“将货物交与”的表述含义相同。

3.“通常”(usual)

“通常”一词在很多术语中出现,如在EXW术语中表示交货时间的条款(A4)中,在C组术语下关于卖方必须提供的单据和必须订立的运输合同的条款(A8、A3)中。当然,说清楚“通常”的含义并非易事,然而在很多情况下,是有可能认定该行业业内人士通常是如何行事的,这种行事惯例即可作为参照。在此意义上,“通常”这个词比“合理的”一词更有帮助。“合理的”要求的不是根据日常实践的评估,而是根据更难界定的善意和公平交易原则的评估,在一些情况下,可能还是需要判断什么是“合理的”。尽管如此,由于上述原因,在INCOTERMS中,一般使用“通常”一词而不是用“合理的”一词。

4.“费用”(charges)

在涉及到办理货物进口手续的义务时,判断货物进口时要支付的“费用”包括哪些内容是很重要的。在 INCOTERMS 1990 中,DDP 术语 A6 使用的是“出口和进口中所需交纳的官方费用”。而在 INCOTERMS 2000 中,删去了“官方”一词,其原因是在决定某项收费是否是“官方”收费时,“官方”一词会造成某种不确定性,虽然删去了“官方”一词,但本意并非改变这一条款的实质意义。必须支付的“费用”仅涉及进口必然发生并按适用的进口管理规定必须支付的费用,其他任何由私人机构在货物进口时收取的费用不应包括在“费用”中,如与清关义务无关的储存费。若承诺义务的一方非亲自履行该义务,则履行此义务可能发生付给海关经纪人或运输行(freight forwarders)的一些费用。

5.“港口”(port)、“地点”(place)、“点”(point)和“所在地”(premise)

在交货地点的问题上,INCOTERMS 中使用了不同的表达方法。只适用于海运的术语,如 FAS、FOB、CFR、CIF、DES 和 DEQ,使用了“装运港”和“目的港”两种表达。在所有其他的术语中使用的是“地点”(place)一词。在某种场合,有必要指明在“港口”和“地点”(place)内的某“点”(point),因为卖方不仅需要知道要把货物交至一个特定地区,例如某个城市,而且也要知道在该地区的什么点将货物交给买方处置。销售合同经常缺少这一方面的信息,于是,INCOTERMS 规定如果在指定地点没有约定交货点,并且有几个点可以选择,则卖方可选择对其最有利的点交货(见 FCA 术语中的 A4 条款)。当交货点是卖方“地点”时,则使用了“卖方所在地”(见 FCA 术语中的 A4 条款)。

6.“船只”(ship 和 vessel)

在使用海上运输货物的术语时,“ship”和“vessel”被当作同义词使用。无需说明,当“ship”作为贸易术语的组成部分时,如“船边交货(FAS)”和“目的港船上交货(DES)”,必然要使用“ship”一词。同样,由于 FOB 术语中传统上使用“越过船舷”的表达,因而必然会将“ship”一词用于相关内容。

7.“查对”(checking)和“检验”(inspection)

在 INCOTERMS 中,A9 和 B8 条款分别使用“查对、包装和标记”和“货物检验”作为条款标题。尽管“checking”和“inspection”是同义词,但是普通认为运用下述方法来区别使用比较合理:在涉及卖方按 A4 交货的义务时使用查对(checking),而后者则用于一些特殊情况,即进行“装运前检验”,因为在通常情况下只有当买方或货物出口(进口)国当局希望货物装运前保证货物符合合同或官方规定时才要求进行“检验”。

七、卖方的交货义务

INCOTERMS 将重点放在卖方的交货义务上。对与卖方交货有关联的责任和费用的准确分配在各当事方有持续商业关系的情况下一般不会有什么问题。他们会在相互之间确立一种习惯做法(course of dealing),而且他们会按这种方式处理以后的交易。然而,当建立一种新的商业关系或通过经纪人的中介订立合同(这在农矿产品销售中是普遍现象)时,当事人一定要按合同规定办事,即将 INCOTERMS 2000 订入合同时,要按照 INCOTERMS 2000

的规定划分责任、费用和风险。

当然,人们希望 INCOTERMS 能够尽可能细致地划分与交货有关的各当事方的义务。与 INCOTERMS 1990 相比,INCOTERMS 2000 在某些具体情况下在这方面有更细致的规定(见 FCA 术语中 A4 条款)。但在 FAS 和 FOB A4 中,不可避免地要援用行业惯例("按港口的习惯方式"),其原因是在 FAS 或 FOB 合同下将货物尤其是农矿产品交运的具体做法在不同的海港是不一样的。

八、与货物有关的风险和费用的转移

当卖方交货后,货物灭失或损失的风险以及负担与货物有关费用的义务便从卖方转移到买方。由于不应给予买方任何拖延风险和费用转移的机会,所以,所有术语都作出规定,当买方没有按约定受领货物或没有给予卖方完成交货义务的必要指示(有关装船时间或交货地点)时,风险和费用甚至在交货之前就可转移。这种提前转移风险和费用的条件就是货物一直为买方准备的,或如术语所规定,已为买方"划出"。

在 EXW 术语下,这一点尤为重要,因为在所有其他术语下,当采取措施为交运、发送货物(F 组和 C 组)或在目的地作交货准备时(D 组),一般即可认为这批货物是专门为买方准备的。但在一些场合例外,如当卖方散装发运货物且未确定每一个买方的数量时,则在货物按前述规定特定化前,风险和费用不发生转移(参见《1980 年联合国国际货物销售合同公约》第 69.3 条)。

九、术语

1. E 组术语

E 组术语下卖方的义务最小:卖方只要将货物在约定地点,通常是在卖方所在地,交给买方处置即可。但是,另一方面,在实务中,卖方经常帮助买方将货物装至买方的运输工具上。如果将卖方的义务扩大到包括装货,那么 EXW 术语将更好地反应这一实务。但是,人们认为理想的状态是仍然保留 EXW 下卖方义务的传统原则,使其适用于那些卖方不愿意承担任何装货义务的情况。若买方希望卖方负担更多的义务,则可在销售合同中写明。

2. F 组术语

F 组术语是指要求卖方按指示将货物交运。在 FCA 术语下,当事各方所希望的交货点造成了困难,其原因是此术语涉及的合同可能会遇到各种的情况。货物可能装上买方派往卖方所在地提取货物的车辆;或者货物也许需要从卖方派往买方指定交货地点的车辆上卸下。INCOTERMS 2000 考虑到了上述可能,规定若合同中指定交货地点是卖方所在地,当货物装上买方的装货车辆时即完成交货,在其他情况下,当货物在卖方的车辆上尚未卸货而交给买方处置时,即完成交货。在 INCOTERMS 1990 中,FCA 术语 A4 条款中提到的各种不同运输方式在 INCOTERMS 2000 中未再重复。

FOB 术语中的交货点与 CFR 和 CIF 术语中的相同，尽管对此有很多争议，但在 INCOTERMS 2000 中仍未作改动。虽然 FOB 术语中的“越过船舷”交货原则在当前许多情况下已不适合，但是既然已为商人们所深知，并根据货物的特点和可用的装卸设备的具体情况加以运用，更改 FOB 的交货点可能会造成不必要的混乱，尤其对于租船合同进行农矿产品运输，更是如此。

不幸的是，FOB 术语被一些商人用来表示“任何”交货点，如“FOB 工厂”、“FOB 卖方工厂”或其他内陆地点，这样就失去了 FOB 术语是“Free on Board”的缩写的意义了。这样使用 FOB 术语会造成混乱，应该避免。

FAS 术语办理货物出口手续的义务出现了重要的变化，因为最普通的做法是由卖方而不是由买方承担这项义务。为了保证这一变化得到足够的重视，在 FAS 序言中使用黑体字标出。

3. C 组术语

C 组术语是指要求卖方按照通常条件自付费用订立运输合同。因此，卖方支付运费运到的地点，必须在 C 组每一项属于后指明。按照 CIF 和 CIP 术语，卖方还要负责办理保险和负担保险费用，由于费用划分地点确定为目的地国家的某个点，因此 C 组术语往往被误认为是到货合同，在到货合同中，卖方要承担货物实际被运到约定地点之前的全部风险和费用。

在此必须强调，C 组术语与 F 组术语具有相同性质的原因，就在于卖方是在装运国或发货国进行合同履行。因此，C 组术语的销售合同和 F 组术语的销售合同一样，属于装运合同。

装运合同的特点是，卖方要支付将货物按照惯例航线和习惯方式运至约定地点所需的通常运输费用，而货物灭失或损坏的风险以及在货物以适当方式交付运输之后发生意外而发生的额外费用则由买方承担。因此，C 组术语包含两个区别于其他所有术语的“分界点”：一是指明卖方必须安排运输，并承担其费用；二是指风险的划分点。因此，凡因增加卖方在 C 组术语下的义务而扩大卖方的责任超出上述风险划分的“分界点”时，应特别注意。按照 CIF 和 CIP 术语，卖方在履行其合同义务、订立运输合同、将货物交付承运人并办理保险后，应免除卖方任何进一步的风险和费用，这正是 C 组术语的实质所在。

C 组术语作为装运合同的本质也通过在此组术语下广泛使用跟单信用证作为人们喜爱的付款方式显现出来。若销售合同的当事方同意，卖方凭跟单信用证向银行提交约定的运输单据后收取货款，则如果卖方在按照跟单信用证得到货款或在货物起运或发货后以其他方式得到货款之后，仍承担进一步的风险和费用，卖方必须支付运输合同的费用；然而，在货物装船或发货后的事件所发生的额外费用必须由买方承担。

如果卖方需要提供包括交纳关税、税款和其他费用在内的运输合同，那么，在合同约定这些费用由卖方支付时，这一点在所有 C 组术语的 A6 条款中已作出明确规定。

若按习惯要订立几份运输合同，以便货物中途转运以抵达约定的目的地，卖方必须支付所有的费用,包括货物从一种运输工具转到另一种运输工具发生的费用。但是,若承担人依据转运合同或类似条款的规定形式及权利以避免意外的阻碍(例如冰块、堵塞、劳工动乱、政府禁令、战争或类似战争行为),则由此发生的所有额外费用应由买方承担,因为卖方的义务只限于订立通常的运输合同。

销售合同的当事人往往希望明确卖方应在什么程度内订立运输合同,包括卸货费用由谁负担。由于当货物由通常的班轮运输时,这些费用一般包括运费之内,所以,销售合同中经常规定,货物必须由班轮运输或至少按"班轮条件"运输。有时在 CIF 和 CIP 术语后加上"到岸上(landed)"。然而,最好不要在 C 组术语中用缩用语,除非在有关行业中,该缩写语为合同当事人或适用的法律或行业惯例所明确理解和接受的。

具体来说,卖方不应当(在不改变 C 组术语本质的情况下,实际上也不能够)承担任何保证货物抵达目的地的义务,因为在运输途中任何迟延的风险都应由买方承担。因此,涉及时间的任何义务都必须表明装船地或发货地,例如"装运(发货)不迟于……"。像"CFR 汉堡不迟于……"这样的一份协议属于用语不当,并会引起不同的解释:当事人的意思可能被认为是货物必须在规定的日期抵达汉堡,在这种情况下该合同不是装运合同而是到货合同;另一种理解可能是,卖方发运货物的时间必须使其在通常情况下能在规定的时间前抵达汉堡,除非发生意外事件耽误运输。

在农矿产品贸易中,若是购买的货物正在海上运输途中,贸易术语后应加上"在途(af loat)"一词。根据 CIF 和 CIP 术语,货物的灭失或损坏的风险这时已从卖方转移到买方,这就可能引起解释上的困难。一种可能是,维持 CIF 和 CIP 术语有关买卖双方风险划分的通常含义,即风险在装运时转移,这意味着买方也许不得不承担销售合同生效时已发生的事件的后果;另一种可能性是让风险转移和合同订立的时间相一致。前一种可能性也许更切合实际,因为确定正在运输途中货物的状况往往是不可能的。鉴于这个原因,《1980 年联合国国际货物销售合同公约》第 68 条规定"如果情况表明由此需要,从货物交付给签发体现运输合同的单据的承运人时起,风险就由买方承担",但是有一种例外情况,即当"卖方知道或理应知道货物已经灭失或损坏,而不讲这一事实告知买方"时。因此,CIF 或 CIP 术语后加上"在途"一词的解释应取决于销售合同适用的法律。建议当事人弄清适用的法律及其可能导致的解决方法,如有疑问,当事人应在合同中明确规定。

在实务中,甲、乙方继续频繁使用 C&F(或 C and F,C + F)这样传统的术语。然而,在绝大多数情况下,交易方视这些传统术语等同于 CFR。为了避免解释合同时的困难,交易方应适用 CFR 术语,因为 CFR 术语是全球广泛接受的"成本加运费(……指定目的港)"的唯一缩写。

在 INCOTERMS 1990 中,CFR 和 CIF 的 A8 条款要求:只要卖方提供的运输单据(通常是提单)中援引了租船合同,例如,通常用表达方式"所有其他条款(terms)和条件(conditions)均按租船合同",这时卖方就有义务提供租船合同的副本。尽管签约人应该总是能够确知合同中所有条款的内容(最好是在订立合同时),但是这种提供租船合同的做法带来了一些问题,尤其是在跟单信用证业务中。所以,在 INCOTERMS 2000 中,删去了 CFR 和 CIF 术语下卖方要随运输单据提供租船合同副本的义务。

虽然 INCOTERMS 中 A8 条款目的在于保证卖方向买方提供"交货凭证",但应该指出,这里强调的只是卖方提供了"通常"的凭证,卖方就完成了这项义务。在 CFR 和 CIF 术语下,卖方要提供"通常的运输单据",即在 CFR 和 CIF 术语下,卖方要提供提单和海运单,运输单据必须是"清洁的",即运输单据上不能出现声明货物和(或)其包装有与合同不符的条款或批注。若单据中出现这样的条款或批注,那么这个单据就被认为是"不清洁的",在跟单信用证交易中就会被银行拒收。但是,一份运输单据,即使上面没有这样的条款或批注,对买方来说通常也不能成为对抗承运人的无可置疑的证据,证明货物在装运时是符合销售合同内容的。一般情况下,承运人会在运输单据的正面以标准文句指明,在运输单据中加入的细节(particulars)是托运人的声明,因此货物情况只是"据称"如其添加的细节所述。承运人以此拒绝承担有关货物状况的责任。根据大多数援助的法律或原则,承运人必须使用合理的方法检验货物是否正确,否则对收货人负有责任。然而,在集装箱中承运人无法检查集装箱内货物,除非承运人负责将货物装入集装箱。

涉及保险的术语只有两个,即 CIF 和 CIP。在这两个术语下,卖方有义务为买方的利益办理保险。在其他情况下,则是由当事方自己决定是否要办理保险以及投保到什么程度。由于卖方要为买方的利益办理保险,卖方不一定知道买方的详细需求。根据由伦敦保险人协会(Institute of London Underwriters)拟订的《协会货物保险条款》(Institute Cargo Clauses),①规定办理"最低程度"的保险,②规定办理中等程度保险,③规定办理最高险别。在 CIF 术语下的农矿产品销售中,买方或许希望将在途货物卖给新的买方,而这个新的买方也许希望再将货物售出,所以,买方不可能了解这些后继买方的保险需求。因此,在 CIF 术语下,传统上选择最低保险,买方可以要求卖方办理附加保险。但最低保险对制成品货物的销售可能不太适宜,因为制成品存在偷盗、不可搬运或保管的风险。由于 CIP 不同于 CIF,一般不用于农矿产品的销售,所以采用 CIP 下最高险别而不是 CIF 下的最低险别,将会是可行的。但若在 CIF 和 CIP 术语下对卖方办理货物保险义务的要求不同,则容易导致混乱。所以,这两个术语要求卖方只限于办理"最低程度"的货物保险。对于 CIP 术语下的买方来说,注意到这一点是非常重要的。如果买方要求附加险别,他可以与卖方协议由卖方办理或自行安排办理个别高的保险。在某些情况下,买方也许会要求获得比《协会货物保险条款》(A)更高的保险,比如战争险、动乱险、民变险、罢工或其他劳工动乱险。若买方希望卖方安排这样的保险,则买方必须明示卖方,而卖方必须在可能情况下负责安排这些保险。

4. D 组术语

D 组术语与 C 组术语有着本质区别。根据 D 组术语,卖方负责将货物运至边境或进口国内的约定目的地或点。卖方必须承担货物运至该地前的全部风险和费用,因此,D 组术语属于到货合同，而 C 组术语属于离港（装运）合同。

在 D 组术语下，除了 DDP，卖方在目的地国交货时无须办理进口手续。

传统的做法是，在 DEQ 术语下，卖方有义务办理货物的进口清关手续，因为货物需要搬运到码头，这样就进入了进口国。但是，由于大多数国家的清关手续发生了变化，所以在该国有居住地的一方办理进口清关手续并交纳关税和其他费用更为合适。因此 DEQ 术语有了一些改变，正如前面提到的 FAS 术语的变化一样，DEQ 术语中的变化在序言中以黑体字标出。

很多国家使用一些没有收进 INCOTERMS 中的贸易术语，尤其是在铁路运输中（如 franco border，franco – frontiere，Frei Granze）等。然而，在这些术语下，通常并不想让卖方承担将货物运至边境前的货物灭失或损坏的风险，在这些情况下，最好使用 CPT 指明边境。如果希望卖方负担运输中的风险，则使用指明边境的 DAF 术语更合适。

DDU 术语是在 INCOTERMS 1990 中新加入的。当卖方准备在目的国交货但不办理进口手续、不交纳关税时，该术语就发挥了重要作用。在那些办理海关手续很困难而且耗时很久的国家里，卖方承担在完成海关清关手续后交货的义务将是有风险的。尽管按照 DDU 术语的 B5 和 B6 条款，买方要承担其为完成货物进口手续情况时可能发生的额外风险和费用，但仍然建议在办理货物进口手续可能会有困难的国家的交易中，卖方不使用 DDU 术语。

十、“无义务”的表示

“卖方须知”和“买方须知”这样的表达方法体现出 INCOTERMS 只涉及当时双方分别对对方承担的义务。这样，“无义务”则被用于一方对另一方不承担义务的情况。如果按该术语中的 A3 条款卖方须安排并支付运输费用，则在 B3（1）的“运输合同”项目下“无义务”的字样即规定了买方的地位。同样，当任何一方对对方都不承担义务时，在双方名下都会出现“无义务”一词，例如有关“保险”的情况。

在上述任何一种情况下，重要的是要指出，即使一方“无义务”为另一方履行某项任务，也并不意味着履行该任务不符合它的利益。例如，CFR 的买方按照 B4 对卖方并无投保的责任，但很明显买方投保符合其利益，因为在该术语下按照 A4 条款卖方也没有义务获取保险。

十一、INCOTERMS 的变体

在实务中，当事双方经常在 INCOTERMS 术语基础上添加词句以求得比术语更精确的约定。需要强调的是，INCOTERMS 对任何这种添加的内容不提供任何规定。这样，如果当事双方无法依赖一个公认的行业惯例来揭示其新增内容时，他们可能会由于无法就新增内容证明有一贯的理解而面临严重的问题。以常用的“FOB 理舱”和“EXW 装车”为例，卖方的义务不仅被扩大至包括负担将货物分别装到船上或装上车辆的费用，而且也包括在装舱和装货期间货物意外的灭失或损坏的风险，这就无法在全世界达成一致的理解。由于上述

原因,强烈建议当事双方明确表示他们是否只打算由卖方承担装舱和装车的任务及费用,还是卖方也需要承担装舱和装车全部结束之前的风险,对此 INCOTERMS 并无答案。假如合同也未对双方意图明确,双方就将面临不必要的麻烦和费用。

尽管 INCOTERMS 2000 未对许多这样的普遍使用的变体作出规定,但某些术语的序言确实在提醒双方,如希望超出 INCOTERMS 的规定来分配双方义务,则需要使用特殊的合同条款。例如:

EXW	关于卖方将货物装上买方的运输工具的额外义务
CIF/CIP	关于买方安排货物额外保险的需要
DEQ	关于卖方支付卸货之后的费用的额外义务

在一些情况下,卖方和买方援引班轮和租船合同中的商业惯例。这样就需要明确地区分当事双方在运输合同中的义务和彼此在销售合同中的义务。但是,对于"班轮条件"(liner terms)和"终点站搬运费"(Terminal Handling Charges,THC)等表达法尚无权威解释。在这些条款下,费用的划分因地点的不同而不同,而且经常变化。建议当事方在销售合同中明确规定如何划分双方应承担的费用。

在租船合同中经常使用的表达法如"FOB 理舱"、"FOB 理舱和平舱"等,有时被用在销售合同中以明确在 FOB 术语下卖方要在何种程度内负担理舱和平舱的义务。有时用此类附加语时,有必要在销售合同中明确额外的义务只限于费用还是包括费用和风险。

如上所述,我们尽量使 INCOTERMS 反映出最通行的国际商业做法。然而,在某些情况下,尤其是在 INCOTERMS 2000 与 INCOTERMS 1990 有不同之处时,当事方也许会希望以不同方式使用贸易术语。在贸易术语的序言中,以"但是"作句子的开头专门提醒注意这些可能性。

十二、港口或特定行业的习惯做法

因为贸易术语要在不同行业和不同地区使用,对双方的义务不能总是规定得很精确,所以,在某种程度上,有必要参考港口的或特定行业的习惯做法,或当事方在先前的交易中已经建立的习惯做法(参见《1980 年联合国国际货物销售合同公约》第 9 条)。对于卖方和买方而言,当协商销售合同时,使自己及时了解这些习惯做法,并在不能确定时,通过在销售合同中适当的条款澄清当事方的法律地位是值得推荐的做法。在具体合同中这些特别条款将取代或改变 INCOTERMS 规定的任何解释规则。

十三、买方关于装运地的选择

在一些情况下,在订立销售合同时可能无法准确地确定卖方将货物交运的点(Point)甚至地点(Place)。比如,在这一阶段,可能只约定在"某一范围"或一个较大的地点,如海港。在这种情况下,通常规定买方随后有权或有义务在这一范围内或地点内指定更精确的地点。若如上文所述买方有义务提供精确点而没做到，则买方就要承担由这种未尽义务而造成的任何额外的风险和费用（如所有术语中 B5 和 B7 条款规定）。除此之外，若买方没能使用自己的权力指示交货点，则卖方可以选择在对卖方最合适的点交货（FCA 中的 A4 条款）。

十四、清关

对“清关”这个词有了一些误解，在本书中明确，“清关”是指无论何时当卖方或买方承担将货物运过出口国或进口国的海关的义务时，这项义务不仅包括交纳关税和其他费用，而且包括履行一切与货物通过海关有关的行政事务以及向当局提供必要信息并交纳相关费用。在某些地区，如欧盟内部或其他自由贸易区，当不再有交纳关税的义务和对进出口的限制时，有人认为使用规定办理货物清关手续义务的术语是不恰当的（尽管这是错误的认识）。为此，“在需要办理海关手续时（where applicable）”的用语被加入了相关术语的 A2 和 B2、A6 和 B6 条款，这样，在无须办理海关手续的情况下，使用该用语就可以避免模棱两可。

清关手续由住所在该国的一方或其代表办理通常是可取的。因此，通常出口商应办理出口清关手续，进口商应办理进口清关手续。

INCOTERMS 1990 中的 EXW、FAS（要求买方办理货物出口清关手续）和 DEQ（要求卖方办理进口清关手续）与上述原则不一致，其表示卖方最低义务的术语 EXW 却未被改动（买方仍承担办理出口清关的义务）。DDP 术语的字面含义即完税后交货（Delivered Duty Paid），采用该术语表示卖方明确同意完成该术语的义务，即办理进口清关手续并交纳全部相关费用。

十五、包装

大多数情况下，当事人事先知道货物安全运至目的地需要何种包装。但是，由于卖方包装货物的义务可能因具体的运输方式和期限而大相径庭，所以有必要规定卖方有义务使货物的包装适合运输方式，但只限于在订立销售合同前已经知道有关运输的情况（参阅《1980 年联合国国际货物销售合同公约》第 35 条 1 款和第 35 条 2 款 b 项规定，即货物包装必须“适用于订立合同时曾明示或默示地同意卖方的任何特定目的，除非情况表明买方并不依赖卖方的技能和判断力，或者这种依赖是不合理的”）。

十六、货物检验

在许多情况下，人们会建议买方在卖方把货物交付运输前或交付运输时安排货物检验（称为“装运前检验”）。除非合同另有规定，买方应承担检验费用，且这种检验是为了他自身利益安排的。但是，若进行的检验是为了使卖方履行在其本国时用于出口货物的任何强制性规定，则卖方应支付检验费用，除非使用的是 EXW 术语，这使买方应负担检验费用。

十七、运输方式和相应的 INCOTERMS 2000 术语

表 1－2　运输方式和相应的 INCOTERMS 2000 术语

(1)适用于任何运输方式

E 组	
EXW	工厂交货(……指定地点)
F 组	
FCA	货交承运人(……指定地点)
C 组	
CPT	运费付至(……指定目的地)
CIP	运费、保险费付至(……指定目的地)
D 组	
DAF	边境交货(……指定地点)
DDU	未完税交货(……指定目的地)
DDP	完税交货(……指定目的地)

(2)只适用于海运及内河运输

F 组	
FAS	船边交货(……指定装运港)
FOB	船上交货(……指定装运港)
C 组	
CFR	成本加运费(……指定目的港)
CIF	成本、保险费加运费(……指定目的港)
D 组	
DES	目的港船上交货(……指定目的港)
DEQ	目的港码头交货(……指定目的港)

十八、推荐使用

在某些情况下,条款的序言推荐使用或者不使用某个术语。注意这一点在选择 FCA 和 FOB 时尤其重要。但是,商人们依然不适当地使用 FOB,使得卖方在将货物交给买方指定的承运人之后依然会遇到风险。FOB 仅在下列情况下适用,即当卖方只打算越过船舷交货,怎样都要交到船上,而不是将货物交给承运人以使货物能被继续运输和装载到船上,例如装到集装箱内或装上卡车等集装运输工具上,若当事方无意超过船舷交货则不应使用该术语。

有时也会出现这样的情况,即当买卖双方考虑使用其他运输方式时却错误地使用了适合于海运的术语,这将会使卖方处于不利的处境,即无法完成向买方提交适合单据的义务

(如提单、海运单或有同等作用的电子信息)。

十九、提单和电子商务

传统做法,在CFR和CIF术语下,装船提单是卖方应提供的唯一可接受的单据,提单起到了三个重要的作用:

(1)将货物交付至船上的证明;

(2)运输合同的证明;

(3)一种通过将纸面单据(paper document)交给另一方而将在途货物的权利转移给另一方的方式。

除提单外的其他运输单据可以完成上述三项作用的前两项,它们无法控制货物在目的地交货或使买方能够通过纸面单据交付给卖方的在途货物。而其他运输方式则将指明在目的地有权接受货物的当事方的名字。为了保证在目的地能够向承运人提取货物,拥有提单是必要的,这使得用电子通信方式取代提单变得尤其困难。

另外,习惯上签发数份正本提单,这时,买方或按其指示向卖方付款的银行,确信所有正本都已由卖方提交(所谓"全套")至关重要。这也是ICC有关跟单信用证的规则(即《跟单信用证统一规则》,在INCOTERMS 2000出版时其版本为UCP 500)的要求。

运输单据不仅必须证明货物已经交付承运人,而且要证明在承运人能够确定的范围内货物被收到时状况良好。在运输单据中任何表示货物并非呈良好状态的批注都将使该单据成为"不清洁"单据,这样的单据根据UCP将无法接受。

尽管提单具有特定的法律性质,但预计在不远的将来其会被电子方式替代。INCOTERMS 1990充分估计了这种可以预期的发展。根据A8条款,若当事方同意以电子方式通信,则可以用具有同等作用的电子信息取代纸面运输单据。这些电子信息可以被直接或经由提供增值服务的第三方传送至有关当事人。提供这种服务的系统,如BOLERO(提单登记组织)的服务,或许需要得到像国际海运委员会电子提单1990年规则第16条、17条和1996年UNCTTRAL电子商务示范法那样的法律规范和原则的进一步支持。

二十、不可转让的运输单据替代提单

近几年,简化单据的做法取得了很大的进展。提单经常被不可转让的运输单据所代替,其类似于海运以外的其他运输方式所使用的运输单据。这些单据被称为"海运单"、"班轮运单"、"货运收据"或其他名称。使用这些不可转让单据也是可以的,但当买方希望通过提交单据给新的买方来出售在途货物时就不行了。为了使出售在途货物成为可能,有必要在CFR和CIF术语下保留卖方提供提单的义务。如果合同当事人知道买方不打算销售在途货物,他们可以达成明确协议来免除卖方提供提单的义务,或者在不需要提供提单时采用CPT和CIP这两种术语。

二十一、对承运人给予指示的权利

在C组术语下，买方支付货款时应确信卖方收款后无权就货物的处置对承运人作出新的指示。有些用于特殊运输方式（空运、公路或铁路）的运输单据通过向买方交付特定的运单正本或两联中的一联，使买方有排除卖方对承运人作出新指示的可能性。但在海运中，用以替代提单的运输单据通常并不包含这种“阻止”功能。国际海事委员会为弥补这一缺陷，引入《海运提单统一规则》，使当事方可以加入一“无处置权”条款，卖方据此放弃指示承运人向其他人或在运单中指定地点之外的地点交货的权利。

二十二、ICC仲裁

若合同当事人愿意在相互间发生争议时提交ICC仲裁，则应在合同（或当没有单独的合同文本时，在达成协议的相互往来函电）中明确清楚地约定采用ICC仲裁。合同中或与之有关的来往函电中订入一种或几种INCOTERMS术语本身并不构成采用ICC仲裁条款。（“与本合同有关的一切争议应根据ICC仲裁规则，由根据该规则指定的一名或几名仲裁员最终裁决。”）

第三节 贸易术语

一、EXW（工厂交货（……指定地点））

“工厂交货（……指定地点）”是指当卖方在其所在地或其他商定的地点（如工厂或仓库等）将货物交给买方处置时，即完成交货，卖方不办理出口清关手续或将货物装上任何运输工具。

该术语是卖方承担责任最小的术语。买方必须承担在卖方所在地受领货物的全部费用和风险。但是，若双方希望在起运时卖方负责装载货物并承担装载货物的全部费用和风险，则须在销售合同中明确写明。在买方不能直接或间接地办理出口手续时，不应使用该术语，而应使用FCA，并应在卖方同意装载货物并承担费用和风险的情况下。在此说明中，A代表卖方义务，B代表买方义务。

1. 提供符合合同规定的货物

A1 卖方必须提供符合销售合同规定的货物和商业发票或有同等作用的电子信息，以及合同可能要求的、证明货物符合合同规定的其他任何凭证。

B1 买方必须按照销售合同规定支付价款。

2. 许可证、其他许可和手续

A2 应买方要求并由其承担风险和费用，在需要办理海关手续时，卖方必须给予买方一切协助，以帮助买方取得为货物出口所需的出口许可证或其他官方许可。

B2 买方必须自担风险和费用，取得任何出口和进口证或其他官方许可，并在需要办理海关手续时，办理货物出口的一切海关手续。

3. 运输合同与保险合同

A3 卖方无义务承担运输合同和保险合同。

B3 买方无义务承担运输合同和保险合同。

4. 交货

A4 卖方必须按照合同约定的日期或期限，或如果未约定日期或期限，按照交付此类货物的惯常时间，在指定的地点将未置于任何运输车辆上的货物交给买方处置。若在指定的地点内未约定具体交货点，或有若干个交货点可使用，则卖方可在交货地点中选择最适合其目的的交货点。

B4 买方必须在卖方按照 A4、A7、B7 条款规定交货时受领货物。

5. 风险转移

A5 除 B5 条款规定者外，卖方必须承担货物灭失或损坏的一切风险，直至已经按照 A4 条款规定交货为止。

B5 买方必须按照下述规定承担货物毁灭或损坏的一切风险。

(1) 自按照 A4 条款规定交货之时起与货物有关的一切风险。

(2) 由于买方未按照 B7 条款规定通知卖方，则自约定的交货日期或交货期限届满之日起，但以该项货物已正式划归合同项下，即清楚地划出或以其他方式确定为合同项下之货物为限。

6. 费用划分

A6 除 B6 条款中规定外，卖方必须支付与货物有关的一切费用，直至已按照 A4 规定交货为止。

B6 买方必须支付：

(1) 自按照 A4 规定交货之时起与货物有关的一切费用；

(2) 在货物交给买方处置而买方未受领货物或未按照 B7 规定给予卖方相应的通知而发生的任何额外费用，但以该项货物已正式划归合同项下，即清楚地划出或以其他方式确定为合同项下的货物为限；

(3) 在需要办理海关手续时，货物进口应交纳的一切关税、税款和其他费用以及办理海关手续的费用。

买方必须偿付卖方按照 A2 规定给予协助时所发生的一切费用。

7. 通知

A7 卖方必须给予买方有关货物将于何时何地交给买方处置的充分通知。

B7 一旦买方有权确定在约定的期限内受领货物的具体时间(或)地点时，买方必须就此给予卖方充分的通知。

8. 交货凭证、运输单据或有同等作用的电子信息

A8 卖方无义务提供相应凭证。

B8 买方必须向卖方提供已受领货物的适当凭证。

9. 查对、包装、标记

A9 卖方必须支付为了货物交给买方处置所需进行的查对费用(如查对货物品质、丈量、过磅、电数的费用)。

卖方必须自付费用提供按照卖方在订立合同前已知的有关该货物运输(如运输方式、目的地)所要求的包装(除非按照相关行业惯例,合同所指货物通常无需包装)。包装应做适当标记。

B9 买方必须支付任何装运前的检验费用,包括出口国有关当局强制进行的检验。

10. 其他义务

A10 应买方要求并由其承担风险和费用,卖方必须给予买方一切协助,以帮助其取得由交货国和(或)原产地国所签发或传送的为买方出口和(或)进口货物可能的要求的、必须要从他国过境所需要的任何单据或有同等作用的电子信息。

应买方要求,卖方必须向买方提供投保所需的信息。

B10 买方必须支付因取得 A10 所述单据或有同等作用的电子信息而发生的一切费用,并偿付卖方给予协助时所发生的费用。

二、FCA(货物承运人(……指定地点))

"货物承运人"是指卖方只要将货物在指定地点交给由买方指定的承运人,并办理了出口清关手续,即完成交货。需要说明的是,交货地点的选择对于在该地点装货和卸货的义务会产生影响。若卖方在其所在地交货,则卖方应负责装货,若买方在其任何其他地点交货,卖方不负责卸货。该术语可用于各种运输方式,包括多式联运。

"承运人"指任何人在运输合同中,承诺通过铁路、公路、空运、海运、内河运输或上述的联合方式履行运输或他人履行运输。若买方指定承运人以外的人领取货物,则当卖方将货物交给此人时,即视为已履行了交货义务。

1. 提供符合合同规定的货物

A1 卖方必须提供符合销售合同规定的货物和商业发票或有同等作用的电子信息,以及合同可能要求的、证明货物符合合同规定的其他任何凭证。

B1 买方必须按照销售合同规定支付价款。

2. 许可证、其他许可和手续

A2 卖方必须自担风险和费用,取得任何出口许可证或其他官方许可,并在需要办理海关手续时办理货物出口所需要的一切海关手续。

B2 买方必须自担风险和费用,取得任何进口证或其他官方许可,并在需要办理海关手

续时办理货物进口和从他国过境的一切海关手续。

3. 运输合同与保险合同

A3 卖方义务

(1)运输合同。卖方无义务承担运输合同。但若买方要求,或者如果是商业惯例而买方未适时给予卖方相反指示,则卖方可按照通常条件订立运输合同,费用和风险由买方承担,在任何一种情况下,卖方都可以拒绝订立运输合同;如果拒绝,则应立即通知买方。

(2)保险合同。卖方无义务承担保险合同。

B3 买方义务

(1)运输合同。买方必须自付费用订立自指定的地点运输货物的合同,卖方按照 A3 订立了运输合同时除外。

(2)保险合同。买方无义务承担保险合同。

4. 交货

A4 卖方必须在指定的交货地点,在约定的交货日期或期限内,将货物交付给买方指定的承运人或其他人,或由卖方按照 A3 选定的承运人或其他人。

交货在以下时候完成:

(1)若指定的地点是卖方所在地,则当货物被装上买方指定的承运人或买方代表提供的其他运输工具时;

(2)若指定的地点不是(1)中指定的地点而是其他任何地点,则当货物在卖方的运输工具上,尚未卸货的承运人或其他人的处置时。

若在指定的地点没有约定具体交货点,且有几个具体交货点可供选择时,卖方可以在指定的地点选择最适合其目的的交货点。

若买方没有明确指示,则卖方可以根据运输方式和(或)货物的数量(或)性质将货物交付运输。

B4 买方必须在卖方按照 A4 规定交货为止受领货物。

5. 风险转移

A5 除 B5 规定外,卖方必须按照规定承担货物毁灭或损坏的一切风险,直至已经按照 A4 规定交货为止。

B5 买方必须按照下述规定承担货物毁灭或损坏的一切风险:

(1)自按照 A4 规定交货时起;

(2)由于买方未按照 A4 规定指定承运人或其他人,或其指定的承运人或其他人未在约定的时间接管货物,或买方未按照 B7 规定给予卖方相应的通知,则自约定的交货日期或交货期限届满之日起,但以该项货物已正式划归合同项下,即清楚地划出或以其他方式确定为合同项下的货物为限。

6. 费用划分

A6 除 B6 规定外,卖方必须支付以下费用:

(1)与货物有关的一切费用,直至已按照 A4 规定交货为止;

(2)在需要办理海关手续时,货物出口应办理的海关手续费用及出口应交纳的一切关税、税款和其他费用。

B6 买方必须支付以下费用:

(1)自按照 A4 规定交货之时起与货物有关的一切费用;

(2)由于买方未能按照 A4 规定指定承运人或其他人、或由于买方指定的人未在约定的时间内接管货物、或由于买方未按照 B7 规定给予卖方相应的通知而发生的任何额外费用,但以该项货物已正式划归合同项下,即清楚地划出或以其他方式确定为合同项下的货物为限;

(3)在需要办理海关手续时,货物进口应交纳的一切关税、税款和其他费用以及办理海关手续的费用及从他国过境的费用。

7. 通知

A7 卖方必须给予买方说明货物已按照 A4 规定交付给承运人的充分通知。若在约定时间内承运人未按照 A4 规定接受货物,则卖方必须相应地通知买方。

B7 买方必须按照 A4 规定指定的人的名称给予卖方充分通知,并根据需要指明运输方式,根据条款指定人,指定货的日期或期限,以及依情况在指定的地点内具体交货。

8. 交货凭证、运输单据或有同等作用的电子信息

A8 卖方必须自担费用向买方提供证明按照 A4 规定交货的通常单据。除非前项所述单据是运输单据,否则,应买方要求并由其承担风险和费用,卖方必须给予买方一切协助,以取得有关运输合同的运输单据(如可转让提单、不可转让海运单、河内运输单据、空运单、铁路托运单、公路托运单或多式联运单据)。

B8 买方必须接受按照 A8 规定提供的交货凭证。

9. 查对、包装、标记

A9 卖方必须支付为按照 A4 交货所需进行的查对费用(如核对货物的品质、丈量、过磅、点数的费用)。

卖方必须自付费用提供按照卖方在订立销售合同前已知的有关该货物运输(如运输方式、目的地)所要求的包装(除非按照相关行业惯例,合同所述货物无需包装发运)。包装应作适当标记。

B9 买方必须支付任何装运前检验的费用,但出口国有关当局强制进行的检验除外。

10. 其他义务

A10 应买方要求并由其承担风险和费用,卖方必须给予买方一切协助,以帮助买方取得由装运地的或原产地国所签发或传送的、为买方进口货物可能要求的或必要时从他国过境所需的任何单据或有同等作用的电子信息(A8 中除外)。应买方要求,卖方必须向买方提供投保所需的信息。

B10 买方必须支付因取得 A10 所述单据或电子信息所发生的一切费用,并偿付卖方按照该条款给予协助以及按照 A3 订立运输合同所发生的费用。

当买方按照 A3 规定要求卖方协助订立运输合同时,买方必须给与卖方相应的指示。

三、FAS(船边交货(……指定装运港))

船边交货是指卖方在指定的装运港将货物交到船边即完成交货。买方必须承担自那时起货物灭失或损失的一切风险。FAS 术语要求卖方办理出口清关手续。

这一点与以前版本的内容相反,以前版本要求买方安排办理出口手续。但是,当事方办理出口手续,需要在销售合同中明确写明。

该术语适用于海运或内河运输。

1. 提供符合合同规定的货物

A1 卖方必须提供符合销售合同规定的货物和商业发票或有同等作用的电子信息,以及合同可能要求的,证明货物符合合同规定的其他任何凭证。

B1 买方必须按照销售合同规定支付价款。

2. 许可证,其他许可和手续

A2 卖方必须自担风险和费用,取得任何出口许可证或其他换防许可,并在需要办理海关出口手续时,办理货物出口所需的一切海关手续。

B2 买方必须自担风险和费用,取得任何进口许可证或其他换防许可,并在需要办理海关出口手续时,办理货物进口和从他国过境所需的一切海关手续。

3. 运输合同和保险合同

A3 卖方无义务承担运输合同和保险合同。

B3 买方义务。

(1)运输合同。买方必须自付费用订立自指定的装运港运输货物的合同。

(2)保险合同。B3 买方无义务承担保险合同。

4. 交货

A4 卖方必须在买方指定的装运港、在买方指定的装货地点、在约定日期或期限内,按照该港的习惯的方式将货物交至买方指定的船边。

B4 买方必须在卖方按照 A4 规定交货时受领货物。

5. 风险转移

A5 除 B5 规定外,卖方必须承担货物灭失或损坏的一切风险,直至已按照 A4 规定交货为止。

B5 买方必须按照下述规定承担货物灭失或损坏的一切风险:

(1)自按照 A4 规定交货时起;

(2)由于买方未按照 B7 规定通知卖方,或其指定的船只未按时到达,或未接受货物,或按照 B7 通知的时间提早停止交货，则自约定的交货日期或期限届满时起，但以该货物已计划拨到合同项下，即明确保留或其他方式确定为合同项下的货物为限。

6. 费用划分

A6 除 B6 规定外，卖方必须支付：

(1) 与货物有关的一切费用，直至已按照 A4 规定交货为止；

(2) 在需要办理海关手续时，货物出口应办理的海关手续费用及应交纳的关税、税款和其他费用。

B6 买方必须支付：

(1) 按照 A4 规定交货时起与货物有关的一切费用；

(2) 由于买方指定的船只未按时到达，或未装载上述货物或比按照 B7 通知的时间提早停止装货，或由于买方未按照 B7 规定给予卖方相应的通知而发生的任何额外费用，但以该货物已正式划归合同项下，即清楚的划出或以其他方式确定为合同项下的货物为限；

(3) 在需要办理海关手续时，货物进口应交纳的一切关税、税款和其他费用，及办理海关手续的费用，以及从他国过境的费用。

7. 通知

A7 卖方必须给予买方说明货物已交至指定的船边的充分通知。

B7 买方必须给予卖方有关船名、装船点和要求交货时间的充分通知。

8. 交货凭证，运输单据或有同等作用的电子信息

A8 卖方必须给予自付费用的买方提供证明按照 A4 规定交货的通常单据，除非前项所述单据是运输单据，否则，应买方要求并由其承担风险和费用，卖方必须给予买方一切协助，以取得运输单据。

如买卖双方约定使用电子方式通信，则前项所述完全可以使用有同等作用的电子数据交换信息代替。

B8 买方必须接受按照 A8 规定提供的交货凭证。

9. 查对、包装、标记

A9 卖方必须支付为按照 A4 交货所需进行的查对费用。

卖方必须自支付费用，提供按照卖方订立销售合同前已知的有关该货物运输所要求的包装，包装应作适当标记。

B9 买方必须支付任何装运前检验的费用，但出口国有关当局强制进行的检验除外。

10. 其他义务

A10 应买方要求并由其承担风险和费用，卖方必须给予买方一切协助，以帮助其取得由装运地国和原产地所签发或传送的，为买方进口货物可能要求的或从他国过境所需的任何单据或有同等作用的电子信息。应买方要求，卖方必须向买方提供投保所需的信息。

B10 买方必须支付因获取 A10 所述单据或有同等作用的电子信息所发生的一切费用，

并偿付卖方因给予协助而发生的费用。

四、FOB(船上交货(……指定装运港))

船上交货是当货物在指定的装运港越过船舷,卖方即完成交货。这意味着买方必须从该点起承担货物灭失或损坏的一切风险。FOB 术语要求卖方办理货物出口清关手续。该术语仅适用于海运或内河运输,如当事各方无意越过船舷交货,则应使用 FCA 术语。

1. 提供符合合同规定的货物

A1 卖方必须提供符合销售合同规定的货物和商业发票或有同等作用的电子信息,以及合同可能要求的、证明货物符合合同规定的其他任何凭证。

B1 买方必须按照销售合同规定支付价款。

2. 许可证、其他许可和手续

A2 卖方必须自担风险和费用,取得任何进口许可证或其他官方许可,并在需要办理海关手续时,办理出口货物所需的一切海关手续。

B2 买方必须自担风险和费用取得任何进口许可证或其他官方许可,并在需要办理海关手续时,办理货物进口和在必要时从他国过境的一切海关手续。

3. 运输合同和保险合同

A3 卖方无义务承担运输合同和保险合同。

B3 买方义务。

(1)运输合同。买方必须自付费用订立从指定的装运港运输货物的合同。

(2)保险合同。买方无义务承担保险公司。

4. 交货

A4 卖方必须在约定日期或期限内,在指定的装运港,按照该港的习惯方式,将货物交至买方指定的船只上。

B4 买方必须在卖方按照 A4 规定交货时受领货物。

5. 风险转移

A5 除 B5 规定外,卖方必须承担货物灭失或损坏的一切风险,直至货物在指定的装运港越过船舷为止。

B5 买方必须按照下述规定承担货物灭失或损坏的一切风险:如果买方未按照 B7 规定通知卖方,或其指定的船只未按时到达,或未接收货物,或比按照 B7 通知的时间提早停止装货,则自约定交货日期或交货期限届满之日起,但以该项货物已正式划归合同项下,即清楚地划出或以其他方式确定为合同项下的货物为限。

6. 费用划分

A6 除 B6 规定外,卖方必须支付:

(1)与货物有关的一切费用,直至货物在指定的装运港越过船舷时为止;

(2)在需要办理海关手续时，货物出口需要办理的海关手续费用及出口时应交纳的一切关税、税款和其他费用。

B6 买方必须支付：

(1)货物在指定的装运港越过船舷之时起与货物有关的一切费用；

(2)由于买方指定的船只未按时到达，或未接收货物，或比按照 B7 通知的时间提早停止装货，或买方未能按照 B7 规定给予卖方相应的通知而发生的一切额外费用，但以该项货物已正式划归合同下，即清楚地划出或以其他方式确定为合同下的货物为限；

(3)在需要办理海关手续时，货物进口应交纳的一切关税、税款和其他费用，以及办理海关手续的费用和货物从他国过境的费用。

7. 通知

A7 卖方必须给予买方说明货物已经按照 A4 规定的充分通知。

B7 买方必须给予卖方有关船名、装船点和要求交货时间的充分通知。

8. 交货凭证、运输单据或有同等作用的电子信息

A8 卖方必须自付费用向买方提供证明货物已按照 A4 规定交货的通常单据。除非前项所述单据是运输单据，否则应买方要求并由其承担风险和费用，卖方必须给予买方一切协助，以取得有关运输合同的运输单据(如可转让提单、不可转让海运单、内河运输单据或多式联运单据)。如买卖双方约定使用电子方式通信，则前项所述单据可以由具有同等作用的电子数据交换(EDI)信息代替。

B8 买方必须接受按照 A8 规定提供的交货凭证。

9. 查对、包装、标记

A9 卖方必须支付为按照 A4 规定交货所需进行的查对费用(如核对货物品质、丈量、过磅、点数的费用)；卖方必须自付费用，提供按照卖方订立销售合同前已知的该货物运输(如运输方式、目的港)所要求的包装(除非按照相关行业惯例，合同所述货物无需包装发运)。包装应作适当标记。

B9 买方必须支付任何装运前检验的费用，但出口国有关当局强制进行的检验除外。

10. 其他义务

A10 应买方要求并由其承担风险和费用，卖方必须给予买方一切协助，以帮助其取得由装运地国和(或)原产地国所签发或传送的、为买方进口货物可能要求的和必要时从他国过境所需的任何单据或有同等作用的电子信息(A8 所列的除外)。

B10 买方必须支付因获取 A10 所述单据或有同等作用的电子信息所发生的一切费用，并偿付卖方因给予协助而发生的费用。

五、CFR（成本加运费(……指定目的港)）

“成本加运费(……指定目的港)”，是指在装运港货物越过船舷卖方即完成交货，卖方

必须支付货物运至目的港所需的运费和费用。但交货后货物灭失或损坏的风险,以及由于各种事件造成的任何额外费用,即由卖方转移到买方。CFR 术语要求卖方办理出口清关手续。该术语仅适用于海运或内河运输。如当事各方无意越过船舷交货,则应使用 CFR 术语。

1. 提供符合合同规定的货物

A1 卖方必须提供符合销售合同规定的货物和商业发票或有同等作用的电子信息,以及合同可能要求的、证明货物符合合同规定的其他任何凭证。

B1 买方必须按照销售合同规定支付价款。

2. 许可证、其他许可和手续

A2 卖方必须自担风险和费用,取得任何出口许可证或其他官方许可,并在需要办理海关手续时办理货物出口所需的一切海关手续。

B2 买方必须自担风险和费用,取得任何进口许可证或其他官方许可,并在需要办理海关手续时办理货物进口及从他国过境的一切海关手续。

3. 运输合同和保险合同

A3 卖方义务。

(1)运输合同。卖方必须自付费用,按照通常条件订立运输合同,经由惯常航线,将货物用通常可供运输合同所指货物类型的海轮(或依情况适合内河运输的船只)运输至指定的目的港。

(2)保险合同。卖方无义务承担保险合同。

B3 买方无义务承担运输合同和保险合同。

4. 交货

A4 卖方必须在装运港、在约定的日期或期限内,将货物交至船上。

B4 买方必须在卖方按照 A4 规定交货时受领货物,并在指定的目的港从承运人处受领货物。

5. 风险转移

A5 除 B5 规定外,卖方必须承担货物灭失或损坏的一切风险,直至货物在装运港越过船舷为止。

B5 买方必须承担货物在装运港越过船舷之后灭失或损坏的一切风险。如买方未按照 B7 规定给予卖方通知,则必须从约定的装运日期或装运期限届满之日起,承担货物灭失或损坏的一切风险,但以该项货物已正式划归合同项下,即已清楚地划出或以其他方式确定为合同项下的货物为限。

6. 费用划分

A6 除 B6 规定外,卖方必须支付:

(1)与货物有关的一切费用,直至已经按照 A4 规定交货为止;

(2)按照 A3 规定所发生的运费和其他一切费用,包括货物的装船费和根据运输合同由卖方支付的,在约定卸货港的任何卸货费;

(3)在需要办理海关手续时,货物出口需要办理的海关手续费用和出口时应交纳的一切关税、税款和其他费用,以及根据运输合同规定,由卖方支付的货物从他国过境的费用。

B6 除 A3 规定外,买方必须支付:

(1)自按照 A4 规定交货时起的一切费用;

(2)货物在运输途中直至到达目的港为止的一切费用,除非这些费用根据运输合同应由卖方支付;

(3)包括驳运费和码头费在内的卸货费,除非这些费用根据运输合同应由卖方支付;

(4)如买方未按照 B7 规定给予卖方通知,则自约定的装运日期或装运期限届满之日起,货物所发生的一切额外费用,但以该项货物已正式划归合同项下,即清楚地划出或以其他方式确定为合同项下的货物为限;

(5)在需要办理海关手续时,货物进口应交纳的一切关税、税款和其他费用,及办理海关手续的费用,以及需要时从他国过境的费用,除非这些费用已包括在运输合同中。

7. 通知

A7 卖方必须给予买方说明货物已按照 A4 规定交货的充分通知,以及要求的任何其他通知,以便买方能够为受领货物采取必要措施。

B7 一旦买方有权决定装运货物的时间和(或)目的港,买方必须就此给予卖方充分通知。

8. 交货凭证,运输单据或有同等作用的电子信息

A8 卖方必须自付费用,毫无迟延地向买方提供表明载往约定目的港的通常运输单据。此单据(如可转让提单,不可转让海运单或内河运输单据)必须载明合同货物,其日期应在约定的装运期内,使买方得以在目的港向承运人提取货物。除非另有约定,否则应使买方得以通过转让单据(可转让提单)或通过通知承运人,向其后手买方出售在途货物。

如此运输单据有数份正本,则应向买方提供全套正本。如买卖双方约定使用电子方式通信,则前项所述单据可以由具有同等作用的电子数据交换(EDI)信息代替。

B8 买方必须接受按照 A8 规定提供的运输单据,但要在该单据符合合同规定的情况下。

9. 查对、包装、标记

A9 卖方必须支付为按照 A4 规定交货所需进行的查对费用(如核对货物品质、丈量、过磅、点数的费用)。卖方必须自付费用提供符合其安排的运输所要求的包装(除非按照相关行业惯例该合同所描述货物无需包装发运)。包装应作适当标记。

B9 买方必须支付任何装运前检验的费用,但出口国有关当局强制进行的检查除外。

10. 其他义务

A10 应买方要求并由其承担风险和费用,卖方必须给予买方一切协助,以帮助买方取得

由装运地国和(或)原产地国所签发或传送的,为买方进口货物可能要求的和必要时从他国过境所需的任何单据或有同等作用的电子信息(A8 所列的除外)。应买方要求,卖方必须向买方提供投保所需的信息。

B10 买方必须支付因获取 A10 所述单据或有同等作用的电子信息所发生的一切费用,并偿付卖方因给予协助而发生的费用。

六、CIF(成本、保险费加运费(……指定目的港))

"成本、保险费加运费"是指在装运港货物越过船舷时卖方完成交货后,卖方必须支付将货物运至指定的目的港所需的运费和费用,但交货后货物灭失或损坏的风险及由于各种事件造成的任何额外费用即由卖方转移到买方。但是,在 CIF 条件下,卖方还必须办理买方货物在运输途中灭失或损坏风险的海运保险,因此,由卖方订立保险合同并支付保险费。买方应注意到,CIF 术语只要求卖方投保最低限度的保险险别。如买方需要更高的保险险别,则需要与卖方明确地达成协议,或者自行作出额外的保险安排。

CIF 术语要求卖方办理货物出口清关手续,该术语仅适用于海运和内河运输。若当事方无意越过船舷交货则应使用 CIP 术语。

1. 提供符合合同规定的货物

A1 卖方必须提供符合销售合同规定的货物和商业发票或有同等作用的电子信息,以及合同可能要求的、证明货物符合合同规定的其他任何凭证。

B1 买方必须按照销售合同规定支付价款。

2. 许可证、其他许可和手续

A2 卖方必须自担风险和费用,取得任何出口许可证或其他官方许可,并在需要办理海关手续时办理货物出口所需的一切海关手续。

B2 买方必须自担风险和费用,取得任何进口许可证或其他官方许可,并在需要办理海关手续时办理货物进口和从他国过境的一切海关手续。

3. 运输合同和保险合同

A3 卖方义务。

(1)运输合同。卖方必须自付费用,按照通常条件发、订立运输合同,经由惯常航线,将货物用通常可供运输合同所指货物类型的海轮(或依情况适合内河运输的船只)装运至指定的目的港。

(2)保险合同。卖方必须按照合同规定,自付费用取得货物保险,并向买方提供保险单或其他保险证据,以使买方或任何其他对货物具有保险利益的人有权直接向保险人索赔。保险合同应与信誉良好的保险人或保险公司订立,在无相反明确协议时,应按照《协会货物保险条款》(伦敦保险人协会)或其他类似条款中的最低险别先投保。保险期限应按照 B5 和 B4 规定。如果能投保,应买方要求,并由其负担费用,卖方加投战争、罢工、暴乱和民变险,如果能投保，最低保险金额应包括合同规定价款另加10%（即110%），并应采用合同货币。

B3 买方无义务承担运输合同和保险合同。

4. 交货

A4 卖方必须在装运港、在约定的日期或期限内，将货物交至船上。

B4 买方必须在卖方已按照A4交货时受领货物，并在指定的目的港从承运人处受领货物。

5. 风险转移

A5 除B5规定外，卖方必须承担货物灭失或损坏的一切风险，直至货物在装运港越过船舷为止。

B5 买方必须承担货物在装运港越过船舷之后灭失或损坏的一切风险。如买方未按照B7规定给予卖方通知，则买方必须从约定的装运日期或装运期限届满之日起，承担货物灭失或损坏的一切风险，但以该项货物已正式划归合同项下，即清楚地划出或以其他方式确定为合同项下的货物为限。

6. 费用划分

A6 除B6规定外，卖方必须支付：

(1)与货物有关的一切费用，直至已经按照A4规定交货为止；

(2)按照A3规定所发生的运费和其他一切费用，包括货物的装船费；

(3)按照A3规定所发生的保险费用；

(4)根据运输合同规定由卖方支付的、在约定的卸货港的任何卸货费用；

(5)在需要办理海关手续时，货物出口所需办理的海关手续费用，及出口应交纳的一切关税、税款和其他费用，以及根据运输合同规定由卖方支付的货物从他国过境的费用。

B6 除A3规定外，买方必须支付：

(1)自按照A4规定交货时起的一切费用；

(2)货物在运输途中直至到达目的港为止的一切费用，除非这些费用根据运输合同应由卖方支付；

(3)包括驳运费和码头费在内的卸货费，除非这些费用根据运输合同规定由卖方支付；

(4)如买方未按照B7规定给予卖方通知，则自约定的装运日期或装运期限届满之日起，货物所发生的一切额外费用，但以该项货物已正式划归合同项下，即清楚地划出或以其他方式确定为合同项下的货物为限；

(5)在需要办理海关手续时，货物进口所应交纳的一切关税、税款和其他费用和办理海关手续的费用，以及在需要时从他国过境的费用，除非这些费用已包括在运输合同中。

7. 通知

A7 卖方必须给予买方说明货物已按照A4规定交货的充分通知，以及要求的任何其他通知，以便买方能够为受领货物而采取通常必要的措施。

B7 一旦买方有权决定装运货物的时间和(或)目的港,买方就必须对此给予卖方充分通知。

8. 交货凭证、运输单据或有同等作用的电子信息

A8 卖方应自付费用、毫无延迟地向买方提供表明载往约定目的港的通常运输单据。此单据(如可转让提单、不可转让海运单或内河运输单据)必须载明合同货物,其日期应在约定的装运期内,使买方得以在目的港向承运人提取货物,并且除非另有约定,否则应使买方能通过转让单据(可转让提单)或通过通知承运人,向其后手买方出售在途货物。如此运输单据有数份正本,则应向买方提供全套正本。

如买卖双方约定使用电子方式通信,则前项所述单据可以由具有同等作用的电子数据交换(EDI)信息代替。

B8 买方必须接受按照 A8 规定提供的运输单据,但要在该单据符合合同规定情况下。

9. 查对、包装、标记

A9 卖方必须支付为按照 A4 交货所需进行的查对费用(如核对货物品质、丈量、过磅、点数的费用)。卖方必须自付费用,提供符合其安排的运输所需求的包装(除非按照相关行业惯例该合同所描述货物无需包装发运)。包装应作适当标记。

B9 买方必须支付任何装运前检验的费用,但出口国有关当局强制进行的检验除外。

10. 其他义务

A10 应买方要求并由其承担风险和费用,卖方必须给予买方一切协助,以帮助买方取得由装运地国和(或)原产地国所签发或传送的、为买方进口货物可能要求的和必要时从他国过境所需的任何单据或有同等作用的电子信息(A8 所列的除外)。应买方要求,卖方必须向买方提供额外投保所需的信息。

B10 买方必须支付因获取 A10 所述单据或有同等作用的电子信息所发生的一切费用,并偿付卖方因给予协助而发生的费用。应卖方要求,买方必须向其提供投保所需的信息。

七、CPT(运费付至(……指定目的地))

"运费付至(……指定目的地)"是指卖方向其指定的承运人交货,但卖方还必须支付将货物运至目的地的运费,亦即买方承担交货之后的一切风险和其他费用。

"承运人"是指任何人,在运输合同中,承诺通过铁路、公路、空运、海运、内河运输或上述运输的联合方式履行运输或由他人履行运输。如果还使用接运的承运人将货物运至约定目的地,则风险自货物交给第一承运人时转移。

CPT 术语要求卖方办理出口清关手续。该术语可适用于各种运输方式,包括多式联运。

1. 提供符合合同规定的货物

A1 卖方必须提供符合销售合同规定的货物和商业发票或有同等作用的电子信息,以及合同可能要求的、证明货物符合合同规定的其他任何凭证。

B1 买方必须按照销售合同规定支付价款。

2. 许可证、其他许可和手续

A2 卖方必须自担风险和费用，取得任何出口许可证或其他官方许可，并在需要办理海关手续时办理货物出口所需的一切海关手续。

B2 买方必须自担风险和费用，取得任何出口许可证或其他官方许可，并在需要办理海关手续时办理货物进口和从他国过境所需的一切海关手续。

3. 运输合同与保险合同

A3 卖方义务。

(1)运输合同。卖方必须自付费用，按照通常条件订立合同，依照惯常路线及习惯方式，将货物运至指定的目的地的约定点。如未约定或按照惯例也无法确定具体交货点，则卖方可在指定的目的地选择最适合其目的的交货点。

(2)保险合同。卖方无义务承担保险合同。

B3 买方无义务承担运输合同和保险合同。

4. 交货

A4 卖方必须向按照 A3 规定订立合同的承运人交货，或如果还有接运的承运人时，则向第一承运人交货，以使货物在约定的日期或期限内运至指定的目的地约定点。

B4 买方必须在卖方按照 A4 规定时受领货物，并在指定目的地从承运人处受领货物。

5. 风险转移

A5 除 B5 规定外，卖方必须承担货物灭失或损坏的一切风险，直至已经按照 A4 规定交货为止。

B5 买方必须承担按照 A4 规定交货时起货物灭失或损坏的一切风险。如买方未按照 B7 规定给予卖方通知，则买方必须从约定的交货日期或交货期限届满之日起，承担货物灭失或损坏的一切风险，但以该项货物已正式划归合同项下，即清楚地划出或以其他方式确定为合同项下的货物为限。

6. 费用划分

A6 除 B6 规定外，卖方必须支付：

(1)直到按照 A4 规定交货时与货物有关的一切费用，以及按照 A3 规定所发生的运费和其他一切费用，包括根据运输合同规定由卖方支付的装货费和在目的地的卸货费；

(2)在需要办理海关手续时，货物出口需要办理的海关手续费用和出口应交纳的一切关税、税款和其他费用，以及根据运输合同规定，由卖方支付的货物从他国过境的费用。

B6 除 A3 规定外，买方必须支付：

(1)自按照 A4 规定交货之时起与货物有关的一切费用；

(2)货物在运输途中直至到达约定目的地为止的一切费用和除非这些费用根据运输合同应由卖方支付；

(3)卸货费,除非这些费用根据运输合同应由卖方支付;

(4)如买方未按照B7规定给予卖方通知,则自约定的装运日期或装运期限届满之日起,货物所发生的一切额外费用,但以该项货物已正式划归合同项下,即清楚地划出或以其他方式确定为合同项的货物为限;

(5)在需要办理海关手续时,货物进口应交纳的一切关税、税款和其他费用和办理海关手续的费用,以及从他国过境的费用,除非这些费用已包括在运输合同中。

7. 通知

A7 卖方必须给予买方说明货物已按照A4规定交货的充分通知,以及要求的任何其他通知,以便买方能够为受领货物而采取必要的措施。

B7 一旦买方有权决定发送货物的时间和(或)目的地,则买方必须就此给予卖方充分通知。

8. 交货凭证、运输单据或有同等作用的电子信息

A8 卖方必须自付费用(如果习惯如此)向买方提供按照A3订立的运输合同所涉及的通常运输单据(如可转让提单、不可转让海运单、内河运输队单据、空运货运单、铁路运单、公路运单或多式联运单据)如买卖双方约定使用电子方式通信,则前项所述单据可以由有同等作用的电子数据交换(EDI)信息代替。

B8 买方必须接受按照A8规定提供的运输单据,但要在该单据符合合同规定情况下。

9. 查对、包装、标记

A9 卖方必须支付为按照A4交货所需进行的查对费用(如核对货物品质、丈量、过磅、点数的费用)。卖方必须自付费用,提供符合其安排的运输所要求的包装(除非按照相关行业惯例合同所述货物无需包装发运)。包装应作适当标记。

B9 买方必须支付任何装运前检验的费用,但出口国有关当局强制进行的检验除外。

10. 其他义务

A10 应买方要求并由其承担风险和费用,卖方必须给予买方一切协助,以帮助买方取得由装运地国和(或)原产地国所签发或传送的、为买方进口货物可能要求和必要时从他国过境所需的任何单据或有同等到作用的电子信息(A8所列的除外)。

应买方要求,卖方必须向买方提供投保所需的信息。

B10 买方必须支付因获取A10所述单据或有同等作用的电子信息所发生的一切费用,并偿付卖方因给予协助而发生的费用。

八、CIP(运费和保险费付至(……指定目的地))

“运费和保险费付至(……指定目的地)”是指卖方向其指定的承运人交货,但卖方还必须支付将货物运至目的地的运费,亦即买方承担卖方交货之后的一切风险和额外费用。但是,按照CIP术语,卖方还必须办理买方货物在运输途中灭失或损坏风险的保险,因此,由卖

方订立保险合同并支付保险费。

买方应注意到,CIP 术语只要求卖方投保最低限度的保险险别。如买方需要更高的保险险别,则需要与卖方明确达成协议,或者自行作出额外的保险安排。

“承运人“指任何人在运输合同中,承诺通过铁路、公路、空运、海运、内河运输或上述运输的联合方式履行运输或由他人履行运输。如果还使用接运的承运人将货物运至约定目的地,则风险自货物交给第一承运人时转移。

CIP 术语要求卖方办理出口清关手续。该术语可适用于各种运输方式,包括多式联运。

1. 提供符合合同规定的货物

A1 卖方必须提供符合销售合同规定的货物和商业发票或有同等作用的电子信息,以及合同可能要求的、证明货物符合规定的其他任何凭证。

B1 买方必须按照销售合同规定支付价款。

2. 许可证、其他许可和手续

A2 卖方必须自担风险和费用,取得任何出口许可证或其他官方许可,并在需要办理海关手续时办理货物出口所需的一切海关手续。

B2 买方必须自担风险和费用,取得任何进口许可证或其他官方许可,并在需要办理海关手续时办理货物进口和从他国过境所需的一切海关手续。

3. 运输合同和保险合同

A3 卖方义务。

(1)运输合同。卖方必须自负费用,按照通常条件订立运输合同,依通常路线及习惯方式,将货物运至指定目的地的约定点。若未约定或按照惯例也不能确定具体交货点,则卖方可在指定的目的地选择最适合其目的的交货点。

(2)保险合同。卖方必须按照合同规定,自付费用取得货物保险,并向买方提供保险单或其他保险证据,以使买方或其他对货物具有保险利益的人有权直接向保险人索赔。保险合同应与信誉良好的保险人或保险公司订立,在无相反明示协约时,应按照《协会货物保险条款》(伦敦保险人协会)或其他类似条款中的最低限度保险险别投保。保险期应按照 B5 和 B4 规定。如果能投保应买方要求,并由其负担费用,卖方应加投战争、罢工、暴乱和民变险。最低保险金额应包括合同规定价款另加 10%(即 110%),并应采取合同货币。

B3 买方无义务承担运输合同和保险合同。

4. 交货

A4 卖方必须在约定日期或期限内向按照 A3 规定订立合同的承运人交货,或如有接运的承运人时,向第一承运人交货,以使货物运至指定目的地的约定点。

B4 买方必须在卖方按照 A4 规定交货时受领货物,并在指定的目的地从承运人处受领货物。

5. 风险转移

A5 除 B5 规定外,卖方必须承担货物灭失或损坏的一切风险,直至已经按照 A4 规定交货为止。

B5 买方必须承担按照 A4 规定交货后货物灭失或损坏的一切风险。买方如未按照 B7 规定通知卖方，则必须从约定的交货日期或交货期限届满之日起，承担货物灭失或损坏的一切风险，但以该项货物已正式划归合同项下，即清楚地划出或以其他方式确定为合同项下的货物为限。

6. 费用划分

A6 除 B6 规定外，卖方必须支付：

(1)与货物有关的一切费用，直至已经按照 A4 规定交货为止，以及按照 A3 规定所发生的运费和其他一切费用，包括装船费和根据运输合同应由卖方支付的目的地的卸货费；

(2)按照 A3 发生的保险费用；

(3)在需要办理海关手续时，货物出口需要办理的海关手续费用，以及根据运输合同由卖方支付的货物从他国过境的费用。

B6 除 A3 规定外，买方必须支付：

(1)自按照 A4 规定交货之时起与货物有关的一切费用；

(2)货物在运输途中直至到达约定目的地为止的一切费用，除非这些费用根据运输合同应由卖方支付；

(3)卸货费，除非这些费用根据运输合同应由买方支付；

(4)如买方未按照 B7 规定给予卖方通知，则自约定的装运日期或装运期限届满之日起，货物所发生的一切额外费用，但以该项货物已正式划归合同项下，即清楚地划出或以其他方式确定为合同项下的货物为限；

(5)在需要办理海关手续时，货物进口应交纳的一切关税、税款和其他费用和办理海关手续的费用，以及从他国过境的费用，除非这些费用已包括在运输合同中。

7. 通知

A7 卖方必须给予买方说明货物以按照 A4 规定交货的充分通知，以及要求的任何其他通知，以便买方能够为受领货物而采取通常必要的措施。

B7 一旦买方有权决定发运货物的时间和(或)目的地，则买方必须就此给予卖方充分通知。

8. 交货凭证、运输单据或有同等作用的电子信息

A8 卖方必须自付费用(如果习惯如此)向买方提供按照 A3 订立的运输合同所涉及的通常运输单据(如可转让提单、不可转让海运单、内河运输单据、空运货运单、铁路运单、公路运单或多式联运单据)。如买卖双方约定使用电子方式通信，则前项所述单据可以由具有同等作用的电子数据交换(EDI)信息代替。

B8 买方必须接受 A8 规定提供的运输单据，但要在该单据符合合同规定的情况下。

9. 查对、包装、标记

A9 卖方必须支付为按照 A4 规定交货所需进行的查对费用(如核对货物品质、丈量、过

磅、点数的费用)。卖方必须自付费用,提供符合其安排的运输所要求的包装(除非按照相关行业惯例该合同所描述的货物无需包装发运)。包装应作适当标记。

B9 买方必须支付任何装运前检验的费用,但出口国有关当局强制进行的检验除外。

10. 其他业务

A10 应买方要求并由其承担风险和费用,卖方必须给予买方一切协议,以帮助买方取得由装运地国和(或)原产地国所签发或传送的、为买方进口货物可能要求的和从他国过境所需的任何单据或同等作用的电子信息(A8 所列的除外)。应买方要求,卖方必须向买方提供办理任何额外投保所需的信息。

B10 买方必须支付因获取 A10 所述单据或有同等作用的电子信息所发生的一切费用,并偿付卖方因给予协助而发生的费用。应买方要求,买方必须向卖方提供办理投保所需的信息。

九、DAF(边境交货(……指定地点))

"边境交货(……指定地点)"是指当卖方在边境的指定地点和具体交货点,在毗邻国家海关边界前,将仍处于交货的运输工具上尚未卸下的货物交给买方处置,办妥货物出口清关手续时,即完成交货。"边境"一词可用于任何边境,包括出口国边境。用指定的地点和具体交货点来准确界定所指定边境是极为重要的。但是,如当事各方希望卖方负责从交货运输工具上卸货并承担卸货风险和费用,则应在销售合同中明确写明。

该术语可用于陆地边界交货的各种运输方式,当在目的港船上或码头交货时,应使用 DES 或 DEQ 术语。

1. 提供符合合同规定的货物

A1 卖方必须提供符合销售合同规定的货物和商业发票或有同等作用的电子信息,以及合同可能要求的、证明货物符合合同规定的其他任何凭证。

B1 买方必须按照销售合同规定支付价款。

2. 许可证、其他许可和手续

A2 卖方必须自担风险和费用,取得任何出口许可证,或其他官方许可和文件中的任意一个,以便交给卖方处置,并在需要办理海关手续时办理货物出口并运至指定的边境交货地点以及从他国过境所需的一切海关手续。

B2 买方必须自担风险和费用,取得任何进口许可证,或其他官方许可和文件中的任意一个,并在需要办理海关手续时办理货物进口所需的一切海关手续,以及后继运输所需的一切海关手续。

3. 运输合同与保险合同

A3 卖方义务。

(1)运输合同。卖方必须自付费用订立运输合同,将货物运至边境指定的交货地点和具体交货地点。如未约定或按照惯例也无法确定边境指定的交货地的具体交货点，则卖方可在制定的交货地选择最适合其目的的交货点；若买方要求，卖方可以同意按照通常条件订立合同，由买方负担风险和费用，将货物从边境指定的地点继续运至由买方指定的进口国的最终目的地。卖方可以拒绝订立此合同，如果这样，应迅速通知买方。

(2)保险合同。卖方无义务承担保险合同。

B3 买方无义务承担运输合同和保险合同。

4. 交货

A4 卖方必须在约定日期或期限内，在边境的指定交货地点，将仍处于交货工具上尚未卸下的货物交给买方处置。

B4 买方必须在卖方按照 A4 规定交货时受领货物。

5. 风险转移

A5 除 B5 规定外，卖方必须承担货物灭失或损毁的一切风险，直至已经按照 A4 规定交货为止。

B5 买方必须承担按照 A4 规定交货之时起货物灭失或损坏的一切风险。如买方未按照 B7 规定通知卖方，则必须从约定的交货日期或交货期限届满之日起，承担货物灭失或损坏的一切风险，但以该项货物已正式划归合同项下，即清楚地划出或以其他方式确定为合同项下的货物为限。

6. 费用划分

A6 除 B6 规定外，卖方必须支付：

(1)按照 A3 规定发生的费用，及以后与货物有关的一切费用，直至已经按照 A4 规定交货为止；

(2)在需要办理海关手续时，货物出口需要办理的海关手续费用，及货物出口时应缴纳的一切关税、税款和其他费用，以及按照 A4 规定交货之前从他国过境的费用。

B6 买方必须支付：

(1)自按照 A4 规定交货时起与货物有关的一切费用，包括在边境的交货地点将货物从交货运输工具上卸下以受领货物的卸货费；

(2)如按照 A4 规定交货而买方未受领货物或未按照 B7 规定给予卖方通知，因此发生的一切额外费用，但以该项货物已正式划归合同项下，即清楚地划出或以其他方式确定为合同项下的货物为限；

(3)在需要办理海关手续时，办理海关手续的费用及货物进口时应缴纳的一切关税、税款和其他费用，以及办理后继续运输的费用。

7. 通知

A7 卖方必须给予买方有关按照 A4 规定指定的船只预期到达时间的充分通知，以及要求的任何其他通知，以便买方能够为受领货物而采取必要的措施。

B7 一旦买方有权决定在约定期限内的时间和(或)在指定的目的港受领货物的点,买方就必须就此给予卖方充分通知。

8. 交货凭证、运输单据或有同等作用的电子信息

A8 卖方义务。

(1)卖方必须自付费用向买方提供说明货物以按照 A3 规定交付至边境指定的地点的通常单据或其他凭证。

(2)如当事各方同意按照 A3 规定越过边境后继续运输,卖方必须根据买方的要求,并由买方负担风险和费用,向其提供费用通常发生在发运国取得的联运单据,订明按照惯常条件从该国的发运地发送至买方指定的进口国最终目的地。如买卖双方约定以电子方式通信,则前项所述单据可以由具有同等作用的电子数据交换(EDI)信息代替。

B8 买方必须接受按照 A8 规定提供的运输单据和(或)其他交货凭证。

9. 查对、包装、标记

A9 卖方必须支付为按照 A4 规定交货所需进行的查对费用(如核对货物品质、丈量、过磅、点数的费用)。卖方必须自付费用提供包装(除非约定或按照相关行业惯例,合同所指货物通常无须包装即可交货),此项包装应符合卖方订立销售合同前一直使用的运输方式(如运输方式、目的地)要求,适合在边境交货及接运运输。包装应作适当标记。

B9 买方必须支付任何装运前检验的费用,但出口国有关当局强制进行的检验除外。

10. 其他义务。

A10 应买方要求由其承担风险和费用,卖方必须给予买方一切协助,以帮助买方取得由装运地国和(或)原产国所签发或传送的、为买方进出口货物可能要求的、必要时从他国过境所需的任何单据或有同等作用的电子信息(A8 所列的除外)。应买方要求卖方必须向买方提供投保所需的信息。

B10 买方必须支付因获取 A10 所述单据或有同等作用的电子信息所发生的一切费用,并偿付卖方因此给予协助而发生的费用。必要时,按照 A3 规定,应卖方要求,买方必须负担风险和费用,向卖方提供外汇管制许可、许可证件、其他单据或经认证的副本,或提供取得联运单据所需的进口国最终目的地地址或 A8 中所指的任何其他单据。

十、DES(目的港船上交货(……制定目的港))

"目的港船上交货(……制定目的港)"是指在制定的目的港,货物在船上交给买方处置,但不办理货物进口清关手续,卖方即完成交货。买方必须承担货物运至指定的目的港卸货前的一切风险费用。如果当时各方希望卖方承担卸货的风险费用,则应使用 DEQ 术语。只有当货物经由海运或内河运输或多式联运在目的港船上交货时,才能使用该术语。

1. 提供符合合同规定的货物

A1 卖方必须提供符合销售合同规定的货物和商业发票或有同等作用的电子信息,以及

合同可能要求的、证明货物符合合同规定的其他凭证。

B1 买方必须按照销售合同规定支付价款。

2. 许可证、其他许可和手续

A2 卖方必须自担风险和费用，取得任何出口许可证或其他官方许可或其他文件，并在需要办理海关手续时办理货物出口和从他国过境所需的一切海关手续。

B2 买方必须自担风险和费用，取得任何进口许可证或其他官方许可，并在需要办理海关手续时办理货物进口所需的一切海关手续。

3. 运输合同和保险合同

A3 卖方义务。

(1)运输合同。卖方必须自付费用订立运输合同，将货物运至指定目的港的指定的点。如未约定或按照惯例也无法确定具体交货点，则卖方可在指定的目的港选择最合适其目的的交货点。

(2)保险合同。卖方无义务承担保险合同。

B3 买方无义务承担运输合同和保险合同。

4. 交货

A4 卖方必须在约定的日期或期限内，在指定的目的港按照 A3 指定的卸货点，将货物在船上交给买方处置，以便货物能够由适合该项货物特点的卸货设备从船上卸下。

B4 买方必须在卖方按照 A4 规定交货时受领货物。

5. 风险转移

A5 除 B5 规定外，卖方必须承担货物灭失或损坏的一切风险，直至已经按照 A4 规定交货为止。

B5 买方必须承担按照 A4 规定交货时起货物灭失或损坏的一切风险。如买方未按照 B7 规定通知卖方，则必须自约定的交货日期或交货期限届满之日起，承担货物灭失或损坏的一切风险，但以该项货物已正式划归合同项下，即清楚地划出或以其他方式确定为合同项下的货物为限。

6. 费用划分

A6 除 B6 规定外，卖方必须支付：

(1)按照 A3 规定发生的费用，以及按照 A4 规定交货前与货物有关的一切费用；

(2)在需要办理海关手续时，货物出口需要办理的海关手续费用和货物出口时应交纳的一切关税、税款和其他费用，以及按照 A4 规定交货前从他国过境的费用。

B6 买方必须支付：

(1)自按照 A4 规定交货时起与货物有关的一切费用，包括为受领货物所需要的将货物从船上卸下的卸货费；

(2)如货物按照 A4 规定交给买方处置而未受领货物，或未按照 B7 规定通知卖方，由此

而发生的一切额外费用,但以该项货物已正式划归合同项下,即清楚地划出或以其他方式确定为合同项下的货物为限;

(3)在需要办理海关手续时,货物进口所需办理的海关手续费用及应交的一切关税、税款和其他费用。

7. 通知

A7 卖方必须给予买方有关按照 A4 规定指定的船只预期到达时间的充分通知,以及要求的任何其他通知,以便买方能够为受领货物而采取必要的措施。

B7 一旦买方有权决定在约定期限内的时间和(或)在指定的目的港受领货物的点,买方就必须就此给予卖方充分通知。

8. 交货凭证、运输单据或有同等作用的电子信息

A8 卖方必须自付费用向买方提供提货单和(或)通常的运输单据(如可转让提单、不可转让海运单、内河运输单据或多式联运单据),以使买方得以在目的港从承运人处受领货物。如买卖双方约定以电子方式通信,则前项所述单据可以由具有同等作用的电子数据交换(EDI)信息代替。

B8 买方必须接受按照 A8 规定提供的提货单或运输单据。

9. 查对、包装、标记

A9 卖方必须支付为按照 A4 规定交货所需进行的查对费用(如核对货物品质、丈量、过磅、点数的费用)。卖方必须自付费用提供为交付货物所要求的包装(除非按照相关行业惯例,合同所指货物无需包装即可交货)。包装应作适当标记。

B9 买方必须支付任何装运前检验的费用,但出口国有关当局强制进行的检验除外。

10. 其他义务

A10 应买方要求并由其承担风险和费用,卖方必须给予买方一切协助,以帮助买方取得由装运地国和(或)原产地国所签发或传送的、为买方进口货物可能要求的任何单据或有同等作用的电子信息(A8 所列的除外)。应买方要求,卖方必须向买方提供投保所需的信息。

B10 买方必须支付因获取 A10 所述单据或有同等作用的电子信息所发生的一切费用,并偿付卖方因给予协助而发生的费用。

十一、DEQ(目的港码头交货(……指定目的港))

"目的港码头交货(……指定目的港)"是指卖方在指定目的港码头将货物交给买方处置,不办理进口清关手续,即完成交货。卖方应承担将货物运至指定的目的港并卸至码头的一切风险和费用。

DEQ 术语要求买方办理进口清关手续并在进口时支付一切办理海关手续的费用、关税、税款和其他费用。这和以前的版本相反,以前版本要求卖方办理进口清关手续。如果当事方希望卖方负担全部或部分进口时交纳的费用,则应在销售合同中明确写明。只有当

货物经由海运、内河运输或多式联运且在目的港码头卸货时，才能使用该术语。但是，如果当事方希望卖方负担将货物从码头运至港口以内或以外的其他点（仓库、终点站、运输站等）的义务时，则应使用 DDU 或 DDP 术语。

1. 提供符合合同规定的货物

A1 卖方必须提供符合销售合同规定的货物和商业发票或有同等作用的电子信息，以及合同可能要求的、证明货物符合合同规定的其他任何凭证。

B1 买方必须按照销售合同规定支付价款。

2. 许可证、其他许可和手续

A2 卖方必须自担风险和费用，取得任何出口许可证或其他官方许可或文件，并在需要办理海关手续时办理货物出口和从其他国过境所需的一切海关手续。

B2 买方必须自担风险和费用，取得任何进口许可证或其他官方许可，并在需要办理海关手续时办理货物进口所需的一切海关手续。

3. 运输合同和保险合同

A3 卖方义务。

(1)运输合同。卖方必须自付费用订立运输合同，将货物运到指定的目的港的指定码头。如未约定或按照惯例也无法确定目的码头，则卖方可在目的港选择最适合其的码头交货。

(2)保险合同。卖方无义务承担保险合同。

B3 买方无义务承担运输合同和保险公司。

4. 交货

A4 卖方必须在约定的日期或期限内，在按照 A3 规定的指定目的港码头上将货物交给买方处置。

B4 买方必须在卖方按照 A4 规定交货时受领货物。

5. 风险转移

A5 除 B5 规定外，卖方必须承担货物灭失或损坏的一切风险，甚至已经按照 A4 规定交货为止。

B5 买方必须承担按照 A4 规定交货时起货物灭失或损坏的一切风险。如果买方未按照 B7 规定通知卖方，则必须自约定的交货日期或交货期届满之日起，承担货物灭失或损坏的一切风险，但以该项货物已正式划归合同项下，即清楚地划出或以其他方式确定为合同项下的货物为限。

6. 费用划分

A6 除 B6 规定者外，卖方必须支付：

(1)按照 A3 规定发生的费用，以及按照 A4 规定在目的港码头交货之前与货物有关的一切费用；

(2)在需要办理海关手续时,货物出口需要办理的海关手续费用和货物出口时应交纳的一切关税、税款和其他费用,以及交货前货物从它国过境的费用。

B6 买方必须支付:

(1)自按照 A4 规定交货时起,与货物有关的一切费用,包括在港口搬运货物以便继续运输或存入仓库或中转站的一切费用;

(2)如货物按照 A4 规定交给买方处置而未受领货物,或未按照 B7 规定通知卖方,则此而引发的一切额外费用,但以该项货物已正式划归合同项下的货物为限;

(3)在需要办理海关手续时,货物进口所需办理的海关手续费用以及应交纳的一切关税、税款和其他费用,以及继续运输的费用。

7. 通知

A7 卖方必须给予买方说明按照 A4 规定的指定船只预期到达时间的充分通知,以及要求的其他任何通知,以便买方能够为受领货物而采取必要的措施。

B7 一旦买方有权决定在约定期限内的时间和(或)在指定的目的港受领货物的点,买方必须就此给予卖方充分通知。

8. 运输单据或有同等作用的电子信息

A7 卖方必须自付费用向买方提供提货单或通常运输单据,如可转让提单、不可转让海运单、内河运输、单据或多式联运输单据,以使买方得以提货,从码头上搬走。

如买卖双方约定以电子方式通信,则前项所述单据可以由具有同等作用的电子数据交换(EDI)信息代替。

B8 买方必须接受按照 A4 规定提供的提货单或运输单据。

9. 查对、包装、标记

A9 卖方必须支付为按照 A4 规定提供的交货所需进行的查对费用(如核对货物品质、丈量、过磅、点数的费用)。卖方必须自付费用提供交货所需要的包装(除非按照相关行业惯例,合同所指货物无须包装即可交货)。包装应作适当标记。

B9 买方必须支付任何装运前检验的费用,但出口国有关当局强制进行的检验除外。

10. 其他义务

A10 应买方要求并由其承担风险和费用,卖方必须给予买方一定协助,以帮助买方取得由装运地国和(或)原产地国所签发或传送的、为买方进口货物所需的任何单据或有同等作用的电子信息(A8 所列的除外)。应买方要求,卖方必须向买方提供投保所需的信息。

B10 买方必须支付因获取 A10 所述单据或有同等作用的电子信息所发生的一切费用,并偿付卖方因给予协助而发生的费用。

十二、DDU(未完税交货(……指定目的地))

“未完税交货(……指定目的地)”是指卖方在指定的目的地将货物交给买方,不办理进口手续,也不从交货的运输工具上将货物卸下,即完成交货。卖方应承担货物运至指定目的地的一切费用和风险,不包括在办理海关手续时在目的地国进口应交纳的任何"税费"(包括办理海关手续的责任和风险,以及交纳手续费、关税、税款和其他费用)。买方必须承担此项"税费"和因其未能及时办理货物进口清关手续而引起的费用和风险。但是如果双方希望卖方办理海关手续并承担由此而发生的费用和风险,以及在货物进口时应支付的一些费用,则应在销售合同中明确写明。

该术语适用于各种运输方式,但在货物目的港船上或码头交货时,应使用 DES 或 DEQ 术语。

1. 提供符合合同规定的货物

A1 卖方必须提供符合销售合同规定的货物和商业发票或有同等作用的电子信息,以及合同可能要求的、证明货物符合合同规定的其他凭证。

B1 买方必须按照销售合同规定支付价款。

2. 许可证、其他许可和手续

A2 卖方必须自担风险和费用,取得任何出口许可证或其他官方许可及文件,并在需要办理海关手续时办理货物出口及他国过境所需的一切海关手续。

B2 买方必须自担风险和费用,以取得任何进口许可证或其他官方许可及文件,并在需要办理海关手续时办理货物进口所需的一切海关手续。

3. 运输合同与保险合同

A3 卖方义务。

(1)运输合同与保险合同。卖方必须自付费用订立运输合同,将货物运至指定的目的地。如未约定或按照惯例也无法确定具体交货点,则卖方可在目的地选择最合适其目的的交货点。

(2)保险合同。卖方无义务承担保险合同。

B3 买方无义务承担运输合同和保险合同。

4. 交货

A4 卖方必须在约定日期或交货期限内,在指定的目的地将在交货的运输工具上尚未卸下的货物交给买方或买方指定的其他人处置。

B4 买方必须在卖方按照 A4 规定交货时受领货物。

5. 风险转移

A5 除 B5 规定者外,卖方必须承担货物灭失或损坏的一切风险,直至已经按照 A4 规定交货为止。

B5 买方必须承担按照 A4 规定交货时起货物灭失或损坏的一切风险。如买方没有履行 B2 规定的义务,则必须承担由此发生的货物灭失或损坏的一切额外风险;如买方未按照 B7 规定通知卖方,则必须自约定的交货日期或交货期限届满之日起,承担货物灭失或损坏的一切风险,但以该项货物已正式划归合同项下,即清楚地划出或以其他方式规定为合同项下的货物为限。

6. 费用划分

A6 除 B6 规定外,卖方必须支付:

(1)按照 A3 规定发生的费用,以及按照 A4 规定交货之前与货物有关的一切费用;

(2)在需要办理海关手续时,货物出口需要办理的海关手续费用和货物出口时应交纳的一切关税、税款和其他费用,以及交货前货物从他国过境的费用。

B6 买方必须支付:

(1)自按照 A4 规定交货时起与货物有关的一切费用;

(2)当买方未履行 B2 规定的义务,或未按照 B7 规定作出通知时,由此而发生的一切额外费用,但以该项货物已正式划归合同项下,即清楚地划出或以其他方式规定为合同项下的货物为限;

(3)在需要办理海关手续时,货物进口时需要办理的海关手续费用及应交纳的一切关税、税款和其他费用。

7. 通知

A7 卖方必须给予买方有关发运货物的充分通知,以及要求的任何其他通知,以便买方能够为受领货物而采取必要的措施。

B7 一旦买方有权决定在约定期限内的时间和(或)在指定的目的地受领货物的点,买方就必须对此给予卖方充分通知。

8. 交货凭证、运输单据或有同等作用的电子信息

A8 卖方必须自付费用向买方提供按照 A4 或 B4 规定受领货物可能需要的提货单和(或)通常运输单据(如可转让提单、不可转让海运单、内河运输单据、空运单、铁路运单、公路运单或多式联运单据)。如买卖双方约定以电子方式通信,则前项所述单据可由具有同等作用的电子数据交换(EDI)信息代替。

B8 买方必须接受按照 A8 规定提供的适当的提货单或运输单据。

9. 查对、包装、标记

A9 卖方必须支付为按照 A4 规定交货所需要进行的查对费用(如核对货物品质、质量过磅、点数的费用)。卖方必须自付费用提供所需要的包装(除非按照相关行业惯例,合同所指货物无需包装即可交货)。包装应作适当标记。

B9 买方必须支付任何装运前检验的费用,但出口国有关当局强制进行的检验除外。

10. 其他义务

A10 应买方要求并由其承担风险和费用,卖方必须给予买方一切协助,以帮助买方取得由装运地国和(或)原产地国所签发或传送的、为买方进口货物可能要求的任何单据或有同等作用的电子信息(A8 所列的除外)。

应买方要求,卖方必须向买方提供投保所需的信息。

B10 买方必须支付因获取 A10 所述单据或同等作用的电子信息所发生的一切费用,并偿付卖方因给予协助而发生的费用。

十三、DDP(完税后交货(……指定目的地))

"完税后交货(……指定目的地)"是指卖方在指定的目的地办理完进口清关手续,将在交货运输工具上尚未卸下的货物交与买方,即完成交货。卖方必须承担将货物运至目的地的一切风险和费用,包括在需要办理海关手续时在目的地应交纳的任何进口"税费"(包括办理一切海关手续、交纳海关手续费、关税、税款和其他费用的责任和风险)。

EXW 术语下卖方承担最小责任,而 DDP 术语下卖方承担最大责任。若当事方希望将任何进口时所要支付的一些费用(如增值税)从卖方的义务中排除,则应在销售合同中明确写明。

若卖方不能直接或间接地取得进口许可证,则不应使用此术语;若当事方希望买方承担进口的风险和费用,则应使用 DDU 术语。

DDP 术语可用于所有运输方式,但当货物在目的港船上或码头交货时应使用 DES 或 DEQ 术语。

1. 提供符合合同规定的货物

A1 卖方必须提供符合销售合同规定的货物和商业发票或有同等作用的电子信息,以及合同可能要求的、证明货物符合合同规定的其他凭证。

B1 买方必须按照销售合同规定支付价款。

2. 许可证、其他许可和手续

A2 卖方必须自担风险和费用,取得任何出口许可证或其他官方许可及文件,并在需要办理海关手续时办理货物的出口、进口及从他国过境所需的一切海关手续。

B2 应卖方要求,并由其负担风险和费用时,买方必须给予卖方一些协助,帮助卖方在需要办理海关手续时取得货物进口所需的进口许可证或其他官方许可。

3. 运输合同与保险合同

A3 卖方义务。

(1)运输合同。卖方必须自付费用订立运输合同,将货物运至指定的目的地。如未约定或按照惯例也无法确定具体交货点,则卖方可在目的地选择最合适其目的的交货点。

(2)保险合同。卖方无义务承担保险合同。

B3 买方无义务承担运输合同和保险合同。

4. 交货

A4 卖方必须在约定日期或交货期限内,在指定的目的地将在交货的运输工具上尚未卸下的货物交给买方或买方指定的其他人处置。

B4 买方必须在卖方按照 A4 规定交货时受领货物。

5. 风险转移

A5 除 B5 规定外，卖方必须承担货物灭失或损坏的一切风险，直至已经按照 A4 规定交货为止。

B5 买方必须承担按照 A4 规定交货时起货物灭失或损坏的一切风险。如买方没有履行 B2 规定的义务，则必须承担由此发生的货物灭失或损坏的一切额外风险；如买方未按照 B7 规定通知卖方，则必须自约定的交货日期或交货期限届满之日起，承担货物灭失或损坏的一切风险，但以该项货物已正式划归合同项下，即清楚地划出或以其他方式规定为合同项下的货物为限。

6. 费用划分

A6 除 B6 规定者外，卖方必须支付：

(1) 按照 A3 规定发生的费用，以及按照 A4 规定交货之前与货物有关的一切费用；

(2) 在需要办理海关手续时，货物出口需要办理的海关手续费用，货物出口时应交纳的一切关税、税款和其他费用，以及交货前货物从他国过境的费用。

B6 买方必须支付：

(1) 自按照 A4 规定交货时起与货物有关的一切费用；

(2) 如买方未履行 B2 规定的义务，或未按照 B7 规定作出通知，则由此而发生的一切额外费用，但以该项货物已正式划归合同项下，即清楚地划出或以其他方式规定为合同项下的货物为限。

7. 通知

A7 卖方必须给予买方有关发运货物的充分通知和要求的任何其他通知，以便买方能够为受领货物而采取措施。

B7 一旦买方有权决定在约定期限内的时间和(或)在指定的目的地受领货物的点，买方必须就此给予卖方充分的通知。

8. 交货凭证、运输单据或有同等作用的电子信息

A8 卖方必须自付费用向买方提供按照 A4 或 B4 规定受领货物可能需要的提货单和(或)通常运输单据(如可转让提单、不可转让海运单、内河运输单据、空运单、铁路运单、公路运单或多式联运单据)，以使买方按照 A4 或 B4 规定受领货物。如买卖双方约定以电子方式通信，则前项所述单据可由具有同等作用的电子数据交换(EDI)信息代替。

B8 买方必须接受按照 A8 规定提供的适当的提货单或运输单据。

9. 查对、包装、标记

A9 卖方必须支付为按照 A4 规定交货所需要进行的查对费用(如核对货物品质、质量过磅、点数的费用)。卖方必须自付费用提供货物需要的包装(除非按照相关行业惯例，合同所指货物无需包装即可交货)。包装应作适当标记。

B9 买方必须支付任何装运前检验的费用,但出口国有关当局强制进行的检验除外。

10. 其他义务

A10 卖方必须支付为获取有同等作用的电子信息(A8 所列的除外)所发生的一些费用,并偿付买方因给予协助而发生的费用。应买方要求,卖方必须向买方提供投保所需的信息。

B10 应卖方要求并由其承担风险和费用时,买方必须给予卖方一切协助,以帮助卖方取得为按照本规则将货物交付买方需要的,由进口国签发或传递的任何单据或有同等作用的电子信息。

第二章　国际货物销售合同的基本条款

第一节　商品的品名与品质

一、商品的品名

国际贸易同国内贸易有着很大差异。在国际贸易中，看货成交的情况较少，交易双方商订合同时，往往很少见到具体商品，一般只是凭借对买卖商品的必要的描述来确定交易标的，因此在合同中列明商品的名称就成为不可缺少的一项主要贸易条件。按照有关的法律和惯例，对交易标的物的描述是构成商品说明的一个主要组成部分，也是买卖双方交接货物的一项基本依据，它关系到买卖双方的权利和义务。若卖方交付的货物不符合约定的品名或说明，买方有权提出损害赔偿要求，甚至可以拒收货物或撤销合同。由此可见，列明合同中商品的具体名称，具有重要的法律和实践意义。品名条款的规定取决于成交商品的品种和特点，它并无统一格式，可由交易双方酌情商定。合同中的品名条款通常比较简单，一般只是在“商品名称”或品名的标题下，列明交易双方成交商品的名称。有时为了省略，也可不加标题，只在合同的开头部分列明交易双方同意买卖某种商品的文句。品名条款的规定，还取决于成交商品的品种和特点。就一般商品来说，有时只要列明商品的名称即可，但有的商品往往具有不同的品种、等级和型号，因此，为了明确起见，有时也把有关具体品种、等级或型号的概括性描述包括进去，作进一步限定。此外，有的品名条款甚至把商品的品质、规格也包括进去，在此情况下，它就不单是品名条款，而是品名条款与品质条款的合并。

二、商品的品质

鉴于品质对商品的效用、市场价格和销路都有重大影响，所以买卖双方为了保证交易商品符合一定的质量要求，都要在协商一致的基础上，在买卖合同中订立品质条款，就商品的品质及双方当事人在这方面的权利和义务作出具体规定，作为卖方交货和买方验收的依据。国际贸易大多是大宗的期货交易，买卖双方又是地处两国，在洽谈交易时，往往没有看到全部商品，因此，需要有某种说明品质的方法，作为洽谈和履行合同的依据。当前，进入国际贸易的商品种类繁多，特点各异，用以说明品质的方法也就不可能一致。概括起来，国际贸易中常用来表示商品品质的方法基本上有两大类。

1. 用实物表示的方法

即由卖方在货物存放地点向买方展示准备出售的货物，经买方现场检视满意后达成交易。以这种方式达成的交易，货物的品质以检视时的状态为准。卖方只要交付经检视的货物，买方就不得对其品质提出任何异议。一般而言，看货成交是在卖方掌握现货，货物数量不太大，买方能够亲临现场的条件下进行的，所以，其通常只适用于一些首饰或工艺品等贵重货物及其他现货交易。

2. 用样品表示的方法

样品（Sample）通常是从一批商品中抽取出来的或由生产、使用部门加工、设计出来的足以反映该批商品平均质量的少量实物。凭样品买卖（Sales by Sample）是指买卖双方约定凭样品作为交货品质依据的交易。用来作为衡量交货品质的样品，即称为标准样品（Standard Sample）。

（1）凡属凭卖方样品的交易，在出口对外寄送样品时，必须注意选择有代表性的样品（Representative Sample），其又称原样（Origin Sample）。样品的质量既不能偏高，也不能偏低。偏高，会给日后交货造成困难；偏低，会使卖方在价格上吃亏。

（2）凡属凭买方样品的交易，即称"来样成交"。在凭买方样品成交时，卖方所交货物的质量，必须以买方样品为准。当买方寄给卖方样品要求按样成交时，卖方也可以根据买方样品进行复制或提出与之相似的样品作为"回样"（Return Sample）或"对等样品"（Counter Sample），寄交对方确认，作为交货时的品质依据，以免在交货时引起争端。如果买方接受了卖方提出的"对等样品"，则交易的性质即由凭买方样品的买卖变为凭卖方样品的买卖，这样卖方就能主动控制交货的品质。

（3）凭样品买卖的商品多属品质难以规格化、标准化的商品，要求其交货品质与样品完全相符，有时是难以办到的。因此，在出口业务中如采用凭样品买卖的做法时，一般应争取以我方提出的样品成交，并在合同中作相应的规定："交货品质与样品大体相符"，或其他类似条款。

（4）在凭样销售交易中，为防止履行合同时发生不必要的纠纷，必要时可使用封样（Sealed Sample）即由公证机构（例如商品检验局）在一批商品中抽取同样品质的样品若干份，在每份样品上烫上火漆或铅封，供交易当事人使用。封样也可由发样人自封或由买卖双方会同加封。

3. 用说明（Description）表示的方法

（1）凭规格、等级或标准的交易（Sales by Specification, Grade or Standard）。在国际贸易中，有很大一部分商品是按一定的规格、等级或标准进行交易的。商品不同，表示商品品质的指标和方法也不同。商品的规格（Specification）是指用来反映商品品质的一些主要技术指标，如成分、含量、纯度。商品特性不同，规格的内容也不同，所以凭规格买卖比较方便、准确，应用较广。商品的等级（Grade）是指同一类商品，按其规格上的差异，用文字、数码或符号将品质分为各不相同的若干等级，如大、中、小，重、轻，甲、乙、丙，一级、二级、三级。凭等级买卖时，如果对方已熟悉每个级别的具体规格，就可以只列明等级，不需要叙述其具体内容。商品的标准（Standard）是将商品的规格和等级标准化。在我国，商品的标准是由国家或有关政府部门规定的。在资本主义国家，商品的标准有的由国家规定，有的由同业公会、交易所或国际性的工商业组织制订。这些标准，有的有约束性，即不符合标准规定品质的商品，不准出口或进口；有的没有约束性，由买卖双方根据需要决定采用或另订规格。

(2)凭牌号或商标的交易。在国际贸易中，对于某些品质稳定有良好信誉的商品，交易时仅凭牌号(Brand)或商标(Trade Mark)即可说明其品质，这些商品可凭牌号或商标交易。这种表示商品品质的方法已被各国广泛使用。

(3)凭说明书和图样的交易。有些商品，如机械、电器、仪表产品等，由于其结构和性能十分复杂，无法用几个简单的具体指标来反映其品质的全貌，因此，必须凭详细的说明书(Descriptions)及图样(Illustrations)来具体说明其构造、用材、性能及使用方法等，必要时甚至还须辅以设计、照片、分析表等来解释。按这种办法进行的买卖，称为凭说明书的买卖。有些凭说明书买卖的机、电、仪产品，除在合同中订有品质检验条款外，还订有品质保证条款和技术服务条款。明确规定卖方需要在一定期限内保证其所出售的商品质量符合说明书上所规定的指标，如在保证期限内发现品质低于规定的指标，或部件的工艺质量不良，或材料内部有隐患而产生缺陷时，买方有权提出索赔，卖方有义务消除缺陷或更换有缺陷的商品或材料，并承担由此引起的各项费用。

(4)凭产地名称的交易。在国际货物买卖中，有些产品因产区的自然条件、传统加工工艺等因素的影响，在品质方面具有其他产区的产品所不具有的独特风格和特色。对于这类产品，一般也可用产地名称(Name of Origin)来表示其品质，如四川榨菜等。

4. 合同中的品质条款

上述国际贸易中一些常见的表示商品品质的方法，根据商品的特点及市场或交易习惯也可以单独运用，也可以酌情将几种方式结合运用。通常，规定商品的品质规格时，还可使用品质机动幅度(Quality Latitude)的办法。即对某些初级产品，由于卖方所交货物品质难以完全与合同规定的品质相符，所以为便于交货，往往在规定的品质指标外，加订一定的允许幅度。只要在允许的幅度内，买方无权拒收，即可根据合同规定调整价格。

(1)规定范围。即对某项商品的品质指标规定允许有一定的差异范围。例如：湿度(Moisture)5% ~10%。

(2)规定极限。即对有些商品的品质规格规定上下极限。规定极限的表示方法常用的有：最大、最高、最多(Maximum 或 Max)和最小、最低、最少(Minimum 或 Min)。例如：羊毛最少98%(Wool 98% minimum)。

(3)规定上下差异。例如：羽绒含绒量16% ±1%(1% more or less)

第二节 商品的数量

一、计量单位

由于各国度量衡制度不同，所使用的单位各异，所以了解与熟悉相互之间的换算方法是很重要的。目前国际贸易中常用的度量衡制度，有国际单位制（国际单位制代号为“SI”即 International System of Units）、公制（The Metric System）、英制（The British System）和美制（The U. S. System）。我国的法定计量单位为国际单位制，但为了适应国外市场习惯，在对外成交时，也有采用对方常用的计量单位的。因此，在洽谈交易和签订合同时，必须明确规定使用哪一种度量衡制度，以免造成误会和纠纷。同时，还要掌握各国度量衡制度之间的换算方法。

二、计量方法

国际贸易中的许多商品是按重量买成交的。按照一般商业习惯，计算重量的方法有以下几种。

1. 毛重（Gross Weight）

毛重即商品本身的重量加包装的重量，一般适用于低值的商品。

2. 净重（Net Weight）

净重是指商品本身的重量，即除去包装后的商品实际重量。在国际贸易中，大部分以重量计量的商品，都是以净重计价的。但是一些价值较低的农副产品，如粮谷、饲料等有时也以毛重计价。这种以毛重计价的办法称为“以毛作净”（Gross for Net）。例如：中国东北大豆，100 公吨，单层麻袋包装，每袋 100 公斤，以毛作净。货物按净重计算时，必须由毛重扣除皮重，计算皮重的方法有四种。

（1）实际皮重（Actual Tare 或 Real Tare）。即商品包装实际重量，是将整批货物包装材料逐一过秤求得的重量之和。

（2）平均皮重（Average Tare）。在皮重相差不大的情况下，从全体商品中抽出若干件包装材料，秤出皮重，然后求出其平均重量，即为平均皮重。

（3）习惯皮重（Customary Tare）。有些比较标准化、规格化的包装，其重量已为市场所公认，因此不必逐件重复过秤，而以习惯上公认的包装重量计算，称为习惯皮重。

（4）约定皮重（Computed Tare）。即指买卖双方事先协商约定的皮重，不必过秤逐一衡量。计算皮重究竟采取哪一种方法，在磋商交易和签订合同时也应明确规定，以免事后引起争议。如在合同中未明确规定用何种方法计算重量和价格，按惯例应以净重计。

3. 公重（Conditioned Weight）

公重即用科学方法除去商品中所含的实际水分，再另加标准水分所求得的重量。这种方法经常用于水分含量不稳定、易受空气湿度影响的商品，如羊毛、生丝、棉花等。

4. 理论重量(Theoretical Weight)

理论重量是对于有固定规格和尺寸的商品，根据其数量推算所得的重量。如马口铁、钢板规格一致，其重量大致相等，可以从张数推算其实际重量。

三、合同中的数量条款

1. 数量条款的重要性

在国际贸易中，买卖双方必须以约定的货物数量作为履行合同的依据，商品数量是买卖合同中不可缺少的主要条件之一。按照《联合国国际货物销售合同公约》规定，卖方所交货物的数量必须与合同规定相符。如卖方所交货物的数量小于合同规定的数量，卖方应在规定的交货期届满前补交，但不得使买方遭受不合理的不便或承担不合理的开支。即使如此，买方也有保留要求损害赔偿的权利。反之，卖方所交货物的数量如大于合同规定的数量，买方除了可以拒收超额部分外，也可以收取多交部分中的一部分或全部，但应按合同价格付款。

2. 溢短装条款

在农副产品和工矿产品的交易中，往往由于商品的特性、生产能力、船舶舱位、装载技术和包装等原因，难以准确地按合同规定的数量交货。因此，买卖双方在商订交货数量时应订有一定的机动幅度，即应在合同中明确规定溢短装条款(More or Less Clause)。按照这一规定，卖方在交货时可以溢交或短交合同数量的百分之几。例如，中国大米 10 万公吨，卖方可溢交或短交 2% (China Rice, 100 000 metric tons with 2% more or less at Sellers' option)。按照国际商会《跟单信用证统一惯例》规定，如是用证付款方式进行的买卖，除非 L/C (信用证)所列的货物数量不得增减，否则在支取金额不超过 L/C(信用证)金额的条件下，即使不准分批装运，卖方交货数量的伸缩幅度也为 5%，但货物数量按包装单位或个体计算时，此项伸缩原则不适用。合同数量的溢短装，一般由卖方决定，也有由买方决定的。在合同数量大、商品价格波动剧烈的情况下，为了防止卖方或买方利用溢短装条款，故意多装或少装，有的合同在规定溢短装条款时，还规定此项条款适应船舱的需要时才适用。

第三节　商品的包装

商品的包装是保护商品在流通过程中品质完好和数量完整的重要措施。由于国际贸易商品一般需要经过长距离辗转运输，所以国际贸易商品的包装比国内销售商品的包装更为重要。在国际贸易中，经过适当包装的商品，有利于储存、保管、运输、装卸、计数、销售和防止盗窃等工作的进行，有利于消费者的挑选和携带。包装良好的商品，还有利于吸引顾客、扩大销路、提高售价、多创外汇。此外，商品的包装还在一定程度上反映出了一个国家的生产水平、科学技术和文化艺术水平。在当前市场竞争空前激烈的情况下，各国出口商更是千方百计地变换包装方式，不断翻新包装花样，以利保持和扩大其商品的销路，排挤和打击竞争对手。因此，包装的作用不仅限于保护商品的品质和数量，而且已发展成为增强商品竞争能力、扩大销路、增加外汇收入的重要手段之一。

一、运输包装的种类

运输包装又称大包装或外包装(Outer Packing)，它的作用主要在于保护商品的品质和数量，使商品便于运输、储存、检验、计数、分拨，有利于节省运输成本。运输包装的方式主要有两种：单件运输包装和集合运输包装。单件运输包装是根据商品的形态或特性将一件或数件商品装入一个较小容器内的包装方式。单件运输包装应坚固结实，具备保护商品品质安全和数量完整的良好性能，如能防潮、防震、防漏、防锈蚀、防碰撞、防盗和通风等等。单件运输包装还应适于运输装卸、储存并符合节省运输费用的要求。单件运输包装所用的材料有木制品、金属制品、纺织纤维制品、陶土制品、纸制品和塑料制品等等。制作单件运输包装时，要注意选用适当的材料，并要求结构造型科学合理，同时还应考虑不同国家和地区的气温、湿度、港口设施和不同商品的性能、特点和形状等因素。

1. 单件运输包装

单件运输包装的种类很多：按照包装外形来分，习惯上常用的有包、箱、桶、袋等；按照制作包装所采用的材料来分，一般常用的有纸制包装、金属包装、木制包装、塑料包装、棉麻制品包装、玻璃制品包装、陶瓷包装，还有竹、柳、草制品包装等。

2. 集合运输包装

随着科学技术的发展，运输包装使用集合包装的方式日益增多。集合包装是将一定数量的单件商品组合成一件大的包装或装入一个大的包装容器内。集合包装可以提高港口装卸速度，便利货运，减轻装卸搬运的劳动强度，降低运输成本和节省运输费用，更好地保护商品的质量和数量，并促进包装的标准化。

二、运输包装的标志

运输标志，习惯上称为“唛头”(Shipping Mark)，它通常是由一个简单的几何图形和一些字母、数字及简单的文字组成，其作用主要是便于识别货物，便于收货人收货，也有利于运输、仓储、检验和海关等有关部门顺利地进行工作。

1. 运输标志

鉴于运输标志的内容差异较大，有的过于繁杂，不适应货运量日益增大、运输方式迅速变革和电子计算机在运输与单据流转方面应用的需要，所以，联合国欧洲经济委员会简化国际贸易程序工作组，在国际标准化组织和国际货物装卸协调协会的支持下，制定了一项运输标志向各国推荐使用。该标准运输标志包括：收货人或买方名称的英文缩写字母或简称；参考号，如运单号、订单号或发票号；目的地；件号。至于根据某种需要而必须在运输包装上刷写的其他内容，如许可证号等，则不作为运输标志的必要组成部分。

2 指示性标志

根据商品的性能和特点，用简单醒目的图形或文字对一些容易破碎、残损、变质的商品提出某些在装卸搬运操作和存放保管条件方面的要求和注意事项，称为指示性标志（Indicative Mark）。例如："此端向上"、"防湿"、"小心轻放"等等。

3 警告性标志

警告性标志（Warning Mark）是针对危险货物，为了在运输、保管和装卸过程中，使有关人员加强防护措施，以保护物资和人身的安全而加在外包装上的危险货物标志。凡包装内装有爆炸品、易燃物品、自燃物品、遇水燃烧物品、有毒品、腐蚀性物品、氧化剂和放射性物品等危险品时，应在运输包装上刷写清楚明显的危险品警告标志，以示警告。

三、中性包装

中性包装（Neutral Packing）是指在商品上和内外包装上不注明生产国别、地名和生产厂名，也不注明原有商标和牌号，甚至没有任何文字的包装。中性包装包括无牌中性包装和定牌中性包装。前者是指包装上既无生产地名和厂商名称，又无商标、牌号；后者是指包装上仅有买方指定的商标或牌号，但无生产地名和出口厂商的名称。在国际贸易中，使用中性包装的目的主要是为了打破某些进口国家和地区实行的关税壁垒、配额限制和其他一些限制进口的歧视性措施。它是推销出口商品的一个手段。目前，某些出口商品使用中性包装已成为国际贸易中的一种习惯做法。

四、合同中的包装条款

在国际贸易中，有些合同对包装条款只作原则性规定，如使用"海运包装"（Sea－worthy Packing）和"习惯包装"（Custom Packing）的术语。此种术语，由于内容不明确，各国理解不同，容易引起争议。因此，在合同中，一般应尽量避免使用，如需使用时，应具体订明使用何种包装材料，以免引起纠纷。包装物料和费用一般包括在货价之内，不另计价。如果在买方对于包装材料和包装方式提出特殊要求的情况下，卖方也可要求另收包装费。如由买方提供包装或包装材料，则应在合同中具体规定，并订明买方包装送交卖方的时间以及由于包装不能及时运到而影响货物出运时对方所应负担的责任。

第四节 商品的价格

国际市场上商品的价格是千变万化的，它受价值规律支配，并随着供求关系的变化而变化。为了正确掌握我国进出口商品的价格，应注意以下几个问题。

一、支付货币的选择

在决定采用什么货币进行交易时，必须充分考虑货币发行国对我国的政治态度。同时在使用其他国家货币时，必须充分考虑货币本身的兑换性和稳定性。这就要求作好调查研究，了解各国外汇的管理情况和币值变动趋势，灵活选择兑换比较方便、市值又相对稳定的货币，以尽量减少由于外汇汇值的变动可能造成的损失，有利于国家外汇的调度和使用。对外贸易一般买卖的都是期货，自合同签定至履约结汇，需要有一定时间，在此期间，用来计价和结算的外国货币的汇价在浮动汇率情况下，随时都会发生变动，有时甚至是重大的变动。因此，如果能在出口方面，采用一些比较稳定或趋于上浮的货币，在进口方面争取用地位相对疲软的外币，则是比较有利的。有时，在对外成交时会出现不得不在进口时使用硬币(Hard Currency)、在出口时使用软币(Weak Currency)的情况，在这种情况下，一般可采取下述两种方法来排除或减轻汇价变动的风险。

(1)在作价时考虑所选用货币的汇价在合同执行期间可能变动的幅度，并且把它包括在进口价格中间。

(2)在合同中订立保值条款。过去在固定汇率时期，流行所谓黄金保值条款，即在出口合同中列入所使用货币的法定含金量。如果该项货币的法定含金量发生变化，即所谓法定升值或贬值，合同价格即按比例相应调整。目前，在浮动汇率制度的条件下，一国货币的汇率的变动往往不是由政府宣布改变其法定含金量来实现，而是听任市场上的供需情况决定它对其他货币的汇率是上浮或是下浮。黄金保值已失去其实际意义，于是人们往往采用汇率保值条款，即在签订合同时，规定合同货币和另一种货币的汇率。付款时，如果汇率发生变动，即按比例调整合同价格。

二、佣金和折扣

佣金(Commission)是中间商为介绍交易或代买代卖而收取的报酬。折扣(Discount, Rebate)是卖方按价格给予买方一定百分比的减让，佣金和折扣都与商品的价格有直接关系。对于佣金和折扣，如果运用得当，有助于灵活掌握价格，可以增强出口商品在市场上的竞争能力，调动外商的经营积极性从而扩大贸易。对于进口商品，除了基价不合理的可以压低基价外，也可通过佣金和折扣的运用争取到有利的价格。佣金和折扣的名目有好多种。例如，由于特殊情况而给予的特别折扣(Special Discount)，因订购数量较大而给予的数量折扣(Quantity Discount)，在年度终了时根据成交金额而给予的年终奖金(Turnover Bonus)，按累进方式而给予的累计佣金(Accumulative Commission)，作为试订而给予的样品折扣(Sample Discount)等。佣金或折扣的百分比应根据不同商品、不同市场、不同对象等具体情况慎重确定。在国际贸易中，凡价格中包括佣金的称为含佣价(Price including commission)，其表示方法可用文字说明。例如“每台 2000 美元 C. I. F. 旧金山包括 2% 佣金"(USD2000 per set C. I. F. San Francisco including 2% Commission),也可以在价格术语后加注英文字母"C",如:"每台2000美元C. I. F. C. 5 %旧金山"(USD2000 per set C. I. F. C. 5 %San Francisco),这种在价格中表明的佣金称为明佣。有时,买卖双方约定的佣金不在价格中表明,习惯上称为暗佣。凡价格中不包含佣金或折扣的,都称为净价。有时为了强调成交价格是净价,可在价格术语后注明"净价"(Net)。例如,"每台2000美元CFR净价旧金山"(USD2000 perset CFR net San Francisco)。

折扣一般用文字表明。例如"每台2000美元C. I. F. 新加坡元减2%折扣"(USD2000 per set C. I. F. Singapore less 2% discount),有时则加注"R"(Rebate)表示,如"每台2000美元C. I. F. R. 2 %新加坡"(USD2000 per set C. I. F. R. 2 %Singapore)。但"R"指的是回扣,这里用作折扣,严格地说是不确切的。佣金和折扣一般是按交易金额的百分比计算的,但佣金有时也可按成交数量来计算,即每成交一定数量收取佣金若干。

三、合同中的价格条款

贸易合同中的价格条款一般包括两项内容,即单价(Unit price)和总值(Total amount)。单价由四个部分组成,即计量单位、单位价格金额、计价货币和价格术语。

第五节　商品的运输

运输方式的种类很多,包括海洋运输、铁路运输、公路运输、航空运输、邮政运输、江河运输、管道运输和联合运输等,具体应由买卖双方在磋商交易时约定。我国对外贸易货物绝大部分通过海洋运输,少部分通过铁路运输,也有一些货物是通过空运等其他运输方式进行的。在我国外贸企业中,根据进出口货物的特点、运量的大小、路程的远近、需要的缓急、运费的高低、风险的程度、装卸的情况、气候与自然条件以及国际政治形势的变化等因素,慎重选择合理的运输方式,对多快好省地完成进出口货物运输任务,有着十分重要的意义。

一、海洋运输

海洋运输(Ocean Transportation)不受道路和轨道的限制,通过能力很大,万吨以上、甚至数十万吨的巨轮都可以在海洋中航行,由于海洋运输的运量很大,而运输成本又较低,所以许多国家、特别是各沿海国家的进出口货物,大部分都采用海洋运输。在国际贸易总量中,通过海洋运输的货物约占80%以上,海洋运输是国际贸易中最主要的运输方式。

1. 班轮运输

班轮(Liner),是指按照固定的航行时间表,沿着固定的航线,停靠在固定的港口,收取固定运费的运输船舶。班轮运输是国际航运中的一种主要运输方式,它有如下一些特点。

(1)船舶行驶的路线和停靠的港口都是固定的。船舶按船期表航行,船舶开航和到港时间都较为固定。

(2)船方负责货物的装卸。船方按班轮运价表收取运费,运费率相对固定。

班轮运费包括基本运费和附加费两部分,基本运费是指货物在预定航线的各基本港口之间进行运输所规定的运价,它是构成全程运费的主要部分。基本运费的计收标准,通常按不同商品分为下列几种。

(1)按货物的重量计收。即1重量吨(Weight ton)为1公吨或1长吨作为计算运费单位。在运价表内用字母W表示。

(2)按货物的体积或按尺码吨(Measurement ton)计收。即1尺码吨以每立方米或40立方英尺作为计算运费单位。在运价表内用字母M表示。

(3)按货物的件数计收。如装运卡车按辆数、活牲畜按头数计收运费等。

(4)按重量或体积来计算运费,即船方从各种计收运费办法中,任选对其有利的一种作为计算运费的标准。例如:在运价表中若用"W/M"表示,即指船方可凭货物的重量或体积收取费用较高的一种计收运费;若用"W/M or A. V. "表示,即指船方可根据货物的重量、体积及货价三者中取收费较高的一种计收运费;也有在运价表中列明"W/M Plus A. V. "字样,即指船方除先按货物的重量或体积中收费较高的一种计收运费外,还需要另收一定百分比的从价运费。

(5)由货主和船公司临时议定。有些班轮公司对承运某些大宗货物(如粮谷、豆类、矿石、煤炭等)采取由船货双方临时议定运价的办法。由于这些大宗货物运量较大,装卸容易,货价较低,所以对这些货物临时议定的运价比一般杂货的班轮费率低。

班轮承运货物除了收取"基本运费"外,往往还要加收种种附加费,以弥补船方在运输上的额外开支或其所蒙受的某些损失。附加费名目繁多,常见的有:超重附加费、超长附加费、转船附加费、直航附加费、洗舱费、选港附加费、港口附加费、港口拥挤附加费、燃油附加费、货币贬值附加费,等等。因此,在对外报价时应充分考虑这一因素,才能使商品的价格定得合理。

2. 租船运输

租船运输通常是指包租整船,大宗货物一般都采用租船运输。租船方式主要包括定程租船和定期租船两种。

(1)定程租船(Voyage Charter)。在定程租船方式下,船方必须按租船合同规定的航程完成货物运输任务,并负责船舶的经营管理及其在航行中的各项费用开支,租船人则应支付双方约定的运费。租船的运费一般按装运货物的数量计算,也有按船次包租总金额计算的。至于货物在港口的装卸费用,究竟由船方还是租方负担,应在租船合同中作出明确规定。租赁定程租船运送货物时,关于装卸费的收取办法,有下列各种不同的规定。

①船方不负担装卸费(F. I. O.)或船方不管装卸、理舱和平舱(F. I. O. S. T.),采用此法

的较为普遍。

②船方负担装卸费(Gross Terms 或 Liner Terms)。

③船方只负担装货费,不负担卸货费(F.O.)。

④船方只负担卸货费,不负担装货费(F.I.)。

(2) 定期租船。定期租船即指按一定期限租赁船舶。在租赁期间,租船人根据租船合同规定的航行区域可自行使用和调度船舶。一般定期租船在各自航次中所产生的燃料费、港口费、装卸费、垫舱物料费等项费用,均由租船人负担。租船运价由船、租双方根据租船市场运价水平协商确定。关于租船运价的计算及支付方法,都应在租船合同中明确规定。

二、铁路运输

在国际贸易货物运输中,铁路运输(Railway Transportation)占着相当重要的地位,特别是在内陆国家之间的贸易,铁路运输的作用更为显著。铁路运输具有许多特点,例如铁路火车运行速度较快,载运量较大,不易受气候条件的影响,能终年正常运行,而且在运输当中遭受的风险较小,所以铁路运输具有高度的连续性。

三、航空运输

1. 航空运输的特点

航空运输(Air Transport)是一种现代化的运输方式,它不受地面条件的限制,航行便利,运输速度很快,航行时间很短,货物中途破损率小。因此,某些急需物资、易损货物和贵重商品适于利用航空运输。航空运输的运费,就其绝对值而言,一般比海洋运输和铁路运输高,但有些商品利用航空运输,其运费反而可以降低。这是因为一方面航空运输计收运费的方法不同于其他运输方式,另一方面,采用航空运输还有助于减少包装费、装卸搬运费、仓储费、保险费和利息开支等项附属费用。由于航空运输具有上述特点和优越性,所以许多国际贸易货物都通过航空运输。随着航空工业技术的迅速发展和国际贸易的不断扩大,航空运输在国际贸易中的使用越来越多。

2. 航空运输的种类

航空运输包括班机运输、包机运输、集中托运三种方式。所谓班机运输,是指客、货班机定时、定点、定线的运输,它适用于载运数量较小的货物。所谓包机运输,是指包租整架飞机运输货物,它适用于载运数量较大、有急需或有特殊要求的货物。集中托运是指航空货运公司把若干单独发运的货物组成一整批货物,用一份总运单整批发运到预定目的地,由航空货运公司在那里的代理人收货、报关、分拨后交给实际收货人。办理货物航空运输时,应填写航空货运单(Airway Bill),并制作其他有关证件。航空货运单是航空运输的正式凭证,承运人收到货物后开立的货物收据,货物运抵目的地后,收货人凭承运人的到货通知及有关证明领取货物时,应在货运单上签收。在随附货物运送的证件中,必须包括发票及装箱单等。由于航空运输要求快捷,故一般航空公司都要求附上这些单证,以利于及时办理海关手续,迅速将货物送交到收货人手中。

四、集装箱运输

集装箱运输是一种新型的现代运输方式。集装箱(Container)是成组运输中比较好的一种工具,采用这种工具进行运输,可以大大提高货运质量和营运效果,所以许多国家都竞相采用这种新的运输方式。

采用集装箱运输,主要有以下优点。

(1)便利货运,简化手续。集装箱运输便于采用海陆(空)联运,货物在中途的一切装卸、搬运工作,全由有关承运人负责,而且货物中途也可以免验,这就大大减少了中间环节,简化了办理货运的手续。

(2)提高装卸效率,扩大港口吞吐能力。国际上通用的集装箱,规格一致,便于机械化操作,而且装卸作业不受气候限制,故装卸速度很快。每艘集装箱船一般在港口只需一天即能装卸完毕。由于装卸效率高,码头使用率也随之提高,从而扩大了港口的吞吐能力。

(3)加速船舶周转,降低营运成本。集装箱运输的装卸效率高,大大减少了船舶的停港时间,加速了船舶的周转,提高了船舶的使用率,并降低了营运成本。一般地说,集装箱运输的货运成本比非集装箱运输的货运成本要降低60% ~70%左右。

(4)加快货运速度,缩短货运时间。采用集装箱运输,货运手续简便,装卸效率高,船舶运转快,可大大提高货运速度,缩短货运时间。

五、国际多式联运

国际多式联运(International Multi - modal Transportation)是指通过两种或两种以上不同的运输方式来完成某项运输任务,它包括陆海联运、陆空联运、海空联运、陆海空联运和国际多式联运。在国际贸易中,有许多货物是通过陆海联运(或海陆联运)方式运输的。近年来,我国部分对外贸易货物也开始采用这种方式运输。目前,这种方式主要应用于内地货物从国内港口装运出口发生困难的场合。其具体做法是,先由内地起运地把货物用火车装运至香港地区,然后由香港代理机构联系二程船舶,将货物转运至国外目的地。

六、运输单据

国际贸易中的运输单据主要是指提单。

1. 提单的目的

提单(Bill of Lading,简称 B/L)是货物承运人(或其代理人)在收到货物后签发给托运人的一种证件,它体现了承运人和托运人之间的相互关系。提单的性质与作用主要表现在以下三个方面。

(1)它是承运人(或其代理人)签发给托运人的货物收据(Receipt for the goods),证实已按提单记载的事项收到货物,承运人应凭提单所列内容向收货人交货。

(2)它是代表货物所有权的凭证。由于提单是一种物权证件(Documents of Titie),是提取货物的凭证,因此占有提单就有支配货物的权利,就等于占有货物。卖方凭提单向银行议付货款,收货人凭提单可以提取货物或背书转证,承运人有责任把货物交与提单的合法持有人。由于提单能起到代替货物本身的作用,因此,提单持有人在货物运抵目的港之前,可以凭提单向银行抵押取得贷款。

(3)它是承运人和托运人双方同意的运输契约的证明。运输契约是在装货前商定的,而提单是在装货后才签发的,因此,提单本身并不是运输契约,而只是运输契约的证明(Evidence of Contract of Carrier)。

2. 提单的种类

在国际贸易业务中,提单可以从各种不同的角度加以分类,主要有以下几种。

(1) 按签发时间分类

根据签发提单的时间是在货物装船之后还是装船以前,提单以分为下列两种。

①已装船提单(Shipped on Board B/L)。已装船提单是指货物装船后,由承运人签发给托运人的提单,它必须载明装货船名称和装船日期。装船日期经常以签发提单的日期来证明。由于已装船提单对收货人按时收货有保障,因此,在买卖合同中一般都规定卖方必须提供已装船提单。按照国际商会的《跟单信用证统一惯例》规定,在信用证没有特别规定的情况下,卖方提供的提单必须是已装船提单。《海上货物运输公约》也规定,货物装船后,如托运人提出要求,承运人必须签发给托运人已装船提单。已装船提单在国际贸易中广泛使用,在我国对外贸易业务中,一般也都是使用这种提单。

②备运提单(Received for Shipment B/L)。备运提单又称收讫待运提单,是承运人在收到托运货物等待装船期间,向托运人签发的提单。这种提单有利于船方争揽货载。由于这种提单没有肯定的装货日期,而且往往不注明装运船只的名称,即使注明也多是拟装船名,将来货物能否装出,以及能否凭单提到货物,都很难预料,加上有时还可能发生根本未收到货物就出具备运提单的欺诈行为,因此,进口商一般都不愿接受这种提单。在跟单信用证支付方式下,银行一般也都不接受备运提单。所以在国际贸易中,这种提单应用不广。备运提单如经承运人加注"已装船"(on Board)字样,注明装船名称、装船日期并签字证明,也可变成"已装船提单"为银行所接受。

(2)按提单有无不良批注分类

①清洁提单(Clean B/L)。清洁提单是指交运货物的外表状况良好(in Apparent Good Order and Condition),承运人未加有关货损或包装不良之类批注的提单。在买卖合同中,一般都明确规定卖方提供的已装船提单必须是清洁提单。卖方提交了清洁提单后,才能取得货款。

②不清洁提单(Unclean B/L or FouI B/L)。承运人为了保护自身利益,对交运货物的外表状况不良或件数、重量与提单记载不符,可以在提单上加注批语,如“包装不固”、“破包”、“×件损坏”等。凡承运人加注了这类表明货物外表状况不良或存在缺陷的批语的提单,叫做不清洁提单。银行为了自身的安全,对不清洁提单,除信用证明确规定可接受外,一般都拒绝接受。

(3)按提单的收货人抬头分类

①记名提单(Straight B/L)。记名提单是指发给指定的收货人的提单,在提单中的收货人栏内,具体填明收货人的名称。这种提单只能是指定的收货人提货,不能转让,因而又称为“不可转让提单”。记名提单虽可避免提单转让过程中的风险,但却失去了其代表货物转让流通的便利,同时银行也不愿接受这种提单作为议付证件,因而在国际贸易业务中极少使用。一般只有在运送贵重物品、援助物资和展览品等物品时才采用。

②不记名提单(Bearer B/L)。不记名提单又称空名提单,是指在提单收货人栏内不填写收货人或指示人的名称而留空,提单持有人可不作任何背书,就能凭提单转让货物所有权或提取货物,承运人只凭提单交货。由于这种提单风险较大,故国际上一般极少使用。

③指示提单(Order B/L)。指示提单是指在提单的收货人栏内只填写:“凭指定书”或“凭某人指定”字样的一种提单。这种提单可以背书转让。背书的方法有两种:单纯签字盖章的,称空白背书;除背书人签字盖章以外,还列有被背书人名称的,称记名背书。提单经背书后可转让给其他第三者,因而又称为“可转让的提单”。注明“凭指定”的提单,在卖方未指定收货人之前,卖方仍保持货物的所有权,如经卖方在提单上空白背书转让后,持有这种提单的人,就有权提货。这样的提单也可称为“不记名提单”。指示提单在国际贸易中较为普遍使用。

(4) 按运输方式分类

按运输方式划分,提单可分为直达提单(Direct B/L)、联运提单(Through B/L)、转船提单(Transhipment B/L)和多式联运单证(Combined Transport Documents,简称 C. T. D.)四种。

①直达提单。承运人对自装运港直接运到目的港的货物所签发给托运人的提单,叫做直达提单。在国际贸易中,如合同和信用证规定有限制转船条款时,则托运人必须取得直达提单,方可向银行结汇。在直达提单中,除列明装运港和目的港名称外,不得有中途转船的批语。

②联运提单。联运提单用于海陆联运、海河联运或海海联运。它是由第一承运人或其代理人在货物起运地签发运往货物最终目的地的提单,并收取全程运费,货物到达转运港后,由前一承运人或其代理人代为将货物交给下一段航程的承运人或其代理人,继续运往目的地。联运提单虽然包括全程运输,但在联运提单中一般都载有一项免责条款,申明签发提单的承运人或其代理人,一般只对第一程运输所发生的货物损害负责,对于货物在卸离第一程运输工具及装上第二程运输工具以后所发生的损失概不负责。

(5) 按提单内容的繁简分类

①全式提单(Long Form B/L)。全式提单是指通常应用的带有背面条款的提单。这种提单除其正面必要的项目外,在背面还列有各项有关装运的条款,以表明承运人和托运人的权利与义务。

②略式提单(Short Form B/L)。略式提单是指内容简略而不带背面条款的提单。这种提单仅保留其正面的必要项目。略式提单又可分为租船合同项下的略式提单和非租船合同项下的略式提单两种。

为了简化提单的备制工作,有些船公司将全式提单留存起来,仅供托运人查阅,而签发给托运人一种略式提单。在这种提单上一般印有"本提单货物的收受、保管、运输和运费等事项,均按本公司全式提单的正面、背面的铅印、手写、印章和打字等书面的条款和例外条款办理"等内容。按一般国际贸易惯例,银行对这种略式提单可以接受。

七、合同中的运输条款

在买卖合同中,涉及装运方面的条款,主要有装运期、装运港和目的港、装卸时间、装卸率、装运通知、分批装运和转船等项内容。

1. 装运期

装运期是买卖合同中的主要条件,如卖方违反这一条件,买方有权撤销合同,并要求卖方赔偿其损失。在买卖合同中,合理地规定装运期是非常重要的。为了使装运期订得明确、合理和切实可行,就必须正确处理贸易和运输的关系,把贸易和运输作为一个整体来考虑,那种只顾成交、不管运输的想法,是十分错误而有害的。

关于买卖合同中的装运期,有以下几种规定方法。

(1) 明确规定具体装运期限。在买卖合同中,一般都订明装运成交货的年度及月份。例如,限于某年某月内(或跨月)装运或交货,或某年某月以前装运或交货。对偏僻港口,装运期或交货期应适当放长一些,以季度为宜。这类规定方法,期限具体,含义明确,既便于安排船、货,又可避免在装运期问题上发生争议和纠纷。因此,它被我国各进出口公司广泛使用。

(2) 规定在收到信用证后若干天装运。这类规定方法,主要适用于下列情况:按买方要求的花色、品种和规格专为某一地区或某商号生产的商品,而这些商品,既不宜于内销,又无法销给国外其他客户。卖方为了避免盲目生产和造成产品积压,可以采用这种规定方法;在一些外汇管制较严的国家和地区,一般都实行进口许可证和进口配额制度,当签订合同时,买方还不能肯定批准进口许可证或外汇配额的具体时间,因而也无法确定具体装运期,为了促进成交,有时采用这种方法;对某些信用较差的客户,为促使其按时开证,也可酌情采用这一方法。

2. 分批装运和转船

(1) 分批装运。凡一笔成交的货物，分若干批次装运，叫做分批装运(Partia1Shipment)。但同一船只、同一航次中多次装运的货物，即使提单表示不同装船日期及(或)不同装货港口，也不视为分批装运。在大宗货物交易时，买卖双方根据交货数量、运输条件和市场销售需要等因素，可在合同中订立分批装运的条款。根据国际商会的《跟单信用证统一惯例》规定："除非信用证有不同规定，可准许分批装运。"为了避免发生争论，买卖双方在商订装运条件时，如限一次装运完毕，即应明确规定不准分批装运的限制性条款；如需分批装运，则对分批装运的时间和数量，应在合同中具体订明。分批装运的数量，关系到买卖双方的利益，因此，买方一般都要求具体规定每批装运的数量。但卖方在货源无充分把握时，一般不愿作此规定，倘若笼统地规定"某年某月底以前分批交清"，则卖方比较主动，因为他可以根据货源情况，灵活安排，但这对买方很不利，故买方一般不轻易接受。此外，对一笔货物在短期内分若干批装运的条款，在船源无把握的情况下，不宜轻易接受，因为在规定期内，如无适当的两条以上的船只，就会影响这笔货物的全部装运。当买卖合同规定有分批、定期、定量装运条款时，买卖双方应当严格按照合同和信用证有关规定办理，否则视为违约。根据国际商会的《跟单信用证统一惯例》规定："如信用证规定在指定期内分期装货，其中任何一期未按期装运，信用证对该期和以后各期货物均告失效，除非信用证另有规定。"

(2) 转船。当国际贸易货物没有直达船或一时无合适的船舶运输，而需通过某中途港转运时，买卖双方可以在合同中商订"允许转船"(Transhipment to be allowed)的条款。由于货物中途转船有可能发生损失，故买方一般不轻易接受货物转船的条款。不仅如此，买方有时还提出限制转船的条款。

第六节　商品的保险

一、海上风险

货物在海上运输及在海陆交接过程中，可能遭遇各种风险和损失，各国保险公司并不是对所有风险都予以承保，也不是对一切损失都予以补偿。海上风险，一般指船舶、货物在海上运输中所发生的各种风险。在各国保险业务中，各保险公司所承保的风险，主要包括"自然灾害"、"意外事故"和其他外来原因所引起的"外来风险"。这些风险，在保险业务中，都有其特定的含义和内容。按照一般的解释，这些风险所指的大致内容如下。

(1)自然灾害(Natural Calamity)。所谓自然灾害，并非指一切由于自然力量所造成的灾害，而是仅指恶劣气候(如暴风雨)、雷电、海啸、地震、洪水及其他人力不可抗拒的灾害。

(2)海上意外事故(Fortuitous Accidents at Sea)。海上意外事故不同于一般的事故，这里所指的主要是船舶搁浅、触礁、沉没、火灾、爆炸、碰撞、船舶失踪或其他类似的事故。

(3)外来风险(Fxtraneous Risks)。所谓"外来风险"，通常是由外来原因引起的，一般仅指偷窃、破碎、雨淋、受潮、受热、发霉、串味、沾污、短量、渗漏、钩损、锈损等。除上述风险外,保险货物还可能遇到一些特殊的风险,如战争、敌对行为或武装冲突等所造成的损失。凡以上所指的各类风险,均属海洋运输保险所承保的范围,买方或卖方可根据需要向保险公司投保。

二、海上损失

1. 全部损失

全部损失简称全损(Total Loss)。全损有实际全损(Actual Totat Loss)和推定全损(Constructive Total Loss)两种。实际全损是指被保险货物完全灭失或指货物完全变质和货物已不可能归还被保险人。例如,货物沉没海底无法打捞,或水泥被水浸泡后变成硬块后完全失去原有用途等。推定全损是指被保险货物受损后进行施救整理或恢复原状所需的费用、超过恢复后的货价,或者施救及修理费用加上续运至目的地费用的总和,或者估计要超过货物在目的地的完好状态的价格。

2. 部分损失

部分损失(Parial loss)是指货物的损失不及上述全部损失的程度。部分损失可以分为共同海损和单独海损。

(1)共同海损(General Average,简写为 G. A.)。在海运途中,载货的船舶遇到危险时,船方为了维护船舶和所有货物的共同安全或使航程得以继续完成,有意采取合理措施会作某些特殊牺牲或支出某些特殊的额外费用。这些特殊的牺牲和额外费用,叫做共同海损。

(2)单独海损(Particular Average,简写为 P. A.)。保险货物遭受海损以后,如未达到全损程度,仅属部分损失,而且这种损失又不属共同海损,不是由多方面的关系人共同分摊,仅由受损方面自己负责,这种损失,称为单独海损。单独海损是与共同海损相对而言。除上述风险损失外,保险货物在运输途中还可能发生其他损失,如运输途中的自然损耗,由于货物本身特点和内在缺陷所造成的货损等。对于这些损失,保险公司一般不予承保。

三、合同中的保险条款

中国人民保险公司根据《协会货物条款》的规定,保险货物的险别分为平安险(Free From Particular Average,简写为 F. P. A.)、水渍险(With Average 或 With Particular Average,简写为 W. A. 或 W. P. A.)和一切险(All Risks)大类。

1. 平安险(F. P. A.)

平安险是我国历史上的习惯叫法,英文原意是"不负单独海损责任"。也就是说,被保险标的所遭受的单独海损的损失,原则上不在保险人承保范围之内。按照《协会货物条款》的规定,承保平安险时,保险人仅对自然灾害和海上意外事故所造成的全部损失负赔偿责任,而对单独海损不负责任。

2. 水渍险(W.P.A.或W.A.)

水渍险也是我国保险业务中的习惯叫法,英文原意为"负单独海损责任"。其责任范围是:第一,平安险责任范围以内的全部责任;第二,由于恶劣气候,如暴风、巨浪等自然灾害引起的部分损失。以上说明,水渍险的责任范围比平安险的责任范围大。

3. 一切险(All Risks)

一切险的责任范围是:除包括平安险和水渍险的各项责任外,保险人对于被保险货物因遭受所有意外事故所发生的损失,不论是共同海损、单独海损、全部损失、部分损失,还是其他外来原因造成的偷窃、淡水雨淋、破碎等损失,均包括在一切险承保责任范围之内。但是,由于货物本身特性所造成的损失、物价跌落的损失等,不包括在一切险承保范围之内。一切险条款的责任范围很广泛,但战争险(War Risks)或罢工险(Risks of Strikcs)则不包括在内。

4. 附加险(Extraneous Risks)

在附加险条款中,有一般附加险条款和特殊附加险条款两类。由于货物种类繁多,各有特点,所以投保附加险的险别各异,投保人可根据需要选择投保一种或若干种附加险。一般附加险的种类很多,其中主要包括:偷窃提货不着险(Theft, Pilferage and Non-delivery,简写为T.P.N.D.)、淡水雨淋险(Fresh and/or Rainwater Damage Risks)、渗漏险(Risk of Leakage)、短量险(Risk of Shortage in Weight)、钩损险(Hook Damage)、污染险(Risk of contamination)、破碎险(Risk of Breakage)、碰损险(Clashing)、生锈险(Risk of Rust)、串味险(Risk of Odour)、受潮受热险(Sweating and/or heating)等。凡保险人对承保这些附加险货物如在运输途中发生损失,均按条款规定的责任范围予以赔偿。战争险(War Risk)属特殊附加险。按照战争险条款的规定,其责任范围包括:由于战争、类似战争行动、敌对行为、武装冲突或海盗等行为,因船舶被捕获、拘押、禁制、扣留等事故所造成的损失,以及水雷、雨雷、炸弹或其他常规武器所造成的损失,均由保险人负责赔偿。此外,对于因上述原因引起的共同海损或救助费用保险人也负赔偿责任,但由于原子或热核武器所造成的损失除外。特殊附加险还包括罢工险、舱面险、进口关税险、拒收险、黄曲霉素险、交货不到险等。

第七节　商品的检验、索赔、不可抗力和仲裁

在国际贸易买卖合同中,检验条款和品质、数量条款是有密切联系的。进、出口商品的检验(Commodity lnspection),就是指对卖方交付商品的品质和数量进行鉴定,以确定交货的品质、数量和包装是否与合同规定的一致。有的检验条款还规定,买方应于货物运抵目的港后若干天内进行检验,如有品质、数量方面的索赔,应当在合同规定的时间内提出,逾期提出索赔,卖方可不予受理。因此,有些进出口公司也把这种条款称为检验与索赔条款(Inspection and Claim Clause)。商品检验是国际贸易中的一个重要环节,不能忽视。在国际

贸易交易过程中,买卖双方往往因彼此间权利与义务等问题产生业务纠纷,引起争议,并有可能导致索赔、仲裁和诉讼等问题的发生。为了防止争议的产生,或者出现争议时能够得到妥善和圆满的解决,买卖双方在磋商交易时就应明确各方的责任和义务,特别是对容易产生争议的条款都应作出明确和详细的规定。除此之外,还要在合同中对于违约后的补救,如索赔、罚金和仲裁以及不可抗力等问题作为合同条款予以详细规定。

一、商品的检验

1. 商品检验的作用

商品检验的作用是为了鉴定商品的品质、数量和包装是否符合合同规定的要求,借以检查卖方是否已按合同履行交货义务,并在发现卖方所交货物与合同要求不符时,给予买方以拒收货物或提出索赔的权利。因此,商品检验对保护买方的利益是十分重要的。在磋商交易中,如何订好检验条款,往往是买卖双方争论较多的问题之一。出口贸易中应当贯彻“平等互利”的原则,按照“重合同、守信用”,“按时、按质、按量”交货的精神,根据不同的商品,公平合理地订好检验条款,并由国家的商检部门监督实施,以保证我国的出口商品符合合同规定,维护和提高我国对外贸易的信誉。在进口工作中,订好检验条款,做好进口商品的检验工作,对于维护国家和人民的正当权益是有重要意义的。因为我国每年要从国外购买大量的生产建设和人民生活需要的物资,要警惕不法商人在对我交货中,以旧顶新、以次顶好、以假充真等行为。这就要求必须注意订好进口合同的检验条款,认真做好进口商品的检验工作,及时发现他们的违约行为,同他们进行必要的斗争,以维护国家和人民的利益。根据《中华人民共和国进出口商品检验法》的规定,我国商检机构的主要任务是:对重要进出口商品进行法定检验,对一般进出口商品实施监督管理和鉴定。

2. 检验时间与地点

关于买卖合同中的检验时间与地点,通常有下列各种不同的规定方法:在出口国产地检验,在装运港检验,在目的港检验,装运港检验重量和目的港检验质量,装运地检验和目的港复验。

(1)离岸品质、重量(或数量)。其由买卖双方在合同中规定,出口货物在装船前进行品质的检验和数量的衡量,以装船口岸商检机构出具的品质证明书和重量证明书作为决定商品品质、重量和包装的最后依据。在采用这种做法时,买方在货物到达目的港后,虽然可以委托检验机构对货物进行检验,但原则上无权对品质和数量提出异议。这种做法对卖方比较有利,它可以使卖方免于负担货物在运输途中品质或重量发生变化的风险。

(2)到岸品质、重量(Landing Quality, Weight)。商品的品质、重量应在目的港卸货后进行检验,以目的港的商检机构签发的品质、重量证明书为准。买方可据此向卖方提出品质或数量上的任何异议。这种做法显然是对买方有利。

(3)离岸重量、到岸品质。这种做法的特点是把品质与数量分别处理。交货的数量,以卖方所委托的装运口岸的商检机构出具的重量检验证明书作为最后依据。货到目的港后，买方有权对商品的品质进行检验，并以目的口岸商检机构出具的品质检验证明书作为检验或索赔的依据。例如，伦敦有些协会制订的“标准合同”就采用这种做法。

3. 检验机构

检验机构的选定关系到交易双方的利益，故交易双方应商定检验机构，并在合同中订明。我国的检验机构是进出口商品检验局。在国际贸易中，从事商品检验的机构大致有以下三类：由国家设立的商品检验机构，由私人或同业公会、协会开设的公证行或公证人，生产、制造厂商或使用单位。在我国，进出口商品检验、鉴定工作是统一由国家设立的中国进出口商品检验局办理的。在其他国家，除了官方设立的检验机构外，还有大量由私人或同业公会、协会开设的公证行。它们都接受买卖双方的委托，对商品的品质、数量和包装进行检验和衡量。应当指出，某些资本主义国家的检验机构所出具的证书，并不完全是公平可靠的，对此我们应当注意。在具体业务中，有时经买卖双方同意，也可采用由出口方的生产制造厂商，或由进口方的使用部门检验出证的办法。在拟订检验条款时，对检验机构必须作出明确的规定。如在我国检验，应订明“由中国进出口商品检验局进行检验”。在出口合同中，如允许国外买方有复验权，最好争取在合同中规定，“须以买卖双方同意的检验机构出具的检验报告作为索赔的依据”。这样规定的好处是，对方在委托办理检验的机构时，必须征得我方的同意，如发现对方所委托的检验机构在政治上对我方不友好，或在业务上缺乏应有的能力，又或者有偏袒对方的行为时，我方有权提出异议，并要求另行委托其他比较合适的检验机构进行复验，以维护我方的正当权益。进出口商品经过商检机构检验后，都要由检验机构发给一定的证明书，以证明商品的品质和数量是否符合合同的规定，这种证件称为商检证书。目前在国际贸易中常见的检验证书主要有检验证明书、品质证明书、重量证明书、卫生证明书、兽医证明书、植物检疫证明书、价值证明书、产地证明书。

商品不同，检验要求及应提供的检验证书也有所不同。如一般轻纺产品只需要提供品质、数量或重量证明书即可；而有些农副土特产品则除需要出具品质（重量）证明书外，还需出具卫生证明书、兽医证明书或植物检疫证明书。因此，在签订合同时，应根据商品的特性，对所需的检验证书作出明确的规定。目前，由于世界各国公害严重，不少国家的政府都制定了许多有关环境保护、卫生检疫、消费者保护等方面的法令和条例，凡不符合规定要求的商品，一律不得进口。例如，美国农产品销售管理处规定，有壳蛋类和蛋制品的进口，均必须受蛋品检查法的限制，并必须附具原产国兽医官签字的证书。对牲畜、肉类和肉食品的进口，也严加管制，要求必须符合美国农业部条例的规定。在未经美国动植物卫生检验处检验合格以前，美国海关一律不予放行，这些都是属于政府颁布的强制性的规章、法令，买卖双方当事人是无权在合同中随意加以改变的。在签订出口合同时，虽然可以不接受要求出口商品的“卫生质量必须符合某国某项法令的规定”的条款。但是，为了做好出口工作，对有关进口国家的这类法令、条例也应有所了解，并且要认真研究对策。如果不给予应有的注意，难免会使我国的出口商品与进口国家的卫生、检疫规定相抵触，那么，即使在出口合同中没有规定必须遵守进口国的卫生检疫条件，但到交货时对方政府不准进口，合同还是无法履行，这是在扩大出口中值得注意的一个问题。

4. 检验方法和检验标准

检验方法和检验标准涉及到检验工作中许多复杂的技术问题。同一商品，如用不同的检验方法和标准进行检验，其结果也会不同。因此，在签订对外合同时，应注意确定适当的检验标准和检验方法。在出口方面，我国的出口商品一般应按我国有关标准规定的方法进行检验。如对方要求按对方或第三国的标准进行检验时，应和商检部门研究，征得有关部门同意后再定，但不宜接受与我国不进行贸易的国家的标准进行检验或复验。

在进口方面，对进口商品的检验一般可按下列原则办理。

(1)按生产国的标准进行检验。

(2)按买卖双方协商同意的标准和方法进行检验，但原则上不能接受在合同中规定用与我国不进行贸易的国家的标准进行检验。

(3)按国际标准或国际习惯进行检验。

如合同规定需按国外标准进行检验，而我国又没有该项商品的有关标准时，应及时向对方索取合同规定的标准，以利于检验工作的进行。同时应在合同中规定我方有取样的权利，因为取样不同，检验结果也往往有所差异。此外，无论是出口商品还是进口商品的检验方法或标准，在合同中均应订明以一种标准或方法为限，不要采用“某种或某种均可”这类带有选择性的条款，以免发生差异时，双方在选用何种标准或方法上引起不必要的纠纷。

二、索赔

索赔，是指在进出口交易中，因一方违反合同规定直接或间接给另一方造成损失，受损方向违约方提出赔偿请求，以弥补其所受损失。当违约的一方受理对方提出的赔偿要求即为理赔(Settlement)。

1. 索赔的含义

对于索赔应该负责的对象主要有卖方、买方、船公司(或承运人)和保险公司。他们所负的责任根据造成损失的原因和有关合同的规定而有所不同。属于卖方的责任有：货物品质规格不符，原装货物数量短少，包装不善致使货物受损，延期交货，卖方不符合合同条款规定的其他行为致使买方受到损失。属于买方的责任有：付款不及时，订舱或配船不及时(指按 F. O. B. 条款成交的合同)或延迟接货，买方不符合合同条款规定的其他行为致使卖方受到损失。属于船公司(或承运人)的责任有：数量少于提单载明的数量，收款人持有清洁提单而货物发生残损短缺。属于保险公司的责任有：在承保范围以内的货物损失，船公司(或承运人)不予赔偿的损失或赔偿额不足以补偿货物的损失而又属承保范围以内的。以上是各个索赔对象应负的单独责任。损失的发生牵涉到几方面，例如保险的货物到达目的港后发生短卸，由于船公司对每件货物的赔偿金额有一定的限制，往往不能赔足，其不足部分就应由保险公司负责。这里涉及船公司和保险公司两方面，因此收货人应向船公司和保险公司同时提出索赔。

2. 合同中的索赔条款

进出口合同中的索赔条款主要内容有索赔的期限、索赔必须具备的证据、出证的机构以及解决索赔的办法等。有时索赔条款还同检验条款合并订在一起。对于买卖大宗商品的机械设备的合同往往还订有罚金条款(Penalty Clause)。索赔的期限是指索赔的一方向违约一方提出索赔要求的有效期限，逾期提出，除经理赔方同意，否则可不予受理，因此索赔期限应根据不同商品结合具体情况作出合理的规定。对于食品、农产品等易腐商品的索赔期可规定得短一些。对于一般货物的索赔期限，通常为货到目的港后30～45天。对于机器设备的索赔期限则应就数量和品质作不同的规定：有关数量方面的索赔期一般为货物到目的港后60天，有关规格、性能等品质方面的索赔期一般为一年或一年以上。对于分批交货的成套机械设备，如需全部设备到货后才能试车，则应规定全部设备的索赔期从最后一批货到目的港后起算。我国进口货物索赔的检验出证机构规定为中国进出口商品检验局。对于出口合同如允许国外买方有复验权，则应争取在合同中规定“必须以买卖双方同意的检验机构出具的检验报告作为索赔的依据”。关于解决索赔的办法，一般合同只作笼统的规定。但如果需要，可由买卖双方商定具体办法，如整修、换货或退货还款等，也可规定赔偿一定的损失和费用。罚金条款的主要内容是一方如果未能履约或未完全履约则应向对方支付一定金额作为罚金以补偿对方的损失。这种条款常用于卖方延期交货或买方延期接货。如我国某进出口公司在进口合同中就“迟交和罚金条款”作如下规定：“如延迟交货除人力不可抗拒者外，卖方应付给买方每一星期按迟交货物总值的0.5%的迟交罚款，不足一星期的迟交日数作为一星期计算。此项罚款总额不超过全部迟交货物总值的5%。在议付货款时，由银行代为扣除，或由买方在付款时进行扣除。如延迟交货超过原定期限10个星期时，买方有权终止合同，但卖方仍应向买方缴付以上规定之罚款。”罚金的支付并不解除违约方继续履行的义务，因此，违约方除支付罚金外，仍应履行合同规定的义务。关于合同的罚金条款，各国法律规定不尽相同。俄罗斯、德国等国的法律承认罚金条款并予以保护。而英、美、澳大利亚、新西兰等国家的法律则对罚金有异议，它们认为对于违约行为只能要求赔偿，而不能惩罚。英、美的法院对于合同中的固定赔偿金额条款，首先要区别这一金额是属于预定的损害赔偿金额，还是属于罚款。如果法院认为属于损害赔偿金额则可按合同规定的固定金额判给；如果法院认为属于惩罚性的罚金，则不予承认而只能按照受损害一方所受损失的证据另行确定其金额。因此我们在与英、美等国商人订立合同时，如需规定罚金或损害赔偿金条款，应注意约定的金额是否合宜，以免在发生纠纷时，使我方处于被动。

三、不可抗力

1. 不可抗力的含义

不可抗力,也称人力不可抗拒,是指在合同签订以后,不是由于当事人的过失或疏忽,发生了当事人所不能预见的、无法预防的意外事故,以致不能履行合同或不能如期履行合同。遭受意外事故的一方可以据此免除履行合同的责任或延迟履行合同,对方无权要求损害赔偿。不可抗力包括两种情况:一是自然原因引起的,如水灾、旱灾、飓风、暴雨、大雪、地震等自然灾害;二是社会原因引起的,如战争行为、政府封锁、禁运等。但不可抗力事故目前在国际上还没有统一的、确切的解释。对于哪些意外事故应订人合同的不可抗力条款,买卖双方可自行商定。但不是所有意外事故都可以构成人力不可抗拒事故的,例如,合同签订后,物价的涨落,货币的升值、贬值等,这些是交易中常见的现象,除买卖双方另有约定外,不属于不可抗力的范围。

不可抗力事故所引起的后果主要有两种:一种是解除合同,一种是延迟履行合同。至于在什么情况下可以解除合同,在什么情况下不能解除合同而只能延迟合同的履行,则要看意外事故对履行合同的影响。也可由买卖双方在合同中作具体规定。如合同中未有规定,一般解释为:如不可抗力事故使合同的履行成为不可能,则可解除合同;如不可抗力事故只是暂时阻碍了合同的履行,则只能延迟履行合同。

2. 合同中的不可抗力条款

不可抗力条款对买卖双方都是同样适用的。在进出口合同中订立了不可抗力条款,一旦发生意外事故影响到合同的履行时就可根据合同规定确定发生的意外事故是否属于不可抗力,防止对方任意扩大或缩小对不可抗力的解释。这对于维护买卖双方正当利益是有好处的。不可抗力条款的内容一般有:不可抗力事故的范围;不可抗力事故发生后,通知对方的期限;出具证明文件的机构;不可抗力事故的后果。常见的不可抗力条款的订法有三种。

(1)概括式规定。即在合同中不具体规定不可抗力事故的种类而是作笼统的规定。例如:"由于公认的不可抗力原因而不履行合同规定义务的一方可不负责任,但应于若干天内通知对方并提供有关的证明文件。"

(2)列举式规定。即逐一证明不可抗力事故种类。例如:"由于战争、洪水、水灾、地震、暴风、大雪的原因而不能履行合同规定义务的一方可不负责任。"

(3)综合式规定。即将概括式和列举式合并在一起的方式。例如在订购成套设备的进口合同中规定:"由于战争、地震、严重的风灾、雪灾、水灾、火灾以及双方同意的其他人力不可抗拒事故,致使任何一方不能履行合同时,遇有上述不可抗力事故的一方,应立即将影响履行合同的不可抗力事故的情况以电报通知对方,并应在 15 天内,以航空挂号信提供事故的详细情况及影响合同履行程度的证明文件。此项文件如由卖方提出时,应由发生不可抗力事故地区的商会出具证明;如由买方提出时,应由中国国际贸易促进委员会出具证明。”上述概括式规定比较笼统,容易产生纠纷。列举式规定虽然明确,但不可抗力的事故举不胜举,如发生了没有列举的事故,就无法引用不可抗力条款。综合性规定则弥补了前两种方式的不足,因此使用比较广泛。

四、仲裁

1. 解决争议的方法

在国际贸易中,买卖双方发生争议后的解决方式有友好协商、调解、仲裁和诉讼等。采用友好协商的方法或第三者调解的方式,气氛比较友好,可以节省仲裁或诉讼的费用,有利于双方贸易的开展。这是买卖双方解决争议常用的两种方法。如果这两种方式不能解决时,才采用仲裁或诉讼的方式。仲裁是由买卖双方根据双方达成的书面协议自愿把双方之间的争议提交双方同意的第三者进行裁决。裁决对双方都有约束力。凡采用仲裁方式处理争议时,双方当事人必须订有仲裁协议。仲裁协议是双方当事人表示愿意将他们之间的争议交付仲裁解决的一种书面协议。它是仲裁机构受理争议案件的依据,仲裁协议可在争议发生前订立,一般是包括在买卖合同的仲裁条款中的,但也可在争议发生后由双方达成。目前大多数国家都承认这两种协议具有同样的效力。仲裁协议的主要作用是使双方当事人发生争议时,只能用仲裁方式解决而不得向法院起诉,这就排除了法院对有争议案件的管辖权。这个原则是被国际上多数国家所承认的。仲裁不同于司法诉讼,仲裁庭也不同于法庭。仲裁必须有双方当事人的仲裁协议才能进行,是自愿性的。而司法诉讼不需要双方当事人的协议,只要一方按照司法程序向有管辖权的法院提出诉讼,另一方就必须应诉,因此是强制性的。仲裁机构一般都是民间性组织,仲裁员不是由政府任命,而是由买卖双方当事人指定的。法院则是国家机器的重要组成部分,法官都是由国家任命的。采用仲裁方式解决争议有以下几个优点:程序简单、费用较少、处理案件时间较短,更重要的是可以较少影响双方之间的关系。因此在国际贸易合同中大多订有仲裁条款,以便在争议无法协商解决时,提交仲裁。

2. 仲裁程序

仲裁程序主要指进行仲裁的手续和做法,包括仲裁的申请、仲裁员的指定、仲裁条件的审理、仲裁裁决的效力和仲裁费用的支付等内容。各国常设的仲裁机构都订有自己的仲裁程序规则。为便于仲裁进行,仲裁条款应明确规定采用哪个仲裁机构的仲裁规则进行仲裁。我国各进出口公司的通常做法是规定在哪个国家的仲裁机构仲裁,就规定按哪个仲裁机构的仲裁规则办理。在资本主义国家,采用哪个仲裁规则可由双方当事人自由选择。进行仲裁时涉及两种法律:一种是上述仲裁程序规则,即程序法;另一种是确定双方当事人权利与义务的实体法。关于实体法问题,资本主义国家一般也允许双方当事人在合同中加以订明。如果没有订明,除仲裁所在国另有规定外,一般由仲裁员按仲裁所在国的法律冲突规则来确定。我国各进出口公司通常不在合同中规定适用的实体法，这就意味着由仲裁员按照上述法律冲突规则予以确定。根据这一原则，既有适用我国法律的可能，也有适用对方国家法律或第三国法律的可能。这点必须引起我们注意。仲裁程序规则一般对仲裁的申请、仲裁员的指定、仲裁案件如何审理都有具体规定。例如，关于仲裁员的指定，我国的仲裁规则规定：仲裁员可由当事人在仲裁委员会委员中选出，也可委托仲裁委员会代为选定。仲裁裁决的效力一般都规定为终局性的，对双方当事人都有约束力，但有些国家的法律允许当事人对明显违背法律的裁决可向法院上诉。仲裁费用一般规定由败诉的一方负担。仲裁的裁决应由当事人自动执行。对于由我国的对外经济贸易仲裁委员会的裁决，一方如果逾期不予执行，另一方可申请中国人民法院依法执行。外国仲裁机构的裁决可以根据具体情况向仲裁所在地国家的法院或与仲裁地国家订有相互承认和执行仲裁公约或条约的国家申请执行。

3. 仲裁地点

仲裁地点是进行仲裁的所在地。根据一些资本主义国家的法律解释，在哪个国家仲裁就适用哪个国家的仲裁规则或程序法，因此确定仲裁地点是仲裁条款的重要内容。国际上对仲裁地点的选择一般有以下几种情况：在买方国家，在第三国，在被诉方国家或原诉方国家，在货物所在地。我国各进出口公司在规定仲裁地点时主要有三种方式：在我国仲裁，在被诉方所在国仲裁，在双方所同意的第三国仲裁。一般来说，首先应当争取在我国进行仲裁，其次才考虑在被诉方所在国仲裁，或在第三国进行仲裁。在选择第三国仲裁时，应注意所选择的国家必须在政治上对我方友好，仲裁机构有一定的业务能力，审理公平合理，我方对该国仲裁程序有所了解。

4. 仲裁机构

国际贸易仲裁机构有临时机构和常设机构两种。临时仲裁机构是为了解决特定的争议而组成的仲裁庭。争议处理完毕，临时仲裁庭即告解散。常设仲裁机构又可分为两种：一种是国际性和全国性的特设机构。国际性的如国际商会仲裁院、全国性的如英国伦敦仲裁院、英国仲裁协会、美国仲裁协会、瑞典斯德哥尔摩商会仲裁院、瑞士苏黎士商会仲裁院、日本国际商事仲裁协会等。中国国际贸易促进委员会附设的对外经济贸易仲裁委员会，也属于全国性的常设仲裁机构。另一种是附设在特定的行业组织之内的专业性仲裁机构。如伦敦谷物商业协会等。常设仲裁机构有负责组织和管理有关事项的人员，为仲裁提供方便，因此在仲裁条款中通常都选用适当的常设机构。如双方同意在中国仲裁，合同内应订明争议由中国国际贸易促进委员会对外经济贸易仲裁委员会仲裁。该委员会受理的案件可分四类。

(1) 对外贸易契约和交易中所发生的争议，特别是外国商号、公司或者其他经济组织同中国商号、公司或者其他经济组织间的争议。

(2) 当事人双方都是外国商号、公司或者其他经济组织间的争议。

(3)中国商号、公司或者其他经济组织间的争议。

(4)有关中外合资经营企业、外国来华投资建厂、中外银行相互信贷等各种对外经济合作方面所发生的争执。

5. 合同中的仲裁条款

国际贸易合同中的仲裁条款主要包括仲裁地点、仲裁机构、仲裁程序、仲裁效力和仲裁费用等。我国对外贸易合同中的仲裁条款常用的有下列三种。

(1)规定在我国仲裁的条款。“凡因执行本合同所发生的或与本合同有关的一切争议,双方应通过友好协商解决;如果协商不能解决,应提交北京中国国际贸易促进委员会对外经济贸易仲裁委员会根据该会的《仲裁程序暂行规则》进行仲裁,仲裁的裁决是终局的,对双方都有约束力。”

(2)规定在被诉方所在国仲裁的条款。“凡因执行本合同所发生的或与本合同有关的一切争议,双方应通过友好协商解决;如果协商不能解决,应提交仲裁。仲裁在被诉人所在国进行,如在中国,由中国国际贸易促进委员会对外经济贸易仲裁委员会根据该会《仲裁程序暂行规则》进行仲裁。如在某国(被诉人所在国家名称),由某仲裁机构(被诉人所在国家的仲裁机构的名称)根据该机构的仲裁程序规则进行仲裁。仲裁裁决是终局的,对双方都有约束力。”

(3)规定在第三国仲裁的条款。“凡因执行本合同所发生的或与本合同有关的一切争议,双方应通过友好协商解决;如果协商不能解决,应提交某国(第三国名称)某仲裁机构(第三国某地的仲裁机构的名称)根据该仲裁机构的仲裁规定进行仲裁。仲裁裁决是终局的,对双方都有约束力。”

第三章 国际货款支付

第一节 支付工具

在国际贸易中，进出口货款如何支付是一个复杂的问题，也是买卖双方密切关心的重要问题之一。首先，国际贸易是国与国之间的商品交换，货物从出口国到进口国需要有一定的运转过程和交接手续，存在着一定的风险；买卖双方又分处两地，很难像国内零售贸易那样，严格地做到交货和付款同时进行。其次，在国际贸易中，双方国家在法律体制、金融管理、货币制度、外汇管制方面，存在各种各样的差别。再次，对于货款的结算，除买卖双方之外，往往还需要有银行或其他金融机构介入，关系复杂。所以，为了保证交易的顺利进行和货款的安全收付，买卖双方有必要事先就货款支付的时间、地点，付款的途径与方法，以及用于支付的货币等一系列与支付有关的问题，作出具体安排。这些问题直接关系到买卖双方的切身利益，其中任何一个方面变化都可能会给双方当事人带来不同的经济后果，因此在磋商过程中，买卖双方要力争订立对自己有利的条件，以保证自身的经济利益。在一笔交易中，有关支付时间、地点和支付货币的选择和确定过程，也就是双方根据各自的贸易政策、市场地位、经营意图，通过磋商谈判，采用各种方式，就这些矛盾进行调整、妥协而达到统一的过程。以上这些因素都决定了国际贸易货款支付方式有多样性。

一、汇 票

1. 汇票的含义

作为国际结算中的一个主要组成成分，国际贸易货款的支付一般是利用汇票这种支付凭据，通过银行进行的。我国在对外贸易中也大量地使用汇票作为支付凭据。汇票(Bill of Exchange, Draft)是一种债权证书，它是由一个人向另一个人签发的无条件的书面支付命令。它要求对方立即或者在一定时间之内，对某人或其指定的人及持票人支付一定的金额。

2. 汇票的基本内容

(1)汇票的当事人。汇票的当事人有三个。

①出票人。即开出汇票的人，在进出口业务中，通常就是出口人。

②受票人。即汇票的付款人(Payer)，在进出口业务中，通常就是进口人。

③受款人。即受领汇票所规定的金额的人，在进出口业务中，通常就是出口人或其指定的人。

(2)金额和货币。汇票必须明确具体地规定受票人应付的金额，并注明使用的货币。在国际贸易中，汇票的金额原则上应在合同或信用证金额的范围内，如无特殊规定，其具体金额和货币一般必须与发票金额和货币一致，否则受票人有权拒付。

(3)付款时间。汇票还需规定明确的付款时间，如"见票即付"、"见票后30天付款"等等。

(4)出票和付款地点。汇票一般应注明开票和付款地点。一般分别以汇票上所列的出票人和受票人的所在地表示。

(5)出票人签字。

3. 汇票的种类

汇票从不同的角度可分为以下几种。

(1)银行汇票(Banker's Bill)和商业汇票(CommercialI Draft)。由银行开立的汇票，即为银行汇票，它一般是银行应汇款人的要求，开立以汇入行为付款人的汇票，这种汇票一般由汇款人直接寄交收款人，凭票向汇入行取款。在国际贸易中，凡由出口商签发，向进口商或银行收取货款或其他款项的汇票，都属商业汇票。

(2)光票(Clean Bill)和跟单汇票(Documentary Draft)。前者是指不附货运单据的汇票，即只凭汇票付款，不附交任何单据。跟单汇票是指附有货运单据的汇票，其作用在于出票人必须提交约定的货运单据才能取得货款；受款人必须在付清货款或提供一定保证后，才能取得货运单据，提取货物。

(3)即期汇票(Sighi Draft)和远期汇票(Time Drafi)。汇票按付款时间的不同，分为即期汇票和远期汇票两种；凡汇票上规定见票即付款的汇票称即期汇票。凡汇票上规定付款人在将来一个可确定的日期付款的汇票，称远期汇票。远期汇票的付款日期有三种规定方法：一种是规定付款人见票后(After Sight)若干天付款，如见票后30天、60天、120天付款；一种是在出票后(After Date)若干天付款；再一种是在提单签发日期后(After Bill of Lading)若干天付款。第一种方法的付款时间的起算是决定于付款人"见票"，因此，对付款人比较有利，他可以避而不见票以推迟付款时间；第二种办法不受付款人见票的限制，而且可节省从出票到见票的时间，对出票人比较有利，但不易为付款人接受；第三种办法是以货物装运签发提单起算，比较客观合理，容易为双方接受。在实际业务上，使用什么办法计算付款日期，需由双方协定，并在合同和汇票中明确规定。

4. 汇票的使用

在国际贸易实际业务中，使用汇票支付货款一般需要经过出票、提示、付款等程序，如是远期汇票，受票人在到期付款之前，还必须办理承兑手续。出票(Issue)是指出口人根据合同签发汇票并交给受款人的行为。汇票是一种无条件支付命令书，体现着一定的债权和债务关系，因此，它们的开立需要有一定的合法前提，从国际贸易的角度来看，这个前提就是双方当事人订立的合同及其履行。提示是持票人将汇票提交付款人要求付款或承兑的行为。付款人看到汇票叫做见票(Sight)。如果持票人提示的是即期汇票，付款人应立即付款；如果是远期汇票，付款人必须在汇票上写上承兑(Accepted)字样，在汇票到期时付款。

承兑是远期汇票到期之前办理的一道手续，按照资本主义国家的解释，远期汇票只有经过付款人承兑，付款人才承担到期付款的义务。在国际金融市场上，汇票既是一种支付凭据，又是一种流通工具。除少数在汇票上书明“仅付××公司”(Pay××Co. only)或“付××公司，不得转让”(Pay××Co. not transferable)的所谓限制性抬头的汇票外，资本主义国家的汇票都可以通过议付或贴现辗转转让。汇票在转让时，除了来人抬头(Bearer)即以持票人作为收款人的汇票，只需交付汇款，无需办理其他手续外，其他汇票的转让都需要通过背书(Endorsement)交付。背书就是由原来的持票人在汇票的背面签上自己的名字，表示该汇票已转让出去。汇票经转让后，受让人还可以通过背书方式再次转让。所以一张汇票在资本主义市场，可以有许多背书人，而对于某一个受让人来说，凡是在他以前背书的人，都是他的前手，在他后面的背书人都是他的后手，前手对后手负有担保汇票必然会被承付的责任。从上述有关汇票的转让和背书可以看出，汇票这种作为债权证书的支付凭据，可以通过转让，也就是债权的转让，来承担一系列债权债务的结算任务，从而避免使用现金。从国际贸易看，汇票的转让，也给买卖双方的资金融通带来方便。它一方面使得卖方可通过汇票的议付或贴现，提前从第三者取得资金；另一方面，也给买方提供了一定的付款期限，避免过早地付出资金。汇票的转让是以转让人向被转让人保证付款人将承担汇票的付款义务作为前提的。在资本主义国家，汇票遭到付款人拒付的现象仍是时有发生的，所以拒付(Dishonour)，包括拒绝付款和拒绝承兑的两个方面。汇票被拒付时，持票人有权向出票人及所有“前手”背书人进行追索(Recourse)。汇票的背书人为了避免承担这种责任，也可以在背书时注明“不受追索”(Without Recourse)。在汇票拒付时，持票人行使其追索权，除出票人已在汇票写明不必开立拒绝证书外，应及时作成拒绝证书(Protest)，其向“前手”追索。拒绝证书是由付款地的法定出证人或其他依法有权作出这种证书的机构作出的，证明付款人拒付的文件，是持票人向其“前手”追索的法律依据。

二、本 票

本票(Promissory Note)是出票人对受款人承诺无条件支付一定金额的票据。本票有由工商企业签发的商业本票和由银行签发的银行本票两种。商业本票有即期与远期之分，银行本票都是即期的。国际贸易结算中使用的本票大多是银行本票。本票的当事人只有两个：出票人和受款人。本票的付款人就是出票人本人，因此远期本票不需承兑。

三、支 票

支票(Cheque, check)是存款户对银行签发的委托银行对受款人在见票时无条件支付一定金额的票据。出票人在签发支票时应在付款银行存有不低于票面金额的存款。支票只有即期，没有远期。用于远期支付的，可将出票日期按需要往后填。支票如在左上角划上两道平行线的，称为划线支票，这种支票的受款人只能通过往来银行代为收款入账；未经划线的支票，受款人可凭其向付款银行提取现款。

第二节　支付方式

一、汇 付

汇付(Remittance)泛指付款人主动通过银行或其他途径将款项汇交收款人。对外贸易的货款如采用汇付，一般是由买方按合同约定的条件(收到单据或货物)和时间，将货款通过银行汇交给卖方。买方在汇款时可以采用以下三种不同的方式。

(1)信汇。信汇是由买方将款项交给进口地银行，由银行开具付款委托书，通过邮递寄交卖方所在地银行，委托其向卖方付款。

(2)电汇。电汇是进口地银行应买方申请，直接用电信方式通知出口地银行向卖方付款。这种方法比信汇快捷，对卖方来说，可以提早收到货款，但是买方却要因此负担较高的费用。

(3)票汇。票汇是由买方向进口地银行购买银行汇票自行邮寄给卖方，由卖方或其指定的人持汇票向出口地有关银行取款。

从我国对外贸易的实践看，在使用汇付时，大多数是通过信汇或电汇的方式进行，但是这两种汇款方式对买卖双方的利害关系却是不同的。电汇对卖方来说可较早收到货款，加速资金周转，增加利息收入，避免汇率变动，是较为有利的，但买方却要多付电信费用和银行费用，所以，在没有明确规定使用电汇的情况下，买方一般只通过信汇付款。在国际贸易中，汇付方式除了用于小额款项费用、佣金支付外，更多的是与其他支付方式结合使用，如预付定金等。从上述的做法，不难看出，汇付是一种最简便的支付方式，它对买卖双方的影响，可因具体采用的办法不同而有很大的差别。

二、托 收

1.托收的概念

托收(Collection)是债权人出具汇票委托银行向债务人代收款项的一种结算方式。在国际贸易中，债权人为出口商，债务人为进口商。出口商根据贸易或商务合同发运货物，产生债权，进口商获得货物而发生债务。为了结清这种债权债务，出口商出具以进口商为付款人的汇票并通常附发票及货运单据(物权凭证)，委托银行收款。托收是基于买卖双方信用的，也就是通常所说的商业信用，银行虽居于其间，但只是处于受委托代理的地位，不作任何关于付款的承诺，只根据委托人或付款人的指示办事。

2.托收的当事人

托收业务通常涉及4个当事人，即委托人(出口商)、托收行、代收行和付款人。

(1)委托人(Principal)。委托人即出口商，是指委托银行办理托收业务的客户。

(2)付款人(Drawee)。付款人是进口商,其基本和主要的义务就是按贸易或商务合同规定付款,以最终结清债权债务。

(3)托收行(Remitting Bank)。托收行是指受委托人的委托,办理托收业务的银行。在托收业务中,托收行处于代理人的地位,重要的责任就是依据委托人的指示办理,在向代收行发出业务委托时,其内容要与委托人的委托书一致。

(4)代收行(Collecting Bank)。代收行是指除托收行以外,参与办理托收指示的任何银行,它通常是与进口商同在一地的某家银行。在托收业务中,代收行也处于代理地位,它受托收行委托办事。因此,其基本的责任义务与托收行类似。

3. 托收的种类

(1)光票托收(Clean Collection)。光票托收指以汇票、本票、支票而不随附其他单据的托收,故也不涉及交单的方式问题。

(2)跟单托收(Documentary Collection)。跟单托收即是指汇票随附其他单据的托收,也是贸易中常用的结算方式。跟单托收按其交单方式又分为付款交单和承兑交单。

① 付款交单(Documents against Payment)。简单地说,付款交单就是付款才能放单给付款人,付款人只有在交付货款后才能取得单据凭借其提货。按支付时间的不同,付款交单又可分为即期付款交单和远期付款交单两种。即期付款交单是指银行提示即期汇票和单据,进口人见票时即应付款,并在付清货款后取得单据;远期付款交单是指银行提示远期汇票,进口人审核无误后在汇票上进行承兑,于汇票到期日付清货款后再领取货运单据。

②承兑交单(Documents against Acceptance)。承兑交单即为汇票付款人承诺到期付款后,代收行可放单给付款人。不难看出,承兑交单有两个特点:一是付款是远期的;二是有远期汇票,无汇票则无法发生承兑的行为。

三、信用证(Letter of Credit,简称 L/C)

1. 信用证的概念

根据国际商会《跟单信用证统一惯例》第 2 条规定,“信用证是指一项约定,不论其名称或描述如何,即由一家银行(开证行)依照客户(申请人)的要求和指示或以自身的名义,在符合信用证条款的条件下,凭规定单据向第三者(受益人)或其指定人付款,或承兑并支付受益人出具的汇票;或授权另一家银行进行该项付款,承兑并支付该汇票;或授权另一家银行议付。”上述定义由于考虑法律上的严谨和完整,表述比较复杂。对于进口商或出口商来说,最主要的是把握住一点,即信用证是一家银行对信用证受益人有条件的付款承诺,这个条件就是受益人提交完全符合信用证所规定的单据。

2. 信用证的当事人

信用证可能涉及的当事人有开证行、受益人、开证申请人、通知行、议付行、保兑行等。

(1)开证申请人(Applicant)。一般来说,信用证的申请人是贸易或商务合同的买方。

申请人与开证行之间以开证申请书作为合同；申请人与受益人(即出口商)之间受贸易或商务合同制约。

(2)开证行(Opening Bank, Lssuing Bank)。开证行是指接受开证申请人的委托，开立信用证的银行，通常与开证申请人同处一地。开证行在信用证业务中承担第一性付款义务，其付款是终局性的，一经付出便无追索权。

(3)通知行(Advising Bank,Notifying Bank)。通知行是指接受开证行的委托，将信用证转交出口人的银行。它只证明信用证的真实性并通知受益人。

(4)受益人(Beneficiary)。受益人是指信用证上所指定的有权使用该证的人，即出口人或实际供货人。受益人应注意认真履行合同义务；如果议付行向受益人垫付了货款而又未能得到开证行的偿付，议付行可向受益人索回有关款项，受益人必须退回。

(5)议付行(Negotiating Bank)。议付行是指愿意买入受益人交来跟单汇票的银行。议付行必须具有垫付货款的行为。

(6)付款行(Paying Bank, Drawee Bank)。付款行是指信用证上指定的付款银行，它代行付款后对受益人或其前手无追索权，但它有权不付款。

3. 信用证操作的程序

在采用信用证支付货款时，一般需经过下述几个程序。

(1)由买卖双方在合同中明确规定以信用证方式结算，这是买方据以开证的基础和前提。

(2)买方向其所在地银行提出申请书，要求银行(开证行)按申请书的内容，向卖方(受益人)开出信用证。买方在申请开证时，一般需交纳相当于信用证金额一定百分比的押金或提供一定的保证，并按信用证的种类交纳与开证有关的费用。目前，有些银行对其下属的企业，或是与其有密切关系、资本雄厚的往来企业，往往可提供一定的信用限额，在此限度内，申请开证的企业可免交押金。

(3)开证行按申请书内容开立以卖方为受益人的信用证，并通过其在卖方所在地的代理行或往来行将信用证通知卖方。

(4)卖方在发运货物时，取得装运单据及信用证要求的其他必备单据后，按信用证规定向其所在地银行(可以是上述通知行，也可以是其他银行，一般是出口人的往来行)议付货款。

(5)议付行议付后即在信用证背面批销议付或议付金额，并将单据寄开证行索偿。

(6)开证行在单据审查无误、符合信用证规定后，偿还议付行付出的款项，同时通知买方付款赎单。

(7)买方向开证行付款赎单，凭单提货。从上述信用证的内容和做法，可以看出信用证是一种银行信用，这是它同汇付和托收的根本区别。在信用证的条件下，银行根据买方的申请书，通过信用证上的保证条款向卖方提出付款保证。这样，银行就不再像托收那样，只是接受卖方的委托代收跟单汇票，对能否收到货款概不负责。在信用证业务中，银行处于首先付款人的地位，只要卖方提交的单据符合信用证的条件，银行就不得无理拒付。因此，只有在银行倒闭或丧失支付能力时，出口人才可以转向进口人要求偿付货款，这就清楚地说明，原来由商人承担付款责任的商业信用已由银行承担付款责任的银行信用所代替。由于进口人在信用证条件下还要负付款的最后责任，所以，更明确地说，信用证是用银行信用来保证商业信用的。由于银行信用一般比商业信用可靠，所以在采用信用证付款的条件下，出口人只要在装运前收到信用证，收到货款就有了保证。这在很大程度上解除了卖方在托收条件下对能否收到货款存在的疑虑，从而对扩大贸易额，发展新客户、新地区的贸易提供了可能。但是，银行信用也不是绝对可靠的，在经济危机和金融货币危机的袭击下，资本主义国家的银行还是会有倒闭的可能。即使在平时，银行凭借各种借口，拒不履行付款义务的现象也是有的。因此，在采用信用证付款时还需注意调查了解开证行的资信情况。

4. 信用证的特点

(1)信用证是一种银行信用凭据。信用证支付方式是一种银行信用，由开证行以自己的信用作出付款的保证。

(2)开证行的第一性付款责任在信用证业务中，只要受益人提交了合格单据，无论是议付行拒绝议付或付款行拒绝付款，还是开证申请人破产倒闭，开证行的付款义务都是确实和不可推卸的。在信用证业务中，各有关当事人处理的是单据，而不是与单据有关的货物、服务或其他行为。

(3)信用证是一种相对独立的文件。就其性质而言，信用证与可能作为其依据的销售合同或其他合同是相互独立的交易，即使信用证中含有此类合同的任何援引，银行也与该合同毫不相关，并不受其约束。

5. 信用证的种类

(1)根据开证行的责任，信用证可分为不可撤销信用证和可撤销信用证。

①不可撤销信用证。不可撤销信用证是指一经开出，未得所有当事人(主要是受益人)同意不能撤销，这对受益人是一个确定无疑的付款承诺和保障。

②可撤销信用证(Revocable L/C)。可撤销信用证是指信用证开立后，不必事先通知或征得受益人同意就有权随时撤销或修改的信用证。《跟单信用证统一惯例》第6条(3)款规定，如果信用证没有明确注明是可撤销的或是不可撤销的，"应视为是不可撤销的"。

(2)根据付款方式划分，信用证可分为付款信用证、承兑信用证和议付信用证。

①付款信用证。付款信用证是指定某一银行付款的信用证，一般不要求受益人开具汇票，而仅凭受益人提供的单据付款。

②承兑信用证。如果信用证规定付款期限为远期，同时要求出具汇票，这种信用证即为承兑信用证。

③议付信用证。议付信用证是指允许受益人向某一指定银行或任何银行交单议付的信用证。又可分为自由议付信用证和限制议付信用证，前者任何银行均可办理，后者则由

指定的银行议付。

(3)其他几种重要的信用证分类。

①循环信用证。循环信用证是指当受益人全部或部分使用完信用证的金额以后,其信用金额又恢复原金额再被受益人使用,直至达到规定次数或累计总金额为止。循环信用证主要用于长期供货,开证申请人为了免交多次开证费用和节省开证押金,才用此种信用证。

②对背信用证。对背信用证是指一个信用证的受益人要求银行以该信用证为保证开出另一信用证。这种方式通常用于第一个信用证的受益人是中间商,需要向实际供货人开出购货的第二个信用证的三角贸易。

6. 合同中的信用证条款

以我国对外出口业务中常用的支付条款为例,将信用证支付条款的主要内容简单介绍。

(1)即期信用证条款。"买方应于××年×月×日前(或接到卖方通知×天内或签约后×天内)通过××银行开出以卖方为受益人的(由××银行保兑的)不可撤销的(可转让可分割的)全部发票金额的即期信用证,信用证有效期延至装运日期后15天在中国到期。"

如果要求电汇,即可在上列条款内加列"信用证应列明在收到议付电报通知后即以电汇偿付"。

(2)远期信用证条款。"买方应于××年××月×日前(或接到卖方通知后×天内或签约后×天内)通过××银行开立以卖方为受益人的不可撤销的(可转让的)见票××天(或装船后×天)付款的银行承兑信用证。信用证议付有效期延至上述装运期后15天在中国到期。"

四、银行保证书

银行保证书是由银行开立的与信用证近似的担保凭证,也属银行信用,但与信用证相比,在使用范围和承担责任上有明显区别。一般的跟单信用证仅用于为进口人开立,银行承担按规定条件付款的第一性责任。保证书则不仅用于进口,还可用于其他场合,其形式、内容和条款也多种多样,银行承担的责任可以是第一性的,也可以是第二性的。

第四章 国际货物销售合同的商订

第一节 交易磋商的程序

国际销售合同的商订是国际货物买卖的首要环节，一般都要经过多次协商才能达成交易。在我国的进出口业务中，要根据国家方针政策和经营意图，按照国际市场上通常使用的方式同国外客户进行交易协商。国际销售合同的交易磋商程序大致可分为 4 个环节：询盘、发盘、还盘和接受。其中发盘和接受是必不可少的两个基本环节。

一、询盘(Inquiry)

询盘，亦称询价，是指交易的一方欲出售或购买某种货物，向另一方发出的探询买卖该项货物有关交易条件的一种口头或书面的表示。在法律中称为“要约邀请”(Invitation for offer)。询盘的内容可涉及价格、规格、品质、数量、包装、装运以及索取样品等，且多数只是询问价格。询盘从发出、入的地位不同，可分为以下两种。

(1)买方发出询盘，也称“邀请发盘”(Invitation to make an offer)。

(2)卖方发出询盘，也称“邀请递盘”(Invitation to make abid)。在国际贸易业务中，询盘并不一定是为了达成交易，有时只是为了建立业务联系或探询某些商品的该国市场行情。

二、发盘(Offer)

发盘，又称发价，是指交易的一方向另一方提出一定的交易条件，并愿意按照提出的交易条件达成买卖该项货物的交易，签订合同的一种口头或书面的表示。《联合国国际货物销售合同公约》(以下简称《公约》)第 14 条对发盘的定义为：“向一个或一个以上特定的人提出的订立合同的建议，如果十分确定并且表明发盘人在得到接受时承受约束的意旨，即构成发盘。一个建议如果写明货物并且明示或暗示地规定数量和价格或规定如何确定数量和价格，即为十分确定。”

三、还盘(Counter Offer)

所谓还盘，是受盘人对发盘内容不完全同意而提出要求更改的表示。在磋商交易中，还盘是对发盘的拒绝，也是受盘人以发盘人的地位所提出的新发盘。因此，一方的发盘经对方还盘以后即失去效用，受盘人不得再接受原发盘。所谓再还盘，就是对还盘的还盘。同上述还盘的性质一样，再还盘是对还盘的拒绝，是被还盘人针对还盘而发出的新发盘，是双方考虑成交的新的基础。一方发盘，另一方如对其内容不同意，可以进行还盘。同样，一方还盘,另一方如对其内容不同意,也可以进行再还盘。一笔交易往往经过还盘及往返多次的再还盘才能达成。

四、接受(Acceptance)

接受是交易的一方完全同意对方发盘中全部交易内容的肯定表示。发盘和接受是达成交易的两个不可缺少的环节。一方的发盘经另一方接受,交易即告达成,合同亦即成立,双方即应分别履行其所承担的义务。接受由我方作出,也可以由国外商人作出。表示接受的电文,内容可以很简单,如仅列明“你10日电我接受(或确认)”,而不重复列出有关的交易条件。

第二节 合同的订立

在交易磋商过程中,一方发实盘或还盘,经另一方接受以后,交易即告成立,买卖双方就构成了合同关系,双方在磋商过程中的往返函电即具有合同的书面证明效用。但根据国际贸易习惯,买卖双方通常还需要照例签订书面的正式合同或成交确认书。

一、发盘

发盘(Offer)是对发盘人具有约束力的“要约”,是发盘人在发盘的有效期限内不得撤回或修改的。是发盘人向受盘人提出各项主要交易条件,并愿按这些条件达成交易的肯定表示。发盘一经对方在有效时限内表示无保留的接受,交易即成立。

1. 发盘的构成

根据《公约》的定义,可以看出一项发盘的构成必须具备下列条件。

(1)向一个或一个以上的特定人发出。发盘是由发盘人向受发盘人(Offeree)发出的。特定的人是指受发盘人必须为指定的人,即发盘人在发盘时必须指明收受该项发盘的公司、企业或个人的名称或姓名。这项规定的目的是把刊载普通商业广告或向广大公众散发商品目录(Catalognes)、价目表(Price List)等行为与发盘区别开来。

(2)发盘的内容必须十分确定。所谓十分确定(Sufficiently definite),是指必须符合《公约》所提出的最低限度要求。

2. 发盘的有效期

发盘的有效期,是发盘人受发盘约束的期限,在此期限内不得任意撤销;发盘的有效期也是受盘人表示接受的期限,在此期限内作出答复才算有效。在国际贸易中,发盘通常都规定有效时间。

3. 发盘的撤回与撤销

发盘的撤回与撤销是两个不同的概念。发盘的撤回是指发盘人在发出发盘后,在其尚未到达受发盘人之前，即在发盘尚未生效之前，将该项发盘收回，使其不发生效力；发盘的撤销则是指发盘人在其发盘已经到达受发盘人之后，即在其发盘已经生效之后，将该项发盘取消，从而使发盘失去效力。关于发盘的撤回，《公约》第15条第2款明确规定："一项发盘，即使是不可撤销的，如果撤回通知于发盘送达被发盘人得予撤回。"按照上述规定，一项发盘是在传达到被发盘人时才发生效力的，因此，在被发盘人收到该项发盘之前，发盘人可以用更为迅速的传递方式声明撤回，只要该声明是早于或与发盘同时送达被发盘人，撤回即可生效。

关于发盘的撤销，《公约》第16条规定："在未订立合同之前，发盘得予撤销，如果撤销通知于被发盘人发出接受通知之前送达被发盘人。"但同时，《公约》规定了两种例外情况下发盘不得撤销，即"发盘写明接受发盘的期限或以其他方式表示发盘是不可撤销的"或"被发盘人有理由信赖该项发盘是不可撤销的，而且被发盘人已本着对该项发盘的信赖行事。"在这种情况下，发盘人如果撤销发盘，将会给受发盘人带来损失。

4. 发盘的终止

按照《公约》的规定，发盘在以下几种情况发生时失效：

(1)发盘因受盘人拒绝而终止；

(2)发盘因发盘人撤回或撤销而终止；

(3)发盘因所规定的接受届满或"合理期限"已过而自然终止。

二、接受

接受是指受盘人在发盘有效期之内同意发盘的全部内容，并愿意签订合同的一种口头或书面的表示，在法律中被称为"承诺"。《公约》第18条第1款对接受的定义是："受盘人声明或做出其他行为表示同意一项发盘，即为接受。"缄默或不行动本身不等于接受。

1. 接受的构成

一项有效的接受必须具备以下条件。

(1)接受必须是被受盘人作出的。一般说来，一项发盘会明确规定受盘人，即一个或一个以上特定的人，只有他们表示接受才可以达成交易。除此之外，任何第三人表示接受均无法律效力。

(2)接受的必须是发盘内容。原则上说，当接受中含有对发盘内容的增加、限制或修改，接受均不能成立。但是，为了促进交易达成和发展国际贸易，《公约》对此作了变通，第19条明确规定了以下内容。

①对发盘表示接受但载有添加、限制或其他更改的答复，即为拒绝该项发盘，并且构成还盘。

②对发盘表示接受但载有添加或不同条件的答复，如所载的添加或不同条件在实质上并不变更该项发盘的条件，除发盘人在不过分迟延的期间内以口头或书面形式通知反对其

间的差异外,仍构成接受。如果发盘人不作出这种反对,合同的条件就以该项发盘的条件以及接受通知内所载的更改为准。

③有关货物价格、付款、货物质量和数量、交货地点和时间、一方当事人对另一方当事人的赔偿责任范围或解决争端等的添加或不同条件,均视为在实质上变更发盘条件。因此,应将还盘与肯定接受前提下的"请求"区分开来。还盘是指对发盘提出了新的附加条件,是对发盘的拒绝,如果发盘人不接受附加条件,就不能达成交易;而请求则不然,无论发盘人同意与否,都不影响交易的达成。

(2)接受必须在一项发盘的有效期限之内或一段合理的时间内作出。

(3)接受必须由受盘人采用声明或实际行动的形式来表示,并且在传达给发盘人时生效。在《公约》18 条第 2 款规定:"接受发盘于表示同意的通知送达发盘人时生效。"第 3 款又规定:"如果根据该项发盘或按照当事人之间确立的习惯做法或惯例,被发盘人可以做出某种行为,例如与发运货物或支付价款有关的行为,来表示同意,而无需向发盘人发出通知,则接受于该项行为做出时生效。"

2. 接受的撤回

《公约》第 22 条规定:"接受得即撤回,如果撤回通知应于接受生效之前或同时送达发盘人。"接受不得撤销。接受通知一经到达发盘人合同即告成立,所以此时撤销接受就等同于违反合同。

三、合同的成立

在国际贸易中,订立合同的形式有三种:一是书面形式,二是口头形式,三是以实际行动表示。《公约》第 11 条规定:"销售合同无须以书面订立或书面证明,在形式方面也不受任何其他条件的限制。销售合同可以用包括人质在内的任何方法证明。"由此可见,《公约》对合同形式没有限制,我国在参加《公约》时对这一条作出了保留,因为这一条与我国法律冲突。《涉外经济合同法》第 7 条规定:"当事人就合同条款以书面形式达成协议并签字,即为合同成立。"因此,我国的进出口销售合同必须采用书面形式。我国对外贸易实践中,书面合同包括合同、确认书和协议书等,其中采用合同和确认书两种形式居多。

国际贸易的买卖合同一般包括三个部分:第一部分是合同的首部,包括合同名称、合同号数、缔约日期、缔约地点、缔约双方名称和地址等;第二部分是合同的主体,包括合同的主要条款,如商品名称、品质、规格、数量、包装、单价和总值、装运、保险、支付以及特殊条款(索赔、仲裁及不可抗力)等;第三部分是合同的尾部,包括合同文字和份数以及缔约双方的签字。合同条款内容应符合政策,做到内容完备、条款明确及前后呼应,与交易磋商内容一致。合同对双方都有约束,应根据重合同、守信用的原则严肃对待合同。

第三节 合同的履行

通过交易磋商达成交易，签订了具体的交易合同，下一步就进入了履行合同过程。“重合同、守信用”是我国对外贸易的重要原则，是我国在进出口业务中具体贯彻“平等、互利”的对外贸易政策的要求，在我国出口业务中，要严格遵守这个原则，按时、按质、按量履行合同，维护国家信誉。我国出口合同，多属 CIF 或 CFR 价格条件和即期信用证支付方式的合同。履行此类合同的程序一般包括货（备货）、证（催证、审证、改证）、船（租船、订舱）、款（制单、结汇）四个主要环节。货、证、船、款四个环节的工作之间是有紧密的不可分割的内在联系的。因此，在进行每个环节的工作时，都必须同其他环节的工作相互配合，保持一致，防止“有货无证、有证无货”或“有货无船、有船无货”或“单证不符”等现象发生。

一、备 货

备货就是根据出口合同的规定，按时、按质、按量准备好应交的货物，以便及时装运。如货物是凭库存现货对外成交的商品，在签约后必须按照所规定的品质、规格、数量、包装、运输标志等条件进行检查核实；如货物属期货，则应及时与生产部门或供货部门联系安排生产，特别要注意备货的时间，除了根据合同的交货期限外，还要与船期紧密衔接，防止交货脱期。

二、催证与审证

国际贸易买卖合同的有效履行，一方面决定于卖方按照合同规定交货，另一方面还决定于买方按照合同规定及时办理开立信用证或付款手续。在对国外出口业务中，由于国外买方遇到资金短缺或市场变化等种种原因，有时可能拖延开证。因此，我们应催促对方遵守合同的规定及时办理开证手续。

信用证开到后，应对信用证内容逐项认真审核，信用证条款必须与合同内容相一致，不得随意改变。在实际业务中，有时由于国外商人（或开证银行）工作上的疏忽差错，或因来证地区不同，信用证另有特殊规定或因国外商人对我国政策不了解，会使信用证所列内容与合同不符，甚至会有同我国政策相违背的条款。因此，我们必须认真做好审证工作，以保证及时装船、安全结汇。审证时，遇到有关政策性的问题，因对于不同国家、不同地区以及不同银行有不同的掌握原则，应先与中国银行共同研究，根据我国的方针政策，区别问题的性质，决定统一的对外措施，以使银贸步调一致。如果属于品质、数量、金额、交货期、港口等交易条件的不符，责任在对方的，不能为我方接受时，应立即要求国外修改。有时由于舱位及备货发生变化等原因不能按期装运，责任在我方的，也应及时商请对方改证，并要在收到对方的修改书后再安排装运交货。这里要注意的是，对于一张信用证中的问题，应尽可能一次提出修改，不应一次只修改一项，造成多次修改的现象，改证过多也会引起不良的政治影响和经济上的损失。

三、装运

按照CIF或CFR价格条件成交的出口合同，租船、订舱工作应由卖方负责。我国进出口公司大多委托中国对外贸易运输公司代为办理。除了数量较大的货物需向国外租船外，一般都是由外运公司代为租订部分舱位。订舱及装船的简单程序为：进出口公司根据国外来证和合同内有关运输条款及货物的性质、数量等向外运公司提出"订舱委托书"。外运公司在收到委托书后，会同外轮代理公司，根据配载原则，结合船期、货物性质、货运数量、目的口岸等因素具体安排船只和舱位。外轮代理公司安排好船只和舱位，并签发"装货单"(Shipping Order)后，船长命令装船。船方在装船后，由大副或船方其他负责人在"大副收据"(Mateis Receipt)即装货单的第二联上签字，交由发货人凭其向轮船公司(或中国外轮代理公司)调换提单。进出口公司收到提单后，便向国外商人发出装船通知。出口货物在装船前，还要办理报关、报验和投保手续。凡是出口货物，都必须按照规定手续，向海关申报，经海关核验放行后，才能装船。凡属国家规定的法定检验的商品和出口合同规定应由商品检验局进行检验并出具检验证明的商品，在装船前必须申请商检局进行检验，并取得有关检验证明。凡属CIF价格条件成交的出口货物，在装船前均需由卖方向保险公司办理投保手续。

四、制单结汇

在出口货物装船后，应立即按照信用证的规定，正确备制各种单据，并在信用证有效期内送交银行议付、结汇。制单时要注意单据与信用证规定相符，单据与单据之间一致，做到"单证相符"、"单单一致"。银行接到单据，审核无误后，一方面向国外银行收款，另一方面按照约定的结汇办法，与进出口公司结汇。在信用证支付方式下，国外银行只凭单据付款，不问货物如何，即使所交货物本身同信用证及合同的要求相符，如果单据所列与信用证规定不一致，银行仍可拒绝付款。因此，各种制单要正确、及时、完备、简明、整洁，以保证安全及时收汇。

第五章　跟单信用证统一惯例

第一节　UCP 600

第一条　UCP 的适用范围

《跟单信用证统一惯例》(2007 年修订本,国际商会第 600 号出版物)(简称“UCP”)一套规则,适用于所有在其文本中明确表明受本惯例约束的跟单信用证(下称信用证)(在其可适用的范围内,包括备用信用证)。除非信用证明确修改或排除,本惯例各条文对信用证所有当事人均具有约束力。

第二条　定义

就本惯例而言,有如下定义。

(1)通知行。指应开证行的要求通知信用证的银行。

(2)申请人。指要求开立信用证的一方。

(3)银行工作日。指银行在其履行受本惯例约束的行为的地点通常开业的一天。

(4)受益人。指接受信用证并享受其利益的一方。

(5)相符交单。指与信用证条款、本惯例的相关适用条款以及国际标准银行实务一致的交单。

(6)保兑。指保兑行在开证行承诺之外作出的承付或议付相符交单的确定承诺。

(7)保兑行。指根据开证行的授权或要求对信用证加具保兑的银行。

(8)信用证。指一项不可撤销的安排,无论其名称或描述如何,该项安排构成开证行对相符交单予以承付的确定承诺。

(9)承付。承付指以下内容。

①如果信用证为即期付款信用证,则即期付款。

②如果信用证为延期付款信用证,则承诺延期付款并在承诺到期日付款。

③如果信用证为承兑信用证,则承兑受益人开出的汇票并在汇票到期日付款。

(10)开证行。指应申请人要求或者代表自己开出信用证的银行。

(11)议付。指指定银行在相符交单下,在其应获偿付的银行工作日当天或之前向受益人预付款项,从而购买汇票(其付款人为指定银行以外的其他银行)及(或)单据的行为。

(12)指定银行。指信用证可在其处兑用的银行,如信用证可在任一银行兑用,则任何银行均为指定银行。

(13)交单。指向开证行或指定银行提交信用证项下单据的行为,或指按此方式提交的单据。

(14)交单人。指实施交单行为的收益人、银行或其他人。

第三条　解释

就本惯例而言,有如下惯例。

(1)如情形相同,单数词形包含复数含义,复数词形包含单数含义。

(2)信用证是不可撤销的,即使未如此表明。

(3)单据签字可用手签、摹样签字、穿孔签字、印戳、符号或其他任何机械或电子的证实方法。

(4)诸如单据必须履行法定手续、签证、证明等类似要求,可由单据上任何看似满足该要求的签字、标记、印戳或标签来满足。

(5)一家银行在不同国家的分支机构被视为不同的银行。

(6)用诸如"第一流的"、"著名的"、"合格的"、"独立的"、"正式的"、"有资格的"或"本地的"等词语描述单据的出单人时,允许除受益人之外的任何人出具该单据。

(7)除非要求在单据中使用,否则诸如"迅速地"、"立刻地"或"尽快地"等词语将被不予理会。

(8)"在或大概在(on or about)"或类似用语将被视为规定事件发生在指定日期的前后五个日历日之间,起讫日期计算在内。

(9)"至(to)"、"直至(until,till)"、"从(from...)"及"在……之间(between)"等词用于确定发运日期时包含提及的日期,使用"在……之前(before)"及"在……之后(after)"时则不包含提及的日期;"从……开始(from)"及"在……之后(later)"等词用于确定到期日不包含提及的日期;"前半月"及"后半月"分别指一个月的第一日到第十五日及第十六日到该月的最后一日,起讫日期计算在内;一个月的"开始(beginning)"、"中间(middle)"及"末尾(end)"分别指第一到第十日、第十一日到第二十日及第二十一日到该月的最后一日,起讫日期计算在内。

第四条　信用证与合同

(1)就其性质而言,信用证与可能作为其开立基础的销售合同或其他合同是相互独立的交易,即使信用证中含有对此类合同的任何援引,银行也与该合同无关,且不受其约束。因此,银行关于承付、议付或履行信用证项下其他义务的承诺,不受申请人基于开证行或与受益人之间的关系而产生的任何请求或抗辩的影响。

受益人在任何情况下不得利用银行之间或申请人与开证行之间的合同关系。

(2)开证行应劝阻申请人试图将基础合同、形式发票等文件作为信用证组成部分的做法。

第五条　单据与货物、服务或履约行为

银行处理的是单据而不是单据可能涉及的货物、服务或履约行为。

第六条　兑用方式、截止日和交单地点

(1)信用证必须规定可在其处兑用的银行,或是否可在任一银行兑用。规定在指定银行兑用的信用证同时也可以在开证银行兑用。

(2)信用证必须规定其是以即期付款、延期付款、承兑还是议付的方式兑用。

(3)信用证不得开成凭以申请人为付款人的汇票对用。

(4)信用证必须规定交单的一个截止日。规定的承付或议付的截止日将被视为交单的截止日。

(5)可在其处兑用信用证的银行所在地即为交单地点。可在一银行兑用的信用证其交单地点为任一银行所在地。除规定的交单地点外,开证行所在地也是交单地点。

(6)除非符合二十九条(1)款规定的情形,否则受益人或者代表受益人的交单也可在截止日当天或之前完成。

第七条　开证行责任

(1)如果信用证符合以下情形,则只要规定的单据被指定交给指代银行,并且构成相符交单,开证行就必须支付。

①信用证规定由开证行即期付款、延期付款或承兑;

②信用证规定由指定银行延期付款但未付款;

③信用证规定由指定银行延期付款但其未承诺延期付款,或虽已承诺延期付款,但未在到期日付款;

④信用证规定由指定银行承兑,但其未承兑以其为付款人的汇票,并未在到期日付款;

⑤信用证规定有指定银行议付但其未议付。

(2)开证行自开立信用证之时起即不可撤销地承担承付人责任。

(3)指定银行承付或议付相符交单并将单据转给开证行之后,开证行即承担偿付该指定银行的责任。无论指定银行是否在到期日之前预付或购买了单据,对承兑或延期付款信用证下相符交单金额的偿付都应在到期日办理。开证行偿付指定银行的责任独立于开证行对受益人的责任。

第八条　保兑行责任

(1)只要规定的单据提交给保兑行,或提交给其他任何指定银行,并且构成相符交单,保兑行就必须履行以下义务。

当信用证为以下情形之一时承付:信用证规定由保兑行即期付款、延期付款或承兑;信用证规定由另一指定银行即期付款,但其未付款;信用证规定由另一指定银行延期付款,但其未承诺延期付款,或虽已承诺延期付款但未在到期日付款;信用证规定由另一指定银行承兑,但其未承兑以其为付款人的汇票,或虽已承兑汇票但未在到期日付款;信用证规定由另一指定银行议付,但其未议付;如果信用证规定由保兑行议付,无追索权地议付。

(2)保兑行自对信用证加具保兑之时起即不可撤销地承担承付或议付的责任。

(3)其他指定银行承付或议付相符交单并将单据转往保兑行之后,保兑行即承担偿付该指定银行的责任。对承兑或延期付款信用证下相符交单金额的偿付应在到期日办理。

无论指定银行是否在到期日之前预付或购买了单据，保兑行偿付指定银行的责任独立于保兑行对受益人的责任。

(4)如果开证行授权或要求一银行对信用证加具保兑，但其并不准备照办，则其必须毫不延误地通知开证行，并可通知此信用证而不加保兑。

第九条　信用证及其修改的通知

(1)信用证及其任何修改都可以经由通知行通知给受益人。非保兑行的通知行通知信用证及修改时不承担承付或议付的责任。

(2)通知行通知信用证或修改的行为表示其已确信信用证或修改的表面真实性，而且其通知准确地反映了其收到的信用证或修改的条款。

(3)通知行可以通过另一个银行(“第二通知行”)向受益人通知信用证及修改。第二通知行通知信用证或修改的行为表明其已确信收到的通知的表面真实性，并且其通知准确地反映了收到的信用证或修改的条款。

(4)经由通知行或第二通知行通知信用证的银行必须经由同一银行通知其后的任何修改。

(5)如一银行被要求通知信用证或修改，但此银行决定不予通知，则其应毫不延误地告知自其处收到信用证、修改或通知的银行。

(6)如一银行被要求通知信用证或修改，但其不能确信信用证、修改或通知的表面真实性，则此银行应毫不延误地通知看似从其处收到指示的银行。如果通知行或第二通知行决定仍然通知信用证或修改，则应告知受益人或第二通知行其不能确信信用证、修改或通知的表面真实性。

第十条　修改

(1) 除第三十八条另有规定外，未经开证行、保兑行(如果存在)及受益人同意，信用证不得修改，也不得撤销。

(2)开证行自发修改之时起，便不可撤销地受其约束。保兑行可将其保兑扩展至修改，并自通知该修改时便不可撤销地受其约束，但是，保兑行可以选择将修改通知受益人而不对其加具保兑。并且此时该保兑行必须毫不延误地将此告知开证行，并在其受益人的通知中告知受益人。

(3)从受益人告知通知修改的银行起至接受修改之前，原信用证(或含有先前被接受的修改的信用证)的条款仍然有效。受益人仍提供接受或拒绝修改的通知。如果受益人仍能未给予通知，当交单与信用证以及尚未表示修改的要求一致时，即视为受益人已作出接受修改的通知，并且从此时起，信用证被修改。

(4)通知修改的银行应将任何接受或拒绝的通知转告发出修改的银行。

(5)对同一修改的内容不允许部分接受，部分接受将被视为拒绝修改的通知。

(6)修改中关于除非受益人在某一时间内拒绝修改否则修改生效的规定已被不予理

会。

第十一条　电信传输的和预先通知的信用证和修改

(1)已经证实的电信方式发出的信用证或信用证修改即被视为有效的信用证或修改文据,任何后续的邮寄确认书应不予理会。

如电信声明"详情后告"(或类似用语)或声明以邮寄确认书为有效信用证或修改,则该电信不被视为有效信用证或修改。开证行必须随即不迟延地开立或修改,其条款不得与该电信矛盾。

(2)开证行只有在准备开立有效信用证或作出有效修改时,才可以发出关于开立或修改信用证的初步通知(预先通知)。开证行作出该预先通知,即不可撤销地保证不迟延地开立或修改信用证,且其条款不能与预先通知相矛盾。

第十二条　指定

(1)除非指定银行为保兑行,否则对于承付或议付的授权并不赋予指定银行承付或议付的义务,指定银行明确表示同意并且告知受益人的情况除外。

(2) 开证行指定一银行承兑汇票或作出延期付款承诺,即为授权该指定银行预付或购买其已承兑的汇票或已作出的延期付款承诺。

(3)非保兑行的指定银行收到或审核并转递单据的行为并不使其承担承付或议付的责任,也不构成其承付或议付的行为。

第十三条　银行之间的偿付安排

(1)如果信用证规定指定银行("索赔行")向另一方("偿付行")获取偿付,则其必须同时规定该偿付是否按信用证开立时有效的 ICC 银行之间偿付规则进行。

(2)如果信用证没有规定偿付遵守 ICC 银行间偿付规则,则按照以下规定操作:

① 开证行必须给予偿付行有关偿付的授权,授权应符合信用证关于兑用方式的规定,且不应设定截止日。

②开证行不应要求索偿行向偿付行提供与信用证条款相符的证明。

③如果偿付行未按信用证条款见索即偿,则开证行将承担利息损失以及产生的任何其他费用。

④偿付行的费用应由开证行承担。如果此项费用由受益人承担,开证行有责任在信用证及偿付授权中注明;如果偿付行的费用由受益人承担,该费用应在偿付时从付给索偿行的金额中扣取;如果偿付未发生,偿付行的费用仍由开证行负担。

(3)如果偿付行未能见索即偿,则开证行不能免除偿付责任。

第十四条　单据审核标准

(1)按指定行事的指定银行、保兑行(如果有)及开证行必须审核交单,并仅基于单据本身确定其是否在表面上构成相符交单。

(2)按指定行事的制定银行、保兑行(如果有)及开证行各有从交单次日起的至多五个银行工作日用以确定交单是否相符。这一期限不因在交单日当天或之后信用证截止日或最迟交单日届至而受到缩减或影响。

(3)如果单据中包含一份或多份受第十九、二十、二十一、二十二、二十三、二十四或二十五条规制的正本运输单据,则必须由受益人或其代表在不迟于本惯例所指的发运日之后的二十一个日历日内交单,但是在任何情况下都不得迟于信用证的截止日交单。

(4)单据中的数据,在与信用证、单据本身以及国际标准银行实务参照解读时,无需与该单据本身中的数据、其他要求的单据或信用证中的数据等同一致,但不得矛盾。

(5)除商业发票外,其他单据中的货物、服务或履约行为的描述(如果有),可使用与信用证中的描述不矛盾的概括性用语。

(6)如果信用证要求提交运输单据、保险单据或者商业发票之外的单据,且未规定出单人或其数据内容,则只要提交的单据内容看似满足所要求单据的功能,且其他方面符合第十四条(4)款,银行将接受该单据。

(7)提交的非信用证所要求的单据将被不予理会,并可被退还给交单人。

(8)如果信用证含有一项条件,但未规定用以表明该条件得到满足的单据,银行将视为未作规定并不予理会。

(9)单据日期可以早于信用证的开立日期,但不得晚于交单日期。

(10)当受益人和申请人的地址出现在任何规定的单据中时,无需与信用证或其他规定单据中所载相同,但必须与信用证中规定的相应地址同在一国。联络细节(传真、电话、电子邮件及类似细节)作为受益人和申请人地址的一部分时被不予理会。然而,如果申请人的地址和联络细节为第十九、二十、二十一、二十二、二十三、二十四或二十五条规定的运输单据上的收货人或通知方细节的一部分时,则其规定应与信用证规定的相同。

(11)在任何单据中注明的托运人或发货人无需为信用证的受益人。

(12)运输单据可以由任何人出具,无需一定为承运人、船东、船长或租船人,只要其符合第十九、二十、二十一、二十二、二十三或二十四条的要求。

第十五条　相符交单

(1)当开证行确定交单相符时,必须承付。

(2)当保兑行确定交单相符时,必须承付或者议付并将单据转递给开证行。

(3)当指定银行确定交单相符并承付或议付时,必须将单据转递给保兑行或开证行。

第十六条　不符单据,放弃及通知

(1)当按照指定行事的指定银行、保兑行(如果有)或者开证行确定交单不符时,可以拒绝承付或仪付。

(2)当开证行确定交单不符时,可以自行决定联系申请人放弃不符点,但不能将其延长至第十四条(2)款所指的期限。

(3)当按照指定行事的指定银行、保兑行(如果有)或开证行决定拒绝承付或仪付时,必须给予交单人一份单独的拒付通知。该通知必须声明：

① 银行拒绝承付或仪付；

②银行拒绝承付或仪付所依据的每一个不符点；

③银行留存单据听候交单人的进一步指示；

④开证行留存单据直到其从申请人处接到放弃不符点的通知并同意接受该放弃，或者其同意接受对不符点的放弃之前从交单人处收到其进一步指示；

⑤银行将退回单据；

⑥银行将按之前从交单人处获得的指示处理。

(4) 第十六条(3)款要求的通知必须以电信方式，如不可能，则以其他快捷方式，在不迟于自交单之翌日起第五个银行工作日结束前出发。

(5)按照指定行事的指定银行、保兑行(如果有)或开证行在按照第十六条(3)款③、④、⑤发出了通知之后，可以在任何时候将单据退还交单人。

(6)如果开证行或保兑行未能按照本条行事，则无权宣称交单不符。

(7)当开证行拒绝承付，或保兑行拒绝承付或者议付，并且按照本条发出了拒付通知后，有权要求返还已偿付的款项和利息。

第十七条　正本单据及副本

(1)信用证规定的每一种单据必须至少提交一份正本。

(2)银行应将任何带有看似出单人的原始签名、标记、印戳或标签的单据视为正本单据，除非单据本身表明其非正本。

(3)除非单据本身另有说明，在以下情况下，银行也将其视为正本单据：

①单据看似由出单人手写、打字、穿孔或盖章；

②单据看似使用出单人的原始信纸出具；

③单据声明其为正本交单据，除非该声明看似不适用于提交的单据。

(4)如果信用证要求提交单据的副本，则提交正本或副本均可。

(5)如果信用证使用诸如“一式两份”、“两份”、“两套”等用语要求提交多份单据，则至少提交一份正本，其余使用副本即可满足要求，但单据本身另有说明情况除外。

第十八条　商业发票

(1)商业发票具有以下特点：

①必须看似由受益人出具(第三十八条规定的情形除外)；

②必须出具成以申请人为抬头(第三十八条(7)款规定的情形除外)；

③必须与信用证货币相同；

④无需签名。

(2)按指定行事的制定银行保兑行(如果有)可以接受金额大于信用证允许金额的商业发票，其决定对有关各方均有约束力，只要该银行对超过信用证允许金额的部分未作承付或者议付。

(3)商业发票上的货物或履约行为的描述应该与信用证中的描述一致。

第十九条　涵盖至少两种不同运输方式的运输单据

(1)涵盖至少两种不同运输方式的运输单据(多式或联合运输单据),无论名称如何,必须具有以下特点。

①表明承运人名称并由以下人员签署:承运人或其具名代理人,船长或其具名代理人。

承运人、船长或代理人的任何签字,都必须标明承运人、船长或代理人身份。代理人签字必须标明其代表承运人还是船长签字。

②通过方式表明货物已经在信用证规定的地点发送、接管或已装运,即事先印就的文字,或者表明货物已经被发送、接管或装运日期的印戳或批注。运输单据的出具日期将被视为发送、接管或装运的日期,也即发运的日期。若单据以印戳或批注的方式表明了发送、接管或装运日期,该日期将被视为发运日期。

③表明信用证规定的发送、接管或发运地点,以及最终目的地,即使该运输单据另外还载明了一个不同的发送、接管或发运地点或最终目的地,或者该运输单据载有"预期的"或类似的关于船只、装货港或卸货港的限定语。

④单据是唯一的正本运输单据,或者如果出具为多份正本,则为运输单据中表明的全套单据。

⑤单据中有承运条款和条件,或提示承运条款和条件参见别处(简式或背面空白的运输单据),银行将不审核承运条款和条件的内容。

⑥单据未表明受租船合同约束。

(2)就本条而言,转运指在从信用证规定的发送、接管或者发运地点至最终目的地的运输过程中,从某一运输工具上卸下运货并装上另一运输工具的行为(无论其是否为不同的运输方式)。

(3)运输单据可以表明货物将要或可能被转运,只要全程运输由同一运输单据涵盖。即使信用证禁止转运,注明将要或者可能发生转运的运输单据仍可接。

第二十条　提单

(1)提单必须有以下特点。

①表明承运人名称,并由承运人或其具名代理人、船长或其具名代理人签署。承运人、船长或代理人的任何签字都必须标明其承运人、船长或代理人的身份。代理人的任何签字必须标明其是代表承运人还是代表船长签字。

②通过两种方式表明货物已在信用证规定的装货港装上具名船只,即预先印就的文字,或以装船批注注明货物的装运日期。

提单的出具日期将被视为发运日期,除非提单载有表明发运日期的已装船批注,此时已装船批注中显示的日期将被视为发运日期。如果提单载有"预期船只"或类似的关于船名的限定语，则需以已装船批注明确发运日期以及实际船名。

③表明货物从信用证规定的装货港发运至卸货港。如果提单没有表明信用证规定的装货港为装货港，或者其载有"预期的"或类似的关于装货港的限定语，则需以已装船批注表明信用证规定的装货港、发运日期及实际船名。即使提单以事先印就的文字表明的货物已装载或装运于具名船只，本规定仍然适用。

④提单为唯一的正本提单，或如果以多份正本出具，为提单中表明的全套正本。

⑤载有承运条款和条件，或提示承运条款和条件参见别处（简式或背面空白的提单）。银行将不审核承运条款和条件内容。

⑥未表明受租船合同约束。

（2）就本条而言，转运是指在信用证规定的装货港到卸货港之间的运输过程中，将货物从一船卸下并再装上另一船的行为。

（3）提单可以表明货物将要可能或可能被转运，只要全程运输由同一提单涵盖。即使信用证禁止转运，注明将要或可能发生转运的提单仍可接受，只要其表明货物由集装箱、拖车或子船运输。

（4）提单中声明承运人保留转运权利的条款将被不予理会。

第二十一条　不可转让的海运单

（1）不可转让的海运单必须具有以下特点。

①表明承运人名称并由承运人或其具名代理人、船长或其具名代理人签署。

承运人、船长或代理人的任何签字都必须标明其承运人、船长或代理人身份。代理人签字必须标明其是代表承运人还是代表船长签字。

②通过两种方式表明货物已在信用证规定的装货港装上具名船只，即预先印就的文字，或者已装船批注表明货物的装运日期。

不可转让海运单的出具日期将被视为发运日期，除非其上带有已装船批注注明发运日期，此时已装船批注注明的日期将被视为发运日期。如果不可转让海运单载有"预期船只"或类似的关于船名的限定语，则需要以已装船批注表明发运日期和实际船名。

③表明货物从信用证规定的装货港发运至卸货港。如果不可转让海运单未以信用证规定的装货港为装货港，或者如果其载有"预期的"或类似的关于装货港的限定语，则需要以已装船批注表明信用证规定的装货港、发运日期和船名。即使不可转让海运单以预先印就的文字表明货物已由具名船只装载和装运，本规定也适用。

④此单据为唯一的正本不可转让海运单，或如果以多份正本出具，为海运单上注明的全套正本。

⑤载有承运条款和条件，或提示承运条款和条件参见别处（简式或背面空白的海运单）。银行将不审核承运条款和条件内容。

⑥未注明受租船合同约束。

(2)就本条而言,转运是指在信用证规定的装货港到卸货港之间的运输过程中,将货物从一船上卸下并装上另一船的行为。

(3)不可转让海运单可以注明货物将要或可能被转运,只要全程运输由同一海运单涵盖。即使信用证禁止转运,注明转运将要或可能发生的不可转让的海运单仍可接受,只要其表明货物装于集装箱、拖船或子船中运输即可。

(4)不可转让的海运单中声明承运人保留转运权利的条款将被不予理会。

第二十二条　租船合同提单

(1)表明受租船合同约束的提单,即租船合同提单。它必须具有以下特点。

①可由船长或其具名代理人、船东或其具名代理人、租船人或其具名代理人签署。船长、船东、租船人或代理人的任何签字必须标明其身份。代理人签字必须表明其是代表船长、船东还是租船人。

②通过以下方式表明货物已在信用证规定的装货港装上具名船只,即欲先印就的文字或已装船批注表明货物的装运日期。

租船合同提单的出具日期将被视为发运日期,除非租船合同提单载有已装船批注表明发运日期,此时已装船批注上注明的日期将被视为发运日期。

③表明货物从信用证规定的装货港发运至卸货港,卸货港也可显示为信用证规定的港口范围或地理区域。

④是唯一的正本租船合同提单,或如以多份正本出具,为租船合同提单注明的全套正本。

(2)银行将不审核租船合同,即使信用证要求提交租船合同,银行也无需审核。

第二十三条　空运单据

(1)空运单据必须具有以下特点。

①表明承运人名称,并由承运人或承运人的具名代理人签署。

承运人或其代理人的任何签字必须标明其身份,代理人签字必须表明其是代表承运人签字。

②表明货物已被收妥待运。

③表明出具日期。该日期将被视为发运日期,空运单据载有专门批注表明实际发运日的情况除外,此时批注中的日期将被视为发运日期。空运单据中其他与航班号和航班日期相关的信息将不被用来确定发运日期。

④表明信用证规定的起飞机场和目的地机场。

⑤是开给发货人或托运人的正本,信用证提交全套正本也不能替代它的作用。

⑥空运单据载有承运条款和条件,或提示条件和条件参见别处。银行将不审核承运条款和条件的内容。

(2)就本条而言,转运是指在信用证规定的起飞机场到目的地机场的运输过程中,将货物从一飞机卸下再装上另一飞机的行为。

(3)空运单据可以注明货物将要或可能转运,只要全程运输由同一空运单据涵盖,即使信用证禁止转运,注明将要或可能发生转运的空运单据仍可接受。

第二十四条　公路、铁路或内陆水运单据

(1)公路、铁路或内陆水运单据必须具有以下特点。

①表明承运人名称,并且由承运人或其具名代理人签署或由承运人或其具名代理人以签字、印戳或批注表明货物收讫。承运人(或其具名代理人)的收货签字、印戳或批注必须标明其承运人或代理人的身份。代理人的收货签字、印戳或批注必须标明代理人是代表承运人签字或行事。

如果铁路运输单据没有指明承运人,可以接受铁路运输公司的任何签字或印戳作为承运人签署单据的证据。

②表明货物在信用证规定地点的发运日期或收讫待运、待发送的日期。运输单据的出具日期将被视为发运日期,除非运输单据上盖有日期的收货印戳,或者注明了收货日期或发运日期。

③表明信用证规定的发运地及目的地。

(2)公路运输单据必须是开给发货人或托运人的正本,或没有任何标记表明单据开给任何人。注明“第二联”的铁路运输单据将被作为正本接受。无论是否注明正本字样,铁路或内陆水运单据都被作为正本接受。

(3)如运输单据上未注明出具的正本数量,则提交的份数即视为全套正本。

(4)就本条而言,转运是指在信用证规定的发运、发送或运送的地点到目的地之间的运输过程中,在同一运输方式中从一运输工具卸下再装上另一运输工具的行为。

(5)只要全程单据由同一运输单据涵盖,公路、铁路或内陆水运单据可以注明货物将要或可能被转运。即使信用证禁止转运,注明将要或可能发生转运的公路、铁路或内陆水运单据仍可接受。

第二十五条　快递收据、邮政收据或投邮证明

(1)证明货物收讫待运的快递收据必须具有以下特点。

①表明快递机构名称,并在信用证规定的货物发运地点由该具名快递机构盖章或者签字;

②表明取件或收件的日期或类似词语,该日期将被视为发运日期。

(2)如果要求显示快递费用付讫或预付,快递机构出具的表明快递费由收货人以外的一方支付的运输单据可以满足该项要求。

(3)证明货物收讫代运的邮政收据或投邮证明,无论名称如何,必须看似在信用证规定的货物发运地点盖章或签署并注明日期,该日期将被视为发运日期。

第二十六条　“货装舱面”、“托运人装载和计数”、“内容据托运人报称”及运费之外的

费用

(1)运输单据不得表明货物装于或者将装于舱面。声明货物可能被装于舱面的运输单据条款可以接受。

(2)载有诸如“托运人装载合计数”或“内容据托运人报称”条款的运输单据可以接受。

(3)运输单据上可以以印戳或其他方式提及运费之外的费用。

第二十七条　清洁运输单据

银行只接受清洁运输单据。清洁运输单据指未载有明确宣称货物或包装有缺陷的条款或批注的运输单据。“清洁”一词并不需要在运输单据上出现,即使信用证要求运输单据为“清洁已装船”的,其也不需要出现。

第二十八条　保险单据及保险范围

(1)保险单据是指保险单、预约保险项下的保险证明书或者声明书,其必须看似由保险公司或承包人,或其代理人或代表出具并签署。代理人或代表的签字必须表明其是代表保险公司还是承保人签字。

(2)如果保险单据表明其以多份正本出具,所有正本均必须提交。

(3)暂保单将不被接受。

(4)可以接受保险单代替预约保险项下的保险证明书或声明书。

(5)保险单据日期不得晚于发运日期,除非保险单据表明保险责任不迟于发运日生效。

(6)保险单据必须表明投保金额并以与信用证相同的货币表示。信用证对于投保金额为货物价值、发票金额或类似金额的某一比例的要求,将被视为对最低保额的要求。如果信用证对投保金额未作规定,投保金额需至少为货物的 CIF 或 CIP 价格的 110%。如果单据中不能确定 CIF 或者 CIP 价格,投保金额必须基于要求承付或议付的金额,或者基于发票上显示的货物总值来计算,两者之中取金额较高者。保险单据需表明承包的风险区间至少涵盖从信用证规定的货物接管地或发运地开始到卸货地或最终目的地为止。

(7)信用证应规定所需投保的险别及附加险(如果有)。如果信用证使用诸如“通常风险”或“惯常风险”等含义不确切用语,则无论是否有漏报的风险,保险单据都将被照样接受。

(8)当信用证规定投保“一切险”时,如保险单据载有任何“一切险”批注或条款,无论是否有“一切险”标题,均将被接受,即使其已声明任何风险除外。

(9)保险单据可以援引任何除外条款。

(10)保险单据可以注明受免赔率或免赔额(减除额)约束。

第二十九条　截止日或最迟交单日的顺延

(1)如果信用证的截止日或最迟交单日适逢接受交单的银行非因第三十六条所述原因而歇业,则截止日或最迟交单日,视适用何者,将顺延至其重新开业的第一个银行工作日。

(2)如果在顺延后的第一个银行工作日交单,指定银行必须在其致开证行或保兑行的面函中声明交单是在根据第二十九条(1)款顺延的期限内提交的。

(3)最迟发运日不因第二十九条(1)款规定的原因而顺延。

第三十条　信用证金额、数量与单价的伸缩度

(1)"约"或"大约"用于信用证金额或信用证规定的数量或单价时，应解释为允许有关金额、数量或单价有不超过10%的增减幅度。

(2)在信用证未以包装单位件数或货物自身件数的方式规定货物数量时，货物数量允许有5%的增减幅度，只要总支取金额不超过信用证金额。

(3)如果信用证规定了货物数量，而该数量已全部发运，如果信用证规定了单价，而该单价又未降低，或当第三十条(2)款不适用时，则及时不允许部分装运，也允许支取的金额有5%的减幅。若信用证规定有特定的增减幅度或使用第三十条(1)款提到的用语限定数量，则该减幅不适用。

第三十一条　部分支款或部分发运

(1)允许部分支款或部分发运。

(2)表明使用同一运输工具并经由同一航程运输的数套运输单据在同一次提交时，只要显示相同目的地，将不视为部分发运，即使运输单据上表明的发运日期不同或装货港、接管地、发送地点不同。如果交单由数套运输单据构成，其中最晚的一个发运日将被视为发运日。含有一套或数套运输单据的交单，如果标明在同一种运输方式下经由数件运输工具运输，则即使运输工具在同一天出发运往同一目的地，也将被视为部分发运。

(3)含有一份以上快递收据、邮政收据或投邮证明的交单，如果单据看似由同一快递或邮政机构在同一地点和日期加盖印戳或签字并且表明同一目的地，将不视为部分发运。

第三十二条　分期支款或分期发货

如信用证规定在指定的时间段内分期支款或分期发运，但任何一期都未按信用证规定期限支取或发运时，信用证对该期及以后各期均告失效。

第三十三条　交单时间

银行在其营业时间外无接受交单的义务。

第三十四条　关于单据有效性的免责

银行对任何单据的形式、充分性、准确性、内容真实性、虚假或法律效力，或单据中规定或添加的一般或特殊条件都概不负责；银行对任何单据所代表的货物、服务或其他履约行为的描述、数量、重量、品质、状况、包装、交付、价值或其存在，发货人、承运人、货运代理人、收货人、货物的保险或其他任何人的诚信、作为或不作为、清偿能力、履约或资信状况，也概不负责。

第三十五条　关于信息传递和翻译的免责

当报文、信件或单据按照信用证的要求传输或发送时，或信用证未作指示而银行自行选择传送服务时，银行对报文传输、信件或单据的递送过程中发生的延误、中途遗失、残缺或其他错误产生的后果概不负责。

如果指定银行确定交单相符并将单据发往开证行或保兑行，则无论指定银行是否已经承付或议付，开证行或保兑行都必须承付或议付，或偿付指定银行，即使单据在指定银行送往开证行或保兑行的途中丢失的情况也不例外。

银行对技术术语的翻译或解释上的错误不负责任，并可不加翻译地传送信用证条款。

第三十六条　不可抗力

银行对由于天灾、暴动、骚乱、叛乱、战争、恐怖主义行为或任何罢工、停工或其无法控制的任何其他原因导致的营业中断的后果概不负责。银行恢复营业时，对于在营业中断期间已逾期的信用证，不再进行承付或议付。

第三十七条　关于被指示方行为的免责

(1)为了执行申请人的指示，银行利用其他银行服务，其费用和风险由申请人承担。

(2)即使银行自行选择了其他银行，如果发出的指示未被执行，开证行或通知行对此亦不负责。

(3)指示另一银行提供服务的银行有责任负担被指示方因执行指示而发生的任何佣金、手续费、成本或开支。如果信用证规定费用由受益人负担，而该费用未能收取或从信用证款项中扣除，开证行依然承担支付此费用的责任。信用证或其修改不应规定向受益人的通知以通知行或第二通知行收到其费用为条件。

(4)对于外国法律和惯例加诸于银行的一切义务和责任，申请人应受其约束，并就此对银行负补偿责任。

第三十八条　可转让信用证

(1)银行无办理信用证转让的义务，除非其明确同意。

(2) 就本条而言有：

①可转让信用证是指特别注明“可转让”字样的信用证。可转让信用证可应受益人（第一受益人）的要求转为全部或部分由另一受益人（第二受益人）兑用。

②转让行指办理信用证转让的指定银行，或当信用证规定可在任一银行兑用时，指开证行特别如此授权并实际办理转让的银行。开证行也可担任转让行的责任。

③已转让信用证指已由转让行转为可由第二受益人兑用的信用证。

(3)除非转让时另有约定，有关转让的所有费用（诸如佣金、手续费、成本或开支）必须由第一受益人支付。

(4)只用信用证允许部分支款或部分发运，信用证就可以分部分地转让给数名第二受益人。已转让信用证不得应第二受益人的要求转让给任何其后受益人。第一受益人不视为其后受益人。

(5)任何转让要求都必须说明是否允许及在何条件下允许将修改通知第二受益人。已转让信用证必须明确说明该项条件。

(6)如果信用证转让给数名第二受益人,其中一名或多名第二受益人对信用证修改的拒绝并不影响其他第二受益人接受修改。对接受人而言该已转让信用证即被相应修改,而对拒绝修改的第二受益人而言,该信用证未被修改。

(7)已转让信用证必须准确转载原证条款,包括保兑(如果有),但有些项目除外,即信用证金额、规定的任何单价、截止日、交单期限和最迟发运日或发运期间。其任何一项或全部均可减少或缩短。

必须投保的保险比例可以增加,以达到原信用证或本惯例规定的保险金额。可用第一受益人的名称替换原证中的开证申请人名称。如果原证特别要求开证申请人名称应在除发票以外的任何单据中出现,已转让信用证必须反映该项要求。

(8)第一受益人有权以自己的发票和汇票(如果有)替换第二受益人的发票和汇票,其金额不得超过原信用证的金额。经过替换后,第一受益人可在原信用证下支取自己发票与第二受益人发票间的差价(如果有)。

(9)如果第一受益人应提交自己的发票和汇票(如果有),但未能在第一次要求时照办,或第一受益人提交的发票导致了第二受益人的交单中本不存在的不符点,而其未能在第一次要求时修正,转让行有权提交从第二受益人处收到的单据。

(10)开证行并不再对第一受益人承担责任。在要求转让时,第一受益人可以要求在信用证转让后的兑用地点,在原信用证的截止日之前(包括截止日),对第二受益人承付或议付。本规定并不损害第一受益人在第本条(8)款下的权利。

(11)第二受益人或代表第二受益人的交单必须交给转让行。

第三十九条　款项让渡

信用证未注明可转让,可不影响受益人根据所适用的法律规定,将该信用证下可能有权或可能将成为有权获得的款项让渡给他人的权利。本条只涉及款项的让渡,不涉及在信用证项下进行履行行为的权利让渡。

第二节　跟单信用证统一惯例关于电子交单的附则

第 e1 条　eUCP

(1)《跟单信用证统一惯例关于电子交单的附则》(eUCP)是对《跟单信用证统一惯例》(UCP)的补充,以适应单独提交或与纸单据混合提交电子记录的情形。

(2)当信用证表明受 eUCP 约束时,eUCP 作为 UCP 的附则适用。

(3)本文中的 eUCP 版本号为 1.1。信用证必须表明适用的 eUCP 版本,否则即受开证日的有效版本约束,或如果信用证因受益人接受的修改而受 eUCP 约束,则受在该修改日期有效的版本约束。

第 e2 条　eUCP 与 UCP 的关系

(1)受 eUCP 约束的信用证("eUCP 信用证")也适用 UCP,而无需将 UCP 明确纳入信用证。

(2)eUCP 使用时,如其与适用 UCP 产生不同结果,则应以 eUCP 规定为准。

(3)如果 eUCP 信用证允许受益人在提交纸单据或电子记录两者之间进行选择,而其选择了只提交纸单据,则该笔交单仅适用 UCP;如果 eUCP 信用证只允许提交纸单据,则仅适用 eUCP。

第 e3 条　定义

(1)为了将 UCP 适用于 eUCP 信用证项下提交的电子记录将作以下解释:

①"表面看似"是指类似用于适用于核审电子记录的数据内容;

②"单据"应包括电子记录;

③电子记录的"交单地点"意指一电子地址;

④"签署"及类似用语应包括电子签名;

⑤"添加的"、"批注"、"盖印戳的"意指在电子记录中其增补特征明显的数据内容。

(2)在 eUCP 中使用的下列用语应具有以下含义:

①"电子记录"意指以电子方法创建的、产生的、发送的、传送的、收到的或储存的数据,其发送人的表面身份、包含的数据的表面来源及是否保持完整和未被更改可以被证实,并且能够根据 eUCP 信用证条款审核其相符性;

②"电子签名"意指附加于或与一份电子记录有逻辑关联的数据过程,被签字人完成或采用以表明签字人身份及其对电子记录的证实;

③"格式"意指表达电子记录的数据组织形式或电子记录提到的数据组织形式;

④"纸单据"意指传统的纸面形式的单据;

⑤"收到"意指电子记录以系统可接受的形式进入相关收件人信息系统的时间,任何对收到的确认并不意味着在 eUCP 信用证下对该电子记录的接受或拒绝。

第 e4 条　格式

eUCP 信用证必须指定应提交的电子记录的格式;如未指定,可以任何格式提交。

第 e5 条　交单

(1)eUCP 信用证中允许提交电子记录的,必须注明提交电子记录的地点;允许提交电子记录和纸单据,必须注明提交纸单据的地点。

(2)电子记录可以分别提交,并且不需要在同一时间提交。

(3)如果 eUCP 信用证允许提交一份或多份电子记录,受益人有责任向接受交单的银行提供表明交单结束的通知。该结束通知可以电子记录或纸单据方式作出,且必须注明其关联的 eUCP 信用证。如果未收到受益人的通知将被认为未曾交单。

(4)在 eUCP 信用证下提交的每份电子记录以及纸单据都必须注明据以交单的 eUCP 信用证,未如此注明的交单可被视为未曾收到。

(5)如果将接受交单的银行在营业中，但在规定的截止日期及(或)发运日后的最迟交单日(视何种情形适用)，使得其系统不能接收传来的电子记录则视其为歇业，最迟交单日及(或)截止日应延展至银行能够接收电子记录的下一个银行工作日。如果尚待提交的电子记录只剩下结束通知，则可以用电信方式或纸单据提交，并被视为及时，但要其在该银行能够接收电子记录之前发出。

(6)不能被证实的电子记录将被视为未曾提交。

第 e6 条　审核

(1)如果电子记录包含一个与外部系统的超级链接，或指明电子记录可参照一外部系统审核，则超级链接中的、或参照的外部系统中的电子记录应被视为是需要审核的电子记录。在审核时，如指明的系统不能提供所需电子记录的读取条件，则构成不符点。

(2)指定银行按指定转递电子记录的行为表明其已确定电子记录的表面真实性。

(3)开证行或保兑行(如果有)无法审核 eUCP 信用证所要求格式的电子记录，或当未要求格式时无法审核提交的电子记录，这一情形不构成拒付的依据。

第 e7 条　拒付通知

(1)审单时限自收到受益人的结束通知至银行工作日的下一个银行工作日起算；如果提交单据或结束通知的时间被延迟，审单时限自接收交单的银行能够接收结束通知的第一个银行工作日起算。

(2)如果开证行、保兑行(如果有)或按其指定行事的指定银行对包含电子记录的交单发出了拒付通知，在发出拒付通知后 30 天内未收到被通知方关于电子记录的处理指示，银行应退还交单人以前尚未退还的任何纸单据，但能够以其认为合适的任何方式处理电子记录而不承担任何责任。

第 e8 条　正本与副本

UCP 或 eUCP 信用证要求提供一份电子记录正本与副本时，提交一份电子记录即满足此要求。

第 e9 条　出具日期

除非电子记录载有具体的出具日期，否则看似出单人发出电子记录的日期即被视为出具日期。如果没有显示其他日期，则电子记录的收到日期将被视为发出日期。

第 e10 条　运输

如果证明运输的电子记录没有表明货物发运或发送日期，则电子记录的发出日期将被视为货物发运或发送日期；但如果电子记录载有证明发运或发送日期的批注时，该批注日期将被视为发运或发送日期。显示附加数据内容的批注无需另外签名或以其他方式证实。

第 e11 条　电子记录在提交后变损

(1)如果开证行、保兑行或其他指定银行收到电子记录看似已经变损，银行可通知交单人，也可要求再次提交电子记录。

(2)如果银行要求再次提交电子记录,则审单时限中止,等交单人再次提交电子记录时恢复;如果指定银行不是保兑行,则必须将其关于再次交单的要求知会开证行和任何保证行,并告知时限中止;如果该电子记录在30天内未被再次提交,则银行可以将该电子记录视为未提交过。

第 e12 条　根据 eUCP 提交电子记录时的额外免责

除通过使用商业上可接受的用于接收、证实和识别电子记录的数据过程即可发现外,银行审核电子记录的表面真实性的行为并不使其对发送人身份、信息来源、完整性或未被更改性承担更多责任。

附　录

附录一　国际贸易实务专业词汇

一、贸易术语

(1)Trade Terms:贸易术语,其是在国际贸易中用来表明商品的价格构成,说明货物交接过程中有关的风险、责任和费用划分问题的专门用语。例如,业务中常用的 FOB,CIF 和 CFR 等。

(2)Delivery Terms:交货条件,即卖方完成其交货义务的具体条件,其中主要包括交货的地点、风险转移的界限,以及卖方承担的各项义务如运输、保险、通关过境等。

(3)《INCOTERMS 2000》:其是《2000 年国际贸易术语解释通则》的英文缩写,简称《2000 年通则》。它是由国际商会制定的有关贸易术语的国际惯例。最早的《通则》产生于 1936 年,后来经过多次修订,现行的《2000 年通则》共包括 13 种贸易术语,即 EXW,FCA,FAS,FOB,CFR,CIF,CPT,CIP,DAF,DES,DEQ,DDU 和 DDP。

(4)《Warsaw - Oxford Rulesl932》:即《1932 年华沙 - 牛津规则》,它也是有关贸易术语的国际惯例之一。该规则是国际法协会专门为解释 CIF 合同而制定的,它对 CIF 合同的性质、特点和双方当事人的权利、义务等,作出了较为详细具体的规定。

二、货物的质量

(1)对等样品:当买卖双方采用凭样成交时,卖方为了减少交货时的风险可根据买方提供的样品,加工复制出一个类似的商品交买方确认,这种经确认后的样品,称为对等样品,也有的称为确认样品或回样。

(2)FAQ:其是 Far Average Quality 的简称,它表示一定时期内某地出口货物的平均品质水平,习惯称"良好平均品质",一般是指中等货或大路货。在国际货物贸易中,某些品质变化较大且难以规定统一标准的农副产品,往往用此术语来表示其品质。在我国出口农副产品时,除用 FAQ 这一术语来表示其品质外,同时还在合同中约定具体规格。

(3)IS09000 系列标准:其是国际标准化组织为适应国际贸易发展的需要而制定的品质管理和品质保证标准。它为国际市场商品的生产企业体系评定提供了统一的标准,具有国际通行证的作用。因此,各国都把质量体系认证作为参加国际市场竞争的手段,它不仅有利于出口商品生产企业提高自身技术和管理素质,而且有利于提高出口商品质量。

(4)商品的品质:是指商品外观形态与内在质量的综合。

(5)样品:是指从一批商品中抽取出来的,或者由生产、使用部门设计加工出来的,能够代表和反映整批商品品质的少量实物。

(6)凭样买卖:是指以样品作为成交和交货品质依据的交易。

(7)对等样品:是指卖方按买方的来样复制或提供品质相近的样品,寄请买方确认后,即作为交货品质的依据。

(8)规格:是指用以反映货物质量的若干主要技术指标,如成分、含量、纯度、尺寸、大小、粗细等。

(9)等级:是指同一类货物,按其品质差异,用文字、数字或符号进行的分类。

(10)标准:是指政府机关或商业团体统一制定和公布的标准化的规格和等级。

(11)品质机动幅度:是指允许卖方所交货物的质量指标在一定的幅度内有所变动。

(12)品质公差:是指在工业制成品中,国际同行业公认的产品品质误差。

三、货物的重量数

(1)毛重:是指商品本身的重量加皮重,即货物重量加上包装的重量。

(2)净重:是指商品本身的重量,即除去包装物后货物的实际重量。

(3)公量:是指用科学方法抽干商品中所含水分,然后再加上一定标准的水分所得出的重量。

(4)理论重量:是指某些商品的规格和尺寸比较固定,重量大致相等,只要根据张数或件数即可推算出的商品重量。

四、货物的包装

(1)包装:是指为了保护商品在品质和数量上的完整性所使用的容器和包装材料。

(2)运输包装:又称外包装或大包装,它的作用主要是保护商品,便于其运输、装卸和储存,方便检验、计数和分拨。

(3)销售包装:又称内包装,是指直接接触商品,直接与消费者见面的小包装。

(4)包装标志:是指在每件货物的外包装上印上一定的文字、图形和数字作为标志。

(5)唛头:又称运输标志,指在运输包装上面书写、压印、刷制简单的图形、文字和数字。

(6)指示性标志:是针对某些容易破碎、损坏、变质的商品用简单醒目的图形和文字,提醒有关人员在装卸、搬运、存储过程中引起注意,它一般用图案表示,并加上英文说明。

(7)警告性标志:又称危险品标志,是指针对某些易燃品、爆炸品、有毒品、腐蚀性物品、放射性物品等危险品,在其货物的外包装上清楚地刷制危险性质的标志。

(8)中性包装:是指商品本身和商品包装上不注明生产国别、生产厂名、原有商标或牌号的包装。

(9)定牌:是指在商品上和包装上不使用卖方指定的商标和牌号。

五、贸易术语与价格核算

(1)贸易术语:又称价格术语或交货条件,它是用一个简短的概念或三个字母的缩写来说明价格的构成及买卖双方有关责任、费用和风险的划分,以确定买卖双方在交接货物过程中应尽的责任和义务 。

(2)进货成本:是贸易商向供货商购买货物的支出。

(3)装运港船上交货:是指货物在指定的装运港越过船舷,卖方即完成交货。

(4)佣金:是卖方或买方付给中间商作为其代买代卖的酬金。

(5)象征性交货:是指卖方按合同规定装运货物后,向买方提交包括物权凭证在内的有关单证就算完成交货义务,无需保证到货。

(6)实际交货:是指卖方按合同规定将实际货物交给买方。

(7)硬币:是币值稳定或具有一定上浮趋势的货币。

(8)软币:是币值不够稳定且具有下浮趋势的货币。

(9)汇率:是用一个国家的货币折算成另一个国家货币的比率。

(10)出口总成本:是指实际成本加上出口前的一切费用和税金。

(11)换汇成本:是出口商获得每一单位外汇的人民币成本。

(12)含佣价:是含有佣金的价格。

(13)FOB Liner Terms:即FOB班轮条件,它是为了解决装船费用的负担问题,而产生的FOB的变形之一。这一变形是指装船费用按照班轮的做法来办,即由船方或买方承担。所以,采用这一变形,卖方不负担装船的有关费用。

(14)Symbolic Delivery:即象征性交货。象征性交货是针对实际交货而言的,在象征性交货方式下,卖方是凭单交货,买方是凭单付款,只要卖方如期向买方提交了合同规定的全套合格单据(名称、内容和份数相符的单据),就算完成了交货义务,即使货物在运输途中损坏或灭失,买方也必须履行付款义务。反之,如果卖方提交的单据不符合要求,即使货物完好无损地运达目的地,买方仍有权拒付货款。

(15)折扣:是指卖方按原价给予买方一定百分比的减让,即在价格上给予适当的优惠。

(16)净价:凡价格中不包括佣金或折扣的则称为净价。

(17)国际市场价格:是指在世界市场上具有代表性的、被普遍承认的国际间商品交换的价格。

六、国际货物运输

(1)班轮:指在预先固定的航线上,按照船期表在固定港口上往来行驶的船舶。

(2)分批装运:是指一笔成交的货物,分若干批次装运。

(3)转船:货物装运后,需要通过中途港转运的称为转船。

(4)国际多式联运:是在集装箱运输的基础上产生和发展起来的一种综合性的连贯运输方式。它一般是以集装箱为媒介,把海、陆、空各种传统的单一运输方式有机地结合起来,组成一种国际间的连贯运输。

(5)装卸率:指每日装卸货物的数量。

(6)滞期费:是指在规定的装卸期限内,租船人未完成装卸作业,给船方造成经济损失后,租船人对超过的时间向船方支付的一定数额的罚金。

(7)速遣费:如果按约定的装卸时间和装卸率提前完成装卸任务,使船方节省了船舶在港的费用开支,船方将其获利的一部分给租船人作为奖励,叫速遣费。

(8)海运提单(B/L):是指船方或其代理人在收到其承运货物时签发给托运人的货物凭证。

(9)清洁提单:是指货物在装船时"表面状况良好",船公司在提单上未加注任何有关货物受损或包装不良等批注的提单。

(10)指示提单:是指在提单收货人栏内填写"凭指示"或"凭某某人指定"字样。指示提单经过背书才能转让。

(11)电子提单:是一种利用 EDI 对海上运输中的货物所有权进行转让的程序。卖方、发货人、银行、买方和收货人均以承运人为中心,利用电子密码来完成在途货物买卖,在整个过程中通常不出现任何书面文件。收货人提货时,只要出示有效证件,由承运人核实即可。

(12)班轮运输:又称定期船运输。它是在一定航线上、一定的停靠港口、定期开航的船舶运输。

(13)集装箱运输:是以集装箱作为运输单位进行货物运输的一种现代化的运输方式。

(14)租船运输:

(15)倒签提单:指货物装船后,应托运人请求承运人签发的早于货物实际装船日期的提单。

(16)空白背书:是指示提单背书的一种方式,指由背书人在提单背面签章,但不注明被背书人的名称。

(17)迟期提单:在信用证条件下,是指错过规定的交单日期或晚于货物到达目的港的提单。卖方超过提单签发日期后 21 天才交到银行议付的提单,按惯例银行拒付。

七、货物的运输保险

(1)单独海损:单独海损仅涉及船舶或货物所有人单方面利益的损失。

(2)共同海损:是指在海洋运输途中,船舶、货物或其他财产遭遇共同危险,为了解除共同危险,采取有效合理的救助措施,直接造成的特殊牺牲和支付的特殊费用。

(3)仓至仓条款:简称 W/W,仓至仓条款是保险责任的起讫条款,即保险责任自被保险货物运离保险单所载明的起运地或储存处所开始,包括正常运输中的海上、陆上、内河和驳船运输在内,直至该项货物运抵保险单所载明的目的地收货人的最后仓库或储存处所,或被保险人用作分配、分排或非正常运输的其他储存处所为止。若被保险货物在最后卸货港全部卸离海轮后 60 天内未完成最后交货,则保险责任以 60 天届满终止。

(4)施救费用:是指被保险的货物在遭受承包责任范围内的灾害事故时,被保险人或其代理人与受让人为了避免或减少损失,采取了各种抢救或防护措施而支付的合理费用。

(5)救助费用:是指被保险货物在遭受了承保责任范围内的灾害事故时,由保险人和被保险人以外的第三者采取了有效的救助措施,在救助成功后,由被救方付给救助人的一种报酬。

(6)保险险别:是指保险人对风险和损失的承保责任范围。

(7)卖方利益险:是中国人民保险公司于1978年开始承包的一种特殊的独立险别。它是针对在CFR或FOB价格条件下或在无证托收支付方式下,万一货物在运输途中受损,买方不赎单付款时,卖方投保此险别就可以弥补因上述风险所带来的损失。保险公司办理此项保险时,按一切险和战争险承保。费率按一切险的1/4再加战争险的费率合并计收。

(8)保险利益:又称可保利益,是指投保人对保险标的物具有的利益。

(9)实际全损(Actual Total Loss):又称绝对全损,凡有下列情况之一者便可构成实际全损,即①被保险货物已经完全灭失;②被保险货物遭受严重损害丧失原有用途,已不具有任何使用价值;⑧被保险货物丧失已无可挽回;④船舶失踪。

(10)推定全损(Constructive Total Loss):是指被保险货物虽未完全灭失,但对被保险人而言已经没有什么用途或价值。凡有下列情况之一者即为推定全损:①被保险货物遭受严重损害,完全灭失已不可避免;②被保险货物受损后,修理费用估计要超过货物修复后的价值;③被保险货物遭受严重损害之后,继续运抵目的地的运费已超过残存货物的价值;④被保险货物遭受保险责任范围内的事故,使被保险人失去被保险货物所有权,而收回这一所有权所需花费的费用,将超过收回后被保险货物的价值。

八、货款的结算

(1)汇票:是指一个人向另一个人签发的,要求受票人即期或定期,或在可以确定的将来时间内,向某人或其指定人或持票人支付一定金额的无条件的书面命令。

(2)出票:是指出票人签发票据并交给收款人的行为。出票人在汇票上一般应填写付款人、付款金额、付款日期和地点、收款人等项目,签字后应交付给收款人。

(3)提示:是指付款人或持票人将汇票提交给付款人要求付款或承兑的行为。

(4)承兑:是指汇票付款人承诺在汇票到期日支付汇票金额的行为。

(5)付款:是指汇票的付款人按汇票金额向持票人支付票款的行为。

(6)背书:是指持票人在汇票背面签上自己的名字,或再加上受让人的名称,并把汇票交给受让人的行为。

(7)拒付:又称退票,是指在汇票提示时,付款人拒绝付款或拒绝承兑的行为。

(8)本票:是指出票人向收款人承诺无条件支付一定金额的票据。

(9)支票:是指在银行有存款的存款人向银行或其他金融机构开出的无条件支付一定金额的票据。

(10)汇付:又称汇款,是指付款人主动通过银行将款项交给收款人的支付方式。

(11)电汇:是指汇出行应汇款人的申请,通过加押电报或电传,委托国外的分行或代理行(即汇入行),指示其解付一定金额给指定的收款人的汇款方式。

(12)信汇:是指汇出行应汇款人的申请,将信汇委托书寄给汇入行,指示其解付一定金额给收款人的汇款方式。

(13)票汇:是指汇出行应汇款人的申请,代汇款人开立以其分行或代理行为解付行的银行即期汇票，并支付一定金额给收款人的汇款方式。

(14)托收：是指出口人依据买卖合同发运货物后，委托当地银行通过其在国外分支机构或代理向进口人收取货款的方式。

(15)付款交单：是指出口人的交单以进口人的付款为条件，也就是说进口商在付款后才能从代收行取得货运单据。

(16)承兑交单：是指出口人的交单是以进口人在远期汇票上承兑为条件的。

(17)信用证：是指银行根据进口人的申请和指示向出口人开立的，在符合信用证条款的条件下，保证付款的书面文件。

(18)信托收据：是指进口人向银行出具的书面信用担保文件，表示愿意作为银行的受托人，代理银行提货、报关、存仓、保险与出售，并承认货物的所有权属于银行，同时保证货物出售后所得款项于汇票到期日按汇票金额偿还给代收银行的凭证。

(19)银行保证书：是指银行根据委托人的请求向受益人开立的，保证委托人履行某项义务的书面文件。

(20)投标保证书：是指银行根据委托人的请求向受益人开立的，保证委托人履行某项义务的书面文件。

(21)履约保证书：是指银行或其他金融机构(保证人)应货物买卖、劳务合作或其他经济合同当事人(申请人)的委托向合同对方(受益人)出具的书面保证，保证委托人履行某项合同义务，否则保证人要保证向受益人支付一定的金额。

(22)付款保证书：是指银行或其他金融机构(保证人)应买方(申请人)的委托，出具给卖方的书面保证，保证卖方在提供劳务或货物后，买方一定按期付款。

(23)还款保证书：是指银行或其他金融机构(保证人)应卖方(申请人)的委托，出具给买方的书面保证，保证卖方按合同规定提供劳务或交付货物。

(24)出口押汇：出口商发货后，将货物单据交给银行，银行在审核单证相符之后，向出口商付款(议付)，银行将单据交开证行索回货款冲回原来垫付的资金。这种议付直到收回货款的全过程就是出口押汇。

(25)国际保理：是指在托收、赊账等情况下，保理商向出口商提供的一项包括对买方资信调查、100%的风险担保、催收应收账款、财务管理以及融通资金等综合性的财务服务。

(26)打包贷款：又叫信用证抵押贷款，是银行在货物出运之前以信用证作抵押向出口商提供的贷款。其是银行凭信用证的开证行有条件的信用承诺而发放的贷款，属于信用放贷。

(27)贴现：在国际市场上，一张远期汇票的持有人如想在付款人付款前取得票款，可以经过背书将汇票转让给贴现的银行或金融公司，由它们将扣除一定贴现利息后的票款付给汇票持有人，这种做法叫贴现。

九、货物的检验

(1)商品检验：是指对商品的品质和数量所进行的鉴定工作。

(2)法定检验:是指国家规定必须经过商品检验后才准许进出口的商品检验。

(3)海关:是由国家设立,对进出国境的货物、邮递物品、旅客行李、货币、金银、证券和运输工具等进行监督检验、征收关税并执行查禁走私任务的国家行政管理机关。

(4)商检证书:是指进出口商品经有商检资格的机构检验、鉴定后所具有的证明文件。

十、货物的索赔

(1)违反要件:违反合同中的主要条款。受害方有权因其解除合同,并要求损害赔偿。

(2)违反担保:通常是指违反合同中的一些次要条件。受害方不能解除合同,只能要求损害赔偿。

(3)根本性违约:是指一方违反合同,使另一方蒙受损害以至剥夺了其依照合同有权得到的东西。

(4)索赔:是指受损的一方向违约的一方提出赔偿要求。

(5)理赔:是指违约的一方受理遭损一方的的赔偿要求。

(6)违约:是指签订合同当事人的一方或双方的过错造成不能履行或不能完全履行合同的行为。

(7)争议:是指买卖的一方认为另一方未能全部或部分履行合同规定的责任和义务所引起的纠纷。

(8)索赔期限:是索赔方向违约方提出索赔的有效期限。

十一、不可抗力

(1)不可抗力事件:是由自然原因和社会原因引起的,当事人在订立合同时无法预见、无法预防、无法避免和无法控制的事件。

(2)不可抗力条款:是指在合同中订明如当事人一方因不可抗力事件不能履行合同的全部或部分义务的,免除其履行合同的责任,不能按期履约的,可以免除其延期履行的责任。另一方不得对此要求损害赔偿的免责条款。

十二、仲裁

(1)仲裁:是指买卖双方达成协议,自愿将有关争议交给双方同意的仲裁机构进行裁决的一种解决争议纠纷的方法。

(2)仲裁条款:是指双方当事人在签订合同时约定将日后可能发生的争议提交仲裁的条款。

(3)仲裁协议:是发生争议的双方当事人表示愿意将它们之间已经发生的或可能发生的争议交付仲裁解决的一种协议。

(4)诉讼:字面上讲是指当事人(原告)向法院起诉,告被告的状。

(5)仲裁效力:是指对仲裁裁决的终局性、约束力和向法院起诉等权力的规定。

十三、出口合同的签订

(1)交易磋商:在国际货物买卖中,交易双方就买卖商品的有关条件进行协商以期达成交易的过程，通常称为贸易谈判。

(2)市场调研：是对于商品或服务的销售问题有关的资料进行系统的收集、记录和分析，是进行营销决策的依据。

(3)订单：是由进口商或实际买主拟制的货物订购单。

(4)委托订购单：是指由代理商或佣金商拟制的代客购买货物的订购单。

(5)询盘：是指试探对方对交易的诚意和了解其对交易条件的意见。因多数是询问价格，故通常称之为询价。

(6)发盘：是指交易一方即发盘人向另一方即受盘人提出购买或出售某种商品的各项交易条件，并表示愿意按这种条件与对方达成交易订立合同的行为。

(7)还盘：是指受盘人不同意或不完全同意发盘人在发盘中提出的条件，为进一步协商对发盘提出修改意见。

(8)接受：是指受盘人接到对方的发盘或还盘后，同意对方提出的条件，愿意与对方达成交易并及时以声明或行为表示出来，在法律上称作承诺。

(9)出口经营方案：是在广泛、深入的市场调研基础上，对市场信息进行筛选、分析、归纳，结合本企业的经营战略目标及自身特点，综合内外可控制的和不可控制的因素所制定的行动方案。

(10)逾期接受：接受通知超过发盘规定的有效期限或发盘没具体规定有效期而超过合理时间才送达受盘人，这项接受为逾期接受。

十四、出口合同的履行

(1)出口报关：出口货物在装船出运之前，出口企业需如实向海关申报货物情况，交验规定的单据文件，办理接受海关监管事宜。

(2)收妥结汇：是指议付行收到外贸公司的单据后，经审查无误，将单据寄交外国付款行索取货款，待收到付款行将货款拨入议付行账户的贷记通知书时，即按当日外汇牌价，折成人民币给外贸公司。

(3)押汇：又称买单结汇，是指议付行收到单据在审查无误情况下，按信用证的条款买入受益人(外贸公司)的汇票和单据，从票面金额中扣除从议付日到估计收到货款日的利息，将余款按议付日外汇牌价折算成人民币，拨交外贸公司。议付行向受益人垫付资金买入跟单汇票后，即成为汇票持有人，可凭票向付款行索取票款。银行作出口押汇，是为了对外贸公司提供资金融通的方式，有利于外贸公司的资金周转。

(4)定期结汇：是议付行根据向国外付款行索偿所需时间，预先确定一个固定的结汇期限，到期后主动将票款金额折成人民币拨交外贸公司。

(5)国际保理：此业务是指在使用托收、赊销等非信用证结算货款时，保理商向出口商提供的一项集买方资信调查、应收账款管理和追账、贸易融资及信用管理等于一体的综合性金融服务业务。

(6)大副收据:是由船长或大副签发的收货单,也是船公司签发给托运人表明货物已经装船的临时收据。托运人凭收货单向外轮代理公司交付运费并换取正式提单。

(7)海运提单:是指船方或其代理人在收到承运的货物时签发给托运人的货物收据,也是承运人与托运人之间所签订的运输契约的证明,在法律上它具有物权凭证的作用。

(8)托运单:是出口商(发货人或托运人)在报关前向船方或其代理人(承运人)申请租船订舱的单据。

(9)议付:是出口方银行买进信用证项下的汇票及所附单据并将票款付给受益人。

(10)装货单:是发票的补充,出口企业报关时提供,便于国外买方在货物达到目的港时核对货物和海关检查验收货物。

(11)原产地证书:是由政府、或公证机构及出口厂商中的任意一方出具的一种证明货物原产地或制造地的证件。其作用主要是实行差别关税、分配和控制进口配额。

(12)海关发票:是由进口国提供空白格式,出口商填写后的结汇单据之一。其主要作为审查货物的原产地、估价完税、征收差别待遇关税或征收反倾销税及编制统计资料的依据。

(13)出口收汇核销:是指对每笔出口业务收汇进行跟踪,直到收回外汇为止。

(14)收货单:又称大副收据,是货物装船完毕后,由船方大副会同理货员签还给托运人表示收妥货物的凭据。

(15)出口退税:是指一个国家为了扶持和鼓励本国商品出口,将所征税款退还给出口商的一种制度。

十五、进口合同的签订与履行

(1)开证申请书:是开证申请人在申请开证时必须填制的文件,是开证银行对外开证的条件和依据,其包括开证申请人的承诺和付款保证(正面)及开证内容(背面)。

(2)预约保险合同:又称开口保险单(Open Cover),是一种长期性的保险单。一般列明保险总金额。

十六、国际贸易方式

(1)国际贸易方式:是指国际间商品流通过程中所采用的交易方式和做法。

(2)经销:是指一国的出口企业和出口经销商与外国经销中间商达成书面经销协议进行商品交易的方式。

(3)包销:是指国际贸易中的卖方与国外包销人通过签订包销协议,给予其在一定时间、一定地区范围内销售某一种或某一类货物的独家专营权利的贸易方式。

(4)非独家经销方式:是指不授予专营权的经营方式,其出口商可同时授权外国的多家经销企业在同一时期和同一地区内经销同一种(类)商品的贸易方式。

(5)代理:是指出口企业与代理商达成代理协议,委托代理商为其在进口国办理或推销商品事宜的贸易方式。

(6)寄售:是指寄售人(委托人)先将寄售的货物运往国外寄售地,交给当地约定的代售人,由代售人根据寄售协议的条件和方法代为销售;货物售出后,所得贷款由代售人扣除佣金和其他费用后,通过银行汇交寄售人。

(7)展卖:是指利用举办或参加各种形式的展览会、博览会、交易会等,展销结合的一种贸易方式。

(8)招标:是指买方(招标人)为了以较低的价格或代价取得高质量的货物或劳务的供应,常常用招标(公开询盘)方式,根据若干供货者的投标书(发盘),择取条件最合意者达成交易的行为。

(9)投标:是指投标人按招标公告中的交易条件,报出最低价格和必要条件争取中标,达成交易的行为。

(10)拍卖:是指专营拍卖业务的机构(拍卖行或拍卖中心)接受货主的委托,在一定时间和固定场所,依据一定的法律,按照一定的章程和规则,以公开叫价竞购的方法,把事先经买主看过的现货卖给出价最高的买主的一种特殊贸易方式。

(11)期货交易:期货交易是指按照交易所的规定,由买卖双方在交易所内达成远期交割的贸易方式。

(12)套期保值:是指在买进或卖出实际商品的同时或前后,在交易所卖出或买进同等数量的期货合同作为保值。

(13)卖期保值:是指在买进实货的同时,在期货交易所卖出同等数量的期货合同,以防止日后该项商品价格下跌而遭受损失。

(14)买期保值:是指在卖出远期交货的实货同时,在期货交易所买进同等数量的期货合约,以避免实货交货时该项商品价格上涨而遭受损失。

(15)空头:是指交易人预测价格将下跌而卖出期货,当价格跌至较低时又买进对销,其买卖数量相等,以买卖价格的差额交割,以完成交易。

(16)多头:是指交易人预测价格即将上涨而买进期货,当价格涨至较高时抛出对销,其买卖数量相等,以买卖价格差额交割,以完成交易。

(17)叫回:是指交易人在作空头卖出期货后发现价格上涨,中途买进平仓,以减少其损失。

(18)推出:是指交易人在作多头买进期货后,发现价格下跌,中途抛空平仓,以减少其损失。

(19)对销贸易:是指贸易双方有买有卖,互为进口人或出口人,把进口与出口有机地结合起来,双方都以自己的出口全部或部分抵偿从对方的进口,使进出口额保持平衡或基本平衡。

(20)互购贸易:是指出口的一方向进口一方承担购买相当于出口货值或一定比例的货物。

(21)补偿贸易:是指买方以信贷形式向国外供货者购进设备、技术、服务等,设立项目,待项目竣工投产后,以该项目的产品或经商定的其他货物偿还的贸易方式。这是一种用货物或劳务抵偿进口货物的一种利用外资的方式。

(22)进料加工:是指外贸生产企业用外汇购买进口的原料、辅助材料、元器件、零部件和包装物料,经加工为成品或半成品后再外销出口的一种贸易方式。

(23)加工装配贸易:是指由国外厂商作为委托方提供一定的原材料、元器件、零部件、辅助材料、包装物料及必要的机器和生产技术,由国内的工厂企业作为承接方,并按照规定的质量、规格、款式、型号、商标、品牌等进行加工装配,成品由委托方负责包销,承接方按合同规定收取工缴费的一种贸易方式。

(24)来料加工:是指由国外厂商作为委托方,提供全部或部分料件,由国内企业作为承接方,按对方的设计与要求加工成成品,再将成品交对方销售,承接方按双方约定的标准收取工缴费的贸易方式。

(25)来料装配:是指由国外厂商提供零部件、元器件、包装物料,必要时还提供设备和技术,由承接方按委托方的设计、工艺等要求,组装成成品交还对方,承接方收取约定的装配费的贸易方式。

附录二　国际贸易实务案例

[案例1]　国际贸易运输单据

正确理解各种运输单据的作用在实际操作中尤为重要。例如,某出口商收到国外某银行的信用证,信用证条款要求提交"clean on board ocean bills of lading full set and 2 non-negotiable copies"。出口商交单时只提交复印件。银行审单无误后寄开证行索汇。开证行收到单据后,提出了不符点:We have found the discrepancies on the terms of the credit:2 photocopies of the original bill of lading presented bill of lading presented I/O 2non - negotiable copies.由于出口商对单据要求理解不透彻和银行审单不严,造成了上述不符点。货款虽然经进口商和出口商协商最后收回,但付出了一定的代价。Bill of lading 具有物权凭证、运输合同、货物收据的作用,而 photocopied B/L 不具备上述功能。

[思考与分析]　不同的运输单据有不同的作用,业务人员应了解和掌握各种不同运输方式下的运输单据的作用,慎重选择运输单据的类型,以防范风险,避免不必要的损失。

[案例2]　提单与托运人

在 FOB 价格条件下,不要接受买方要求将他们的名称作为"托运人"打在提单上。也可以说这种要求代表着潜在的巨大风险。

中国某出口公司(A 公司)与新加坡某进口公司(B 公司)以 FOB 价格条件签订了一份国际货物销售合同。因为是 FOB 价格条件,所以由 B 公司租船订舱。B 公司开来的信用证上要求将 B 公司名称作为托运人打在提单上,A 公司为了满足信用证对单据的要求以便顺利结汇,于是在填制提单的时候,便将 B 公司作为托运人填在了提单上。后来因其他问题发生单证不符,银行拒绝付款并退单。承运人在卸货港把货物放给了提单中记名的托运人,致使 A 公司虽持有提单,但既无法得到货款,又无法取回货物。于是 A 公司起诉中国的船公司(C 公司)。法院一、二审来来回回好几遍,最后由某高院判决驳回 A 公司对 C 公司的全部诉讼请求,理由是 A 公司不是提单关系中的当事人,无权向 C 公司主张索赔权利。

[思考与分析]　尽管我们不认为该判决是合法和合理的,但是对于 A 公司来说教训是深刻的。编者在几年前曾做过一个类似的案件,那个案件中也是将买方名称作为托运人打在了提单上,我们收集了有关证据证明我们的委托人虽不是提单上记载的"托运人",但却是"实际托运人"和合法的"提单持有人"。相关海事法院接受了我们的观点并支持了我们的索赔主张,即判决船公司赔偿我们的委托人因承运人无提单放货而遭受的全部损失

[案例3]　多式联运提单

所谓多式联运,是指使用两种以上的运输方式完成的运输服务,其中之一是海上运输。随着物流业的兴起,多式联运提单的应用将与日俱增。实践中这种提单出现的机率已大大提高。因此,从事经济贸易的人员有必要对其有所了解。

多式联运的“主体”名称被定义为“经营人”，而非“承运人”。其含义既包括承运人又不仅限于承运人，主体范围扩大了。多式联运对托运人来说，经营人的责任期间为自接收货物时起直至交付货物为止的全部运输过程。通常的做法是：多式联运经营人将全程运输分包给不同的专业运输公司。对于这些公司来说，多式联运的经营人是货物运输的“托运人”，“收货人”也是多式运输经营人指出的“收货人”，即他们的“代理人”。专业运输公司向多式联运经营人签发的提单通常是记名提单，即是不可以转让的。在发生货损货差的时候，多式联运经营人的责任适用于“该区运输的法律”，包括责任限制。如损失发生在海运分阶段，则适用海商法；如损失发生在公路运输阶段，则适用公路运输法。解决索赔的步骤通常是由多式联运经营人向托运人或收货人等作出赔偿，然后多式联运经营人再向发生损失的有关区段的承运人即“实际承运人”追偿。

中国法律关于多式联运的托运人是否可以直接向“实际承运人”主张索赔未作明确规定。一般认为这是困难的。但是根据《海商法》的精神，应当认为其可以对当事船采取法律行为，也就是向“实际承运人”采取法律行为。显然，这里有些矛盾。目前交通部正在组织修改中国《海商法》，希望就多式联运的有关问题在此次修改中得到完善。

还有一个问题是复杂而隐蔽的，即上述的多式联运的承运人对各区段运输产生的损害赔偿责任适用该段运输法律的规定。此项规定看似很清楚，比如一项多式联运涉及海运和陆运，在海运期间发生损失适用海商法；在陆运期间发生损失适用公路运输法或者铁路运输法。但是有这样一种情况，假如多式联运的提单适用乙国法律，那么多式联运经营人依照哪国法律向货方赔偿呢？假如乙国法律比甲国法律对多式联运的经营人有利，那么多式联运的经营人可否要求按乙国法律确定较低的法律责任呢？这种要求看似符合《海商法》的规定，但对货方不利。或者，在多式联运经营人行将破产的情况下，多式联运的托运人可否向有偿付能力的海运“实际承运人”主张索赔呢？这些重大问题，在现行法律下是未知的。因此，各方均存在较大的商业风险，此时就会涉及到保险公司。

[思考与分析] 以上提及的两个相反的案例告诉我们：①FOB 价格条件下，将买方的名称作为托运人打在提单上，风险巨大；②同样的问题，法律上的理解和判决结果可能存在严重的分歧；③不掌握全面的和综合性的法律知识而做生意是要付出代价的；④进出口公司应当为业务部门强制性的设立法律顾问，遇到对方客户提出非常规交易条件的要求时，不要心存侥幸，而应该请法律顾问审查交易条件的潜在风险；⑤把学习法律当作继续自我教育的投资活动。

[案例 4] 指示提单与记名提单

国际货物买卖合同中约定的价格条件为 CIF，即由卖方租船订舱。由于是远洋大宗散杂运输，为使买方的“实际收货人”在单证迟晚的情况下也能及时提货，卖方在与承运人订立的租船合同中约定：“如果船抵目的港时，正本提单未到，承运人应当依照租船人的放货指示凭提单副本加提货人保函放货。”实际情况是，货到目的港而信用证下的单证(包括正本指示提单）尚未到达。故租船人即卖方指示承运人按租约约定向"实际收货人"放货，但是"实际收货人"不是买卖合同下的买方，而是"外贸进口代理制"下的委托方，买方代理商得知承运人"无单放货"之后，对承运人起诉。一种观点认为根据《海商法》第95条，即应视为同意了承运人"无单放货"的行为，无权向承运人主张权利；另一种观点认为根据《海商法》第71条和国际惯例，承运人和租船人订立的"无单放货"条款无效。

与本案有关的规定是进口代理中的委托方不得直接与出口商订立合同条件，或者说任何此类约定无效。即对进口代理商而言，这些约定无约束力。所谓的"进口代理商"对出口商而言，就是合法的买方。本案中进口代理的委托方，即"实际收货人"绕过"进口代理商"要求出口商即买主在租约中加入该条约定，在货到后又根据该条约定无单提货，造成善意提单受让人即"进口代理商"持有提单却无法主张提单下的物权。

如果提单持有人是该租船人，则该项约定有效。这时双方的关系实际是租约关系，而非提单下的法律关系。如果提单持有人是善意的提单受让人，则该约定无效，即对该提单的受让人无约束力。因为此时提单持有人与承运人之间的关系依据只有提单，而提单条款的效力是有法定限制条件的，即《海商法》第44条的规定。该条款规定："海上货物运输合同和作为凭证的提单或者其他运输单证中的条款，违反本章（第四章）规定的无效。"该第四章第71条规定，承运人应凭提单交货。

［思考与分析］ 发生本案纠纷的关键问题在哪，或者说造成承运人"叫屈"的关键是什么？编者认为是承运人不懂用法。正确的做法应当是：在承运人接受租船要求在租约中约定"如果船抵目的港时，正本提单未到，承运人应当依照租船人的放货指示凭提单副本加提货人保函放货"时，对于该"提货人"应当指明，应是本案的实际收货人公司。同时不签发指示提单，签发记名提单，即提单记名的收货人为"本案的实际收货人公司。"这样，承运人在放货时只要核对"实际收货人"名称即可。签发这样的记名提单，本案中的进口代理商银行就可以发现单证中的不符点并拒绝付款赎单，因此单证必将退回给出口商。

［案例5］ 提单下承运人责任限制

在国际货物交易当中，成交的价格条件是各不相同的，有CIF、C&F和FOB等等。受损的货物赔偿金额是否依照买卖合同的价格计算呢？《海商法》第55条对此作出了明确的规定：对于灭失的货物，即"货差"损失，以在装货港的货价加保险费和运费计算。也就是说，即使买卖合同价为FOB，贷方仍然可以依据FOB价加运费和保险费计算出总的索赔金额，通常情况下相当于"CIF"价。对于货损的赔偿金额依照受损前后的实际价差额计算。如果发生修理，则按货物的修复费用计算。必须指出，对于在国外港口发生货损和货差的损失计算，大多采用当地的市价作为计算损失的依据，或者按照修复费用加合理的处理费来确定赔偿金额。中国和国外的做法不同，按中国的做法不包括预期利润损失，按国外的做法包括预期利润损失。

上面讲了损害赔偿的计算方法，承运人是不是按此计算的结果照赔呢？不是《海商法》

赋予了承运人责任限制的保护,为什么要给承运人责任限制的保护呢? 一是长期的历史习惯造成的;二是海运仍属风险较大的行业,目前仍需要保护它的存在。为转移此种可能不足额赔偿的风险,货方可以通过购买保险来解决。对于承运人责任限制,《海商法》是这样规定的:即每件或每个运输单位为666.67个“计算单位”,或按毛重每公斤2个“计算单位”,以高者为准。这是法定的承运人最高赔偿责任限制。所谓“计算单位”是指在数字上与特别提款权相等的经折算的人民币金额,即按照判决之日的汇率将特别提款权数额折算出的人民币币值。

[思考与分析] 在按照在述的“CIF”价格计算出货价损失或在修理费确定之后,与承运人的责任限制相比较,如果不超过限额,则按损失额计算赔偿额;如果超过限额,则超过部分承运人可以免赔。例如,如果实际损失超过责任限额,是否可按责任限制计算赔偿为A个“特别提款权”,再将A个“特别提款权”折算出受责任限制保护呢? 答案是否定的,即在货方证明了承运人有故意或明知可能造成损失而轻率地作为或不作为导致发生损失时,承运人无权享受责任限制保护,但是货方通常很难完成举证责任。

[案例6]　承运人与实际承运人

所谓“承运人”一般是指与托运人订立运输合同的当事人。也就是说,在法律上是他与托运人订立运输合同。可以是直接以其名义与托运人订立运输合同,也可以委托代理人以其名义与托运人订立运输合同。

所谓“实际承运人”是指接受“承运人”委托从事运输的人,可以是全部也可以是部分的运输。可以这样理解,承运人与托运人订立运输合同之后,可以使用自己的船完成约定的运输,也可以委托其他船公司或运输公司使用他们的船舶完成约定的运输。这种接受“委托”的人还包括接受“转委托”从事约定运输的人。这种“委托”和“转委托”运输关系定义的实际承运人可以涵盖运输关系链上的任何人。

按照中国《海商法》对承运人责任的规定,其适用实际承运人。也就是说法律规定承运人必须做到的事情,实际承运人也必须做到,如使船舶适航、尽速遣返等。此外,对于某一损失,如果承运人和实际承运人都被认定为应承担赔偿责任,则这种责任为连带责任,即提单持有人有权从承运人和实际承运人中任意一人得到足额赔偿。

托运人甲与承运人乙订立了一份运输合同,承运人乙又委托实际承运人丙从事约定的运输。货到卸货港后实际承运人凭保函将货物放给了托运人甲的买方丁。托运人甲在发运货物之后依据提单等单据,通过银行信用证渠道结汇。银行发现存在不符点,故而拒付。甲通知丁支付货款,丁不理睬。甲后来发现货物已经被非法放掉给了丁。于是甲来找乙要求赔偿损失。乙说无单放货者是丙不是乙,让甲去找丙。丙说,我与你没有关系,是乙委托我运输,你与乙有运输关系,你去找乙。甲该怎么办呢?

[思考与分析] 根据前述中国《海商法》,编者认为甲既可以找乙也可以找丙。这种运输情况下,无单放货既构成违约又构成侵权。为什么既构成违约,又构成侵权呢? 因为运

输合同下承运人有在卸货港交货的义务，承运人未履行，故构成违约；又《海商法》规定提单承运人据以交货的凭证，而承运人违反该项法律规定，侵害了提单持有人的权利，故构成侵权。有一点应当提醒，也有人有不同看法，认为这种情况下，实际承运人应承担侵权责任，而承运人无需承担责任。

[案例7]　提单下该告谁

案例分析一　A公司以FOB价格条件向一家香港公司B公司出口大白云豆。因为是FOB条件出口，所以船舶应由B公司负责租用。B公司租用了C公司的舱容。A公司委托在装港的D公司协助集港。D公司又委托C公司在装港的代理C′公司具体操作集港工作，提单由C′公司以C公司的名义签发。A公司获得提单以后便通过银行向B公司结汇，后B公司拒绝结汇，原因是B公司已经从C公司凭保函提走货物。5个月后，结汇单又通过银行退回给A公司。A公司根据提单在装港的海事法院以C′公司作为被告提起诉讼。法院立案室人员告诉A公司，以C′公司为被告起诉，法院将不受理，除非将被告名称改为C公司。A公司以为法院是帮助他们，故直接以手写将起诉状被告名称改为C公司。法院随后办理了立案和支付诉讼费等手续。之后，法院通知A公司，称因为C公司无地址、电话等，无法通知C公司应诉，要求以公告方式送达法律文书，为此要加收公告费。A公司此时开始担心，照此下去，即使判决胜诉，C公司也找不到，因此也不可能得到赔偿。这时，他们已经不知所措。

[思考与分析]　在此案中A公司应当将C公司和C′公司列为共同被告为宜，单列其中任何一个，都将造成案情难以查清的局面。将该公司列为共同被告的理由是他们都存在可能的法律责任。起诉被告不意味着被告一定有法律上的赔偿责任，而只是存在可能的法律上的责任，正是因为可能存在法律上的责任，所以才需要到法院去，由法院经过审理而判决和认定责任的有无和大小。

本案法院的立案同志告诉A公司，若以C′公司为被告将不受理，这是严重的误导，或是严重侵害了A公司起诉的权利。“不受理”或“驳回起诉”，应当在受理之后以裁决方式作出，以便原告有上诉的机会和实现上诉的权利。一句“不受理”迫使A公司将被告名称由C′公司改为C公司，但却出现无法向C公司送达法律文书的局面，有失周到。

案例分析二　1979年3月，美国Beyene公司出口一批货物给阿拉伯共和国的Moham—ITled Sofan，当时，进口人通过也门开发银行开出信用证给美国出口公司，并指定美国欧文银行为该信用证的保兑银行。1979年5月货物运出后，出口公司将单据提交给欧文银行请求付款，欧文银行发现提单中所载通知人名字是Mohamed Sofan而非Mohammed Soan，认为不符信用证规定，虽然欧文银行也曾向也门复兴开发银行请求授权其付款，但复兴开发银行坚持拒绝授权付款。

Beyene公司（受益人）认为仅一个字母打错而遭开证行拒绝付款是开证行过分挑剔，随即向法院起诉，要求保兑行付款并负担因其未按信用证付款而使原告遭受损失，欧文银行则以多项理由请求其地方法院驳回原告的起诉。

Beyene 公司不服地方法院的驳回，声称仅名字拼错不足以解除保兑行的付款责任并以此为理由再行上诉，上诉法院结果作出了判决：通常信用证条款要求受益人向开证行交付有关单据，使开证人相信他可以得到所购的货物才能据以付款。只要受益人严格遵照信用证条款履行，开证行或保兑行应承担“绝对付款的义务”。为维护开证行或保兑行的权益，其绝对付款义务只有在信用证条款被严格遵守时才能发生。

[思考与分析] 银行对出口商的付款承诺是严格建立在“单单相符、单证相符”的基础上的。

[案例 8]　提单下承运人责任期间

提单下承运人的责任期间分为两种情况。一种是对于集装箱货物，其责任期间为托运人向承运人在装港交付货物时起，至在卸港承运人向收货人交付货物时止，货物处于承运人掌管之下的全部期间。另一种是非集装箱货物，非集装箱货物的范围是很广的，如杂货、散货、液体货等等。对于这些货物，承运人的责任期间为自货物在装货港装上船舶时起，至在卸货港下船舶时止，货物处于承运人掌管之下的全部期间。根据《海商法》的规定，承运人只对在其掌管货物期间发生的货物灭失或损坏承担赔偿责任。货方无论是托运人或发货人，还是收货人或提货人，都有必要了解法定的承运人责任期间，并根据具体情况判定损失是否发生在该期间，以便确定承运人是否应承担损害赔偿责任。

对于集装箱货物，如何理解承运人自托运人“接收”货物呢？例如，由承运人提供集装箱、陆运车辆前往托运人或发货人货场收货装箱，则承运人责任期间从此时刻起；托运人自备集装箱并装箱，将装好的集装箱交付给承运人，承运人责任期间从此刻起。这是两种货船双方有关集装箱运输交接中常见的情况，不包括其他可能的例外情况。因此，有必要根据个案具体情况研究分析确定承运人责任的起始时间。相应地，承运人的责任终止时间也要具体情况具体分析，不能一概而论。

另外，如果发生因收货人原因导致承运人交货时间迟晚的情况，承运人的责任期间是否顺延呢？答案是否定的。例如，对于集装箱货物，承运人已通知收货人去集装箱场站提货，但由于收货人原因未及时提取货物，则承运人责任期间终止于承运人应当交付货物时止，此后货物灭失或损坏的风险由收货人承担。

对于货方来说，量重要的是应当知道承运人的责任期间是有限度的。因此，不能认为只要货物在承运人手上，不在自己手上，一旦出事（发生损失）就是承运人的责任。与其把货物留在一个可能“不尽职”的承运人手中，不如晚些向承运人交货或早些把货物提走。特别是在买卖合同收付款发生问题时，应尽快采取措施控制在承运人手中的货物。

[案例 9]　制单、交单违规错漏怎么办？

“上次秋交会期间，我们同尼加拉瓜客人成交了一份合同，对方通过银行开来 L/C，目的港是南圣胡安（SAN JUAN DELSUR）。货物按期装运出口，单子也送到了中行议付，一切都很顺利。单证科的同志在制单时把'DELSUR'漏掉了，只打上了'SAN JUAN(圣胡安)'。我方中行和开证行，审单时都没有发现这个错误，我们也收到了货款。三个月之后，客人来电说没有收到货物，要我们赶快查清情况后告诉他们。我们通过有关部门一查，这才知道我们把目的港打错了，南圣胡安命名的港口就有三四个，最后才弄清这批货已经卸到美属波多黎各的圣胡安了！"

"哎呀！从尼加拉瓜的南圣胡安港，到美属波多黎各的圣胡安，中间隔着浩瀚的加勒比海，这真是漏打一个字，相差十万八千里啊！"

"后来，我们费了很大劲，花了不少钱，把货转运到南圣胡安，并向客人表示歉意。客人因为金额不大，总共才两万美元，所以没有向我们索赔，但从此不跟我们做生意了！"

"虽然是个小差错，但带来损失却是很大的呀！"

"所以，打合同、打单证，一定要十分小心，九分九都不行啊！"

[案例10]　委托方可否直接对外承担法律责任

日本甲公司为从中国进口铝锭，通过中国乙公司向新疆丙工厂联系，日本表示愿意通过融资的方式，向丙工厂提供资金支持，由丙工厂生产铝锭，由日方出口。丙工厂因无外贸经营权，特委托乙公司与日本甲公司签约。1995年4月，日本甲公司同中国乙公司经协商签订了货物（铝锭）买卖合同。

该合同规定，日方预先支付50万美元和接受铝锭，中国乙公司同意以出售和提供1000吨铝锭的方式偿还。双方约定，日方支付50万美元作为铝锭交易的预付款，在合同签订之时起15日内汇往乙公司账户。该项预付款的利息按照伦敦同业拆借利率计算。合同规定，中国乙公司必须以书面形式担保上述款项及利息的偿还。此外，双方就货物的规格、数量、装运、价格、保险、仲裁等问题加以规定。丙工厂作为生产一方在该货物买卖合同上附签。

合同签订后，日本甲公司依约向乙公司汇出50万美元，乙公司收到后即汇往丙工厂账户。同时，为支持丙工厂生产，乙公司与丙工厂在委托出口协议上增加有关乙公司向丙工厂提供400万人民币资金支持的条款。在将甲公司的预付款汇出后，乙公司又依照委托协议向丙工厂支付400万人民币。

在合同履行期间，由于国际市场的价格变化和丙工厂的生产调整，致使合同第一批货物交付后发生履行困难，丙工厂不能依照规定交付货物。为此三方就后续问题多次协商，1997年3月，上述三方签订《还款协议》。该《还款协议》规定，因丙工厂不能及时供货，三方同意中断铝锭出口合同。对于剩余资金的归还，三方同意在1997年5月30日前，丙工厂应偿还欠日本甲公司的融资款的全部本息；在1997年6月30日前，丙工厂应偿还乙公司代垫资金的全部本息。三方一致同意，如丙公司未能按上述规定如期偿还甲公司和乙公司的资金，由丙工厂承担由此引起的一切法律责任。三方当事人签字盖章后该《还款协议》生效。

至1997年7月1日，丙工厂仍未向日方偿还资金款，日方提起仲裁，称依照货物买卖合同和中国外贸代理制度规定，要求中国乙公司偿还丙工厂欠该公司资金的全部本息。中国乙公司辩称,三方已就还款达成协议,乙公司不承担任何归还甲公司向丙工厂提供的融资款本息的义务,应由委托方(丙工厂)直接对外承担责任。

[思考与分析] 本案的核心问题是甲公司的资金本息的偿还义务应由谁承担。

[案例 11] 跟单信用证中的各种偿付条款

(1)单到付款(或见单付款)条款,就是议付银行取得议付单证以后,向开证银行或偿付银行寄单索汇,当开证银行或偿付银行收到了议付银行寄来的单证以后,如果审核单证相符,开证行或偿付行就按照议付行的指示,支付货款。信用证中常见的单到付款条款如下:

①IN REIMBURSEMENT, WE SHALL REMRT PROCEEDS IN ACCORDANCE WITH YOUR INSTRUCTIONS UPON OF THE DOCUMENTS.

②ON RECEIPT OF CONFORM DOCUMENTS AT OUR COUNTER, WE WILL REMIT COUER TO YOU AS PER YOUR INSTRUCTIONS.

③UPON RECEIPT BY US OF DOCUMENTS WHICH ARE IN CONFORMITY WITH TERMS AND CONDITIONS OF THE CREDIT, WE SHALL PAY TO THE NEGOTLATING BANK AS INSTRUCTED BY T. T. AFTER DEDUCTING OUR CHARGES, IF ANY.

④ WE SHALL COVER THE NEGOTLATING BANK AT BEST CONVENIENCE AT RECEIPT OF CORRECT DOCUMENTS AT OUR COUNTERS.

⑤ REIMBURSEMENT INSTRUCIONS: FOR THE VALUE OF DOCUMENTS WHICH COMPLY WITH CREDIT TERMS, KINDLY: REMTTANCE WILL BE MADE BY US BY TELEX/MALL UPON RECEIVING THE DOCUMENTS STRITLY IN COMPLIANCE WITH D/C TERMS.

⑥WE SHALL COVER YOU AS PER YOUR INSTRUCTIONS FOLLOWING DESPATCH OF SHIPPING DOCUMENTS IN COMPILANCE WITH CREDIT TERMS.

(2)单到授权偿付条款,就是单据到达开证行以后,开证行审核单证相符,然后再授权议付银行向其开证行指定的偿付行索汇的条款。也就是议付银行取得议付单证以后,将所有单据寄给开证银行,当开证银行收到单据并认为单证相符时,来函授权议付银行向其开证行指定的偿付银行索汇。议付行虽然知道偿付行的名称,但不能直接向其索汇。例如,某银行信用证摘录条款如下:

INFORMATIONS: PLS SEND DOCUMENTS DIRECTLY TO UNICREDITO ITALANO. TORINO IN TWO LOTS, IST BY DHL, 2ND BY REGISTERED AIRMAIL.

INSTRUCTIONS: ONLY UPON RECEIPT OF REGULAR DOCUMENTS AT OURCOUNTERS, WE SHALL AUTHORIZE YOU TO REIMBURSE YOURSELVES THROUGH THE CHASE MANHATTAN BANK, NEW YORK, U. S. A.

REIMBURSING BANK :THE CHASE MANHATTAN BANK, NEW YORK, U. S. A.

(3)单到开证银行后,开证行再发出偿付指示或告知偿付银行名称的条款,也就是开证银行收到议付银行寄去的单据以后,经过开证行的审核,认为单证相符。然后,开证行再发给议付银行的偿付指示或告知其指定的偿付银行名称，举如下例子。

①某银行信用证摘录条款如下：

ON RECEIPT OF ORIGINAL DOCUMENTS CONFORMING TO THE TERMS OF THIS DOCUMENTARY CREDIT, WE SHALL INSTRUCT YOU TO CLAIM REIMBURSE MENT IN THE CURRNCE OF THIS DOCUMENTARY CREDIT.

②某银行信用证摘录条款如下：

DEFERRED PAYMENT DETALLS: PAYMENT TO BEEFECTED 45 DAYS AFTER TRANSPORT DOCUMENTS DATE.

INSTRUCS TO PAY/ACCPT/NEGOT BANK:

UPON PRESENTATION OF DOCUMENTS YOU ARE REQUESTED TO ADVISE US BY SWIFT MT750/MT754 AMOUNT AND VALUE DATE OF YOURCLAIM, NAME OF VESSEL AND B/L NO . AND DATE. PLS ALSO ADVISE MATURITY DATE. UPON RECEIPT OF CONFORMING DOCUMENTS WE WILL AUTHORIZE YOU TO CLAIM REIMBURSEMENT. DOCUMENTS MUST BE SENT BY COURIER TO BANK HAPOALIM B. M FOREIGN TRADE OPS. CENTER 40, HAMASGER STREET TEL-AVIV 67131 ISRAEL.

(4)向第三家银行索偿的条款，也就是开证行在其开出的信用证中指明了偿付行名称，并要求议付银行取得议付单据以后，将单据直接寄给开证行，同时向其指定的偿付银行索汇，举如下例子：

①某银行信用证摘录条款如下：

REIMBURSING BANK: BIC. BANK OF NEW YORK. NEW YORK, U. S. A.. INSTRUCTIONS TO PAY/ACCPT/NEGOT BANK:

THE NEGOTLATING BANK MUST AIRMAIL THE DRAFIS AND ALL DOCUMENTSDIRECTLY TO US IN TWO CONSECTIVE LOTS ··· IN REIMBURSEMENT, PLEASE CLAIM BY YOURSELVES TO REIMBURSEMENT BANK.

②某银行信用证摘录有关条款如下：

REIMBURSING BANK: ARAB BANK PLC. , NEW YORK U. S. A.

REIMBURSEMENT INSTRUCTIONS: FOR THE VALUE OF DOCUMENTS WHICH COMPLY WITH CREDIT TERMS, KINDLY: REIMBURSE ON YOUR JORDAN BRANCHES CENTER ACCOUNT WITH ARAB BANK PLC, NEW YORK. , U. S. A.

[案例12]　议付银行在索汇中应注意的问题

由于开来的信用证来自世界各个地方，性质又不尽相同，加上各种货币有不同清算的特点，所以在单证相符的情况下，议付银行在索汇中应特别注意，谨慎操作。

(1)议付银行在审核信用证时，要注意信用证中的偿付条款，这样才能使我方的收汇有保障。若信用证规定的偿付方式不符合国际惯例或偿付路线不明确，应要求开证银行修改或澄清,以便索汇。

(2)议付银行要正确理解信用证中的偿付条款。随着我国加入WTO(世界贸易组织)以及对外贸易的不断扩大,开证来自世界各地各家银行,这就使得信用证的性质各不相同,各种货币的清算特点以及索汇路线各异使得偿付条款也各有不同。为了正确、及时、安全收汇,就必须正确理解信用证偿付条款,确保采取正确的索汇办法。

(3)在实际操作中要仔细认真,以便正确制作。在有些信用证中,虽然开证行指定了偿付银行名称,但议付行议付单证以后,不能同时向其(偿付银行)索汇,而要等待开证行再来授权后,议付银行才能向其索汇。

(4)应注意信用证中的索汇方式是用电报还是用航邮信函索汇。如果信用证规定不能电索,就应用航邮信函索汇,如果信用证中没有明确或没有禁止电报索汇字样,就应看信用证是否有适用证中规定"Reimbursement under this L/C is Subject to ICC URR 525"。如果有,则可采取电报索汇,以加速收汇。

[案例13] 巧用假远期信用证

按信用证受益人收到货款时间分类,信用证可分为即期信用证和远期信用证。即期信用证是开证行或付款行收到符合信用证的即期汇票及符合信用证条款的单据立即履行付款义务的信用证;远期信用证(Usance Credit)是开证行或付款行收到符合信用证的单据时,不立即付款,而是等到汇票到期履行付款义务的信用证。远期信用证有两种,一种是承兑信用证,一种是远期议付信用证。这两种信用证都必须要汇票,但承兑信用证的汇票付款人必须是银行,远期议付信用证的汇票付款人可以是开证行、申请人或其他银行。使用远期信用证应明确是承兑信用证还是远期议付信用证。同时远期信用证中又可分为假远期信用证和真远期(即远期)信用证。

1. 假远期信用证

所谓假远期信用证是指受益人出具远期汇票并提供单据后,议付行可按即期议付并索汇的信用证。利用这种方式,买方(开证人)负担贴现利息和手续费就可享受银行给予的融资便利。这种信用证对受益人来说,与即期信用证无异,其实质是开证行为解决进口商资金周转困难,对开证人使用的一种融资方式。

2. 假远期信用证与远期信用证的区别

假远期信用证与远期信用证虽然都是跟单信用证,但它们仍然有些区别。

(1)假远期信用证是以即期付款的贸易合同为基础,而远期信用证是以远期付款的贸易合同为基础的。

(2)假远期信用证的受益人能即期收汇,而远期信用证的受益人必须要汇票到期才能收汇。

(3)假远期信用证规定远期汇票的贴现息及承兑手续费等由开证人负担,而远期信用证由于是远期付款交易,由远期收汇而发生的利息、贴现息不涉及开证人,受益人如欲即期取得货款,贴现息及费用必须自行负担。

假远期信用证中的有关条款举例。

假远期信用证一般都在信用证的主要条款或特殊指示中附加某些特定条款来说明,例如:

"…Available for acceptance of your drafts at 90 days sight drawn on us . Drawee Bank's discount or interest charges and accptance commission are for the applicant and therefore the beneficiary is to receive value for usance drafts as if drawn at sight."

"…Available by acceptance of your drafts at 60 days sight drawn on us. The drafts must be negotiated by advising Bank of fecting payment to beneficiary sight basis. Discount at our bank and discount charges for buyer's account."

"…Available by acceptance of your drafts at 150 days sight on B. O. C. Interest for buyer's account. Drafts are payable at sight and to be discounted at the Drawee Bank."

Beneficiary's time draft shall be negotiated on at sight Basis and should be forwarded to the drawee bank for their acceptance and discount, together with your certificate of compliance.(受益人的远期汇票将是即期议付,并寄给付款承兑和贴现连同你的相符证明)

Usance Drafts to be negotiated at sight basis and discounted by us (Issuing Bank),discount charges and acceptance commission are for Importer's account.(远期汇票按即期议付,由本银行'开证银行'贴现,贴现息及承兑费由进口商承担)

从上面条款可知,开证银行在开立假远期信用证时,付款人为出口地银行,这是开证行利用出口方银行的资金为进口商提供融资方便。一般来说,如果开证行是资信情况良好的大银行,而且双方有良好的协作关系,在资金允许的情况下,出口地银行是可以接受贴现向受益人即期付款的。贴现息及有关费用均要向开证行索取,转而由开证申请人负担,并且应是单独即期付款,而不是在远期汇票到期时一并支付。

开证银行把汇票付款人做成进口地银行,一般有两种情况:一是选定一家其所在地金融市场贴现率较低的银行作为远期汇票的付款人,当然该银行应与开证行有良好的协作关系,或是其分支机构,当这张汇票经过被指定银行的承兑后,便可拿到当地的贴现市场上去贴现,从而获得成本较低的资金;二是开证行承兑后,再到当地金融市场出售,以取得付汇资金。后一种情况更容易操作,因此在实际工作中经常碰到。

韩汇银行假远期信用证实例

开证行:HANVIT BANK,SEOUL,KOREA(汉城韩汇银行)

信用证号:MDIF3004

期限:at 90 days sight

金额:USD 3,500,000

MT700

4ID/AVAILABLE WITH. . BY…NAME/ADDR

42C/DRAFTS AT…

090 DAYS AFTER SIGHT

42A/DRAWEE – BTC

HVBKHKHH HANVIT BANK (FORMERLY HANIL AND COMMERCIAL BANK OF KOREA. HONGKONG)

78/INSTRUCS TO. PAY/ACCPT/NEGOT BANK;

TO PAY/ACC/NEG/BK:

THE AMOUNT OF EACH DRAFT MUST BE ENDORSED ON THE REVERSE OF THE CREDIT.

ALL DOCUMENTS MUST BE FORWARDED TO US BY COURIER SERVICE IN ONE LOT …

BENEFICIARY' S TIME DRAFT SHALL BE NEGOTIATED ON ATSIGHT BASIS AND SHOULD BE FORWARDED TO THE DRAWEE BANK FOR THEIR ACCEPTANCE AND DISCOUNT, TOGETHER WITH YOUR CERTIFICATE OF COMPLIANCE.

ACCEPTANCE COMM. AND DISCOUNT CHARGES ARE FOR ACCOUNT OF APPLICANT.

[案例 14]　法院裁定冻结信用证项下货款

1995 年 5 月 5 日,中国甲公司和德国乙公司签订钢材买卖合同。双方约定,乙公司在收到甲公司开出的不可撤销信用证后 40 天内装船,目的港为广州黄埔。之后,甲公司于 5 月 10 日从中国银行湖北分行开出以乙公司为受益人的不可撤销信用证,金额为 345 万美元。5 月 25 日,双方签订补充协议,将装船期限改为 7 月 2 日。7 月 4 日,甲公司收到乙公司的装船通知,告知货物已按照装船期装船。7 月 5 日,甲公司与中国丙公司签订购销合同,甲公司将从乙公司购买的钢材转售给丙公司。合同约定,丙公司于 8 月 15 日前在黄埔港提货,之后,丙公司支付定金 1000 万元人民币。7 月 25 日,中行湖北分行收到信用证项下的全套提单,表示予以承兑,约定付款时间是 9 月 1 日。8 月 25 日,货船才抵达目的港。经检查乙公司未能依据钢材买卖合同的规定,在 7 月 2 日装船,是提供的提单倒签所致,实际装船期为 7 月 20 日,导致货船无法依照合同到达目的港。

由于货船抵港期迟延,导致甲公司未能依据购销合同的约定向丙公司交货。丙公司以交货迟延,市场行情暴跌为由,拒绝收取货物,并向人民法院提起诉讼,要求甲公司双倍返还定金和支付违约金,以补偿其经济损失。与此同时,甲公司为维护自身合法权益,向广州海事法院提交诉前扣船申请并提供了担保,然后向海事法院提起诉讼,要求货船的承运人赔偿损失。同时,依据钢材买卖合同的规定,向仲裁机构提起仲裁,要求乙公司赔偿因违约给自身造成的经济损失,并向仲裁机构申请对中行湖北分行业已承兑的信用证项下的款项予以冻结。仲裁机构向法院提请作出财产保全的裁定,丁公司为甲公司提供了担保函。

法院经审查裁定,准许甲公司的财产保全申请,自即日起冻结中行湖北分行已承兑尚未支付的信用证和乙公司的代理行签署和解协议,约定乙公司支付给甲公司450万美元解决所有的各项赔偿,甲公司接受货物,湖北分行在接到德国银行的确认后向法院申请解除对信用证的冻结等。10月11日,甲公司向法院申请解除财产保全措施,法院裁定准许解除对信用证的冻结。

[思考与分析] 本案涉及在涉外仲裁程序中的提请财产保全的法律问题。

1. 有关财产保全的法律规定

财产保全是指法院根据利害关系人或当事人的申请,依据职权对当事人的财产采取保护措施,以保证将来生效和法律裁决得以执行的一种制度。财产保全分为诉前财产保全和诉中财产保全两种形式,本案属于在仲裁程序进行过程中的财产保全。

《中华人民共和国民事诉讼法》第九章对"财产保全"作了详细的规定。提请财产保全的程序如下。

(1)申请:《民事诉讼法》第94条规定,财产保全限于请求的范围或与本案有关的财物,这是指法院在采取保全措施时,保全的范围应当限于当事人争议的财产或被告的财产;对于财产保全的措施,主要是采取查封、扣押、冻结或者法律规定的其他方法。

(2)提供担保:《民事诉讼法》第92条规定,法院采取财产保全措施,可以责令申请人提供担保,申请人不提供担保的,驳回申请。

(3)裁定:法院在审查后,认为不符合条件的,应及时裁定采取保全措施,对于情况紧急的,必须在48小时内作出裁定。

(4)交付执行。

《民事诉讼法》第95条规定,被申请人提供担保的,人民法院应当解除财产保全。由于提供了担保,消除了无法执行法律裁决的可能性,财产保全已经没有必要,因此应裁定解除财产保全措施。对于申请财产保全所遭受的损失,其是对申请人权利滥用的制裁,体现了法律的公平。

对于涉外民事诉讼中有关财产保全的规定,适用有关《民事诉讼法》第九章关于"财产保全"的规定。本案中,人民法院采取财产保全措施时,在程序上完全满足了法律的规定,是合法的。

2. 本案法院采用冻结信用证项下货款的保全措施是否合法

关于涉外民事法律关系的法律适用,我国《民法通则》第142条规定,中华人民共和国法律和中华人民共和国缔结或参加的国际条约没有规定的,可以适用国际惯例。这一规定是指导涉外审判和涉外仲裁的一项基本原则。在目前的国际贸易实践中,有关信用证的法律适用主要是适用《跟单信用证统一惯例》(国际商会第500号出版物)。在本案中,法院采用冻结信用证项下货款的措施实施财产保全是否符合国际惯例的规定已成为首要问题。

有人认为,信用证是独立于其所依赖的销售合同或其他合同以外的交易,银行不应受信用证之外的合同的约束,因此,对本案中行湖北分行已承兑且准备支付的信用证项下的款项,法院不应准许申请人的财产保全。但是,本案中已经确知乙公司伪造并倒签提单,其违反了国际贸易的通行惯例,其行为已经构成欺诈,尤为重要的是其尚未对外付款,因此法院可以对信用证项下的款项采取冻结的保全措施。

《跟单信用证统一惯例》第3条(2)款规定,受益人在任何情况下,不得利用银行之间或申请人与开证行之间存在的合同关系。据此,作为国际货物买卖的卖方是不能利用信用证法律关系实施任何损害买方合法权益的违法行为的。在发生违法行为后,如果信用证已经由开证行表示承兑,在尚未付款的情形下,实施冻结信用证项下的款项的措施是可以最大限度地保护另一方合法权益的。这样,可以有效地防止卖方欺诈行为而导致不良后果的发生。正确的信用证国际惯例应当是维护信用证法律关系的独立性和银行承兑及付款的无因性的,但这也是建立在禁止任何信用证欺诈行为的前提下的。

最高人民法院在有关"财产保全"的司法解释中明确说明,如果有充分证据证明卖方是利用合同进行欺诈,中国银行在合理时间内尚未对外付款,在这种情况下,人民法院可以根据买方的请求,冻结信用证项下的款项。对于中国涉外仲裁机构提交的冻结信用证项下货款的请求,人民法院也应当照此办理。

由此可见,本案中人民法院采取的裁定,准许中国涉外机构提交的、仲裁申请人甲公司关于冻结信用证项下货款,防止卖方的欺诈行为的财产保全申请,是符合国家惯例和我国法律规定的。

[案例15] 法院裁定冻结信用证项下货款

1995年6月20日,香港甲公司和中国乙公司在广州签订035号合同,在甲公司接受乙公司报价的基础上,双方约定乙公司向甲公司购买日本生产的汽车零配件和维修设备。合同的总金额为10万美元,分批装运。最迟不应晚于7月10日装船发运。甲公司对产品的质量保证期为货物到达目的地后的12个月。

合同签订后,甲公司于6月15日电话通知乙公司,由于香港市场的日本产汽车零配件短缺,且价格猛涨,询问可否接受其他国家或地区的产品。乙公司于6月20日回函称,同意在保证产品质量的前提下,接受台湾或韩国产品,并要求立即供货。双方未就改变零配件产地条件后的产品价格问题进行协商。6月27日,甲公司向乙公司提供价值15万港币的产品,乙公司因外汇问题,仅先行支付10万港币。

货到后乙公司进行了检验,9月25日取得商检部门的检验证书。经中国商检部门的检验,上述零配件均是中性产品,包装及零件上均未标产地。10月5日,乙公司致函甲公司,称此批货物非日本产品,要求换货,如不能换货,则要求退货,并要求甲公司承担有关费用损失。甲公司回函称,乙公司已经同意接受非日本产品,不能以产品为非日本产而索赔。10月15日,乙公司再次致函要求赔偿,甲公司回函称,货物已经海关检验,货证相符,乙公司在货物入库前已详细检查、核对，且已投入使用，因而再次拒绝赔偿。

甲公司因为一直未收到货款，12 月 25 日提起仲裁，要求乙公司立即还所欠的货款 5 万港币及利息并承担全部其他经济损失，要求解除 035 号合同。

乙公司辩称，甲公司的赔偿请求不能成立。因为货款的价格是以日本生产的产品的标准来制定的，而甲公司提供的并非日本生产的产品，价格差别很大，不能以非正品交货而收取正品的价金。同时，甲公司的品质存在异议，1996 年 10 月 25 日，即在收货 15 个月后，自行将 035 号合同项下的货物再次送交商品检验机构检验。检验机构出具的检验证书证明，该批货物有 10 项存在缺陷，发货前已有，是制造不良所致，乙公司据此要求拒付货款及利息。甲公司认为，乙公司不能证明第二次送检的产品是交货时产品，并且第二次商检的时间已经超过索赔有效期，商检证书不能发生效力。

[案例 16] 《国际货物销售合同》的案例分析

1995 年 1 月 4 日甲公司与香港乙公司、丙电梯公司（乙公司在大陆的独资公司）签订了《电梯供货合同》，该合同的仲裁条款约定“在合同执行过程中，若出现任何争执，则由买卖双方通过友好协商解决。若争执经友好协商得不到解决，则提交中国国际经济贸易仲裁委员会，根据仲裁程序规定进行仲裁。”在合同签订后，甲公司即向丙公司支付货款 102 万元。在合同履行过程中，当事各方认为合同条款不完善，决定对合同进行修改。鉴于甲公司没有外贸经营权，改由丁外贸公司与丙公司签订电梯供货合同。9 月 22 日，甲公司和丁公司分别签订了与前述合同内容基本一致的《电梯供货及安装合同》。两份合同的第十一条第 1 款约定：“买卖双方在执行合同过程中如发生争执，应友好协商解决。如经友好协商不能解决时，该争执案件将提交仲裁进行裁决。仲裁地点为香港，仲裁委员会将由买卖双方认可及指派，仲裁程序和法律皆按香港现有的有关法例进行。”上述合同的签署日期仍沿用 1995 年 1 月 4 日，只是在合同尾注明“本合同修改日期：1995 年 9 月 25 日”。合同修改后，丙公司未能供货，仅于 1996 年 6 月退回甲公司货款 51 万元人民币，余款未能退回。甲公司在催款未果的情况下，于 1997 年 1 月向中国法院提起诉讼。要求乙公司和丙公司退回剩余货款并支付相应的利息。

某市中级人民法院在受理本案后，乙公司和丙公司在答辩期间提出了管辖异议，认为 1995 年 1 月 4 日签订的合同没有实际履行，且合同中订有仲裁条款，因此，人民法院没有管辖权。甲公司则称，当事人于一天签订两份合同，而且两份合同选择不同的仲裁委员会，属于对仲裁委员会约定不明，人民法院对该案有管辖权。

[案例 17] 《国际备用信用证惯例》（ISP98）的案例分析

由于用途的广泛性和运用的灵活性，备用信用证的业务量早已超过了商业信用证。以 1998 年为例，国际商会于 1998 年 4 月 6 日正式颁布了《国际备用信用证惯例》（International Standby Practices，简称 ISP98，为国际商会第 590 号出版物），并已于 1999 年 1 月 1 日起正式实施。自 1999 年以来，国内有关企业已经开始接到国外依据 ISP98 开立的备用信用证，但由于目前我国国内尚未就 ISP98 进行深入研究和广泛宣传，致使备用信用证在我国的使用受到了很大限制。因此，研究和学习 ISP98 这一备用信用证的“国际游戏规则”已经成为我们的当务之急。

案例分析一 一开证行开立一份不可撤销的备用信用证，通过 A 行通知给受益人。信用证要求受益人提供如下单据。

(1) 申请人违约声明书，注明：“按照 XXX 与 YYY 公司之间达成的第 111 号、日期为 1994 年 1 月 1 日的合同，我方已于 1994 年 2 月 2 日装运了 SSS 加仑的油。发货后，我方等待 YYY 方按上面提及的合同规定付款长达 120 天之久。YYY 方没有支付应付之款，因此，YYY 方违反了合同条件。根据该备用信用证规定，我方有权支取申请人（YYY 公司）所欠 USD 的款项。”

(2) 一份注明装运商品的商业发票副本。

(3) 一份证明装运了货物并标明了装运日期的运输单据副本。

根据商业合同的要求，受益人装运了货物，按照销售合同，受益人对于应付给他的款项向 YYY 方开立了发票，付款期限是 120 天。装运后第 121 天，受益人按照备用信用证的要求备妥单据并提交给开证行索款。

开证行收到单据后，经审核认为单据不符拒绝接受，理由如下：按照 UCP500 第四十三条规定，单据必须不迟于装运日后 21 天内提交，装运日期是 1994 年 2 月 2 日，而单据直至 1994 年 6 月 3 日才提交，受益人的交单构成延迟交单。

请根据 UCP500 的规定，分析开证行的拒付是否有理？

案例分析二 G 银行于 1993 年 3 月 1 日开立一份以 B 为受益人的备用信用证，规定于 4 月 1 日生效。3 月 14 日申请人指示开证行撤销备用信用证。

请论据 ISP98 的规定，分析上述做法是否正确。

[思考与分析] G 银行必须拒绝执行该项指示。备用信用证自 3 月 1 日开立后即不可撤销，而备用信用证的生效日即 4 月 1 日，代表的是可凭备用信用证提出索款要求的最早日期，但该日期与备用信用证变为不可撤销的时间无关。

所谓“独立性”，是指尽管备用信用证是为担保申请人和受益人之间的基础合同而开立，且备用信用证条款中常引述基础合同，但备用信用证一经开立，即独立于基础合同。也就是说，开证人对受益人的付款责任是以受益人提交的与备用信用证条款表面相符的“单据”为依据，而不介入确定申请人是否违约的事实。可见，“凭单付款”这一“单据化”特征，是包括备用信用证在内的所有跟单信用证的共同本质。

案例分析三 应 B（潜在业主）之邀，P 递交了一份标价为 1000 万德国马克的建筑工程投标书，随附一份 G 银行开立的金额为 50 万德国马克的备用信用证。最后，B 在证下提出索款要求，P 抗辩道：B 已与 T 签约，所以备用信用证已经失效。请依据 ISP98 分析 G 银行可否拒付。

[思考与分析] 按照 ISP98 的规定,备用信用证具有独立性和单据化的特点,开证人对受益人的付款责任是以受益人提交的与备用信用证条款表面相符的"单据"为依据,而不介入确定申请人是否违约的事实。因此,除非 P 能证明 B 方的欺诈或其他权利滥用行为,并以此凭有关适用法律构成对 B 方索款要求的有效抗辩,否则 G 银行必须付款。

案例分析四 有一备用信用证要求受益人分期支款时必须提供申请人违约的如下声明:"因为在到期日申请人没有对以下本票中的一张付款,因此,所开立汇票之金额代表开证申请人应该支付而未付的金额。"申请人早于分期付款日,即 1999 年 1 月 1 日、1999 年 2 月 1 日、1999 年 3 月 1 日之前,在备用信用证外,直接向受益人支付了应付的分期支款金额。因此,受益人不需要在备用信用证项下开立特殊的分期支款汇票。

1999 年 4 月 2 日,在分期支款第四张本票到期后,申请人没有像前三次那样如期付款,因此受益人向开证行提交了信用证所要求的违约声明书和汇票,以便在备用信用证项下向开证行索取申请人所欠款项。

请问:按照 ISP98 规定,开证行收到单据后可否拒绝付款?

[思考与分析] 开证行不能拒绝付款。这是因为,与 UCP500 不同,ISP98 明确规定了每次交单均具有独立性,即受益人未能按期交单,并不影响下次交单。国际商会 511 号文件特地提请备用信用证各当事人注意 UCP500 第 41 条"分期支款(分期装运)"的规定:"信用证规定在指定的不同期限内分期支款及(或)装运,则信用证对该期及以后各期均视为无效。信用证另有规定者除外。"有些限定分期支款的备用信用证是保证申请人直接向受益人分期付款的,当申请人未能向受益人按期付款时,受益人才能在备用信用证项下向开证行索取该期款项。在这种备用信用证下,有时因申请人业已在备用信用证外向受益人支付了某一期款项,受益人便不能再向开证行索取该期款项。根据本条,此时信用证就失效了。如申请人事后违约,未直接向受益人支付以后各期款项,受益人也不能向开证行索取以后各期款项。为避免这种情况的发生,UCP500 工作小组向各国委员会建议,银行开出备用信用证限定分期支款时,应注意本条,或在信用证内规定不适用本条,或在信用证内另作规定。在某些案例中,银行时常争论到 UCP500 第 41 条适用于需要分期支款的备用信用证。因此,如果开立需要分期支款的备用信用证时,谨慎的做法是在备用信用证中明确排除 UCP500 第 41 条的适用,或直接注明该备用信用证受 ISP98 约束。

开证人或其指定人对某一不符点交单的付款,无论是否已通知不符点的存在,都不构成其放弃该备用信用证下其他不符点交单的拒付权力。

ISP98 规定,受益人在提交单据时必须确认该单据是某备用信用证项下提交。确认方法包括注明备用信用证完整号码和开证人名称或附上正本或副本备用信用证;否则,受益人的交单视为无效。

[案例 18] **CIC 与 ICC 险别责任范围比较**

在我国国际贸易实践中,进出口货物的保险一般要求采用"中国保险条款"(China

Insurance Clause, CIC),但随着我国对外经济贸易的发展,目前,我国企业以 CIF 价格条件对外出口时,有些外商也常会要求采用国际保险市场上通用的英国伦敦保险协会所制订的"协会货物条款"(Institute Cargo Clauses, ICC)新条款进行投保,我国出口企业有必要对 CIC 和 ICC 新条款险别的责任范围进行比较,这样既有助于我们掌握各险别的精神实质,也有助于在工作中作好投保的选择。

1. 一切险(All Risks, AR) 和 ICC(A)险

ICC 新条款的(A)险对应于 CIC 的一切险,其承保范围采用"承保除规定的除外责任以外的一切风险所造成保险标的损失",看起来承保范围很广,但仔细分析其所列的除外责任后,便会发出其实 ICC(A)险的承保范围与一切险几乎等同,但对(A)险的有些规定还是值得注意的。

(1)在(A)险的一般除外责任中规定:对归因于被保险人故意的不法行为造成的损失或费用,保险人不负赔偿责任,对并未规定归因于其他人的故意不法行为造成的损失或费用,保险人不负赔偿责任,说明(A)险对除被保险人以外的其他人的故意行为造成保险标的损失或费用是负责赔偿的。这与我国海洋运输货物保险条款的除外责任并无差别。

(2)在(A)险的战争除外责任规定中,将"海盗行为"排除在除外责任之外,说明(A)险对"海盗行为"的损失是负赔偿责任的,这一点比我国一切险的范围大,因为在我国海洋运输货物保险中只有加保战争险时才对"海盗行为"的损失予以负责,如未加保战争险是不予负责的。

2. 水渍险(With Particular Average, WPA) 和 ICC(B)险

ICC 新条款的(B)险对应于 CIC 的水渍险,其承保范围采用"列明风险"的方式,从总体上来看,(B)险承保的风险与水渍险并无实质性差别,但就其列出的承保风险责任来说,有两点是必须注意的。

(1)(B)险承保范围中规定:"货物在船舶或驳船装卸时落海或跌落造成任何整件的全损",说明它对装卸时落海或跌落造成的整件全损负责赔偿,对部分损失是不予负责的。我国海洋运输 CIC 责任范围规定:"在装卸或转运时由于一件或整件货物落海造成的全部或部分损失",说明 CIC 对全损和部分损失都是负赔偿责任的。

(2)在(B)险的除外责任中规定:对"由任何个人或数人非法行为故意损坏或故意破坏保险标的或其他任何部分"不负赔偿责任。对"任何人"可以理解为包括被保险人及其他一切人的故意行为所造成的损失都是不负赔偿责任的。被保险人如要获得此保障,需加保新附加险"恶意损害条款"。而我国 CIC 的除外责任中规定对"被保险人的故意行为或过失所造成的损失"是不负赔偿责任的,这说明我国条款仅限于对被保险人(包括被保险人的代理人)的故意行为或过失造成的损失不予负责,而对其他人的故意行为造成的损失是负责赔偿的。以上两点说明,(B)险的责任范围小于我国现行的水渍险。

3. 平安险(Free from Particular Average)与 ICC(C)险的比较

ICC 新条款的(C)险对应于 CIC 的平安险，其承保范围也采用"列明风险"的方式，就两者承保的责任范围来看，差别也不大，但(C)险的实际保障范围明显小于平安险。这可从以下三方面说明。

(1)(C)险对自然灾害和一般性的意外事故均未列入责任范围，如"地震、火山爆发、雷电"以及"海水、湖水或河水进入船舶、驳船、运输工具、集装箱、大型海运箱或贮存处所"所致的损失都是不予赔偿的。

(2)(C)险对装卸或转运时由于一件或数件整件货物落海造成的损失没有列入责任范围，是不负赔偿责任的。

(3)在(C)险的除外责任中，与(B)险规定相同，"由任何个人或数人非法行为故意损坏或故意破坏保险标的或其他任何部分"不负责赔偿。如获得这些保障，同样需加保新附加险"恶意损害条款"。

4. 附加险的比较

ICC 新条款的附加险只有三种，即协会战争险、协会罢工险和恶意损害险。而我国 CIC 的附加险分为一般附加险(11 种)、特别附加险(6 种)和特殊附加险(3 种)。就承保责任范围来看，两者无实质性差别。

(1)协会战争险在除外责任中对敌对行为用原子武器造成货物的损失有些变化。ICC 新条款仅规定由于敌对行为使用原子武器等所致灭失或损害不予赔偿，但对由于非敌对行为使用原子武器等造成的灭失或损失必须负责。所谓"非敌对行为"，主要指敌对双方以外的海轮遭受他们使用的原子武器造成的灭失或损害，保险人仍负赔偿责任。

(2)协会罢工险只是在除外责任中增加了一条'航程挫折"条款，主要对由于罢工而使航程受挫折所造成的额外费用不予负责。

(3)协会恶意损害险是新增加的附加险，其承保范围主要是对被保险人以外的其他人(如船长、船员等)的故意行为所致保险标的灭失或损害负赔偿责任。但如果恶意损害是出于有政治动机的人的行为所致保险标的损失，不属本险别的保险责任，该项损失应属于罢工险的承保范围。协会恶意损害险的承保范围在 ICC(A)险的责任中已经包括，只适用于在 ICC(B)险和 ICC(C)险的基础上加保。

[案例 19]　联营组成部门——因外贸代理产生的民事责任由谁承担

1986 年 3 月，为进一步扩大对外贸易，A 省纺织、机械、土畜和轻工等进出口公司决定联合在国外设立贸易公司。经协商一致，各方在组建过程中签订《章程(草案)》，规定在国外设立新新贸易联合公司，该联合公司由纺织进出口公司主办，对外为有限责任公司，其他进出口公司可以在联合公司下设立各自的商品业务部，联合公司和各商品部均为独立核算单位，自负盈亏，各商品业务部与其在国内的有关外贸公司对口负责，独立经营，接受其外贸母公司的人事、经营和业务管理和指导。

1986 年 11 月，外经贸部作出《同意设立新新贸易联合公司的批复》，同意在国外设立新新贸易联合公司,由纺织公司统一组织和管理,各外贸公司在公司内设立商品部,实行独立核算,自负盈亏。

1991 年 6 月,国内甲公司与 A 省土畜进出口公司在新新联合公司的商品部——新新贸易联合公司土畜商品部签署外贸代理协议,委托土畜商品部代理出口价值 300 万美元的茶叶,由甲公司组织货源,土畜商品部负责对外销售。

合同生效后,甲公司依约将货物交付土畜商品部,履行了自身的义务。货到后,新新贸易联合公司土畜商品部将货物销售后,因国外客户的原因,无法依约向甲公司支付货款,从而产生争议。

后甲公司向 A 省土畜进出口公司所在地的人民法院起诉,要求该公司依法承担因未履行有关偿付货款的合同义务造成的全部损失。A 省土畜进出口公司辩称,新新贸易联合公司的土畜商品部是独立中间商,自主经营,自负盈亏,是外贸代理合同的一方当事人,其与 A 省土畜进出口公司无任何关系,甲公司应依约向新新贸易联合公司索赔。

[案例 20]　国际商事欺诈及风险防范案例分析

案例分析一　1994 年,中国内地 A 公司与美国 D 公司、中国台湾 R 公司分别签订了如下 3 份合同。

(1) 内地 A 公司与美国 D 公司的购销合同规定由 A 公司向 D 公司出口各类运动承兑交单(D/A),也就是说,A 公司出货后,D 公司对 A 公司的汇票予以承兑后即可从代收银行取得装运单据,凭此提取货物,到汇票 90 天到期支付货款。

(2) 国内 A 公司与台湾 R 公司的合同规定,由台湾 R 公司提供一部分健身器材产品,由 A 公司收购后出口给美国 D 公司,另提供一部分零配件由中国公司自行在中国组织生产后出口给美国 D 公司。A 公司与 R 公司的付款条件是远期信用证 120 天付款。

(3) 台湾 R 公司向国内 A 公司出具的保证书保证美国 D 公司付款。如 D 公司不能按时、按期付款,则 R 公司负责偿还 A 公司的货款本金,还要加付利息。

在此之前,A 公司曾经对 D 公司的资信进行了调查,确认该公司为股票上市公司,且有 30 多年经营体育器材的历史,在台湾和东南亚采购中没有发生过不付款的恶性记录。而且,D 公司承诺对承兑交单的货款,可通过其代理银行发电给中方银行进行贴现,提前支付给 A 公司。

A 公司认为,他向美国 D 公司收回货款和向台湾 R 公司付款均为无期,其中有 30 天的时间差,其资金周转应没有问题。而且美国 D 公司承诺其在亚洲的采购均通过 A 公司,包括台湾 R 公司生产的产品当然也应通过 A 公司出口美国。A 公司认为这是一项"优惠政策",便欣然接受。合同签订后,A 公司即开始积极执行,对台湾 R 公司开出 120 天远期信用证收购其产品后每台健身器加价 8 美元直接转单售往美国。货物出口集中在该年 8 月至 12 月份。除了少部分货款外,大部分货款美方均以种种借口未予支付。次年 1 月,美国 D 公司电告中国 A 公司,出口产品有部分不合格,美国 D 公司宣布全面停止支付货款。此时

A 公司已有数百万美元的货款无法回收。

于是,A 公司又与 R 公司签订了一个协议,内容是:有关美国 D 公司货款拒付一事,已委托美国律师提起诉讼,双方要保持一致行动,任何一方不得单独行动与 D 公司私下和解。甲方(即 A 公司)开出信用证,如有必要时,乙方(即 R 公司)得协助台湾相关银行同意付款日期展延。双方各持一份留存。这时,国内 A 公司以为,一个联手共同讨伐美国 D 公司的"神圣同盟"已经形成。只等到美国的官司胜诉后,再对台湾 R 公司付款,了结此事。然而,事与愿违,两方面的事情发展都出乎 A 公司的意料之外。在对 R 公司信用证付款方面,R 公司并没有遵守其延期收款的承诺,而是想在远期信用证到期之前,就将信用证进行承兑,将款提走。A 公司知道后想在付款期在香港法院申请禁止付款令,但被告知其成功希望几近为零,因为信用证一般情况下是不能止付的。A 公司又想到台湾对 R 公司起诉,要求履行不兑付信用证的承诺。但又了解到国内公司到台湾法院起诉台湾企业,难度很大,因为在台湾和祖国大陆无任何来往期间,台湾法庭不承认 A 公司和法人地位,特别是国有企业。另外一个途径是,A 公司将债权转让给在香港注册的关联公司或台湾代理人,如律师,由债权受让人通过台湾法院起诉,追讨欠款。上述方式都需和台湾当地律师商讨后方能确定。除了此项费用,官司打到最后,能拿回来多少钱也是个未知数。而且据了解,该担保合同的效力本身也是值得怀疑的。所以 A 公司最后也就放弃了到台湾诉讼追款的可能性。

A 公司在美国的诉讼情况也不顺利。在马里兰地区法院 A 公司以妨碍交易、商业欺诈等为由,要求美国 D 公司赔偿 720 万美元。D 公司不甘示弱,以迟延交货,货物品质缺陷,以及由此给 D 公司造成商誉损失等为由,对 A 公司提出 1100 万美元的反诉。根据美国的民事诉讼规则,法庭开庭前,双方律师可以对事实和法律问题进行充分的调查取证。为此,双方律师进行了半年多的准备工作,A 公司律师费颇多。在法院准备开庭审理之前,事情又发生了戏剧性的变化。美国 D 公司在其公司注册地纽约的破产法院,依据美国破产法第 11 章提出公司债务重组的申请。美国的破产法规定两种情况:第 7 章规定的是,对债务人财产进行清算以抵偿债权人的债务。而第 11 章则规定,在一定的条件下,可以暂时冻结债权,由债务人提出新的经营计划,让债务人可以通过新的经营活动,逐步还清债务。本案中 D 公司之所以提出第 11 章债务重组的请求,是有其深远考虑的。

从 D 公司当时债务结构来看,可分为三类。

(1)有担保的债权。该债权主要属于美国的一家投资公司,约占 D 公司全部债权的 40%,但占全部可偿债资产 90% 以上,也就是说,如果 D 公司清盘,其资产主要应由担保的债权人银行接收,而银行经过审查后认为,如采取清算的方式,D 公司的资产根本不足以抵偿其债,而如采用债务重组的方式,投资 D 公司可获得 D 公司 94% 以上的股份从而控制该公司,并由此达到逐步收回其债权的目的。此外,债务重组至少使银行账面上的不良资产率得以降低。所以,银行作为 D 公司的第一位债权人,不希望 D 公司清算。如 D 公司进行债务重组,银行还可以提供新的贷款,这是 D 公司求之不得的。

(2)无担保的债权人。这类债权人排在有担保的债权人之后。这类债权人与有担保的债权人的利益有矛盾,同时也不希望排列在其后的债权人能够升格到同等地位与其分享破产财产。

(3)无担保而且有争议的债权。这类债权最后能否成立,往往需要由法院经审理后作出判定。A 公司的债即属于这一类。

由此可见,A 公司在与 D 公司的诉讼中处于十分不利的地位。

在马里兰州地方法院的诉讼,A 公司起诉 D 公司的金额为 720 万美元,而 D 公司的反诉金额为 1100 万,如果 A 公司不将官司继续进行下去,D 公司的反诉可能反而成立,A 公司讨债不成,反而成了欠债人。如果 A 公司将官司继续打下去,据估计,A 公司有可能打赢这场官司,但由于 D 公司已在纽约提出破产债务重整,根据其提出的债务重整计划,A 公司最多只能拿到重组后的 D 公司 1% 左右的股份,既不能参与公司的经营管理,又无红利可分。

该股份的账面价值不过 10 万美元。而市值比这个数字还要低。即使将股票出售,根据行情,也只能收回 2 ~ 3 万美元,还不足以支付律师费。A 公司此时处于进退两难的境地。

最后,经过反复的考虑和论证,并和美国律师进行了充分的讨论,权衡利弊后,在美国法院的推动下,A 公司和 D 公司达成和解协议,双方各自撤回其在美国马里兰州地方法院的货物买卖合同的起诉与反诉,D 公司对 A 公司提供少量金额的赔偿。A 公司撤回其在纽约破产法院的债权申请。

案例分析二 香港人周某与某地某电器厂合资创办企业,周某以合资企业所需部分设备作为资产进行投资。在合资企业建立过程中,周某以购买设备款项不足为由,要求该电器厂以自己的名义,并由他作为代理人到国外购买合资企业所需设备。由于该电器厂急需从国外进口电器机械设备,且对国外市场不了解,便同意了周某的意见。但该厂将货款(实为银行贷款)汇出境外时,周某神秘失踪,贷款也随之石沉大海。

[**思考与分析**] 这是一宗代理进口设备诈骗案,周某在此案中先以小额资金购买设备作为股本与大陆厂家建立合资企业,从而取得该企业的信任,然后提出以自己作为代理人去购买进口设备,最后携货款潜逃。之所以会出现此种诈骗案件,主要原因在于我方企业缺乏对周某的资信调查,也缺乏对国际市场的了解,在周某提出作为代理人到国外购买设备时,对其缺乏防范措施。

[案例 21] 《购销合同》实为外贸代理合同

1998 年 5 月 13 日,山西甲外贸公司就乙公司向甲公司购进菲律宾铬矿石签订了合同。双方约定了商品的规格、数量和价格。运输方式采用铁路运输,由甲公司代理乙公司委托天津新港的货运公司发运。于 1998 年 6 月 30 日前在天津新港铁路车板交货。货物运输保险费、银行开证费、承兑汇票贴息费、商检费、海关手续费、港务港杂费等由乙公司自行承担。合同履行后,乙公司付给甲公司劳务费按照货物进口的到岸价值的 1% 计算。双方还约定,合同签订后 10 日内乙公司向甲公司开出 200 万元银行承兑汇票,作为甲公司对外开证的费用,剩余部分由甲公司向银行贷款,乙公司作担保。货物到港后,乙公司一次性即期汇票付清全部货款及货物的港杂港务费、铁路运费和劳务费。甲公司则应向乙公司提供包括代理费收据在内的各项单据。关于货物质量检验,以 CCIB 在天津港的检验为准,如检验不合格而甲公司对外付款,乙公司可以拒绝付款,甲公司应承担责任并支付 10% 的违约金。最后,双方以《购销合同》的名义签署了上述合同。

合同签订后,甲公司在接到乙公司的 200 万元汇票后依约向银行申请剩余贷款 250 万元的贷款,用于开立信用证,以购买铬矿石。与此同时,乙公司以公司厂房作为抵押为甲公司的 250 万元贷款提供担保。由于甲公司的申请开证行认为甲公司和乙公司处于异地,乙公司不能为甲公司的贷款提供担保,致使信用证未能按照甲公司与菲客商签订买卖合同的约定开出信用证,致使货物不能按期发货。

由于无法按期开出信用证,甲公司不能按期履行与国外客商签订的合同,导致在《购销合同》规定的交货时间到来时,双方产生纠纷,乙公司要求甲公司赔偿由于其违约引起的全部损失和各项费用。甲公司辩称,甲公司违约的根本原因在于乙公司未能依约履行其提供货款以开立信用证的义务,导致货物买卖合同无法履行,而《购销合同》实质上是《外贸代理协议》,乙公司应当按照《关于对外贸易代理制的暂行规定》第 10 条和第 11 条的规定,承担全部责任。

人民法院在审理中认定,尽管《购销合同》中存在有关代理的条款,但根据合同的大多数条款规定,特别是乙公司先行支付 200 万元款项的行为,表明乙公司为履行合同已经支付了预付款,因此该合同属于《购销合同》,故甲公司应当承担由于其不能按期供货而导致乙公司产生的全部损失。

[案例 22]　合同双方混合过错发生后的责任承担

中国甲公司(买方)通过中国乙公司得知美国丙公司(卖方)可供豆油后,于 1996 年 10 月 29 日将签过字的 647 号合同寄给丙公司。合同规定:卖方售给买方初榨豆油和精炼豆油 500 吨,单价 350 美元,产地为泰国,CFR 中国海口交货;买方在 1996 年 11 月 8 日委托中国银行开出以卖方为受益人的合同全额不可撤销信用证,货物装船期为卖方收到信用证后 50 天之内;全部货物为中性包装,单据(包括发票)以一套空邮、两套随船寄交买方。11 月 3 日丙公司在接到合同文本后,加注了"可以接受的信用证",签字寄回甲公司。

11 月 6 日,甲公司按合同条款的规定开出信用证。丙公司于 11 月 10 日发电报,要求甲公司对信用证作如下修改:增加"接受第三方单证";删除"中性包装";删除"发票随船寄交买方"条款,但未说明理由。次日,甲公司发出电报,要求丙公司解释"接受第三者单证"的含义。丙公司回电称,货从泰国发出,除发票和汇票外,均为第三者单证,同时声称,由于不合适信用证而致发货迟延或价格上升,由甲公司承担责任。11 月 12 日,丙公司又电催修正事宜,甲公司未答复,却于 11 月 18 日同中国乙公司签订关于修改信用证的补充协议,作为 467 号合同的附件。11 月 20 日,甲公司发出修改信用证函,只同意加入"除发票和汇票外,可接受第三者单证”的条款。

1997 年 1 月 3 日,丙公司致函甲公司,称因甲公司未及时开具可以接受的信用证,使丙公司不能在泰国供货商规定的最后期限以前开出信用证,供货商已无法供货,且价格上涨,故建议撤销合同,重新订立合同。甲公司坚持认为丙公司有交货义务,双方协商未果。甲公司于是提起仲裁,要求丙公司赔偿包括银行利息、管理费用、转售损失及利润损失等经济损失,又主张丙公司应赔偿全部合同货物交货日期国际市场价格与合同价格之间的差价。

丙公司辩称,甲公司未对该公司回寄的合同文本再次确认,合同条款存在矛盾,因此合同根本没有成立。乙公司不是丙公司的代理人,其与甲公司的协议行为对丙公司不具有约束力;合同确立的信用证为可以接受的信用证,甲公司未依照规定修改信用证,导致合同不能履行等。

[案例 23]　因一方根本违约导致合同解除

1994 年 12 月,深圳甲公司与英国乙公司签订 451 号合同,甲公司向乙公司购买法国产青霉素针剂 15 万瓶,总价款 8 万美元。

1995 年 3 月 20 日,乙公司向中国卫生部申请并取得了 333 号进口药品许可证。许可证规定,青霉素针剂的生产厂为:Teajon Co. 原产地为法国。甲公司在得到乙公司已获取许可证的通知后于 1995 年 4 月 10 日开出信用证。信用证规定了唛头标志、药品产地、单价、总价款和价格术语。

1995 年 5 月 30 日,货到目的港。经目的港海关查验,发现该批药品的标签、批号、合同号、唛头标志与 333 号许可证允许进口的药品完全不符。1995 年 8 月 28 日,目的港所在地的药品检验机关出具药品检验证书,确认“本品由于生产厂牌与提供的进口药品许可证的生产药厂名称不符,不准进口。”

甲公司在得知上述书面文件后立即通知乙公司。乙公司致函甲公司表示,将重新申请临时进口许可证。双方为此进行了多次协商,但时至 1995 年 11 月 13 日仍未有结果。于是甲公司不得不将货物退至法国马赛港,乙公司拒绝收回该批货物,货物又被退至中国大连港。

由于双方的争议得不到解决,甲公司于 1996 年 3 月 4 日提起仲裁。甲公司称,乙公司的行为已经构成根本违约,要求解除 451 号合同,请求乙公司返还货款及利息、总货款价值 10% 的预期利润,承担退货运费及利息和货在马赛港因乙公司无理拒收而发生的仓储保管费用以及中国海关关税等。

乙公司辩称,已经正确履行 451 号合同,所交货物完全符合合同规定。由于甲公司迟开信用证,导致生产厂商无法及时通知甲公司,但商品的实际品质与乙公司向中国卫生部申报的样品品质完全一致。在货物未能通关的情况下,甲公司不积极向中国医药部门申请一次性进口许可证,导致货物最终未能入关。乙公司要求甲公司承担自交货时至目前的利息和全部损失,要求甲公司接受货物,不同意承担甲公司提出的任何损失。

[案例24] 合同条款解释的基本原则

案例分析一 1992年5月20日，中国甲公司和香港乙公司签订《补偿贸易合同书》。双方约定，在为期6年的时间内，乙公司提供美国最新制造的大理石开采生产线和技术及相关设备；甲公司使用上述设备和技术，生产符合质量要求的大理石板材，并全部返销给乙公司。合同第二条第2款规定，乙公司在合同生效起3个月内将所有设备和配件运至中国大连港。第四条规定，必须由甲公司申请××信托投资公司担保。

6月15日，该合同经甲公司所在地主管机关批准后，正式生效。合同生效后，甲公司遂向××信托投资公司提出申请。××信托投资公司于7月1日开出了以乙公司为受益人的担保书。乙公司在收到担保书后，通知甲公司，因其银行不能接受该担保书，要求甲公司对担保书进行修改。8月1日××信托投资公司对担保书作出修改。之后，乙公司再次通知甲公司不能接受其担保书，要求甲公司按照乙公司在香港找到的贷款机构——××租赁国际公司的格式担保书中的条件提供担保。8月25日，乙公司以传真形式将××租赁国际公司的格式担保书通知给甲公司。根据该格式担保书的规定，××租赁国际公司将成为《补偿贸易合同书》中约定的设备出租人，甲公司成为设备的承租人，而乙公司成为设备的供货人。在接到上述文件后，甲公司立即向乙公司表示，把补偿贸易改为设备租赁违背了补偿贸易合同的本意，不能接受，但同意开立可转让的以××租赁国际公司为受益人的担保书。对此，乙公司和××租赁国际公司表示不能接受。此后，甲公司与乙公司就如何开立担保书的问题多次协商。11月26日，乙公司致电甲公司，甲公司所提供的担保书必须为××租赁国际公司或任何其他的金融机构能接受，否则合同将无法继续履行。但此后双方仍未能就如何出具担保书问题达成一致，于是乙公司未能提供开采大理石的生产设备和技术。

1993年1月18日，甲公司提起仲裁，认为作为补偿贸易的合作形式，买方开具担保书，只能担保其对卖方的履约义务，此担保不是融资担保，担保书的受益人应是乙公司，而不是乙公司的银行。甲公司多次修改担保书的目的在于想使合同尽快履行，但乙公司却多次以担保书未办妥为由，不履行合同规定的供货义务，给甲公司造成经济上的损失。故要求乙公司赔偿因为履行该合同而支付的各项费用，包括为项目的可行性研究支出的费用及预期利润。

乙公司辩称，乙公司只有在甲公司开具的担保书能为银行接受的情况下，才能得到贷款以购买设备。甲公司的担保书不能为乙公司的金融机构接受，而甲公司不按照金融机构的要求开具担保书，致使乙公司无法得到贷款，也不能按照合同的规定交付设备，因而要求甲公司赔偿由此导致的经济损失。

案例分析二 2002年5月初，我国某进出口公司（简称A公司）就某种有色矿产品出口一事向国外一家公司（简称B公司）发盘：可供氧化锑500吨，USD 2,850/MTCIF价，即期装运。B公司接到A公司的发盘后，没有明示接受，只来电要求A公司货物数量增加到600吨，并适当降低货物价格，并要求A公司延长发盘的有效期。A公司5月15日将货物增加至600吨,价格为USD 2,800/MTCIF价,有效期为5月25日。B公司5月23日来电接受该发盘,但附加条件"需提供适合海洋运输的良好包装"。A公司接到B公司的接受时,发现国际市场上氧化锑的价格猛涨,所以,A公司拒绝B公司的接受,并复电:"由于国际市场氧化锑产品行情变化,在接到接受之前货物已出售。"B公司坚持合同已经成立,要求A公司履行合同,或者赔偿损失15万美元。

本案结果是:双方经过多次争议和磋商,A公司承认合同成立,赔偿B公司12万美元。

[思考与分析] 本案A公司承认理亏,合同成立,并赔偿B公司的损失是合理的,有几点值得注意。

(1)A公司的业务人员知识和经验都不足,对国际市场行情没有认真分析和对B公司的工作意图不了解。首先,该产品在那段时间价格肯定有向上趋势,但不明显。其次,B公司要求延长有效期是为了进一步观测市场的变化情况,所以不表示是否接受。

(2)A公司的业务人员对发虚盘和发实盘还不完全了解。B公司接受的附加条件实际是对原发盘要件(包装条件)的修改,已经不是接受,而是还盘,A公司可以不接受。

(3)A公司的复电也不对。没有针对B公司改变原发盘的要件,而是说货物已出售,实际上默认合同已成立,那么赔偿当然就合理了。

[案例25] 跟单信用证中的"about"

在进出口业务中,国外银行开来的跟单信用证中,常有使用"约"(about)字,例如,在金融前面加上about(about USD. XXXX)或在货物的数量前面加上"about"(about 2,120 dozen of men slipper…)或在"装运"后面加上"on or about "(shipment on or about)等等,由于它的修饰位置不同,就有不同的意义。如用在装运条款中,则解释为以所提及的日期为依据,自该日期前五天起至该日期后五天止,起讫日期包括在内,前后共11天。如果用在其他方面,则应解释为允许对有关金额、数量或单价有不超过10%的增减幅度。按照国际商会跟单信用证所列的数量或单价时,应解释为允许对有关金额、数量或单价有不超过10%的增减幅度。这里要注意的是:"例如,信用证中货物的单价与数量条款中有"约"词语,但金额中没有此类词语,金额就不允许有上述幅度的增减。另外,在UCP 500第46条C款规定,如果信用证用"于或约于(on or about)"一词来规定装运日期,则解释为所提及的日期为依据,自该日期前五天起至该日期后五天止,起讫日期包括在内,前后共11天。例如,信用证规定"约于1月10日装运(shipment on or about January 10)则从1月5日起至1月15日止,在这11天内装运货物,即为符合信用证要求。

然而,在实际工作中,各人对于增减幅度的看法,也有不同的理解。例如,在货物的数量中,如果有许多品种,是指货物的总数量还是指每一品种的数量呢?香港汇丰银行有的审单员认为,是指每一项品种的数量,而不是指货物的总数量,但有的银行审单员则与此相反,即按货的总数量来掌握,而不是以每一项品种的数量来掌握。对此,有的出口企业提出问题,假如信用证规定是货物的数量有"about",即不超过10%的增减幅度,但未规定每一品种的货物数量有10%的增减幅度,受益人提交的发票中有的品种数量超过10%,有的品种开证行拒付,拒付是否合理。国际商会认为,货物数量有10%幅度,可以是指总货量数,也可指每一品种的货物数量,因此,开证行可以拒付。知道UCP500是处理信用证业务的"圣经",为了执行UCP500惯例,也就是为了避免开证行以此为由拒付,在出口审单时应同时掌握每一品种的数量和总货量数,ICC 565号出版物R238已明确单项超过或少于10%的拒付是有理的。在进口开证时,为了明确起见,最好在信用证条款中规定每一品种货物的数量可以有10%的浮动。

[案例26]　L/C陷阱条款坑人怎么办?

案例分析一　"内地的H公司同一个港商订了一份合同,港商通过银行开出总金额100万美元的L/C,受益人是H公司。L/C规定装船前由买方检验货物并签发检验证明书,证明书上的签字,必须由开证行证实。又规定装船后,H公司要将1/3正本提单交给买方代表。等到货物快要出厂时,港商果然派了代表来验货,当场确认货的品质没有问题,并签发了证明书。后来,货物装船,H公司拿到提单后,按照L/C规定,又把1/3正本提单给了港商代表。当H公司把单据送中行,中行向开证行寄单,开证行收到单据后,认为检验证明书上的签字,同开证行存档的签字不符,说这个签字是假的,不能接单付款。

案例分析二　有一进出口公司出口一批货物,合同规定6月份装船,5月中旬接到对方的L/C,规定:"Shipmentaher June 20th till 30th"该公司6月20日装船并取得B/L,但到银行议付时被拒绝。

[思考与分析]　UCP500中对"aher"的解释为:不包括所提及的日期。因此,6月20日的B/L,就与L/C的规定不符,所以遭拒绝议付。如果是6月21日的B/L就可以。

[案例27]　信用证法律关系中保兑行的法律责任

1991年4月,中国甲公司与美国乙公司签订钢材销售合同。根据合同的规定,乙公司在美国的丙银行申请开出了不可撤销即期信用证一份,通知行为美国丁银行在华的分行。

8月25日,甲公司将货物以多式联运方式,从内地装运火车到香港转海船运往旧金山港,并由当地外运公司签发了陆海联运提单。8月27日,甲公司将全套单据寄交丁银行在华分行议付,9月1日,丁银行在华分行向甲公司发出了"银行付款通知单"。

9月12日,全套单据遭丙银行拒付,理由是有2个不符点:第一,提单未显示"已装船"字样;第二,装运标志上表示的是整批货物的总数量而不是每一纸箱中的数量。鉴于上述原因,丙银行要求丁银行退回货款。9月26日,丁银行将丙银行的第二份通知传真给甲公司,通知中称,如果甲公司降价25%,开证申请人可接受所提示的有不符点的单据。甲公司传真答复:本公司提供的单证并无任何不符点,不同意退单;信用证是独立于合同之外的法律文件,丙银行的降价要求不应在信用证项下予以解决;丁银行在华分行作为保兑行应按照国际惯例履行付款责任。

12月1日,丁银行在华分行致函甲公司,"请示是否同意退单?"12月5日,甲公司回函丁银行表示,“我公司不同意降价,也不同意退单。作为保兑和议付行,你行负有及时付款的责任。”1992年1月丁银行将全套单据退回给甲公司,甲公司则向丙银行投诉,要求保兑行履行支付货款的责任。同年底,丁银行在华分行将全部货款连同理赔支付给甲公司。

[案例28] 单证不符不能成为拒收货物和拒付货款的理由

1995年6月,甲外贸公司与乙公司签订代理进口协议,约定由甲公司代理进口1000吨苯乙烯,目的港张家港,CFR价为每吨1200美元,交货时间为7月30日。货物到港后由甲公司通知乙公司,乙公司凭甲公司办理的海关放行手续自行负责到港区提货,甲公司收取进口货物总价款的1%为代理费。

之后,甲公司与美国的丙公司签订货物进口合同,约定购买丙公司1000吨苯乙烯,采用的价格术语为CFR每吨1200美元,目的港为张家港;约定采用信用证方式付款,在货物装运前30天通过中国银行开立以美国丙公司为受益人的不可撤销信用证,货物装运后,美国丙公司应立即将合同号、商品名称、数量、毛重、船名和开船日期电告甲公司。甲公司于7月6日开出总金额为120万美元的信用证。7月11日,丙公司将船情资料等电传给甲公司。收到电传后的同日,甲公司电复称,鉴于苯乙烯市场行情低迷,甲公司无法继续经营,恳请暂缓装运,装运日期另定;考虑到长期合作关系,希望降低货物价格并修改信用证条款。丙公司在收到后仍按照合同约定装船发运。7月25日,船抵张家港,并于当日开始卸货。甲公司和乙公司代表均在现场。7月28日,乙公司持甲公司交付的提单副本、发票、合同及加工手册等资料委托一公司向海关报关。海关认为涉嫌走私将全部货物扣押。

8月5日,信用证开证行中国银行收到美国银行的单据,经审核后认为单证存在不符点而拒付。美国银行予以反驳。8月10日,甲公司致电丙公司称,由于信用证项下单证有不符点,我公司无法赎单,我公司在没有赎单的情况下不会对货物采取任何行动,报送与我公司无关。中国海关后致函甲公司,表明所扣押的货物涉嫌走私,故予以查封。鉴于苯乙烯保质期较短,为避免损失,海关同意甲公司将货物在海关核定后变卖处理,否则由甲公司承担全部损失。甲公司在收到该函后未按照海关要求处理货物,并于8月29日要求中国银行拒付信用证项下的所有货款。次日,中国银行通知美国银行并退回全套单据。同年10月15日,美国丙公司以甲公司拒不履行应尽的付款义务为由向中国法院提起诉讼。甲公司辩称,甲公司以信用证不符为由的拒付行为符合法律规定,乙公司擅自提货和报送的行为属于违约违规的行为,与甲公司无关,甲公司并未实际接受货物,不应承担支付货款的义务。

[案例29] 用好信用证开拓中东贸易

中东地区是我国纺织品出口的主要市场之一,近年来随着中东局势的缓和,经济的迅速发展,石油收入稳定,与我国进出口贸易不断扩大,开来我国的信用证逐渐增加,为进一步促进我国企业与中东贸易的顺利开展,有必要探讨中东地区各国各银行信用证的情况,本书对该地区来证的一般特点以及缮制单据应注意的事项作简要介绍,供读者参考。

中东银行开证有如下特点:

(1)用证币别一般是美元。

(2)各银行开来的信用证,一般都是即期不可撤销信用证,不限制议付银行,而是可由任何银行议付的自由议付信用证。同时,开证行也不要求通知信用证的通知行对其信用证保兑。

(3)信用证价格条款一般是CFR(成本加运费)或FOB(离岸价),一般不使用CIF(到岸价或叫做成本加运费价)。同时,信用证规定,进口商在当地办理保险。

(4)信用证中一般都有收取单证不符费用的条款(当每次提单有不符单据时,开证行将从货款中扣除不符点费用),但各家银行的标准不一样。有的收取40美元,也有的收取100美元,例如Habib Band AG Dubai就收取100美元。

(5)信用证中一般都规定所有银行费用均由受益人负担。另外,也有的信用证规定快邮费用、偿付行的偿付费用,电报费或电传费用也由受益人负担,对于这些条款,如果受益人不接受,应及时联系买方洽谈,通过开证行来函或来电修改或取消,以便顺利出运货物和安全及时收汇。

(6)中东地区各银行信用证中除了有效日期外,一般还规定了交单日期,而且它必须在信用证的有效日期之内。但各家银行的信用证规定时间不一样,有的规定15天,也有的规定21天,对此应特别注意。假如信用证没有规定交单日期的期限,在这种情况下,就应该按照UCP500第43条A款来掌握,即除规定交单到期日以外,每一要求提交运输单据的信用证还应规定一个装运日期后必须按照信用证条款交单的特定期限,如未规定期限,银行将接受晚于装运日21天后提交的单据,但无论如何,单据不得晚于信用证到期日提交。

(7)信用证中一般都有明确的寄单索汇条款,而且有详细的寄单地址和索汇地址。

(8)信用证中除了具有一般的保证付款条款外,还具有明确而详细的偿付条款,但各家银行信用证的偿付条款不一样,一般有以下四种情况。

第一种是信用证中规定"单到付款"的条款,即议付银行议付单据以后,应把所有的单据用一次或二次航邮或快邮寄给开证行,当开证行收到单据相符的单据以后,再按照议付银行的交款指示,交给议付银行的账户行,然后收账。

第二种是向索的条款,即议付银行议付单据以后应把所有的单据分二次或一次用快邮寄给开证行,同时,向其指定的偿付银行索汇。

第三种情况是信用证中虽然规定有偿付名称,但是议付银行不能向其索偿的条款,需要开证行收取单据以后,再授权向索。

第四种情况是开证行收单以后,再通知偿付银行的名称,然后要求议付行向其偿付行索汇。

(9)信用证中规定由国外开证申请人办理投保,因此,受益人在货物装船以后应在信用证中规定的时间内,将所有的装运情况直接通知开证人指定的保险公司以及开证申请人。

(10)信用证中一般规定不允许分批装运,若允许转运,也有的信用证限制只能在香港转运。

(11)中东地区银行开来的信用证中一般都有附加条款或者特殊条款:如运输行出具的单据不接受;过期的单据和信用证日期以前出具的单据不接受;所有单据和信用证必须用英文制作;所有单证必须注明开证行名称、开证日期和信用证号码等等。

(12)信用证中一般都没有信用证金额、数量和单价增减幅度和条款。

[案例30] 信用证诈骗案例

1. 预借提单

案例分析一 某年某公司向科威特出口白瓜子10公吨,原定装"ELDINA"轮,由于信用证即将到期,该公司向外运公司预借提单,并向银行议付了货款。但事后"ELDINA"轮未按时到达装货港口,该货改装其他船名的轮船,造成十分被动的局面。最后只得由中国银行硬着头皮商请开证行用新的提单替换旧的提单,并由我方补偿开证行由此而产生的包括利息在内的费用。这个案子虽然得到解决,但对外已产生不良影响。

案例分析二 某年7月,我某公司向利比亚出口货物一批,货在仓库尚未装船,公司即向船方预借提单办理结汇,在外轮开航一周以后,公司才发现货物仍在仓库内。于是要求银行退回全套单据,但此时单据已经全部寄出,只得将货物交火车补运香港,再由华夏公司在港代办转船。

2. 倒签提单

案例分析一 某年11月,我国某进出口分公司先后与伦敦B公司和瑞士S公司签订两个出售农产品合同,共计3,500万吨,价值82,750英镑。装运日期为该年12月至次年1月,目的港均为鹿特丹,付款条件为保兑的不可撤销信用证。该货于次年2月11日装船完毕。当时外轮代理公司应我某公司的请求,按次年1月31日签发"已装船提单",并凭此向中国银行办理结汇待续,货物到鹿特丹,经买方聘请律师上船查阅航行日志,查实提单的签发日期是伪造的,立即凭律师拍摄的证据,向当地法院控告,并由法院发出通知扣留该船。经过4个月的协商,最后以我方某分公司同意赔款20,600英镑,买方才撤回上诉。

案例分析二 某商品是我国对某一地区的传统出口商品,我国某出口公司根据合同上规定的交货期并参照该地区客户来证情况(来证规定装船期为4月份)和货源情况,于3月底4月初先后托运该商品一批。由于数量较大,当时按4月份船期表计配载于4条船上,分别为溧阳号轮(4月15号船期)、凤鸣号轮(4月30日船期)、太行山号轮(4月15日船期)、龙山号轮(4月30日船期),但因4月份港口拥挤,进口货不能及时卸货,出口货的船舶泊位不足,以致海运出口跨月船达27艘之多。结果上述4船离港时间均大大推迟,溧阳号轮为5月21日,凤鸣号轮为5月13日,太行山号轮为5月5日,龙山号轮为5月19日。该公司为了能按来证规定的装运期顺利结汇,均倒签提单。国外客户鉴于货物迟到,加之适逢国外市况下疲,于是要求我方补偿损失。我方该商品对该地区业务一般均在每年两次交易会上订价,春交会上订价适用于从5月份起至秋交会,秋交会订价适用于10月至翌年4月。

该年春交会价较前一年秋交会价格低2%，客户提出上述四轮货应按调低后的价格结算，结果我方只好退汇42,800元，且在国外造成不良影响。

[案例31] 可转让与不可转让信用证

信用证分为可转让与不可转让两种。不可转让信用证的利益只能是受益人本人享用，如受益人不能执行信用证条件，信用证只能过期作废。凡未注明可转让字样的信用证都是不可转让信用证。

在可转让信用证下，开证行在开立信用证时，授权出口地银行在受益人提出转让申请后，可将信用证的部分或全部权利，转让给他人。此时原证的受益人为第一受益人，实际供货商为第二受益人。

1. 出现可转让信用证的技巧

在贸易实务中，常会出现货物的卖主(受益人)不是货物的制造商的情况，他要从制造商或供货人那里先买进货物，然后才能向买主交货。这个中间商买进货物需要一定的资金，但他手中并不始终掌握资金。如果实际供货人要求在交货时立即付款，而他无法通过信贷途径取得融资时，他的资金周转就会出现困难。另外，中间商想通过这笔交易谋取利润，又不愿让实际供货人与进口商拉近关系。为了这个目的，中间商要求进口商开立可转让信用证，从而使出口中间商能够把转售货物得来的货款中的大部分转让给实际供货人，货款的另一部分就是他的利润。而作为开证申请人的进口商之所以接受这种信用证，是因为他同意另一个供货人向他供货，因为他不认识这个供货人，需要依靠他原来的贸易伙伴作为供货渠道。

2. 可转让信用证的转让技巧

一般情况下，办理转让的银行即转让行都会打一份"新证"，以便将某些内容作适当的调整，新证的大部分内容与原证是相同的，尤其是两份信用证的最终付款银行都是原证的开证行。因此，两份信用证实际上可以看作是一证，但在以下几个方面可以有变化。

(1)第一受益人可以用自己的名字换下原证的申请人，即进口商。这样可以防止第二受益人与进口商拉近关系。

(2)货物单价和信用证金额可以被减小。这样，新证与原证的差额就是中间商的利润。

(3)新证的投保比例可以有所增加。由于信用证金额减少了，要达到原证的保险金额要求，就应提高新证的投保比例。

(4)货物的装运期与有效期可以提前，交单期可以缩短。这样做是为了保证在第二受益人交单以后，第一受益人有足够的时间替换发票和汇票。

[案例32] 限制议付信用证

限制议付信用证是议付信用证的一种，一般来说限制议付的银行是由开证行在异地，即出口商所在地的分行、代理业务银行、往来银行或通知行其中之一来承担议付，其优点是开证银行与限制议付银行往来可靠、手续简便以及受益人为其汇票寻求付款的贴现费用一般少于自由议付信用证项下所需费用的优越性。另外,限制议付信用证的有效日期及地点都在议付行所在地,信用证项下的汇票付款人可以是开证行或信用证规定的其他银行。

[案例33]　出口商应如何交单议付

开证行开出限制议付信用证的原因不外乎有下述三点:一是开证行有意识地要把该笔业务给他自己的联行或它指定的代理行来做,不准别家银行沾光,即所谓的"肥水不流外人田",如议付时收取费用等;二是由于信用证条款本身复杂或有些问题,需要特别注意审查,开证行希望由指定的银行或代理行独家代办,可以体会开证行的意图,从严掌握;三是由于开证行本身的资信问题或有些小银行害怕自己开出的信用证在有关地点不能被任何银行议付。

出口商对于限制议付信用证项下的单证必须严格审查、严格把关,做到严格相符、四个一致,即单证一致、单单一致、单货一致、单同一致。虽然信用证项下的单据银行只考虑单证一致和单单一致,但就出口商而言,单货一致、单同一致也同样重要,否则即使银行已付款,事后进口商仍可根据合同向出口商索赔。另外,必须按信用证的要求将单据交给其指定的银行议付,决不能交给其他任何银行议付,否则,开证行会提出不符点或者退回单据。

[案例34]　限制议付信用证中的限制条款

限制议付信用证的限制议付条款大致有如下几方面内容:

(1)信用证中的"标题"表示其功能。这是以信用证类别和信用证标题表示其限制的,如不可撤销、跟单、限制议付。

(2)信用证以"承诺"条款表示其功能。不同功能的信用证,开证银行会书写不同的内容"承诺"条款,以适应和表示其功能。限致议付信用证的"承诺"条款:WE HEREBY ENGAGE WTTH YOU THAT ALL DRAWN IN CONFORWITY WITH THE TERMS OF THIS RESTRICTED NEGOTLATION CREDIT WILL BE DULY HONOURED ON PRESEITATION.(开证行对受益人的承诺并说明付款银行只能向签发汇票的出票人付款)

自由议付信用证的"承诺"条款:WE HEREBY ENGAGE WITH DRAWERS,ENDORSERS AND BONA FNDE HOLDERS THAT DRAFTS DRAWN AND NEGOTLATED IN COMPLIANCE WITH THE TERMS AND CONDITIONS OF THIS CREDIT WIILBE DULY HONOURED ON PRESENTATION.(凡根据本证开具与本证条款相等的汇票,并能按时提示和交出本证规定的单据,我行保证对出票人、背书人和正当持有人承担付款责任(必须在本证有效期内开具汇票并议付))

不得议付信用证的"承诺"条款:WE HEREBY ENGAGE WITH YOU(BENEFICIARY) THAT ALL DRAFTS DRAWN UNDER AND IN COMFLIANCE WITH THE TERMS OF THIS CREDIT WILL DULY HONOURED ON PRESENTATION AND ON DELIVERY OF DOCUMENTS AS SPECIFIED TO THE DRAWEE BANK.(凡根据本证开具与本证条款相符的汇票,并能按照提示和按规定交出单据给付款行时,开证行要保证依时付款)

(3)信用证的"汇票"条款表示其限制的:具有不同类型的信用证,且要求在汇票下面和汇票背面列有不同的条款。如:DRART(S) DRAWN UNDER IRREVOCABLE DOCUMENTARY RESTRICTED NEGOTLATION CREDIT NO …OF ISSUING BANK.(依不可撤销跟单限制议付信用证所签发的汇票必须注明开证银行名称和信用证号码)

DRARIS SO DRAWN MUST BE INSCRIBED WTTH THE NUMBER AND DATE OF THIS RESTRICTED NEGOTIATION CREDTT.(开具汇票必须注明本限制议付信用证的号码和日期)

(4)信用证的"正文条款"表示其限制。如:WE(THE ISSUING BANK)HEREBY ISSUE IN YOUR FAVOUR THIS IRREVOCABLE DOCUMENTARY BESTRICTED NEGOTIATION CREDIT WHICH IS AVAILABLE BY NEGOTLATION OF YOUR DRAFT(S).(开证银行开立贵公司为受益人的不可撤销跟单限制议付信用证,并授权贵公司签发汇票,以供议付)

(5)信用证中以"限制议付"条款表示其限制。限制议付的条款种类繁多,表达方式不一。有的信用证是用一种具体的限制议付条款来限制议付的,例如"本信用证限制由某某银行议付",也有的信用证是使用更加间接的方式,例如"偿付时,请借记我行开在你行的账户"。显然,这条指示是针对通知行说明的,这就构成了限制文句,由于种类很多,现将条款一一介绍。

①NEGOTIATION OF THIS CREDIT RESTRICTED TO THE XXX BANK WHOHAS SPECLAL REIMBURSEMENT ARRANGEMENT WITH CREDIT ISSUING BANK.(本信用证限制某银行议付,某银行与信用证开证行已有特殊偿付协议)

②THE NEGOTIATION OF THIS CREDIT MUST THROUGH XXXX BANK.(本信用证议付必须通过某某银行)

③NEGOTIATIONS UNDER THIS CREDIT ARE RESTRICTED TO XXX BANK.(本信用证限制某某银行议讨)

④NEGOTIATION UNDER THIS CREDIT IS RESIRICTED TO ADVISING BANK.(本信用证限制通知行议付)

⑤DRAFIS DRAWN UNDER THIS CRDEIT ARE NEGOTIABLE…BANK…PLACE(依本信用证签发的汇票限某地某银行议付)

⑥PLEASE CLAIMS REIMBURSEMENT BY DRAWING ON OUR A/C WITH YOUR NEW YORK.(请贵行向你的纽约行索债,并在我的账户支取)

⑦TRANSMITTED THROUGH XXX BANK WHO ARE AUTHORISED NEGOTIATION YOUR DRAFTS.(本证由某银行转递,该某银行被授权议付你的汇票)

⑧XXX FROM THE BANK THROUTH WHICH THIS CREDIT HAS BEEN ADVISED WHO SHOULD REIMBURSE THEMSELVES ON ACCORDANCE WITH STANDING ARRANGEMENT.(本证由通知行通知,该行可按照标准协议索偿)

⑨RAFT DRAWN ON ADVISING BANK.（本信用证项下的汇票做成以通知行为付款人）

⑩ NEGOTLATNON UNDER THIS GREDIT ARE RESTRICTED TO XXX BANK ONLY.（本信用证仅限于某某银行议付）

⑪ LETTER OF CREDIT IS NEGOTIATED THROUGH GROUP OFFISES ONLY.（本信用证仅限于集团内银行议付）

⑫ NEGOTLABLE THROUGH YOU ONLY.（本信用证仅由你行议付）

⑬ NEGOTLATIONS ARE RESTRNCTED ON XXX BANK ONLY, DOCUMENTS NEGOTLATED BY OTHERS BANKS MAY BE RETURNED BY US AT THEIR RISKS.（本信用证仅由某银行议付，如其他银行议付，开证行将要退单，风险由他行承担）

⑭ DATE AND PLACE OF EXPIRY; XXX WITH YOURGOODSELVES FOR PRESENTATION OF DOCUMENTS.（本信用证在有效期内在贵行交单）

⑮AFTER NEGOTIATION, PLEASE PRESENT DRAFTS AND DOCUMENTS TO XXX BANK WHO HOLDS SPECIAL INSTRUCTIONS REGARDING DOCUMENTS XXX DISPOSAL AND REIMBURSEMENT OF THE LETTER OF CREDIT.（议付以后，交单据和汇票给某银行，该行有处理本信用证项下的单证和偿付的指示）

[案例 35]　如何审核信用证

审证是一项原则性和技术性都很强的工作，直接关系到执行政策和受汇的安全，因此，一定要认真地进行，应以国家当前的方针政策为依据（外贸服从外交），以合同为基础，参照国际商会跟单信用证统一惯例第 500 号出版物（以下简称 UCP500）来进行，必须对信用证的全文和附件（如果有）以及证实书等，从头到尾、从左到右、从上到下，前前后后，逐条、逐句、逐字地仔细审核，如果有信用证修改，也要依次与原证对照分析是否为对原证的修改、补充或删除，求得应按其执行后的条款。

1. 有关当事人对信用证的审核

开证行依照开证申请人的指示开出信用证，委托另一家银行（通知行）将信用证通知受益人，以便受益人能够利用信用证做证下业务。信用证开出以后，开证申请人、通知行和受益人都要对开证行开出的信用证进行仔细地审核。银行与出口商双方应分工合作，既要共同认真审核信用证的总内容，又要对审核重点各有所侧重，银行应侧重于议付、受汇方面，如对开证行、偿付行或保兑行的资信、态度和经营作风以及对付款办法、使用货币、汇率、利率等条款的审核；出口商（受益人）侧重于交货履约方面，如对货运单据、价格条件、运输方式、装运等条款进行审核，并特别要与有关合约、函电进行核对，以确保货物如期出运与安全收汇，现分述如下。

2. 开证申请人对信用证的审核

开证申请人的审核主要是检查开证行是否严格遵守他的指示，并进一步确定信用证与基础合同是否相符，如果经审核信用证发现问题，可以及时要求开证行对信用证进行修改，以确保信用证符合买卖双方签订的基础合约。

3. 受益人对信用证的审核

受益人审查信用证的一般内容，并应注意以下问题。

(1) 审查开证期和开证地点。如果开证行漏填开日期和开证地点，或开证日期和开证地点不正确，应当及时要求开证行证实。

(2) 严格审核信用证受益人的名称地址。如果有错应立即电汇开证行予以证实，并及时修改更正，避免制单议付时影响收汇。

(3) 审查议付行地点和到期地点，开来信用证的议付地和到期地点一般应在我国境内。如果在国外，应提醒受益人注意，再由受益人斟酌是否要求开证行修改。

(4) 审查信用证所列货币和金额。开来信用证的货币必须是自由兑换的货币，来证金额的大小写应该一致。

(5) 信用证保兑的审查。如开证行来证要求通知行加具保兑，通知行应根据总行代理行政策和开证行资信，可以接受来证者，如条款清楚，金额并不太大，原则上可以加具保兑。如经研究不能加保，应根据 UCP500 第 9 条 C 款的规定，即如果另一家银行经开证行授权或应其请求，对信用证加具保兑，当它不准备照办时必须不迟延地通知开证行。除非开证行在授权或请求保兑时另有规定，否则通知行可不加保兑地将信用证通知受益人。

(6) 生效条款的审核。有的国外银行开来的信用证上加注："This credit will become operative only on receipt of the mail confirmation."等等字样或在修改上注明"Important note : This amendment will not become operative until conformity and payment of our charges ."等等字样，这些都是生效条款，对于有条件生效的信用证或有条件生效的修改，应提醒公司注意，待生效条件实现后，才能办理发货或交单议付。

(7) 审查开证行的责任条款。国外开证行一般遵守跟单信用证统一惯例，并愿意依照"惯例"解释信用证条款，在信用证上通常注明"本证受跟单信用证统一惯例的约束"，如果国外开证行没有保证付款的声明，或没有注明"本证受跟单信用证统一惯例的约束"或额外附加某种"保留"和"限制"条款，银行将不予接受，应要求开证行修改。因此，信用证的开证行必须有明确的保证付款责任的条款，如信用证由第三家银行保兑，保兑行承担的责任也必须明确，以利安全受汇。

(8) 审查开证行的偿付条款。信用证中除了有开证行的保证付款责任条款外，还应该有具体的偿付条款，而且偿付条款必须明确、合理，对于索汇路线迂回，环节过多以及其他影响及时收汇的条款，要及时联系开证行修改。

4. 对装运港和目的港的审核

(1) 装运港。也称起运港口，除来证指定的装船港口名称外，都必须与提单所列明者完全一致。例如来证规定装运口岸为新港，虽然天津与新港同属于天津市范围，但我们不能向银行提供以天津港作为装船口岸的提单，在这种情况下或将货物运往新港装船或与开证人商谈办理信用证的修改。另外，有些银行开来的一些信用证，往往在证上不列明具体的装船港口岸，而在信用证上的起运地点一栏中写上“从你地”字样。这里所指的“你地”应理解为该证的受益人所在地。如受益人地址写广州，则该证项下货物的起运口岸只能是广州，假如货物必须在汕头或其他口岸装运，则应该修改信用证装运口岸。

(2)目的港。目的港是指信用证规定的货物最终御货港口，在核对信用证与合同是否相符时，应注意以下几点。

①如原成交合约未列有具体港名称，仅笼统写成“某国家的主要港口”字样，诸如“英国主要港口”甚至“欧州主要港口”等等，但是在买方开来的信用证上都指定有具体的装货港口，在这种情况下，如卸货港为通常的知名大港则无问题，否则应弄清该指定的目的港是否确属主要港口或偏僻小港，以及船期如何，同时还要了解船公司在收取费用上是否比一般主要港口高。如果在经济上对我们不利，则需要视具体交易情况，向客户交涉办理修改或要买方增加运费。由于对主要港口的含义，有时买卖双方解释不一致，最好在争取成交时，能将目的港确定并在合同上注明。

②在发现买方开来的信用证上擅自变更原合约所规定的目的港时，除应考虑上述的经济后果外，还必须注意，改变后的目的港所在国家对所装运的货物有无规定有配额或进口许可证等限制的做法。并对此所造成的后果应特别留心，不能大意。

5. 对各种单据的审核

由于开证银行不同，信用证的要求各异，故要求受益人提供的单据也不一样，但信用证都有规定单据的要求，也有非规定单据的要求。对此要根据惯例行事。惯例规定或要求的单据是运输单据、保险单据和商业发票这三种单据，非规定单据是指惯例所规定的运输单据、保险单据和商业发票这三种单据以外的其他单据，这类单据种类繁多，各有不同的使用条件，因此，必须按信用证的要求以及商品性质来决定与审核，例如有的单证是否能够提供，单据的要求内容是能否办到等等。现进行如下阐述。

(1)提单：提单是证明有关货物已装船的正式文件，买主往往为了能及时取到货物，投放市场，便在信用证上加添一些限制性条款。主要有下列两种情况。

①不接受过期提单。所谓过期提单是指货物到达目的的港的时间早于买方从银行收到提单的时间，这样，商人就因未能及时提货而增加开支。特别是在所订货物价格呈下跌的趋势或具有较强季节性及花色流行性的商品，如不能马上提货销售，商人要遭受不少损失，因此，买方多不愿接受过期提单，造成过期提单的原因，一是由于受益人因各种原因未能早日将货物装船后向银行交单议付，因而延误了议付行向开证行寄单的时间；二是装货港与目的港距离很近，例如：广州至香港、天津至日本港口等，一般都能很快到达，况且出口商与议付银行之间还有一个合理的时间办理交单、审单及寄单事宜，在这种情况下，造成过期提单是不可避免的。因此，应该洽谈商议予以修改或删除。

②指定班轮或船公司来承运货物。这种情况多见于远洋地区如南、北欧等国家的来证，主要原因据说是这些被开证人指定装其货物的班轮或船公司属下的船有的是靠港比较准时，有利于商人在销售上的安排，也有的是进口商在这些船公司参与股份，或业务上来往的特殊关系。但是这种限制给出口商带来了不便，因此，对来证中指定的班轮或船公司必须事先进行了解，如是 CIF 或 C&F 的价格条款，则需了解其运输费用是否高于我们自行洽谈的船公司。另外，在其规定的装运期内能否逢有该指定班轮或船公司的航轮班，以及载位的可能性等，如果有对卖方不利之处，均应协商修改或不接受这种条款。

(2)保险单证(保险单或保险证明)

信用证中以 CIF 为价格条件的交易中，出口商(受益人)欲提交保险单证，保险的内容必须按照信用证要求缮制。但是，进口商怕货物在运输途中受损，往往在信用证的保险条款中增加一些合同规定投保险别以外的要求，企图把一些风险转嫁给保险公司，因此，我们必须对信用证的保险条款认真深入的审核，对那些含义不明的或陌生的条文应随时与保险公司联系，决定可否接受。就一般情况来说，开证人在来证中所列，在合同规定之外要求的保险责任范围，大概有以下几种。

①加大被保商品的投保金额。按照一般商品的国际惯例凡以 CIF 价格条件成交的合同，均由卖方按发票金额增加 10% 作为投保额，但是，有些商人认为，一旦所保货物在运输途中受到损失，而从保险公司所得到的 10% 的货物赔偿，在扣除一切应付费用后尚不足以弥补该项交易应获得的利润。因此，要求将保险金额增大，以求在万一情况下，能从保险公司取得较多的赔偿。按照我国保险公司目前的做法，对质量认可的增保金额最多不能超过发票金额的 130%，并需增收保险费用，对超过该限额者，否则被认为是不合理的要求，因此对保险金额是否可以接受，事先必须征得保险公司的同意。

②改变货物的最终目的地。由合约规定的目的港伸延至某一内陆城市。遇有这种情况，来证必须明确列明有关该内陆城市的名称及其所在国国名和运输方式，在无特殊情况下，保险公司可以接受承保，但买方必须支付伸延至内陆城市运段保险费用。

③要求承保由于货物内在质量问题所造成的损失。根据国际惯例和保险公司规定，保险公司对承保的货物，仅负责赔偿按约定的险别并限于因外来因素所造成货物的损失，至于货物内在质量方面的保险要求是不被保险公司接受的。

④成交合约的价格条件为 C&F 而来证为 CIF 条款，或合约为 CIF 而来证要求扣除保险费改为 C&F 条款。对于前者为信用证规定应付的保险费用可以在来证项下支付者，对我方可以增加外汇收入，并无不利，则可以接受代为投保。至于后者，因为国际贸易的保险费是国家无形贸易外汇收入的来源之一，最好说服买方仍按 CIF 条件履约，由我方代办保险。

⑤要求延长货物运抵目的港卸后到进入买方仓库这段保险期。按照一般惯例，在仓至仓条款下货物运抵保险单所列的目的港卸货后，如不能在 60 天期限内进入买方仓库，逾期保险公司则将终止其保险责任。但是，买方有时由于某些原因，在开证时将上述期限注明

为90天或更长一些，如有的在货物已出运后，再通知银行修改延长上述60天的期限，有时还要增保火险险别。在这种情况下，事先也必须征得保险公司同意和客户承担应负的加保费用后方可进行。

6. 信用证的修改及银行费用的审核

(1)信用证的修改

信用证的任何修改，都属于原来信用证的不可分割部分，有关条款将以修改后的内容为准。信用证有关条款的修改有的是应卖方要求来进行的，有的是买方主动作出的，因此，卖方在收到银行送来的信用证修改通知书后，必须毫不迟延地与原证进行核对，并要注意以下各点。

①与原信用证号码是否相符，修改次数的顺序号是否要连续，如发现错号、跳号应向银行进行重调以免遗漏。

②信用证修改书上所列各项修改后的条款都应该被视为一组不可分割的整体。这就是说不能对于一次所列修改内容，有的接受、有的拒绝，只能是全部接受或全部拒绝。对不能接受的信用证修改书，按照惯例卖方应在收到银行正式电报或函件修改书后三个工作日内，将该修改书退回银行，并说明不能接受，否则作为接受处理，卖方必须按照修改后条款，无条件地照办。

③有时，我们在日常出口业务中会遇到虽然买方已应要求正在办理信用证修改的答复为"修改中"或"展期中"，但在尚未收到银行正式通知书的情况下，船期在即，货物急待出运，为证实买方是否确实办理了修改或展期手续，以确保收汇的安全，我们可与银行洽商，在征得他们的协助和同意后，通过银行途径，如请银行主动致电开证行，说明应受益人的要求询问有关信用证的开证人是否已办理修改及内容如何等，并要求开证行用电报答复。一般来说，这种属于银行之间的查询往来，开证行是会给予答复的。如果电复是肯定的回答，并列明修改内容，则该项回电就可作为信用证的修改来使用。如果电复是否定的回答，则说明买方根本未办任何修改手续，上述的"修改中"或"展期中"的答复不过是蒙骗卖方而已。以上所述，尚属银行电询开证行的逆向做法，在急等托运的情况下是值得考虑采用的。

(2)关于银行费用的负担

国外开来的信用证上，不少加注有银行费用由受益人负担的条款。所谓银行费用，一是指开证行以外银行的有关服务费用，诸如议付费、信用证及其修改的通知费、邮寄费用等等。所有这些费用金额不大，但积累起来，还是一笔为数不少的国家外汇收入，一般来说，这些费用应由开证申请人负担。UCP500的新规定也明确了开证行利用其他银行的服务是为执行开证审请人的指示，并代开证申请人办理的。由此而产生的一切费用和风险应由开证申请人承担。但是，卖方也要从实际出发，根据不同情况分别对待，例如来证装期短促或所装货物有滞销或降价趋势。在此情况下，不能因小失大，可先办理出运，同时来证的装期较长，一时货又未备妥或来证尚有其他条款需要修改时，可一并提出。

7. 有关当事人应注意的问题

有关当事人在审核信用证时，除了审查有关项目外，还必须注意以下三点，即完整性、合规性、明确性。

(1)信用证的完整性

信用证的完整性包括两方面的内容，一是信用证本身的完整性，二是具体条款内容的完整性。按国际商会 UCP500 号的规定，信用证必须不延误地提供必要的内容，否则银行无法通知有关当事人保兑或修改信用证，有时甚至会危及申请人的利益。因此，信用证本身内容要完整，如信用证金额、到期日及地点、交单期限、单价及装运期限等必要的内容应完整列明。信用证的内容、修改与原证、修改书内容保持完整一致，延长装运期，并应相应延长信用证有效期，改变目的港应相应修改价格条款(如改目的港上海为广州，应同时改 CIF 上海为 CIF 广州)；另一方面是具体条款内容的完整性，例如提单条款就有很多内容，每一项内容都应该清楚指明。完整的条款内容不但使银行和当事人处理单据有充分的依据，而且还能保证当事人的利益。例如，如价格条件是 CIF，就要求受益人提交保单；又如，要求受益人装船后全套单据传真给申请人，那就应指明传真号码。信用证经常有以“buyer”买方或“payee”(付款人)作为提单或装运详情的“被通知人”，而未列明其联络地址、电传或传真号码，其实，若将“buyer”或“applicant”(申请人)，条款便完整了。这样既符合买方意图又方便受益人操作及银行审单，同时，各项要求应合逻辑(如信用证有效期应是装运期限加交车期限)，便于买卖双方业务的合理操作。

(2)信用证条款的合规性

信用证是一种自足的文件，它不受制于其他任何规定、规则及惯例，即使信用证注明“根据 UCP500 规则”开立，但如果信用证条款与 UCP500 规则相抵触，银行和受益人仍然以信用证的具体规定为准。国际贸易的有关规定、规则及惯例是长期实践中形成或确立的，一般都合法、合理，得到普遍接受，而且能保证当事人的利益，所以信用证条款要合规。例如，信用证规定“接受第三者单据”，那么应注明“汇票和发票除外”，这才符合 UCP500 的规则，又如，信用证应要求提单是“清洁”的，提单正本一式二份(或以上)，保单应全套提交，这样才符合有关操作惯例。

(3)信用证要求的明确性

受益人和银行是依照信用证的表面规定处理单据，而无需解释或推敲有关规定的深层意义，因此，信用证要求应具体、明确。例如，对单据的份数、出票人、禁止及批量装运等要求应加以明确，以便制作单据和安全及时收汇。

总之，审证是一项政策性、原则性和技术性都强的工作，直接关系到执行政策和安全收汇，一定要认真仔细地进行，同时应以国家的政策为依据，以合同为基础，参照 UCP500 条款来进行，并对信用证的全文和附件以及修改等，从头到尾、上下前后、逐条逐句地仔细审核，以便正确缮制单证，做到单证相符，顺利出运和安全收汇。

[案例36] 卖方因审征不慎而遭受拒付

我国甲公司与美国乙公司签订一笔以L/C为付款条件的合同。对方来证对部分单据作出规定:“签字的商业发票,由商检局出具的格式A普惠制产地证书(FORMA)。全套清洁已装船的提单做成我行抬头,通知开证申请人,并以‘ABC’公司作为提单的发货人。除发票以外,所有单据不得表示发货人或受益人的地址。”

甲公司按规定装运,并向商检局申请FORMA,商检局称FORMA上的发货人详细地址必须列出,此栏不得留空是带有强制性的。甲公司立即把此事电告乙公司,并要求乙公司修改L/C的条款为:“除发票、普惠制产地证书以外,所有单据不表示受益人地址。”

乙公司来电称:“货物是转销其他国家的,非在本地销售,所以难以修改L/C。如一定要修改L/C,必须有一个条件,即FORMA上不能表示发货人的真实地址,需设计一个虚拟地址。”

甲公司考虑到货物已装运完毕,急待制单议付,所以同意乙方的条件,也收到银行修改的L/C条款:“除发票、普惠制产地证书外,所有单据不表示受益人的地址。”

甲公司根据修改后的L/C制作全套单据后到银行交单议付。银行发现发票与FORMA的地址不一致,甲公司只好将发票上的地址临时删除掉,才办理交单手续。

单据寄到开证行后,对方以单据不符为理由拒付货款,因为L/C规定:“除发票、普惠制产地证外,所有单据不表示受益人的地址。”寄来的单据发票上地址已删除,也就是没有地址,所以单据与L/C规定不符。

甲公司与乙公司和银行多次协商仍然无效,最后货物只好降价处理。

[思考与分析] 本案甲公司审证不慎,后来又同意乙公司的不合理要求,最后遭到开证银行以“单证不符”为由拒付,其教训是深刻的。

本案问题的产生是甲公司没有考虑到FORMA要求必须列出发货人的详细地址,而简单地认为L/C要求单据不表示发货人的地址是可以接受的。而且装船后才发现该问题,为时已晚,所以只能受制于人。后来,甲公司把发票的地址临时删除也是不明智的,又被开证行以“单证不符、单单不符”为借口拒付。本案例实际上是乙公司出于某种原因,企图拒付或拖延付款,所以与开证行配合,有意设计“陷阱”,由开证行以“名正言顺”的“单证不符”理由拒付货款。

在实际国际贸易业务中,这类案例屡见不鲜,千万要引以为戒。

[案例37] 把握好贸易谈判和贸易结算的尺度

案例分析一 2001年我国公司同英国一家公司签订了一万件棉服的订单,我们当时仅同中间商发生往来,但是信用证确是从直接买方开出的,信用证上没有任何中间商的字样。而我们的贸易合同都是同中间商签订的,所以这个信用证不是转让或转开信用证。根据这个信用证,我们开始生产发货。单据最后出现不符点,此时中间商都签了出面的担保,但最终的英国公司拒付,造成了我方的损失。由此可得出教训:直接谈判的公司开出的信用证或由中间人转开的信用证都是需要的。

案例分析二 1998年A公司介绍一家工厂同国外B公司直接签订了合同，但是信用证是从第三国开出的，信用证上还规定了B公司的检验证书，B公司开出了检验证书，在议付行却遭到拒付，理由是B公司检验证书的签字同银行保留的不符。可是这个时候货物是直接发到目的地的。因此，第三国开出的信用证不可取，并且一般也不可能没有附加条件。

[案例38] 开证行有权从信用证款项中扣款

对于UCP500第3条(1)款，信用证含有允许开证行从信用证项下的付款中扣除一定金额的条款。

申请人：C公司、C国。

被申请人：B银行、C国。

1997年11月25日，被申请人应申请人的要求开立了一份金额为USK2,217,000的信用证，以E公司为受益人，有效期至1999年12月31日。

该证通过S银行通知，可在任何一家银行议付，受UCP500约束。

根据信用证条款，有一笔USD 966,800的付款于1998年12月18日到期(最后一批装运的提单日后360天)。

应受益人的指示，F银行于1998年12月18日要求开证行延长1998年12月18日的到期付款。根据开证申请人的协议，开证行于1999年1月1日将到期付款的时间改为最后一批装运货物的提单日后455天(即1999年3月25日)。

1999年3月16日，被申请人通知F银行，USD 966,800的单据已收到，但不会被兑付，原因是由于严重的货物质量问题开证申请人要求拒付。

[思考与分析] 问题的起因是由于信用证中含有“开证行有权直接根据开证申请人的要求从上述议付款项中扣除索赔金额”的条款。开证行正是基于该条款拒付的。

信用证含有授权开证行根据开证申请人的指示而从相符单据的议付款项中扣除索赔金额的条款是很不常见的(当然也违背了UCP500的精神)。并且该条款的措辞也没有任何具体的关于可能的最高索赔金额、最迟的索赔时间的规定，也没有关于该索赔条件的详细规定，以确定其是否可接受作为扣款的依据。

信用证是独立于其基础合同的交易(UCP500第3条(1)款)，银行的付款义务不受开证申请人因与受益人之间的关系而导致的索赔或抗辩的约束。

因此，只考虑信用证条款，而非基础合同的任何细节。上述条款中“开证行”的措辞应解释为赋予开证行根据开证申请人的指示从付款中扣除一定金额的权力。

我们认为受益人已接受了含有允许开证行从信用证款项中扣除的信用证，则受益人就应自行承担其风险。

信用证的该条件是不受欢迎的，我们的结论是开证行有权从信用证的款项中扣除索赔金额。

[案例39]　正确对待信用证软条款

案例分析一　1993年某月，国内某省医保进出口公司，与泰国A进口商签订合同，出口15吨维生素C，付款方式是L/C AT SIGHT。当时国际市场货物紧俏，可能是由于中间出口商拿不到货物的缘故，采取了替换货物的方式。进口商提货后发现，其中10吨货是扑热息痛，5吨货是维生素C。国际市场行情是维生素C每公斤12美元，扑热息痛每公斤3美元。这一换货给进口商带来非常大的损失。

案例分析二　1993年某月，国内某贸易有限公司，与泰国B进口商签订合同，出口2吨CAF产品，付款方式是L/C AT SIGHT，客户提货后发现其中有两桶沙子，至今仍存放在仓库，出示给所有与其谈生意的中国供货商。

案例分析三　1998年某月，国内某进出口贸易公司，与泰国C进口商签订合同，出口5吨维生素C，付款方式是L/C ATSIGHT，信用证规定发新货，所提供单证也标明新货，可进口商收到货后4个月就发现货物变质，颜色发黑。由于维生素C国际市场价格下跌，所以向进口商提供的是库存积压时间已久的旧货。

[案例40]　信用证软条款陷阱

2001年7月，湖北一家生产云母的工厂找到外贸公司，称在交易会上遇到一个香港客商，这个香港客商非常欣赏云母厂的产品，准备大量进口。云母厂希望外贸公司代理出口或收购云母后再出口到香港。

当年8月，外贸公司见到了香港进口商。通过谈判，双方签订了总值140万美元的合同，此时外贸公司面临的选择是：如果外贸公司代理出口，风险很小，但收益只有1.5%；如果外贸公司收购后再出口，利润可达到20%，但风险较大。权衡之后，外贸公司决定采用先收购后出口的方式。这时云母厂提出，由于资金不足，希望在外贸公司接到信用证后向银行申请打包贷款，并将此贷款预付给云母厂，否则很难完成生产任务。外贸公司为保证按时出口，在接到香港进口商的信用证后，向银行申请了打包贷款，并按总货值的80%付给了云母厂。

当年10月，全部货物备妥，外贸公司取得全套单据后即交银行议付，然而不久即遭到拒付，理由是其中一个单据和信用证不符。原来信用证上有一个条款规定，出口商需提供一份由当地商检部门出具的载有香港进口商签字认可的商检证明（即客检单），正是这个单据出了问题——商检单上的签字和议付行留存的签字不符。拒付后，香港进口商拿出香港当地机构的商检证明，声称货物质量存在严重问题，要求大幅度降价。外贸公司开始不肯退步，请云母厂从中协调，但一直没有结果，最后外贸公司不得不低价出售该货物。银行此时也着急，打包的贷款由于信用证拒付没有收回，向外贸公司索要，外贸公司一时也无法还贷。至此，银行和外贸公司均遭受了巨额损失。

事后，外贸公司认为此笔交易有诈骗嫌疑，于是委托有关咨询公司进行了资信调查。发现云母厂曾在一年前就和该香港进口商做过一笔类似的业务，也同样发生了上述的问题,只不过是由另一家外贸公司负责出口。再去调查香港进口商,发现该公司付款记录极差,所有开出的信用证都得不到议付。该公司注册资金只有10,000港币,实投资本只有2,000港币,是一个信誉非常不好的客户。

[思考与分析] 同一个事件发生了两次,不能排除进口商和厂家内外勾结,坑骗外贸公司和银行的可能性。但从法律角度讲,云母厂和香港进口商的行为很隐蔽,并没有违反合同规定。问题的关键是,外贸公司和银行应该从自身找原因。第一,像客检单这样的信用证软条款本应坚决不予接受,不给客户可乘之机。第二,如果外贸公司能够事先委托资信调查部门作一次详细的资信调查,那么这个进口商的真实面目也就一目了然了。

[案例41] 国际贸易术语

案例分析一 有一份CIP合同,出售小公牛,按CIF莫桑比克港口条件成交。合同规定:"半数价金由装船时支付,以换取装运单据;其余半数价金在到货时付清。"后来货物因遇到风险而发生损失,未能到达目的港。买方则以此为理由拒绝支付余数货款,双方发生激烈争论。在上述情况下,买方有无拒付余数货款的权利呢?

[思考与分析] 注意CIF合同的性质。在CIP合同中,卖方只要是按期在约定地点完成装运,并向买方提交合同规定的包括物权凭证在内的有关单据,就算完成了交货义务,而无需保证到货。而且,在CIF合同中,卖方是凭单交货,买方是凭单付款。只要卖方如期向买方提交了合同规定的全套合格单据,即使货物在运输途中损坏或丢失,买方也必须履行付款义务。

案例分析二 有一份CIF合同,出售一批一级咖啡豆,合同规定:"CIP纽约每公吨500美元,6月份装船,卖方在纽约提供单据,由买方支付现金。"货物于6月15日装船,但卖方一直拖延到6月20日才把单据交给买方。由于当时咖啡豆国际市场价格下跌,所以买方拒绝接受单据,除非卖方赔偿差价损失。问买方有无拒绝接受单据的权力,为什么?

[思考与分析] 1. CD贸易术语条件下,卖方的责任是什么,卖方是否违反合同规定?

2. 卖方为什么不及时把单据交给买方?

[案例42] 品名、品质、数量和包装条款

案例分析一 商品的包装:中国台湾的一家公司往中东运输玻璃杯,用木箱作为包装箱,用干草作为填充物。然而,等货物运到目的地时,大部分玻璃杯都碎了。因为,中东地区的天气比较干燥,当木箱运抵中东地区时,木箱里作为填充物的干草里的潮气全散发掉后干草体积变小了,结果在箱子里就有了多余的空隙,船的来回颠簸使得玻璃杯互相碰撞而破碎。

[思考与分析] 这说明在不同地点对包装的要求是不一样的,同样的包装方法,一个地方有效,另一个地方可能无效。

另一个中国台湾公司也遇到了类似的问题。当这家公司将一批羊毛运到伊朗时,伊朗人拒绝接受货物,他们认为这家公司在货物的重量上欺骗了他们。在拖延了很长时间后,他们才发现羊毛在从中国台湾这样的气候比较潮湿的地区发出时含有许多潮气，当运到伊朗时由于这里的气候比较干燥，原来羊毛里的潮气都散发掉后，重量当然就轻了。而到这时，双方都已浪费了许多宝贵的时间，在经济上造成了很大的损失。

［思考与分析］ 该案例说明在不同的气候条件下，对商品的包装要进行专门设计。

案例分析二 某企业生产并出口颜料中间体，其产品质量非常好，深受海外客户的好评。一次，一家美国客户来询购，厂方按照外商要求，从刚生产出来的一批货物中取了样品寄给了这家公司，该客户不久便确认了样品，并按照样品的指标和含量下了价值近 10 万美元的订单。厂方按期将货物生产了出来。由于与这家外商是首次合作，因此厂方在生产上格外注意，经检验所有的指标都达到出口合同的要求，而且其主含量超过了合同规定的 99.6%，达到 99.8%。货到美国用户手中时，却来电告知“货物与样品不符，不能使用，我方要求退货”。这家出口商急忙回电客户：“我们所交货物比合同规定的还要好，我们没有涨价主要是考虑我们首次合作，希望长期合作有一个好的开始，而你方为什么竟要求退货?”外商来电说，他们的车间是按照所提供的样品及其指标来调配产品的，生产出来的颜料的颜色已经用户确认，现交来的货物由于主含量超过生产出来的颜料，颜色就变了，从而造成他们无法按时向用户交货，要求赔偿损失。最后，这批货由于退回中国的成本太高，只好作半价委托客户在当地作了处理。工厂直接和间接共损失了近 8 万美元。

［思考与分析］ 本案例中，卖方在确定检验内容的时候，规定商品的品质指标要科学合理，并要结合行业或技术上的需要。国内这家工厂自己应该清楚，每一批货物的含量不可能完全一样，在给客户寄送样品时应向客户声明“样品仅供参考”，而在签订正式的出口合同时，应在确定的检验内容中规定主含量指标为“99.6%”，其他杂质含量规定为“××%”，这样，客户如有实际需要就会提出来。本例中，美国公司可能会要求 99.6% 为其能接受的水平。如外商不提出来，出口企业根据合同中确定的检验条款交货，外商就没有理由提出异议或索赔。

［案例 43］ 大豆为何屡遭韩国退运

2001 年 1、2 月份，大连口岸就收到了 11 批总量 845 吨从韩国退运回来的中国大豆。这些大豆原来经大连、连云港、天津等地装船运往韩国之前，各地检验检疫机构根据合同规定，都曾对其实施过检疫并出具了植物检疫合格证书，有的运货时间已有 8 个月之久。据辽宁省检验检疫局介绍，这些大豆产自黑龙江、吉林两省，东北大豆在世界上极有盛誉，品质良好、无虫害。在此之前，我国大豆接连被韩国退运的情况极为少见。

据了解，韩方退运的主要理由是大豆品质不好、货物与样品不符、价格有分歧。据分析，这基本“都是合同惹的祸”。首先，这些遭退运大豆的出口合同在检验上仅限于水分、杂质不超标；其次，合同中只要求出具植物检疫证书，没有要求出具品质检验证书；再次，合同中规定的是 T/T 结汇方式(见提单电汇付款)。这为一些信誉度较低的韩国客商违约提供了可乘之机。

［思考与分析］ 检验检疫部门提醒有关外贸企业和主管机构：在签订出口大豆合同时，品质条款要详细且完整，合同中应有要求检验检疫局出具品质证书的条款。这样，检验检疫机构对出口大豆的杂质、水分、不完整粒、千粒重、发芽率等品质实施检验，并出具证书，中方企业既可避免遭遇因所谓“品质问题”的退运，又能凭证书对外索赔。

业内人士建议，为避免退运事件的频频发生，中方出口企业应多与国外正规的大型进出口公司进行合作，尽量避免与一些信誉度较低的民间小商社联系，同时，在合同付款方式上应要求全额或部分预付款。有关专家认为，市场经济是契约经济，国内企业应学习掌握有关的国际商法知识，学会用法律保护自己。

［案例 44］ 国际货物运输保险

案例分析一 国内某公司进口一批货物，已投平安险加战争险。运载该批货物的海轮在航行途中遇到敌对两国交战，船舶被炮火击中，但货物未受损害。当该船驶到附近港口修理时，却因遭遇恶劣气候，船舶沉没，货物全部损失。那么，本案中保险公司是否应当承担赔偿责任？如果本案中卖方投保的是一切险，但来加保战争险，保险公司是否应该赔偿？

［思考与分析］ 保险公司理赔时遵循“近因原则”，即被保险货物所遭受的损失必须是由承保范围内的风险直接导致的，保险人才负责赔偿。本例中，货物遭到全部损失的直接原因是战争而不是恶劣气候，因为在船沉没前，船舶被炮火击中的部位未得到修复，因而货物一直处于战争的风险之中，所以导致货物受损的直接原因是战争，而该公司又已经投保了战争险，故保险公司应予赔偿。战争险的责任范围不包括在一切险的责任范围内，因此，被保险人如果投保了一切险而未加保战争险，则保险公司不予理赔。

案例分析二 中方按 CIP 出口冷冻食品一批，合同规定投保平安险加战争险、罢工险。货到目的港后恰逢码头工人罢工，港口无人作业，货物无法卸载。不久货轮因无法补充燃料以致冷冻设备停机。等到罢工结束，该批冷冻食品已变质。那么这种由于罢工而引起的损失，保险公司是否应该赔偿？

［思考与分析］ 保险公司只对因罢工引起的直接损失负责赔偿，对于间接损失不负责任。在本例中，货物遭受的是间接损失，因此，保险公司不予赔偿。假如是在罢工中因工人与政府武装力量发生冲突，货物因被当做掩体而受到损失，则属于直接损失，保险公司就要予以赔偿了。

［案例 45］ 合同中计价货币选择不当而受损

2002 年 10 月，中国某进出口公司（A 公司）与日本一家贸易公司（B 公司 ）签订一份货物买卖合同。在双方磋商买卖合同的计价货币条款时，A 公司为业务人员按照国际贸易的习惯做法，主张采用美元计价和付款，但 B 公司代表要求采用日元计价，按美元付款。付款时按付款当天美元对日元的汇率折算成美元付给 A 公司。A 公司业务人员开始时不同意，但在 B 公司业务代表的坚持下，同意 B 公司的做法，合同中没有加订保值条款。合同规定交货期为 2002 年年底之前，付款方式为 30 天的远期 L/C。

因本买卖合同执行时间较长，而且采用远期 L/C，我方 A 公司收汇的时间更长。在本买卖合同履行过程中，日元与美元的汇率发生了变化。因日元是“软币”，到付款时日元对美元的汇率下降，使 A 公司少收将近 10 万美元。

［思考与分析］ 本案例的中方 A 公司由于对支付工具的变化未作详细的预测，贸然同意日方 B 公司的要求，最后少收外汇近 10 万美元。说明了选择合同计价货币和在合同中加订保值条款的重要性。

保值条款又称外汇保值条款，是一种在各国货币大多实行浮动汇率、货币的上浮与下降直接影响合同当事人利益的情况下，作为抵消或减少汇率风险的一般措施。软货币一般是指在国际金融市场上呈现疲软的货币，即币值下降的货币。硬货币一般是指在国际市场上呈现坚挺趋势的货币，即币值上浮的货币。

在制定合同中的保值条款时，原则上出口宜采用硬货币计值和支付，进口宜用软货币计值和支付，以减少汇率变动的损失。运用好保值条款，关键在于选择好支付货币，预测好有关货币的汇率走势，否则就会吃亏上当。外汇市场上，汇率经常变化，有时软货币也可能在短期内由于种种原因而发生暂时性的下降。因此，选择不当就会产生不良后果。

附录三　国际贸易实务操作流程

(一)案例基本资料

外贸公司(简称思科):南京思科纺织服装有限公司

NANJING SICO TEXTILE GARMENT CO., LTD.

HUARONG MANSION RM2901 NO.85 GUANJIAQIAO, NANJING 210005, CHINA

TEL: +86-25-35784312 FAX: +86-25-35784513

国外客户(简称FF):

FASHION FORCE CO., LTD

P.O. BOX 8935 NEW TERMINAL, ALTA, VISTA OTTAWA, CANADA

TEL: +1-613-4563508 FAX: +1-613-4562421

交易商品:

COTTON BLAZER 全棉运动上衣

成交方式:

CIF

付款方式:即期信用证(L/C AT SIGHT)

通知行:中国银行江苏省分行

出口口岸:

上海

服装加工厂:

无锡季节制衣有限公司

面、辅料工厂:

无锡百合纺织有限公司

货运代理公司:

上海凯通国际货运代理有限公司

承运船公司:

中国远洋集装箱运输有限公司

(二)备注说明

本案例涉及思科公司的部门有三个:业务部、单证储运部、财务部。其中,业务部负责接洽业务,单证储运部负责出运安排、制单、核销,财务部门负责应收、应付账款。

这是一笔南京思科纺织服装公司和加拿大客户就女式全棉上衣交易的贸易实务案例。

出口到加拿大的纺织品有配额限制,在准备单证时需注意及时申请"输加拿大纺织品出口许可证”,另需注意缮制“加拿大海关发票”等单证,及时寄出给客户用于进口清关。

本案例涉及贸易公司业务部、单证储运部、财务部三个部门,以及工厂、货运代理公司等。在实际业务中,租船订舱、报验、申领核销单、申请配额等工作往往是贸易公司的各个部门在同时进行的,次序不分先后。

(三)出口操作流程

1. 交易磋商

南京思科纺织服装有限公司(NANJING SICO TEXTILE GARMENT CO. ,LTD,以下简称思科公司)成立于1992年,是经国家外经贸部批准的具有进出口经营权的贸易公司,从事纺织服装等产品进出口业务。公司拥有多家下属工厂,产品主要销往欧洲、美加地区及日本等国家和地区。

加拿大客户 FASHION FORCE CO. , LTD(以下简称 F. F. 公司)与思科公司是合作多年的业务伙伴。2000 年 12 月 2 日,F. F. 公司传真一份制作女式全棉上衣的指示书,并邮寄面料、色样及一件成衣样品给思科公司,要求思科公司 2001 年 3 月 25 日前交货,并回寄面料、色样及两件不同型号的成衣样品确认。

2000 年 12 月 8 日上午,思科公司收到该样件后,立即联络无锡百合纺织有限公司(面、辅料工厂,以下简称百合纺织),根据 F. F. 公司提供的样件打品质样和色卡,然后用 DHL 邮寄给 F. F. 公司确认。

2001 年 12 月 12 日,F. F. 公司收到思科公司寄去的样件,回复确认合格,要求思科公司再寄两件不同型号的成衣样品供其确认。接此通知,思科公司立即联络无锡季节制衣有限公司(服装加工厂,以下简称季节制衣)赶制成衣样品。12 月 17 日下午,服装加工厂将两件不同型号的成衣样品送到思科公司。当天,思科公司又将该成衣样品用 DHL 邮寄给 F. F. 公司确认。

12 月 22 日,F. F. 公司收到思科公司寄去的成衣样品,确认合格,要求思科公司报价。当天,思科公司根据指示书要求,以面辅料工厂和服装厂的报价、公司利润等为基础向 F. F. 公司报价。

经过多次磋商,12 月 26 日,双方最终确定以每件 USD12. 80 的报价成交。F. F. 公司要求思科公司根据该份报价单制作合同传真其会签,同时传真形式发票供其开具信用证。

合同签订后,双方就成衣细节进行修改和最终确认。

2. 落实信用证

2001 年 1 月 31 日,中国银行江苏省分行通知思科公司收到 F. F. 公司通过 BNP PARIBAS (CANADA) MONTREAL 银行开来的编号为 63211020049 的信用证电开本。

其中与缮制单据有关的条款如下。

(1)开证行:BNP PARIBAS (CANADA) MONTREAL。

(2)通知行:中国银行江苏省分行。

(3)不可撤销信用证号:63211020049。开证日期:2001 年 1 月 29 日。

(4)信用证有效期及地点:2001 年 4 月 10 日,中国。

(5)申请人:

FASHION FORCE CO., LTD

P.O.BOX 8935 NEW TERMINAL, ALTA, VISTA OTTAWA, CANADA

(6)受益人:

NANJING SICO TEXTILE GARMENT CO., LTD.

HUARONG MANSION RM2901 NO.85 GUANJIAQIAO, NANJING

210005, CHINA

(7)信用证金额:USD32640.00.

(8)商品描述:

SALES CONDITIONS: CIF MONTREAL/CANADA

SALES CONTRACT NO. F01LCB05127

LADIES COTTON BLAZER (100% COTTON, 40SX20/140X60)

STYLE NO. PO NO. QTY/PCS USD/PC

46－301A 10337 2550 12.80

(9)分批装运及转船运输:不允许分批装运,允许转运,从中国运至加拿大蒙特利尔港港口。

(10)最后装船期:2001 年 3 月 25 日。

(11)议付单据要求:

①商业发票六份,受益人代表签名;

②加拿大海关发票四份;

③3/3 全套正本已装船的清洁海运提单,抬头人为“TO THE ORDER OF BNP PARIBAS (CANADA)”,显示运费预付,通知人为开证人的名称和地址;

④明细装箱单三份;

⑤普惠制产地证一份副本(FORM A);

⑥输加拿大纺织品出口许可证一份副本;

⑦受益人证明,证明装运后 5 天内,将普惠制产地证正本、输加拿大纺织出口许可证正本、商业发票副本和明细装箱单副本和正本提单的复印件已经由快递方式直接寄送给开证人,并附快件回执;

⑧提供开证人的传真确认函,确认货物在装运前生产的样品由开证人认可;

⑨印有承运人抬头的证明,显示承运公司的名称和地址、海运提单号、集装箱号,本次承运人的集装箱内不含有任何原生木料制成的支撑物或托盘,以及其他任何原生木制包装材料;

⑩客检证正本一份，其要求出运前 15 天用 DHL 寄四件不同型号的成衣样品，经检验合格后由 F. F. 公司出具客检证；

⑪中国人民保险公司出具的保险单一份正本、一份副本。

(12)附加条款

①如果提供的单据不符合信用证条款的规定，每个不符点 55 美金。

②一切结算费用由受益人支付。

③本信用证的数量和金额有 3% 的溢短。

④所有的单据、证明、申明必须签字及标明日期。

⑤以下内容仅作参考：从 1999 年 1 月 4 日开始，所有从中国运往加拿大的货物，如果包装物中含有木制成分，将被加拿大海关禁止。因为，原生木质中含有一种亚州长角甲虫（LONG HORNED）。

⑥加拿大政府现在坚持所有进入加拿大的货物必须提供上述所有文件。

⑦海运提单和商业发票必须证明以下内容：集装箱内不含有任何原生木料制成的支撑物或托盘，以及其他任何原生木制包装材料。

⑧受益人的银行账号为 0777103281054。

注意：议付单据中有关客检证条款项对我方公司极为不利。如果客户信誉良好，多会在样品检验合格后及时签发客检证明，但有些客户会故意拖延签发客检证的时间，导致我方不能及时交单议付。因此，遇到有此项条款的信用证，我方公司需特别注意及时寄样和催客户及时签发客检证。

3. 出口备货

收到信用证后，2001 年 2 月 1 日，思科公司立即与早已联络好的服装加工厂签订订购合同，指定服装厂使用百合纺织的面辅料。2 月 5 日，服装厂正式生产。

根据信用证规定，3 月 2 日，思科公司寄出四件不同型号的成衣样品给 F. F. 公司检验。3 月 6 日，F. F. 公司收到后，经检验合格，签发客检证正本一份并用 DHL 寄回给思科公司。

注意：关于品质检验和客检证的签发，视客户检验的具体状况而定。一般不外乎有两种方式。第一种，客户派人员亲自来厂检验，检验合格后当场签发客检证，或该人员将检验结果向客户汇报后，由客户将客检证寄给我方。在此种方式下，客户一般是在出运前 4 ~ 5 天来厂检验，此时工厂的加工、包装已基本结束。验货通过后即可安排出运。第二种，将样品寄给客户检验，检验合格后，客户签发客检证并寄给我方。在此种方式下，一般客户会要求我方在出货前 10 ~ 15 天寄样品供其检验。

4. 租船订舱

本批出口商品是采用集装箱班轮运输，故在落实信用证及备货时，思科公司即向上海各家货运代理公司询价，最终确定委托上海凯通国际货运有限公司（以下简称上海凯通）代为订舱，以便及时履行合同及信用证项下的交货和交单义务。

2001年3月9日，服装全部生产、包装完毕，工厂制作装箱单传真给思科公司。思科公司根据工厂报来的装箱单，结合合同及信用证货物明细描述，开列出仓通知单，单证储运部门根据出仓通知单、工厂制的装箱单及信用证统一缮制全套的出运单据。出运单据包括出口货物明细单、出口货物报关单、商业发票和装箱单。

单证储运部门先将出口货物明细单传真上海凯通配船订舱，确认配船和费用后，准备全套报关单据（出口货物明细单、报关委托书、出口货物报关单、商业发票、装箱单、出口收汇核销单、输加拿大纺织品出口许可证（海关联））寄到上海凯通用于报关、出运。同时，准备普惠制产地证用于出运后寄客户作进口清关。

上海凯通在确认配船和费用后，传真送货通知给思科公司，要求思科公司3月16日中午前将货物运至指定仓库。

注意：在FOB条件下，运输公司大多由客户指定。

5. 出口报验

由于思科公司出口的全棉女式上衣属于法定检验的商品范围（属于《种类表》商品范畴），在商品报关时，报关单上必须有商检机构的检验放行章方可报关。因此，2001年3月9日，思科公司寄出商业发票、装箱单、报检委托书，委托服装加工厂向无锡市商检局申请出口检验。

申请出口商品检验时，工厂必须填写出口商品检验申请单，并随附报检委托书、外销合同、信用证复印件、商业发票、装箱单、纸箱证等单据。

3月13日，此批货物经检验合格，无锡商检局出具换证凭单给工厂。当天，工厂将换证凭单寄给思科公司指定的上海凯通国际货运公司用于报关。

6. 申领核销单

由于思科公司有计划内的核销单，2001年3月9日，单证员凭出口货物明细单在本公司申领核销单。

注意：如果核销单已用完，需到外汇局申领出口收汇核销单。具体有如下操作：

（1）在到外汇局申领核销单前，先上网向外汇局申请所需领用核销单份数。

（2）外汇局确认思科公司已上网申领核销单后，凭思科公司核销员所持本人操作员IC卡、核销员证向该核销员发放核销单。

（3）外汇局根据思科公司网上申领的核销单份数和外汇局本地核销系统确认的出口企业可领单数两者中的较小数，向思科公司发放核销单。

7. 申请配额

2001年3月9日，思科公司向外经贸委申领纺织品配额。3月13日，拿到已签发的输加拿大纺织品出口许可证。

注意：对没有配额的公司而言，必须要申领到配额后方能出口。申领纺织品配额一般有以下几种方式：

(1)外经贸部、地方的外经贸厅每年下发给外贸公司的配额。

(2)外贸公司加入纺织品商会,通过商会每年举办的配额招标、投标获取配额。

(3)找有配额的公司调济:一种是纺织商会组织的公开的调济,一种是私下的不规范的转卖。

8. 出口报关

单证部门拿到核销单和输加拿大纺织品出口许可证后,2001 年 3 月 13 日,将上海凯通报关所需的报关委托书、出口货物报关单、出口收汇核销单、商业发票、装箱单、外销合同、输加拿大纺织品出口许可证用快件寄出。

3 月 14 日,上海凯通收到思科公司寄来的上述单据。

3 月 15 日上午,上海凯通收到工厂寄来的商检换证凭单,当天下午即凭此单到上海出入境检验检疫局换取出境货物通关单。

3 月 16 日上午,思科公司根据上海凯通的送货通知按时将货物送到上海凯通指定的仓库。

根据新的海关报关规定要求:货物的出口报关必须在货物进入港口仓库或集装箱整箱进入堆场后才能进行。由于 17、18 号是周六、周日,故 3 月 16 日下午,上海凯通即向上海海关报关,以免耽误 3 月 20 日的船期。

上海凯通在报关前,先上网向上海海关进行核销单的口岸备案,并如实向海关申报成交方式(CIF),按成交方式申报成交总价、运费等,以后外汇局即根据实际成交方式及成交总价办理收汇核销手续。

报关时需填写中华人民共和国海关出口货物报关单(白色的报关联和黄色的出口退税联),并随附报关委托书、商业发票、装箱单、出口收汇核销单、出境货物通关单、输加拿大纺织品出口许可证等单证向海关报关,海关依此份报关单验货,并退回已盖章的核销单和两份报关单。报关通过后,上海凯通安排集装箱拖货至船公司指定的码头。

注意事项:

(1)未进行口岸备案的核销单不能用于出口报关,对已备案成功的核销单,还可变更备案。

(2)报关时必须要"出口收汇核销单",否则海关不予受理。货物出境后,海关在核销单上加盖"放行章"或"验讫章",并随同加盖海关"验讫章"的一份带有海关编号的白色报关单、一份黄色的报关单连同出口退税联一同返还口岸代理上海凯通(从上海海关退回一般需 1 个月左右),最后口岸代理上海凯通寄给思科公司用于向外汇管理部门核销。

(3)纺织品出口许可证是政府机关批准配额纺织品出口的证明文件,其作用是出口商凭此办理出口报关和进口商凭此申领进口许可证并办理进口报关手续。因此,出口加拿大的纺织品在报关时必须要附加拿大纺织品出口许可证,否则海关不予受理。

9. 出口保险

按 CIF 条件成交,保险由思科公司办理。因此,2001 年 3 月 16 日,思科公司按约定的保险险别和保险金额,向保险公司投保。投保时应填制投保单和支付保险费(保险费 = 保险金额×保险费率)，并随附商业发票，保险公司凭其出具保险单。

注意：实际业务中，一些和外贸公司长期合作的保险公司，有时只需外贸公司提供商业发票，甚至可以不填制投保单，直接凭商业发票出具保险单。

10. 装船出运

上海凯通接受思科公司的订舱委托后，2001 年 3 月 12 日，根据思科公司提供的出口货物明细单缮制集装箱货物托运单，这是外运机构向船公司订舱配载的依据。该托运单一式数联，分别用于货主留底、船代留底、运费通知、装货单、缴纳出口货物港务费申请书、场站收据、货代留底、配舱回单、场站收据副本(大副联)等。其中比较重要的单据有装货单(Shipping Order：S/O)和场站收据副本(Mate's Receipt：M/R)。

3 月 19 日，货物离港前，上海凯通传真海运提单给思科公司确认。

3 月 20 日，在确定货物安全离港后，思科公司传真装运通知给 F. F. 公司。

3 月 22 日，思科公司将海运提单复印件、输加拿大纺织品出口许可证(正本)、商业发票、装箱单、加拿大海关发票、普惠制产地证用 DHL 寄给 F. F. 公司供其作进口清关用，同时将 DHL 回执留存准备缮制议付单据。

注意：将来船公司签发的提单上相应栏目的填写也参照订舱委托书的写法，因此，托运人、收货人、通知人这三栏的填写应该严格按照信用证提单条款的相应规定填写。

11. 制单结汇

在办理货物出运工作的同时，思科公司也开始了议付单据的制作。2001 年 3 月 20 日，上海凯通国际货运代理有限公司作为承运人中国远洋运输公司下属的中远集装箱运输有限公司的代理，签发了 COS6314623142 号提单。根据信用证的规定，思科公司备齐了全套议付单据(3/3 海运提单正本、商业发票、装箱单、普惠制产地证、受益人证明、客检证、货物运输保险单)，于 4 月 2 日向议付银行——中国银行江苏省分行交单议付。

12. 财务付款

3 月 22 日，思科公司的财务人员收到上海凯通寄来的海运费发票和港杂费发票。

3 月 27 日，收到服装厂寄来的增值税发票和出口专用缴款书。

议付单据交单后，3 月 30 日，财务人员向服装厂支付货款，并和上海凯通结清海运费、港杂费等费用，同时催上海凯通退核销单。

13. 收汇核销

4 月 20 日，思科公司收到上海凯通寄来的上海海关退回的出口收汇核销单和报关单。当天，核销员在网上将此核销单向外汇局交单，并在进行网上交单时，对核销单、报关单的电子底帐数据进行了认真的核对。

4 月 23 日，思科公司收到银行的收汇水单，开证行已如数付款。至此，该笔交易已安全收汇。

网上交单成功之后，4 月 24 日，核销员持纸质的收汇水单(即出口收汇核销专用联，经银行盖有“出口收汇核销专用章”)、出口收汇核销单(已经出口海关盖章,第三联)、报关单(白色报关联,海关已盖章)、商业发票及自制的核销单送审登记表(外汇局留存联)到外汇局办理核销手续。核销完毕后,外管局当场将加盖“已核销章”的核销单(出口退税联)退回给思科公司。核销完成后,核销员将上述单据转交财务办税人员办理退税事宜。

14. 出口退税

2001 年 4 月 25 日,思科公司的财务办税人员将公司需要办理认证的增值税发票整理后一并申报国税局进行发票认证。当天,拿到国税局认证结果通知书和认证清单。

4 月 26 日,财务办税人员将退税要用的单据收集齐全无误后装订成册。其中,核销单(外管退回的出口退税专用联)、报关单(黄色出口退税联)、商业发票为一册,增值税发票(抵扣联)、出口专用缴款书、认证结果通知书、认证清单为一册,并在退税申报软件中逐条录入进货明细及申报退税明细。录入完毕,核对无误后打印并生成退税处所需要的表格及软盘,连同“外贸企业出口货物退税汇总申报审批表”送交外经委稽核处加盖稽核章。

2001 年 5 月 7 日,财务办税人员将上述资料送交国税局稽核部门待批。5 月 28 日,接到国税局通知,于 5 月 7 日申报的资料已通过。5 月 29 日,财务人员到银行查询,查到申报退税额已足额退回。

至此,该笔业务顺利完成。

参考文献

1 姚大伟,袁海君编著.新编国际贸易实务教程.上海:复旦大学出版社,1997.

2 张素芳编著.国际贸易理论与实务.北京:对外经济贸易大学出版社,2007.

3 刘舒年主编.国际贸易实务.北京:中国人民大学出版社,2006.

4 韩玉珍编著.国际贸易与国际金融.北京:北京大学出版社,2002.

5 国际商会中国国家委员会译.2000年国际贸易术语解释通则.北京:中信出版社,1999.

6 国际商会中国国家委员会译,跟单信用证统一惯例及关于电子交单的附则.北京:中国民主法制出版社,2003.

7 世界贸易组织秘书处.贸易走向未来.北京:法律出版社,1999.

8 联合国贸发会议,世界贸易组织国际贸易中心,英联邦秘书处.WTO企业指南.北京:企业管理出版社,2001.

9 曹建明,贺小勇.世界组织基本法律制度讲话.北京:中国青年出版社,2000.

10 对外贸易合作部国际经贸司译.世界贸易组织乌拉圭回合多边贸易谈判结果.北京:法律出版社,2000.

11 夏国政主编.经贸谈判指南.北京:世界知识出版社,1999.

12 杰弗里·埃德蒙·柯里著.国际谈判.朱丹,陆小红等译.北京:经济科学出版社,1999.

13 韩玉珍编著.现代国际贸易实务.北京:首都经济贸易大学出版社,2000.

14 严思忆主编.中小企业国际贸易实务.北京:中国人民大学出版社,1999.

15 黎孝先主编.国际贸易实务.北京:对外经济贸易大学出版社,2000.

16 世界贸易组织秘书处.乌拉圭回合协议导读.北京:法律出版社.2000.

17 Shen Jinchang, Xu Xiuqiong, Li Baohua and Lu Meiqi. International Payments and Settlements. Shanghai: Shanghai Foreign Language Education Press, 1996.

18 Sun Nanshen. WTO Rues Chinese Economic Law on Foreign Business. Beijing: Law Press, 2002.

19 Michael R Czinkota, Ilkka A Ronkainen, Michael H Moffett. International Business. 4th ed. Harcourt Brace and Company Asia Pte Ltd. the Dryden Press, 1998.

20 Susan Hodges. Cases and Materials on Marine Insurance Law. Gavendish Publishing Limited, 1999.

21 Jonathan Reuvid, Li Yong. Doing Business with China. Kogan Page in association with China's Ministry of Foreign Trade & Economic Co. ,2006.

22 Chen Shenquan and Chen Yue. The English Reading of WTO. Beijing: China Finance Press, 2002.

23 Paul T Vout, Ye Jingsheng and Yi Yiwu. China Contract Handbook. Sweet & Maxwell Asia, 2002.

24 Joseph C H Chai. The Economic Development of Modern China. Edward Elgar Publishing, 1979.

25 Ray August. International Business Law. 3rd ed. Beijing: Higher Education Press, 2002.

26 Chao Lin. International Trade Practices. Beijing: Foreign Language Teaching and Research Press, 2000.

27 Zhu Gelin, Ma li, Zhang Xiaoquan. Documentary Credit. Beijing: China Foreign Economic Relations & Trade Press, 2000.

28 Lu Mozhu. Communicating in International Business. Beijing: University of International Business and Economics Press, China, 1994.

29 Gao Fei. Arbitration Agreement. Beijing: China's Foreign Trade, 2001.

30 Corrie Dosh. Where do we go from here? Beijing: China International Business, 2002. ts. Harper Collins College Publishers New York, 2000.

31 Dennis R Appleyard, Alfred J Field, Jr. International Economics. 3rd ed. Beijing: China Machine Press/McGraw - Hill Companies, 1998.

32 Edward G Hinkelman. Dictionary of International Trade. 4th ed. Beijing: Economic Science Press, 2002.